Piecework Magazine Presents

A FACSIMILE EDITION OF

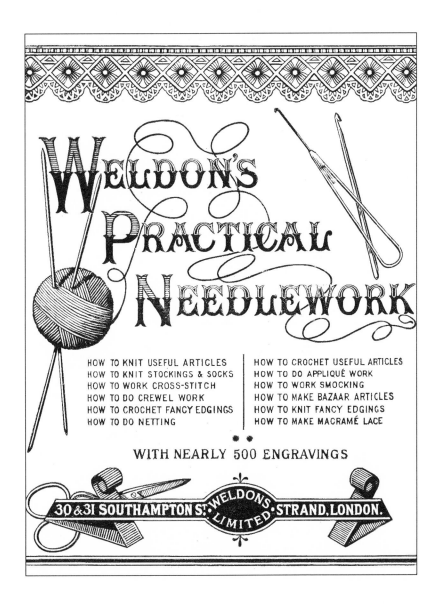

WELDON'S PRACTICAL NEEDLEWORK

HOW TO KNIT USEFUL ARTICLES
HOW TO KNIT STOCKINGS & SOCKS
HOW TO WORK CROSS-STITCH
HOW TO DO CREWEL WORK
HOW TO CROCHET FANCY EDGINGS
HOW TO DO NETTING

HOW TO CROCHET USEFUL ARTICLES
HOW TO DO APPLIQUÉ WORK
HOW TO WORK SMOCKING
HOW TO MAKE BAZAAR ARTICLES
HOW TO KNIT FANCY EDGINGS
HOW TO MAKE MACRAMÉ LACE

WITH NEARLY 500 ENGRAVINGS

30 & 31 SOUTHAMPTON St. WELDONS LIMITED STRAND, LONDON.

VOLUME 2

Sincere thanks to Lilo Markrich for her help,
encouragement, and support.

Weldon's Practical Needlework, Volume 2

Project editor, Jeane Hutchins

Cover design, Dean Howes

Interweave Press

201 East Fourth Street

Loveland, Colorado, 80537-5655

USA

Printed in the United States of America

ISBN 1–883010-82-9

First printing: 5M:IWP:WP

*T*his book opens a window on another time and another place. the time is the turn of the twentieth century and the place is London, England. In an effort to bring needlework to a then emerging middle class, several companies in the late 1800s in London began publishing patterns and instructions for various needlework projects. Unlike other magazines available at the time, which ran one or two needlework projects in an issue filled with other editorial (including fiction, recipes, and housekeeping hints), these new publications were devoted solely to needlework.

Many of the companies involved in these publishing ventures were thread companies, and their purpose, of course, was to sell more thread by making patterns and instructions more readily available. One company, however, Weldon's, began as a paper pattern company and became one of the most recognized needlework publishers in Victorian England.

In approximately 1885, Weldon's began publishing monthly newsletters, available by subscription, featuring patterns and instructions for projects. Each fourteen-page newsletter was devoted to one technique and cost 2 pence. Thus, there was *Weldon's Practical Knitter*, *Weldon's Practical Patchwork*, *Weldon's Practical Crochet*, *Weldon's Practical Cross-Stitch*, and so on. By about 1915, Weldon's had published 159 issues of *Practical Crochet* and 100 issues of *Practical Knitting*.

Around 1888, the company began to publish a series of books titled *Weldon's Practical Needlework*, each volume consisting of twelve issues of the various newsletters (one year of publications) bound together with a cloth cover; each book cost 2 shilling/6 pence.

Editions feature instructions for making flowers from crinkled paper or leather, items suitable for selling at bazaars (pincushions, for example), tatting, smocking, netting, beading, torchon lace, and much more. In addition to knitting and crocheting, which were frequently covered, *Weldon's Practical Needlework* books contain extensive coverage of decorative needlework, including crewel work, appliqué, cross-stitch, mountmellick embroidery, drawn thread work, ivory embroidery, hardanger, and canvas work. Each volume is filled with hundreds of projects, illustrations, information on little-known techniques, fashion as it was at the turn of the century, and brief histories of needlework.

PIECEWORK magazine is pleased to present this limited edition, exact reproduction (neither alterations nor corrections were made to the original) of *Weldon's Practical Needlework*, Volume 2. It is a fitting example of needlework and history, hand in hand.

The Staff of PIECEWORK

WELDON'S
PRACTICAL NEEDLEWORK

COMPRISING—

KNITTING, CROCHET, MACRAMÉ LACE, STOCKING KNITTING, CROSS-STITCH
EMBROIDERY, CREWEL WORK, BAZAAR ARTICLES, SMOCKING,
APPLIQUÉ WORK, NETTING, EDGINGS AND INSERTIONS
IN KNITTING AND CROCHET, &c., &c.,

With Full Working Descriptions and Complete Instructions for Beginners.

NEARLY 500 ILLUSTRATIONS.

* *

LONDON:

WELDON & Co., 7, SOUTHAMPTON STREET, STRAND, W.C.

INDEX.—Vol. II.

STOCKING KNITTER.

CROSS-STITCH EMBROIDERY.

CREWEL WORK.

BAZAAR ARTICLES.

KNITTING.

CROCHET.

SMOCKING.

APPLIQUÉ WORK.

INDEX—*Continued.*

NETTING.

MACRAMÉ LACE.

CROCHET (EDGINGS).

KNITTING (EDGINGS).

WELDON'S
PRACTICAL STOCKING KNITTER.
(THIRD SERIES.)

How to Knit Plain and Fancy Stockings for Ladies, Gentlemen, and Children.

TWENTY-ONE ILLUSTRATIONS.

⁎ *The Knitting Needles used in our directions are regulated by* Walker's Bell Gauge.

The Yearly Subscription to this Magazine, post free to any Part of the World, is 2s. 6d.
Subscriptions are payable in advance, and may commence from any date and for any period.

The Back Numbers are always in print. Nos. 1 *to* 240 *now ready, Price* 2d. *each, or bound in* 20 *Vols., price* 2s. 6d. *each.*

CHILD'S PLAIN KNIT FIRST SOCK.

PROCURE 2 balls of white Cocoon wool, and 4 steel needles No. 15. Cast 23 stitches on the first needle, 16 on the second. and 15 stitches on the third needle, 54 stitches in all. **1st round**—Knit 1, purl 1, alternately, on each needle. **2nd round**—Purl 1, knit 1, alternately, on each needle. It will be seen that the stitches knitted in one round are purled in the next. Knit 16 rounds in this manner. Then on first needle—knit 11, purl the next stitch for the seam stitch, knit to the end of the needle (11 stitches), knit along the other two needles. Knit 19 more rounds the same. **21st round**—Begin decreasing for the leg—on first needle, knit 8, knit 2 together, knit 1, purl the seam stitch, knit 1, slip 1, knit 1, pass the slipped stitch over, and knit plain to the end of the round. Knit 5 plain rounds. **27th round**—On first needle, knit 7, knit 2 together, knit 1, purl the seam stitch, knit 1, slip 1, knit 1, pass the slipped stitch over, and knit plain to the end of the round. Knit 5 plain rounds. **33rd round**—On first needle, knit 6, knit 2 together, knit 1, purl the seam stitch, knit 1, slip 1, knit 1, pass the slipped stitch over, and knit plain to the end of the round. Knit 5 plain rounds. **39th round**—On first needle, knit 5, knit 2 together, knit 1, purl the seam stitch, knit 1, slip 1, knit 1, pass the slipped stitch over, and knit plain to the end of the round. This finishes the reductions, and now there are 15 stitches on the first needle, 16 stitches on the second, and 15 stitches on the third needle, 46 stitches in the round. Knit 19 rounds, always purling the seam stitch. Now for the **Heel**—On first needle, knit 7, purl the seam stitch, knit 7, knit 4 from the next needle, turn the work, slip the first stitch, purl 10, knit the seam stitch, purl 11; this brings 23 stitches on the heel needle, and the remaining 23 stitches are to be left upon the two needles just as they are until wanted for knitting the instep. Turn the work. **3rd row of the Heel**—Slip the first stitch, knit 10, purl the seam stitch, knit 11. **4th row**—Slip the first stitch, purl 10, knit the seam stitch, purl 11. Repeat these two rows till you can count 10 loops down the side of the knitting, when 20 rows will be done. **To turn the Heel**—Slip the first stitch, knit 10, purl the seam stitch, knit 2, slip 1, knit 1, pass the slipped stitch over, turn, slip the first stitch, purl 2, knit the seam

Child's Plain Knit First Sock.

stitch, purl 2, purl 2 together ; * turn, slip first stitch, knit 2, purl seam stitch, knit 2, slip 1, knit 1, pass slipped stitch over, turn, slip first stitch, purl 2, knit seam stitch, purl 2, purl 2 together ; and repeat from * till side stitches are knitted in, and 7 stitches remain on the needle for top of heel. Knit these 7 stitches, and on the same needle pick up, and as you pick up knit, 12 stitches along the side of the flap, knit the 23 instep stitches all off on to one needle, and on another needle pick up and knit 12 stitches along the other side of the flap, and knit 3 stitches off the heel needle. The stitches are now arranged upon three needles, with 54 stitches in the round, ready for knitting the gussets. Knit along the next needle, knit the instep needle. Then, * on first foot needle, knit 1, slip 1, knit 1, pass the slipped stitch over, knit till within 3 stitches of the end of the second foot needle, knit 2 together, knit 1, knit plain along the instep needle ; knit 1 plain round, and repeat from * till reduced to 42 stitches. If the gusset decreasings have been knitted correctly, the 23 instep stitches remain intact upon one needle, and there are 19 stitches divided between the two foot needles ; slip a stitch from each end of the instep needle upon a foot needle to make the stitches equal, 21 for the instep and 21 for the foot. Knit for the foot 23 rounds. Then for the **Toe**—* On first foot needle, knit 1, slip 1, knit 1, pass the slipped stitch over, knit to within 3 stitches of the end of the second foot needle, knit 2 together, knit 1, on the instep needle, knit 1, slip 1, knit 1, pass the slipped stitch over, knit to within 3 stitches of the end of the needle, knit 2 together, knit 1 ; knit 1 plain round ; repeat from * till reduced to 8 stitches. Slip the foot stitches all on one needle, turn the sock wrong side out, place the two needles parallel with each other, and cast off by knitting together a stitch from each needle.

GENTLEMAN'S BICYCLE STOCKING.
CABLE AND RIB PATTERN.

REQUIRED, 8 ozs. of good quality Scotch Fingering, and four steel knitting needles No. 14. Cast 40 stitches on each of three needles, making a total of 120 stitches, and knit 36 rounds thus—Knit 2 purl 2, knit 4, purl 2, and repeat; there are 10 stitches in a pattern. **1st Pattern round**—Knit 2, purl 2, slip the next 2 stitches on to a spare pin, knit the 2 next, then replace the 2 slipped stitches on the left-hand needle and knit them, purl 2, and repeat. **2nd round**—Knit 2, purl 2, knit 4, purl 2, and repeat. Knit 6 more rounds the same as the second round. These eight rounds constitute the pattern, continue them till 96 rounds are knitted. **97th round**—Same as the first round. Knit 3 rounds the same as the second round. **101st round**—Decreasings begin; with a piece of cotton mark the second line of cable on the first needle, this cable and the cable on each side of it are to be knitted entirely out; beginning the round at the first needle, knit 2, purl 2, knit 4, purl 2, knit 2, purl 2 together, knit 4, purl 2 together, knit 2, purl 2, knit 4, purl 2, and finish this needle and knit the two other needles the same as previous rounds. **102nd round**—Beginning on the first needle, knit 2, purl 2, knit 4, purl 2, knit 2, purl 1, knit 4, purl 1, knit 2, purl 2, knit 4, purl 2, and continue in pattern to the end of the third needle. Knit 2 more rounds the same as the last round. **105th round** — Knit 2 purl 2, twist the cable, purl 2, knit 2, purl 1, twist the cable, purl 1, knit 2, purl 2, twist the cable, purl 2, and continue in pattern. **106th round** —Knit 2, purl 2, knit 4, purl 2, knit 2, purl 1, knit 4, purl 1, knit 2, purl 2, knit 4, purl 2, and continue in pattern. **107th round** —Knit 2, purl 2, knit 4, purl 2, knit 2, purl 1, slip 1, knit 1, pass the slipped stitch over, knit 2 together, purl 1, knit 2, purl 2, knit 4, purl 2, and continue in pattern. **108th round**—Knit 2, purl 2, knit 4, purl 2, knit 2, purl 1, knit 2, purl 1, knit 2, purl 2, knit 4, purl 2, and continue in pattern. Knit 4 more rounds the same as the last round. **113th round**—Knit 2, purl 2, twist the cable, purl 2, knit 2, purl 1, slip 1, knit 1, pass the slipped stitch over, purl 1, knit 2, purl 2, twist the cable, purl 2, and continue in pattern. **114th round** —Knit 2, purl 2, knit 4, purl 2, knit 2, purl 3, knit 2, purl 2, knit 4, purl 2, and continue in pattern. **115th round**—Knit 2, purl 2, knit 4, purl 2, knit 2, purl 3 together, knit 2, purl 2, knit 4, purl 2, and continue in pattern. **116th round**—Knit 2, purl 2, knit 4, purl 2, knit 2, purl 1, knit 2, purl 2, knit 4, purl 2, and continue in pattern. Knit 4 more rounds the same as the last round. **121st round**— Knit 2, purl 2, twist the cable, purl 2, knit 1, slip 1, knit 2 together, pass the slipped stitch over, knit 1, purl 2, twist the cable, purl 2, and continue in pattern. **122nd round**—Knit 2, purl 2, knit 4, purl 2, knit 3, purl 2, knit 4, purl 2, and continue in pattern. Knit 6 more rounds the same as the last round. **129th round**—Knit 2, purl 2, twist the cable, purl 2, slip 1, knit 2 together, pass the slipped stitch over, purl 2, twist the cable, purl 2, and continue in pattern. **130th round**—Knit 2, purl 2, knit 4, purl 5, knit 4, purl 2, and continue in pattern. **131st round**—Knit 2, purl 2, knit 3, slip 1, knit 1, pass the slipped stitch over, purl 3, knit 2 together, knit 3, purl 2, and continue in pattern. **132nd round**—Knit 2, purl 2, knit 4, purl 3, knit 4, purl 2, and continue in pattern. Knit 4 more rounds the same as the last round. **137th round**—Knit 2, purl 2, twist the cable, purl 3, twist the cable, purl 2, and continue in pattern. **138th round**—Knit 2, purl 2, knit 4, purl 3, knit 4, purl 2, and continue in pattern. **139th round**—Knit 2, purl 2, knit 3, slip 1, knit 1, pass the slipped stitch over, purl 1, knit 2 together, knit 3, purl 2, and continue in pattern. **140th round**—Knit 2, purl 2, knit 4, purl 1, knit 4, purl 2, and continue in pattern. Knit 4 more

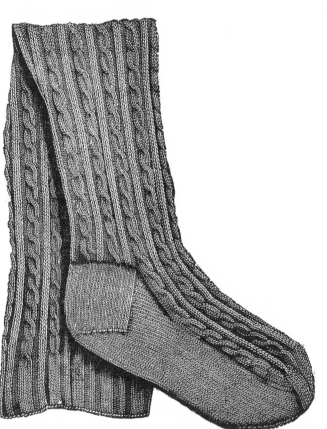

Gentleman's Bicycle Stocking. Cable and Rib.

rounds the same as the last round. **145th round**—Knit 2, purl 2, twist the cable, purl 1, twist the cable, purl 2, and continue in pattern. **146th round**—Knit 2, purl 2, knit 4, purl 1, knit 4, purl 2, and continue in pattern. **147th round**—Knit 2, purl 2, slip 1, knit 1, pass the slipped stitch over, knit 2, purl 1, knit 2, knit 2 together, purl 2, and continue in pattern. **148th round**—Knit 2, purl 2, knit 3, purl 1, knit 3, purl 2, and continue in pattern. Knit 2 more rounds the same as the last round. **151st round**—Knit 2, purl 2, slip 1, knit 1, pass the slipped stitch over, knit 1, purl 1, knit 1, knit 2 together, purl 2, and continue in pattern. **152nd round**—Knit 2, purl 2, knit 2, purl 1, knit 2, purl 2, and continue in pattern. **153rd round**—Knit 2, purl 2, slip the next 2 stitches on the spare pin, knit 2 together, knit 1, replace the 2 slipped stitches on the left-hand needle and knit them, purl 2, knit 2, and continue in pattern. **154th round**—Knit 2, purl 2, knit 4, purl 2, knit 2, and continue in pattern. Knit 6 more rounds the same as the last round. **161st round**—Knit 2, purl 2, twist the cable, purl 2, knit 2, and continue in pattern. **162nd round**—Knit 2, purl 2, knit 4, purl 2, knit 2, and continue in pattern. **163rd round**—Knit 2, purl 2, slip 1, knit 1, pass the slipped stitch over, knit 2 together, purl 2, knit 2, and continue in pattern. **164th round**—Knit 2, purl 2, knit 2, purl 2, knit 2, and continue in pattern. Knit 2 more rounds the same as the last round. **167th round**—Knit 2, purl 2 together, knit 2, purl 2 together, knit 2, and continue in pattern. **168th round**—Knit 2, purl 1, knit 2, purl 1, knit 2, and continue in pattern. **169th round**—Knit 2, purl 1, slip 1, knit 1, pass the slipped stitch over, purl 1, knit 2, and continue in pattern. **170th round**—Knit 2, purl 3, knit 2, and continue in pattern. Knit 2 more rounds the same as the last round. **173rd round**—Knit 1, slip 1, knit 1, pass the slipped stitch over, purl 1, knit 1 together, knit 1, and continue in pattern. **174th round**—Knit 2 purl 1, knit 2, and continue in pattern. Knit 2 more rounds the same as the last round. **177th round**—Knit 1, slip 1, knit 1, pass the slipped stitch over, knit 2, and continue in pattern. **178th round**—Knit 4, purl 2, knit 4, purl 2, and continue in pattern. **179th round**—Slip 1, knit 1, pass the slipped stitch over, knit 2 together, purl 2, knit 4, purl 2, and continue in pattern. **180th round**— Knit 2, purl 2, knit 4, purl 2, and continue in pattern. There are now 90 stitches in the round, and the pattern is all straight on as it began, the only difference being that now there are nine cable twists round the leg instead of 12; re-arrange the stitches, keeping the same knit 2 stitches at the beginning of the first needle, and placing 30 stitches on each needle. Knit 4 more rounds the same as the last round. Then knit the 1st pattern round and the 7 following rounds eight times, making 64 rounds for the ankle. For the **Heel**—Beginning on the first needle, knit 2, purl 2, knit 4, purl 2, knit 2, purl 2, knit 4, purl 2, knit 2, purl 2; turn the work, slip the first stitch, knit the next, purl 2, knit 2,* purl 4, knit 2, purl 2, knit 2, repeat from * three times, and there will be 46 stitches on one needle for the heel. Divide the remaining 44 stitches equally upon two needles, and leave them, as they will not be wanted till the heel is finished. Knit plain and purl in ribbing upon the 46 heel stitches, always slipping the first stitch in every row, till 34 rows are done. **To turn the Heel**—Slip the first stitch, knit plain 25 stitches, slip 1, knit 1, pass the slipped stitch over, knit 1; turn, slip the first stitch, purl 7, purl 2 together, purl 1; turn, slip the first stitch, knit 8, slip 1, knit 1, pass the slipped stitch over, knit 1; turn, slip the first

WELDON'S PRACTICAL STOCKING KNITTER.

stitch, purl 9, purl 2 together, purl 1 ; and continue thus working 1 more stitch each time of turning, till all the side stitches are knitted in, and 26 stitches remain on the needle for the top of the heel. Knit plain across the heel, and on the same needle pick up 20 stitches along the side of the flap, knitting each stitch as you pick it up; rib the 44 instep stitches all on to one needle ; and on another needle pick up 20 stitches along the opposite side of the flap, and knit 13 stitches from off the top of the heel. You now have 33 stitches on this needle, 33 stitches on the next foot needle, and 44 stitches on the instep needle. Knit plain along the foot needle, knit ribbing along the instep needle. For the **Gussets**—* On the first foot needle, knit 1, slip 1, knit 1, pass the slipped stitch over, knit plain to within 3 stitches of the end of the second foot needle, knit 2 together, knit 1 ; rib along the instep needle. Knit 1 round plain on foot and ribbed on instep. Repeat from * till reduced to 88 stitches in the round. Continue plain on foot and ribbed on instep till the foot measures 8½ or 9 inches, about 70 rounds. For the **Toe**—Knit plain along the first foot needle, and with the last stitch knit also the first stitch from off the next needle ; from this re-arrange the stitches, placing 29 stitches on each of the three needles ; the rounds now begin in the centre of the foot—knit 1, slip 1, knit 1, pass the slipped stitch over, knit plain to within 3 stitches of the end of the needle, knit 2 together, knit 1 ; knit the same on each of the other needles. Knit 1 plain round. And continue a decrease round and a plain round till reduced to 15 stitches in the round. Break off the wool, and with a rug needle sew the stitches up securely for the point of the toe.

GENTLEMAN'S STOCKING,

KNITTED IN A BERLIN PATTERN WITH THREE COLOURS.

THIS stocking is given for the benefit of really good knitters, as, though after the ribbing is done it is worked entirely in plain knitting, it is rather a difficult matter to be using wool from three balls at the same time, the pattern being introduced as in woolwork by the variety of colours employed, but when successfully accomplished this stocking is quite a work of art. As will be seen in the engraving, the pattern is arranged to represent diamonds—white diamonds on a brown stripe separated from each other by a line of white, and brown diamonds on a blue stripe separated from each other by a line of brown—the wool that is not in immediate use is passed along on the inside of the stocking and serves to make the fabric doubly thick and warm. Any small set Berlin pattern can be knitted in this way, remembering always that each square in the Berlin pattern represents a stitch in the knitting

Procure 4 ozs. each of blue and brown, and 2 ozs. of white Fingering wool; 4 steel needles No. 14. With blue wool cast 40 stitches on each of three needles, 120 stitches in all, and first of all knit in ribbing in the usual manner, doing 2 stitches plain and 2 stitches purl alternately, 2 rounds with blue, 2 rounds with brown, and 2 rounds with white, till 38 rounds are knitted, ending with blue. Now move round the stitches so that you get the *first stitch* of the round in the *centre* of the *first needle*, and *here* every round is to begin; mark the stitch with a thread of cotton to easily recognise it, as there will be nothing to denote it from any other stitch till the decreasings begin. Blue will not be wanted again just yet, and may be broken off and the end run in. **1st round of Pattern**—Knit 5 stitches with brown, 1 stitch with white, * 9 stitches with brown, 1

Gentleman's Stocking. Berlin Pattern.

stitch with white, and repeat from * to the end of the round, where there will be 4 brown stitches to knit to bring the pattern in. **2nd round**—1 stitch white, 4 brown, 1 white, 4 brown, and repeat. **3rd round**—1 stitch brown, 1 white, 3 brown, 1 white, 3 brown, 1 white, and repeat. **4th round**—1 white, 1 brown, 1 white, 2 brown, 1 white, 2 brown, 1 white, 1 brown, and repeat. **5th round**—1 stitch brown and 1 stitch white alternately all round. **6th round**—1 white, 1 brown, 1 white, 2 brown, 1 white, 2 brown, 1 white, 1 brown, and repeat. **7th round**—1 brown, 1 white, 3 brown, 1 white, 3 brown, 1 white, and repeat. **8th round**—1 white, 4 brown, and repeat. **9th round**—5 brown, 1 white, * 9 brown, 1 white, and repeat from *, ending with 4 brown stitches. **10th round**—Break off the white wool and join on blue, knit 5 stitches with blue, 1 stitch with brown, * 9 with blue, 1 with brown, and repeat from * to the end of the round, where there will be 4 stitches to knit with blue to bring the pattern in. **11th round**—1 stitch brown, 4 blue, 1 brown, 4 blue, and repeat. **12th round**—1 stitch blue, 1 brown, 3 blue, 1 brown, 3 blue, 1 brown, and repeat. **13th round**—1 brown, 1 blue, 1 brown, 2 blue, 1 brown, 2 blue, 1 brown, 1 blue, and repeat. **14th round**—1 stitch blue and 1 stitch brown alternately all round. **15th round**—1 brown, 1 blue, 1 brown, 2 blue, 1 brown, 2 blue, 1 brown, 1 blue, and repeat. **16th round**—1 blue, 1 brown, 3 blue, 1 brown, 3 blue, 1 brown, and repeat. **17th round**—1 brown, 4 blue, and repeat. **18th round**—5 blue, 1 brown, * 9 blue, 1 brown, and repeat from *, ending with 4 brown stitches. Break off blue wool and tie on white, and repeat from the first pattern round till you have knitted the seventh round of the fifth brown stripe, that is 79 rounds from the ribbing. You will by this time see how the pattern is progressing; the decreasings are now to begin, and the three patterns, 30 stitches, 15 each side the seam stitch, in the centre of the first needle, are to be gradually knitted out ; these decreasings are given stitch by stitch in the rounds in which they occur, in the intervening rounds the diamonds are to be preserved as accurately as possible, but there will be a stitch or two less each side the seam stitch in consequence of the decreasing ; of course the front of the stocking is continued in the complete pattern as detailed above. **80th round**—Knit same as the eighth round, and when 5 stitches before the seam stitch knit 1 white, knit 2 together, knit 2 with brown, seam stitch white, knit 2, slip 1, knit 1 with brown, pass the slipped stitch over, 1 white and proceed in pattern. In next round there are 7 brown stitches to knit at the seam. In the next round 7 blue stitches. **83rd round**—When 4 before the seam stitch, knit 1 brown, 3 blue, seam stitch brown, 3 blue, 1 brown, and continue. **84th round**—When 4 before the seam stitch, knit 1 brown, knit 2 together with blue, 1 brown, seam stitch blue, 1 brown, knit 2 together with blue, 1 brown, and continue. **85th round**—When 3 before the seam stitch, knit 1 brown, 1 blue, 1 brown, seam stitch blue, 1 brown, 1 blue, 1 brown, and continue. **92nd round**—When 3 before the seam stitch, knit 1 white, knit 2 together, knit 1, knit 2 together with brown, 1 white, and continue. **93rd round**—When 2 before the seam stitch, knit 1 white, 3 brown, 1 white, and continue. **100th round**—When 2 before the seam stitch, knit 1 brown, slip 1, knit 2 together with blue, pass the slipped stitch over, 1 brown, and continue. **101st round**—When 1 before the seam stitch, knit 1 brown, seam stitch blue, 1 brown, and continue. **108th round**—When 1 before the seam stitch, with brown slip 1 knit 2 together, pass the slipped stitch over. Now knit the brown stripe straight in pattern, you will see it fits in, one pattern being quite knitted away. **118th round**—When 10 before the seam stitch, knit 1 brown, with blue knit 5, knit 2 together, knit 5, knit 2 together, knit 5, knit 1 brown, and continue. **119th round**—When 9 before the seam stitch, knit 1 brown, 8 blue, 1 brown, 8 blue, 1 brown, and continue. **120th round**—When 9 before the seam stitch, knit 1 brown, 7 blue, 1 brown, 1 blue, 1 brown, 7 blue, 1 brown, and continue. **121st round**—When 9 before the seam stitch, knit 1 brown, with blue knit 2, knit 2 together, knit 2, 1 brown, 1 blue, 1 brown, with blue knit 2, knit 2 together, knit 2, 1 brown, and continue. **122nd round**—When 8 before the seam stitch, knit 1 brown, 4 blue, 1 brown, 1 blue, 1 brown, 1 blue, 1 brown, 1 blue, 1 brown, 4 blue, 1 brown, and continue. **126th round**—When 8 before the seam stitch, knit 1 brown, with blue knit 4, knit 2 together, knit 3, knit 2 together, knit 4, 1 brown, and continue. **127th round**—When 7 before the seam stitch, knit 1 white, 13 brown, 1 white, and continue. **128th round**—When 7 before the seam stitch, knit 1 white, knit 2, knit 2 together, knit 2 with brown, 1 white, knit 2, knit 2 together, knit 2 with brown, 1 white, and continue. **129th round**—When 6 before the seam stitch, knit 1 white, 4 brown, 1 white, 1 brown, 1 white, 4 brown, 1 white, and continue. **135th round**—When 6 before the seam stitch, knit 1 white, with brown knit 2, knit 2 together, knit 3, knit 2 together, knit 2, 1 white, and continue. Now the pattern again comes in evenly, knit the blue stripe without decreasing till the last round. **144th round**—When 5 before the seam stitch, knit 1 brown, with blue knit 2, knit 2 together, knit 1, knit 2 together, knit 2, knit 1 brown, and continue. **145th round**—When 4 before the seam stitch, knit 1 white, 7 brown, 1 white, and continue. **146th round**—When 4 before the seam stitch, knit 1 white, 3 brown, seam stitch white, 3 brown, 1 white, and continue. **147th round**—When 4 before the seam-stitch, knit 1 white, 2 brown, 1 white, seam stitch brown, 1 white, 2 brown, 1 white, and continue. **148th round**—When 4 before the seam stitch, knit 1 white, knit 2 together with brown, 1 white, seam stitch brown, 1 white, knit 2 together with brown, 1 white, and continue. **149th round**—When 3 before the seam stitch, knit 1 white, 1 brown, 1 white, seam stitch brown, 1 white, 1 brown, 1 white, and continue. **150th round**—When 3 before the seam stitch, knit 1 white, 2 brown, 1 white, 2 brown, 1 white, and continue. **154th round**—When 3 before the seam stitch, knit 1 brown, with blue knit 2 together, knit 1, knit 2 together, knit 1 brown, and continue. **155th round**—When 2 before the seam stitch, knit 1 brown, 3 blue, 1 brown and continue. **159th round**—When 2 before the seam-stitch, knit 1 brown, with blue slip 1, knit 2 together, pass the slipped stitch over, knit 1 brown and continue. **160th round**—When 1 before the seam stitch, knit 1 brown, seam stitch blue, 1 brown, and continue. **162nd round**—When 1 before the seam stitch, with brown slip 1, knit 2 together, pass the slipped stitch over, and continue. **163rd round**—This round begins a brown stripe, and the pattern comes in evenly, with 90 stitches in the round. Knit 5 stripes (45 rounds) straight on in pattern for the ankle. When you have finished the last of these rounds, which will be the ninth round of the twelfth brown stripe, from the top, break off the wool and run the ends in. Now re-arrange the stitches, place the seam stitch with 20 stitches to the right on one needle, and the 20 stitches to the left of the seam stitch on another needle, these are for the heel and include four patterns, a white line stitch being at the beginning and at the end; the remaining 49 stitches are to be

Lady's Ribbed Stocking, No. 2.

all on one needle for the instep. The instep and the foot are to be knitted separately and sewn up, thus when the foot is worn out it can easily be unpicked and renewed. Proceed with the pattern upon the 49 stitches for the instep, working with two needles in this manner, * knit 9 stitches with blue, 1 brown, 9 blue, 1 brown, and repeat from * ending with 9 blue stitches; turn, * purl 4 blue, 1 brown, 4 blue, 1 brown, and repeat from * ending with 4 blue stitches; turn, * knit 3 blue, 1 brown, 1 blue, 1 brown, 3 blue, 1 brown, and repeat from * ending with 3 blue; turn, * purl 2 blue, 1 brown, 1 blue, 1 brown, 1 blue, 1 brown, 2 blue, 1 brown, and repeat from * ending with 2 blue. Continue a plain row and a purl row preserving the pattern, and do four blue and four brown stripes. Then for the **Toe**—which is to be all blue—slip 1, knit 1, slip 1, knit 1, pass the slipped stitch over, * knit 2, slip 1, knit 1, pass the slipped stitch over, repeat from * 4 times, knit 1, * knit 2 together, knit 2, repeat from * 5 times, 3 stitches now on; turn, purl a row; turn, slip 1, knit 1, * slip 1, knit 1, pass the slipped stitch over, knit 4, repeat from * once, slip 1, knit 1, pass the slipped stitch over, knit 5, * knit 2 together, knit 4, repeat from * once, knit 2 together, knit 2, 31 stitches now on; turn, purl a row; * turn, slip 1, knit 1, slip 1, knit 1, pass the slipped stitch over, knit plain to within four stitches of the end of the pin, knit 2 together, knit 2; turn, purl a row; repeat from * till reduced to 11 stitches on the pin, and cast off. Now for the **Heel**—Take the blue wool and knit the 41 heel stitches plain on to one needle, turn, slip 1, purl, knit 40; turn, slip 1, knit 40, turn, slip 1, purl 40, and continue till 32 rows are done for the flap: then to turn heel, still with blue, slip 1, knit 24, slip 1, knit 1, pass the slipped stitch over, knit 1, turn, slip 1, purl 10, purl 2 together, purl 1; * turn, slip 1, knit 10, slip 1, knit 1, pass the slipped stitch over, knit 1, turn, slip 1, purl 10, purl 2 together, purl 1, and repeat, from * till all the side stitches are knitted in and 13 remain for the top of the heel. Knit the 13 stitches, pick up 20 along the side of the flap, knitting each stitch as you pick it up; turn, purl 33, pick up 20 along the other side of the flap, purling each stitch as you pick it up, turn, slip 1, knit 52, turn, slip 1, purl 52; * turn, knit 1, slip 1, knit 1 pass the slipped stitch over, knit to within three stitches of the end of the needle, knit 2 together, knit 1, turn, purl a row, knit a row, purl a row, and repeat from *, doing the first 9 rows with blue, the next 9 rows with brown, and so on, so as to be level with the instep stripes when sewn up, and reduce to 31 stitches. Then continue stripes till the fourth brown stripe is completed. For **Toe**—Knit all blue, first a plain row and then a purl row, and *then* decrease from 31 stitches to 11 stitches as described for the upper portion of the toe, and cast off, and sew the foot up neatly.

LADY'S RIBBED STOCKING, No. 2.

REQUIRED, 7 balls of black Cocoon wool and four steel knitting needles, No. 16. Cast on 120 stitches: 51 on the first needle, 36 on the second needle, and 33 on the third needle. Knit in ribbing 3 stitches plain and 1 stitch purl, round and round, till 11 inches are worked. Now with a thread of cotton mark the 1 purl stitch in the centre of the first needle and consider it as the seam stitch, and on each side of this decreasings are to be made—rib to within 4 stitches of the seam stitch, then knit 3 together, knit 1, purl the seam stitch, knit 1, slip 1, knit 2 together, pass the slipped stitch over, and finish the round as usual. * Knit 11 ribbed rounds. Next round decrease again in the same way. Repeat from * till the stocking is reduced to 88 stitches. Then knit for the ankle straight on in ribbing for 5 inches. For the **Heel**—Rib to the seam stitch and 23 stitches beyond, turn the work, slip the first stitch, and again rib 23 stitches beyond the seam stitch, thus bringing 47 stitches upon one needle wherewith to knit the heel, and leaving 41 instep stitches divided upon two needles. Continue ribbing upon the heel needle forwards and backwards, always slipping the first stitch in every row for 40 rows. **To turn the Heel**—Leave off ribbing, slip the first stitch and knit 22 plain, purl the seam stitch. knit 1, slip 1, knit 1, pass the slipped stitch over, knit 1; turn, slip the first stitch, purl 2, knit the seam stitch, purl 1, purl 2 together, purl 1; turn, slip the first stitch, knit 2, purl the seam stitch, knit 2, slip 1, knit 1, pass the slipped stitch over, knit 1; turn, slip the first stitch, purl 3, knit the seam stitch, purl 2, purl 2 together, purl 1; turn, slip the first stitch, knit 3, purl the seam stitch, knit 3, slip 1, knit 1, pass the slipped stitch over, knit 1; turn slip the first stitch, purl 4, knit the seam stitch, purl 3, purl 2 together, purl 1; and continue thus doing one stitch more each time on each side the seam stitch till all the side stitches are knitted in, and 23 stitches remain on the needle for the top of the heel. Knit plain along the 23 stitches, and on the same needle pick up and knit 23 stitches along the side of the flap; on another needle rib the 41 instep stitches; and on the next needle pick up and knit 23 stitches along the other side of the flap, and knit 11 stitches from the top of the heel. There now are 110 stitches in the round. Knit plain along the foot needle. Rib along the instep needle. For the **Gussets**—* On the first foot needle, knit 1, slip 1, knit 1, pass the slipped stitch over, knit plain to within 3 stitches of the end of the second foot needle, knit 2 together, knit 1; rib along the instep needle. Knit 2 rounds plain on foot and ribbed on instep. Repeat from * till reduced to 88 stitches. Continue plain on foot and ribbed on instep till the foot including the heel measures 8 inches. For the **Toe**—Knit along the first foot needle and take the last stitch of it together with the first stitch from the next needle; the rounds of the toe are to begin here, exactly in the centre of the sole of the foot; from this arrange the stitches equally, 29 stitches upon each needle, and knit, **1st round**—Knit 1, slip 1, knit 1, pass the slipped stitch over, knit plain to within 3 stitches of the end of the needle, knit 2 together, knit 1; do the same on each of the other needles. **2nd round**—Knit plain, no decrease. Repeat these two rounds till the toe is reduced to 12 stitches. Take a rug needle and run the wool through the stitches, and sew up neatly.

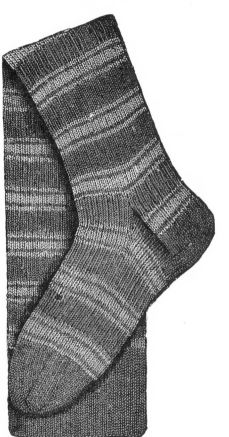

Lady's Silk Stocking, Ribbed in Stripes.

GENT'S CABLE KNIT STOCKING.

THIS stocking is the same pattern as gent's cable knit stocking on page 7 of No. 12, but is knitted in an easier way, and does not involve so much counting of stitches, the decreasings take place at regular intervals round the leg instead of being as usual all at the back, and by this means the cable stripes are held intact from knee to ankle, and the effect is very good. Select wool and needles as advised for the gent's cable knit stocking, and cast 36 stitches on each of three needles, 108 stitches in all. Knit in ribbing, 2 stitches purl and 2 stitches plain, for 40 rounds, and be sure and *begin* each round with the 2 *purl* stitches. **1st Pattern round**—Purl 6, knit 6. and repeat. Knit 8 more rounds the same as this round. **10th round**—Purl 6, slip the next 3 stitches on to a spare pin, knit the three next stitches, knit the 3 stitches off the spare pin, and repeat. Repeat these ten pattern rounds 7 more times. **81st round**—Purl 6, knit 6. and

repeat. Knit 4 more rounds the same as this round. **86th round**—Purl 3, purl 2 together, purl 1, knit 6 and repeat. **87th round**—Purl 5, knit 6, and repeat. Knit 2 more rounds the same as this round. **90th round**—Purl 5, knit cable twist on 6 stitches, and repeat. **91st round**—Purl 5, knit 6, and repeat. Knit 8 more rounds the same as this round. **100th round**—Purl 5, knit cable twist on 6 stitches, and repeat. Repeat the last 10 rounds. **111th round**—Purl 5, knit 6, and repeat. Knit 4 more rounds the same as this round. **116th round**—Purl 1, purl 2 together, purl 2, knit 6, and repeat. **117th round**—Purl 4, knit 6, and repeat. Knit 2 more rounds the same as this round. **120th round**—Purl 4, knit cable twist on 6 stitches, and repeat. **121st round**—Purl 4, knit 6, and repeat. Knit 8 more rounds the same as this round. **130th round**—Purl 4, knit cable twist on 6 stitches, and repeat. Repeat the last 10 rounds. **141st round**—Purl 4, knit 6, and repeat. Knit 4 more rounds the same as this round. **146th round**—Purl 1, purl 2 together, purl 1, knit 6, and repeat. **147th round**—Purl 3, knit 6, and repeat. Knit 2 more rounds the same as this round. **150th round**—Purl 3, knit cable twist on 6 stitches, and repeat. **151st round**—Purl 3, knit 6, and repeat. Knit 8 more rounds the same as this round. **160th round**—Purl 3, knit cable twist on 6 stitches, and repeat. There are now 81 stitches in the round, 27 stitches on each needle. Repeat the 10 pattern rounds till you can count 21 cable twists down the leg, when 210 rounds will be knitted. Then proceed with the heel and foot in accordance with the former instructions; or, if you like, finish off the instep first, and then knit the heel and sole separately and sew up, so as to be easily refooted.

LADY'S SILK STOCKING.

THIS stocking is ribbed in stripes of colour, and for an evening stocking is particularly bright and effective; fewer colours may be employed if preferred, as black and crimson alternately, or black and gold, or it may be worked entirely with one colour. Required, 5 oz. of black Imperial Knitting Silk, 3 oz. of deep bright blue, and 2 oz. each of crimson, pink, and old gold. Four steel knitting needles, No. 17 for a gentleman's size. No. 18 for a lady. With black silk cast 44 stitches on the first needle, and 38 stitches on each of two other needles, making a total of 120 stitches. Knit round and round in ribbing, 3 stitches plain and 1 stitch purl, for 50 rounds. After the 50th round is complete rib 23 stitches along the first needle, this brings you to a purl stitch which if to be the seam stitch of the stocking, and here all rounds are to begin, and when changing colours purl the seam stitch with both colours taken together, not breaking off the colour last used, but leaving it at the back till wanted again. Now from this seam stitch work, still in ribbing, 2 rounds with crimson, 2 rounds with pink, 2 rounds with gold, 6 rounds with blue, 2 rounds with gold, 2 rounds with pink, 2 rounds with crimson, 12 rounds with black, and repeat these colours in due succession for the whole length of the stocking. In the 2nd round of the black stripe, after purling the seam stitch, knit 1, increase 1, knit 2, and continue ribbing till within 1 stitch of the seam stitch again, when increase 1, knit 1; increase again the same way in the 11th round of the same black stripe, and in the 2nd round of the next blue stripe. Also increase in the 2nd round and in the 11th round of the next black stripe, and in the 2nd round of the following blue stripe. Now there are 132 stitches in the round, and the plain rib each side the seam stitch consists of 9 stitches instead of 3 stitches. Continue in ribbing on the 132 stitches till you have completed the fourth coloured stripe. Then decrease in this manner: In the 2nd round of the fourth black stripe, after purling the seam stitch, knit 1, slip 1, knit 1, pass the slipped stitch over, rib round till within 3 stitches of the seam stitch, knit 2 together, knit 1 ; decrease again in the 11th round of the same black stripe, and in the 2nd round of the next blue stripe. And continue decreasing in the same manner till reduced to 104 stitches. The ribbing now comes in evenly, 3 plain, 1 purl, all round. Knit on in stripes of colour for the ankle till you have done 6 rounds of the tenth black stripe. Now for the **Heel**—Having purled the seam stitch, rib 27 stitches beyond ; turn the work, slip the first stitch, rib to the seam stitch and rib 27 stitches beyond ; this brings 55 stitches on one

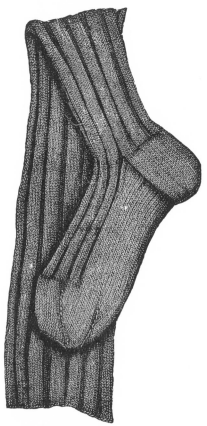

Gentleman's Ribbed Stocking.

needle for the heel, and 49 stitches are left standing as they are upon two needles till required for knitting the instep. Rib on the heel needle forwards and backwards, and slipping the first stitch in every row for 40 rows, working one set of stripes and then finishing the heel with black. **To turn the Heel**—Slip the first stitch, knit plain 26 stitches, purl the seam stitch, knit 5, slip 1, knit 1, pass the slipped stitch over ; turn, slip the first stitch, purl 5, knit the seam stitch, purl 5, purl 2 together ; * turn, slip the first stitch, knit 5, purl the seam stitch, knit 5, slip 1, knit 1, pass the slipped stitch over ; turn, slip the first stitch, purl 5, knit the seam stitch, purl 5, purl 2 together ; and repeat from * till all the side stitches are knitted in, and 13 stitches remain on the needle for the top of the heel. Knit 6, purl the seam stitch, knit 6, and on the same needle pick up and knit 22 stitches along the side of the flap ; rib the 49 instep stitches all on one needle, and on another needle pick up and knit 22 stitches along the opposite side of the flap, and knit 6 stitches from the top of the heel. The stitches are now again arranged upon three needles, 106 stitches in the round. On account of the stripes, a seam stitch (the first stitch on the next needle) is to be continued down the sole, and all rounds are to begin at it, and the colours changed at it as in the leg. Still with black silk, purl the seam stitch, knit plain to the end of the needle ; rib along the instep needle ; knit plain the next needle. For the **Gussets—1st round**—Purl the seam stitch, knit to within 3 stitches of the end of the needle, knit 2 together, knit 1 ; rib along the instep needle ; on the right-hand foot needle, knit 1, slip 1, knit 1, pass the slipped stitch over, knit to the end of the needle. **2nd round**—Purl the seam stitch, knit plain to the end of the needle ; rib along the instep

needle ; knit plain the next needle. **3rd round**—Same as the second round. Repeat these three rounds, keeping the colours in regular order, till reduced to 94 stitches for the round of the foot ; and proceed on the 94 stitches till the foot is the length required. Slip 1 stitch from each end of the instep needle on to each foot needle, so you get 47 stitches on the instep and 47 stitches divided between the two foot needles. For the **Toe**—All black— Knit plain to the end of the needle, discontinuing the seam stitch ; * on the instep needle, knit 4, slip 1, knit 1, pass the slipped stitch over, knit plain to within 6 stitches of the end of the needle, knit 2 together, knit 4 ; on the foot needle, knit 4, slip 1, knit 1, pass the slipped stitch over, knit to within 6 stitches of the end of the second foot needle, knit 2 together, knit 4 ; knit 1 plain round ; repeat from * till reduced to 26 stitches. Slip the 13 foot stitches all on to one needle, hold this parallel with the instep needle, and cast off by knitting a stitch from each needle.

GENTLEMAN'S RIBBED STOCKING.

REQUIRED, 8 ozs. of Alloa yarn or Scotch fingering, and four steel knitting needles, No. 15. Cast 37 stitches on the first needle, 32 stitches on the second needle, and 35 stitches on the third needle, making a total of 104 stitches. Knit in ribbing, 5 stitches plain, and 3 stitches purl, for 50 rounds. Mark with a thread of cotton the 3 purled stitches which stand fourteenth, fifteenth, and sixteenth in the centre of the first needle, these are to be considered as seam stitches, and are to be kept straight in line to the heel of the stocking. In the **51st round**, * when 2 stitches before the seam stitch, pick up a thread and knit it to form an extra stitch on the needle, knit 2, purl 3 seam stitches, knit 2, increase another stitch, and finish the round as heretofore ; knit the next 7 rounds in

Striped Sock for a Boy of Five.

ribbing as before, only now there will be an extra stitch in the plain ribs on each side of the seam ; repeat from * till there are 4 stitches increased each side, 112 stitches in the round. Knit on in ribbing till the stocking measures 10 inches or 11 inches from the commencement. Then to decrease the **Leg**—* Knit in ribbing till within 3 stitches of the seam stitches, knit 2 together, knit 1, purl the 3 seam stitches, knit 1, slip 1, knit 1, pass the slipped stitch over, and rib to the end of the round. Knit 7 ribbed rounds. Repeat from * till you come to knit only 1 plain rib stitch on each side the seam. For the next decrease, purl the 3 seam stitches together. Knit 7 ribbed rounds. For the next decrease, slip the 1 plain rib stitch to the right of the seam, knit together the 1 purl seam stitch and the 1 plain rib stitch to the left, and pass the slipped stitch over them, this joins the ribs neatly. Knit 7 ribbed rounds. For the next decrease, purl 2 together, purl 3, purl 2 together. Knit 7 ribbed rounds. For the next decrease, purl 2 together, purl 1, purl 2 together. And now the stocking is reduced to 88 stitches in the round, and the ribbing comes in evenly, 5 plain, 3 purl, all round, as it did at the commencement of the stocking, 3 purl stitches being sixth, seventh, and eighth upon the first needle for the seam. Knit 66 rounds on the 88 stitches for the ankle. For the **Heel**—Beginning on the first needle, knit 5, purl the 3 seam stitches, knit 21; turn the work, slip the first stitch, purl 20, knit the 3 seam stitches, purl 21; * turn, slip the first stitch, knit 20, purl the 3 seam stitches, knit 21 ; turn, slip the first stitch, purl 20, knit the 3 seam stitches, purl 21 ; and repeat from * till 34 little rows are knitted. While doing this let the 43 instep stitches remain divided upon two needles till again wanted. **35th row of Heel**—Slip 1, knit 8, slip 1, knit 1, pass the slipped stitch over, knit 8, knit 2 together, purl 3 seam stitches, slip 1, knit 1, pass the slipped stitch over, knit 8, knit 2 together,

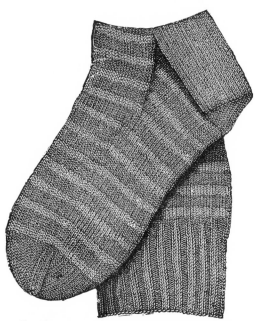

Gentleman's Plain Knit Striped Sock.

knit 9 **36th row**—Slip 1, purl 18, knit 3 seam stitches, purl 19. **37th row**—Slip 1, knit 8, slip 1, knit 1, pass the slipped stitch over, knit 6, knit 2 together, purl 3 seam stitches, slip 1, knit 1, pass the slipped stitch over, knit 6, knit 2 together, knit 9. **38th row**—Slip 1, purl 16, knit 3 seam stitches, purl 17. **39th row** —Slip 1, knit 8, slip 1, knit 1, pass the slipped stitch over, knit 4, knit 2 together, purl 3 seam stitches, slip 1, knit 1, pass the slipped stitch over, knit 4, knit 2 together, knit 9. **40th row**—Slip 1, purl 14, knit 3 seam stitches, purl 15. **41st row**—Slip 1, knit 8, slip 1, knit 1, pass the slipped stitch over, knit 2, knit 2 together. purl 3 seam stitches, slip 1, knit 1, pass the slipped stitch over, knit 2, knit 2 together, knit 9. **42nd row**—Slip 1, purl 12, knit 3 seam stitches, purl 13. **43rd row**—Slip 1, knit 8, slip 1, knit 1, pass the slipped stitch over, knit 2 together, purl 3 seam stitches, slip 1, knit 1, pass the slipped stitch over, knit 2 together, knit 9. **44th row**—Slip 1, purl 10, knit 1 : fold the needles together the wrong side out, put the 43 instep stitches all on one needle, and with the spare needle thus obtained knit the centre stitch of the three seam stitches, and cast off a stitch from each needle together till all are cast off; break off the wool. This is a Balbriggan heel. Now, hold the right side of the heel towards you, and beginning at the right-hand corner pick up on one needle 27 stitches thence to the centre of the heel, knitting each stitch as you pick it up; on a second needle pick up and knit 28 stitches from the centre of the heel to the left-hand corner of the heel ; then rib on a third needle the 43 instep stitches. For the **Gussets**—First knit 1 round plain on foot and ribbed instep. Then * on first foot needle, knit 1, slip 1, knit 1, pass the slipped stitch over, knit plain to within 3 stitches of the end of the second foot needle, knit 2 together, knit 1 ; rib along the instep needle. Knit 2 rounds plain on foot, and ribbed instep. Repeat from * till reduced to 84 stitches in the round. And continue without any more decreasing, plain on foot and ribbed on instep, for 75 rounds. For the **Toe**—This is a pointed toe. Beginning on the first foot needle for the **1st round**—

Knit 9, slip 1, knit 1, pass the slipped stitch over, knit 10 ; repeat three times. Knit 3 plain rounds. **5th round**—Knit 9, slip 1, knit 1, pass the slipped stitch over, knit 9 ; repeat. Knit 3 plain rounds. **9th round**—Knit 9, slip 1, knit 1. pass the slipped stitch over, knit 8 ; repeat. Knit 3 plain rounds. **13th round**— Knit 9, slip 1, knit 1, pass the slipped stitch over, knit 7 ; repeat. Knit 2 plain rounds. **16th round**—Knit 9, slip 1, knit 1, pass the slipped stitch over, knit 6 ; repeat. Knit 2 plain rounds. **19th round**—Knit 9, slip 1, knit 1, pass the slipped stitch over, knit 5 repeat. Knit 2 plain rounds. **22nd round**—Knit 9, slip 1, knit 1, passed the slipped stitch over, knit 4 ; repeat. Knit 2 plain rounds. **25th round**—Knit 9, slip 1, knit 1, pass the slipped stitch over, knit 3 ; repeat. Knit 1 plain round. **27th round**— Knit 9, slip 1, knit 1, pass the slipped stitch over, knit 2 ; repeat. Knit 1 plain round. **29th round**—Knit 9, slip 1, knit 1, pass the slipped stitch over, knit 1 ; repeat. Knit 1 plain round. Now decrease in *every* round in the same places, knitting 1 plain stitch less between the decreasings each time, till reduced to 4 stitches only. Break off the wool, and with a rug needle run the wool through the 4 stitches and sew them up securely.

STRIPED SOCK FOR BOY OF FIVE.

REQUIRED, 2 ozs. each of cardinal and grey soft Fingering wool. Four steel knitting needles, No. 15 or No. 16. With cardinal wool cast 34 stitches on the first needle, and 25 stitches on each of two other needles, 84 stitches in all, and knit in ribbing, 2 stitches plain and 1 stitch purl, for 28 rounds. This done, rib 17 stitches along the first needle, the *next stitch*, the purl stitch, is to be the seam stitch, each round is to commence here, and the colours are to be changed here every two rounds. Join on the grey wool, purl the seam stitch with both wools together, and knit with grey, 2 stitches plain and 1 stitch purl, for 2 rounds. Then purl the seam stitch with both wools, and knit with cardinal, 2 stitches plain and 1 stitch purl, for 2 rounds. Continue thus, 2 rounds with grey and 2 rounds with cardinal, not breaking off the wool but carrying it on at the back

Boy's Knickerbocker Stocking.

from stripe to stripe till you get to the tenth stripe of cardinal. where, after purling the seam stitch with both wools, slip 1, knit 1, pass the slipped stitch over, purl 1, and continue ribbing till within 2 stitches of the end of the round, where knit 2 together ; next round also with cardinal, purl the seam stitch, knit 1, purl 1, rib round, and there will be only 1 stitch to knit on the opposite side of the seam stitch. Knit 2 rounds with grey, 2 rounds with cardinal, 2 rounds with grey. In the next cardinal stripe, the twelfth decrease again in the same way; and again in the fourteenth cardinal stripe. There will now be 78 stitches in the round. Knit straight on in ribbing for the ankle, 2 rounds with each colour, till you begin the twenty-second stripe of cardinal, and there you commence the heel. Knit, still in ribbing, with cardinal, 21 stitches beyond the seam stitch, turn ; slip the first stitch and rib back (to do this you knit the purled stitches and purl the knit stitches) till 43 stitches are on this needle for the heel; let the remaining stitches (35) be divided equally upon two needles for the instep ; and go on ribbing upon the 43 stitches, always slipping the first stitch in every row for 30 rows, all cardinal. **To turn the Heel**—Slip the first stitch, knit 20, purl the seam stitch, slip 1, knit 1, pass the slipped

Shell Pattern Sock for Child of Two.

stitch over, knit 1 ; turn, slip the first stitch, purl 1, knit the seam stitch, purl 2 together, purl 1 ; turn, slip the first stitch, knit 1, purl the seam stitch, knit 1, slip 1, knit 1, pass the slipped stitch over, knit 1, turn, slip the first stitch, purl 2, knit the seam stitch, purl 1, purl 2 together, purl 1 ; turn, slip the first stitch, knit 2, purl the seam stitch, knit 2, slip 1, knit 1, pass the slipped stitch over, knit 1 ; turn, slip the first stitch, purl 3, knit the seam stitch, purl 2, purl 2 together, purl 1 ; turn, and continue in this manner, knitting one more stitch each time till all the side stitches are knitted in, and 23 stitches are on the needle for the top of the heel. Knit plain the 23 stitches (the seam stitch is discontinued), and on the same needle pick up 15 stitches along the side of the flap, knitting each stitch as you pick it up ; rib the 35 instep stitches all on to one needle ; and on another needle pick up 15 stitches along the other side of the flap and knit 11 stitches from off the heel needle ; there are now 88 stitches in the round arranged upon three needles. Knit plain along the next needle, rib along the instep needle, Now for the **Gussets** —The stripes are to continue as down the leg. * On first foot needle, knit 1, slip 1, knit 1, pass the slipped stitch over, knit plain to within 3 stitches of the end of the second foot needle, knit 2 together, knit 1, rib along the instep needle. Knit 1 round without decrease plain on the foot and ribbed instep. Repeat from * till the foot is reduced to 70 stitches in the round. Then continue plain on foot and ribbed on instep, and still knitting in stripes till you can count thirty-nine grey stripes down the whole sock. Knit the **Toe** with cardinal—Beginning on the first foot needle, knit 8, knit 2 together, and repeat to the end of the third needle. Knit 6 plain rounds. **8th round**—Knit 7, knit 2 together, and repeat. Knit 6 plain rounds. **15th round**—Knit 6, knit 2 together, and repeat. Knit 5 plain rounds. **21st round**—Knit 5, knit 2 together, and repeat. Knit 4 plain rounds. **26th round**—Knit 4, knit 2 together, and repeat. Knit 3 plain rounds. **30th round**—Knit 3, knit 2 together, and repeat. Knit 2 plain rounds. **33rd round** —Knit 2, knit 2 together, and repeat. Knit 1 plain round. **35th round**—Knit 1, knit 2 together, and repeat. Break off the wool, and with a rug needle sew up the stitches firmly for the point of the toe.

GENTLEMEN'S PLAIN KNIT STRIPED SOCK.

FOR this nicely-fitting sock 2½ ozs. of cardinal and 2 ozs. of grey Merino wool, or German fingering, will be required, also four steel knitting needles, No. 15. With cardinal wool cast 36 stitches on the first needle, and 24 stitches on each of two other needles, and knit in ribbing, 2 stitches plain and 2 stitches purl, for 36 rounds. Then work in plain knitting, and in the first round of plain knitting in the centre of the first needle, pick up a thread of the stocking and purl it for a seam stitch, and henceforward all the rounds are to commence at this stitch, which is to be purled in every round

From the seam stitch knit 4 rounds with cardinal ; then four rounds with grey ; then six rounds with cardinal and 4 rounds with grey for the whole leg of the sock, beginning each colour at the seam stitch, which purl with both wools taken together, and carry on the colours from stripe to stripe at the back without breaking off the wool. When three grey stripes are knitted (28 rounds), in the next round, the 1st round of cardinal, commence the decreasing, thus, after purling the seam stitch, knit 1, slip 1, knit 1, pass the slipped stitch over, knit plain round, and when 3 stitches before the seam stitch again, knit 2 together, knit 1. Decrease in the same way in the 1st round of each successive cardinal stripe till five decreasings have been made, when there will be 75 stitches in the round. Proceed on these 75 stitches till you have knitted 4 rounds of the tenth cardinal stripe. For the **Heel**—Knit on with cardinal 19 stitches past the seam stitch ; turn the work. slip the first stitch, purl to the seam stitch and 19 stitches beyond ; turn, and continue a plain row, and a purl row alternately on these 39 stitches, always slipping the first stitch in every row, till 36 rows are knitted. While doing this, let the 36 stitches for the instep remain as they are upon two needles till wanted. **To turn the Heel**—All cardinal—Slip the first stitch, knit 19, slip 1, knit 1, pass the slipped stitch over, knit 1 turn, slip the first stitch, purl 2, purl 2 together, purl 1 ; turn, slip the first stitch, knit 3, slip 1, knit 1, pass the slipped stitch over, knit 1 ; turn, slip the first stitch, purl 4, purl 2 together, purl 1 ; turn, and proceed, working one more stitch each time of turning, till all the side stitches are knitted in, and 21 stitches are on the needle for the top of the heel. Knit plain these 21 stitches, and on the same needle pick up, and as you pick up, knit 20 stitches along the side of the flap, knit the 36 instep stitches all on one needle ; and on another needle pick up and knit 20 stitches along the opposite side of the flap, and knit 10 stitches from off the top of the heel. Now there are 97 stitches arranged upon three needles. Purl the first stitch on the next needle, which is the centre stitch of the foot and is to be considered as a seam stitch and the colours changed at it as in the leg, knit plain round. For the **Gussets**—Beginning with grey wool, * purl the seam stitch, knit plain to within 3 stitches of the end of the needle, knit 2 together, knit 1 ; knit along the instep

Child's Fancy Sock.

needle ; on next needle, knit 1, slip 1, knit 1, pass the slipped stitch over, and knit plain to the end. Knit 2 plain rounds only purling the seam stitch. Repeat from * till reduced to 75 stitches, continuing in stripes of colour as in the leg. Knit round and round on the 75 stitches till the foot measures 9 inches in length ; and in the last round knit the seam stitch together with the last stitch of the round, and *from this* divide the stitches equally, placing 25 stitches on each of the three needles. For the **Toe**—All cardinal—Beginning in the centre of the foot, **1st round** —Knit 1, slip 1, knit 1, pass the slipped stitch over, knit to within 3 stitches of the end of the needle. knit 2 together, knit 1 ; work similarly upon each of the other needles. **2nd round**—Plain. Repeat these two rounds till the toe is reduced to 4 stitches on each needle. Break off the wool, and with a rug needle run the wool through the stitches and sew them neatly together.

BOY'S KNICKERBOCKER STOCKING.

REQUIRED, 5 ozs. of grey Penelope knickerbocker yarn, or Beehive yarn, and four steel knitting needles, No. 16 or No. 17. Cast 35 stitches on the first needle, 31 stitches on the second, and 30 stitches on the third needle, making a total of 96 stitches. Knit in ribbing, 2 stitches plain and 1 stitch purl, for 30 rounds. With a thread of cotton mark the 1 purl stitch in the centre of the first needle, it is to be the seam stitch, and in this stocking is in future always to be knitted *plain*. **Pattern for the Leg—1st round**

—Beginning on the first needle, purl 2, knit 1, and repeat all round. Knit 5 plain rounds. Repeat these six rounds seventeen times, that is doing 102 rounds in pattern. **103rd round**—Purl 2, knit 1, and repeat all round. **104th round**—Plain. **105th round**—Knit plain to within 6 stitches of the seam stitch, then slip 1, knit 1, pass the slipped stitch over, knit 2 together, knit 2, knit the seam stitch, knit 2, slip 1, knit 1, pass the slipped stitch over, knit 2 together, knit plain to the end of the round. **106th round**—Plain. **107th round**—Plain. **108th round**—Knit plain to within 4 stitches of the seam stitch, then knit 2 together, knit 2, knit the seam stitch, knit 2, slip 1, knit 1, pass the slipped stitch over, knit plain to the end of the round. * Repeat the pattern of the leg three times (18 rounds), then from the 103rd to the 108th rounds. * Continue from * to * till the stocking is reduced to 72 stitches, which will be when 78 rounds are knitted. Then continue the pattern on these 72 stitches for 60 rounds for the ankle. For the **Heel**—Beginning on the first needle, knit in pattern to the seam stitch and also knit 20 stitches beyond; turn the work, slip the first stitch, purl 40; and now knit a row and purl a row alternately on these 41 stitches for 16 rows. (The 31 instep stitches are meanwhile to stand as they are upon two needles till the heel is finished.) Then knit 40; purl 39; knit 38; purl 37; and so on, turning, and each time doing 1 stitch less, always slipping the first stitch in every row, till you purl 13 only; then knit 14; purl 15; knit 16; purl 17; and so on, widening each row, and *with the* stitch you knit from the side pick up

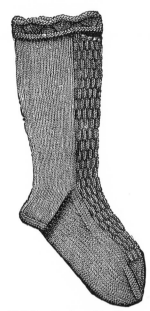

Child's Sock with Fancy Knit Front.

and knit also a thread of the stocking to prevent a little hole being formed, proceed till the heel is brought to its former proportion of 41 stitches, ending with a purl row. Knit plain these 41 stitches, and on the same needle pick up and knit 9 stitches along the side of the flap; knit the 31 instep stitches in pattern all on one needle; and on another needle pick up and knit 9 stitches along the opposite side of the flap, and knit 20 stitches off the top of the heel. You now have the stitches arranged, 29 stitches on this which is the first foot needle, 30 stitches on the second foot needle, and 31 stitches intact upon the instep needle. Knit plain along the second foot needle. Knit pattern along the instep needle. For the **Gussets**— * Beginning on the first foot needle, knit 1, slip 1, knit 1, pass the slipped stitch over, knit plain to within 3 stitches of the end of the second foot needle, knit 2 together, knit 1; knit pattern on the instep needle. Knit 2 rounds plain on foot and pattern on instep. Repeat from * till reduced to 70 stitches in the round. Now continue plain on foot and pattern on instep till the foot measures about 5½ inches, 66 rounds being done. When the foot is the right length slip 2 stitches from each foot needle on to the instep needle, so that you now have 35 stitches on the instep and 35 stitches divided between the two foot needles. For the **Toe**— * On the first foot needle, knit 2, slip 1, knit 1, pass the slipped stitch over, knit plain to within 4 stitches of the end of the second foot needle, knit 2 together, knit 2; on the instep needle, knit 2, slip 1, knit 1, pass the slipped stitch over, knit plain to within 4 stitches of the end of the needle, knit 2 together, knit 2; knit 8 plain round; and repeat from * till the toe is reduced to 22 stitches. Place the needles parallel with each other, 11 stitches to the top and 11 stitches to the bottom, and cast off by knitting together a stitch from each needle.

SHELL PATTERN SOCK FOR CHILD OF TWO.

REQUIRED, 3 skeins of Coat's crochet cotton, No. 24, and four steel knitting needles, No. 20. Cast 42 stitches on the first needle, and 28 stitches on each of two other needles, 98 stitches in all. **1st round**—Knit 1, purl 2, knit 9, purl 2, and repeat. Knit 15

more rounds the same as this round. Then for the **Shell Pattern—1st round**—Beginning on the first needle, knit 1, purl 2, slip 1, knit 1, pass the slipped stitch over, knit 1, make 1 and knit 1 four times, knit 2 together, purl 2, and repeat. **2nd round**—Knit 1, purl 2, knit 11, purl 2, and repeat. **3rd round**—Knit 1, purl 2, slip 1, knit 1, pass the slipped stitch over, knit 7, knit 2 together, purl 2, and repeat. **4th round**—Knit 1, purl 2, knit 9, purl 2, and repeat. Repeat these four rounds till you can count 26 shells knitted down the leg. There are no decreasings. For the **Heel**—Beginning on the first needle, knit 1, purl 2, slip 1, knit 1, pass the slipped stitch over, knit 1, make 1 and knit 1 four times, knit 2 together, purl 2, repeat this twice, then knit 1, purl 2, turn the work. **2nd row**—Knit 2, purl 1, knit 2, purl 11, repeat this twice, knit 2, purl 1, knit 2. **3rd row**—Purl 2, knit 1, purl 2, slip 1, knit 1, pass the slipped stitch over, knit 7, knit 2 together, repeat this twice, purl 2, knit 1, purl 2. **4th row**—Knit 2, purl 1, knit 2, purl 9, repeat this twice, knit 2, purl 1, knit 2; there are 47 stitches on the heel needle. Repeat these four rows three times, slipping the first stitch in every row. Then knit a plain row and a purl row alternately for 16 rows. **To turn the Heel**—Slip the first stitch, knit 25, slip 1, knit 1, pass the slipped stitch over; turn, slip the first stitch, purl 5, purl 2 together; turn, slip the first stitch, knit 5, slip 1, knit 1, pass the slipped stitch over; turn, slip the first stitch, purl 5, purl 2 together; turn, and continue thus till all the side stitches are knitted in, and 7 stitches remain on the needle for the top of the heel. Knit plain these 7 stitches, and on the same needle pick up and knit 19 stitches along the side of the flap; knit the 51 instep stitches in pattern on one needle; and on another needle pick up and knit 19 stitches along the other side of the flap, and knit 3 stitches off the top of the heel. The stitches are now arranged upon three needles; knit plain along the foot needle; knit pattern along the instep needle. For the **Gussets**— * Beginning on the first foot needle; knit 1, slip, 1, knit 1, pass the slipped stitch over, knit plain to within 3 stitches of the end of the second foot needle, knit 2 together, knit 1; knit in pattern along the instep needle. Knit 2 rounds plain on foot and pattern on instep. Repeat from * till reduced to 82 stitches in the round. Continue plain knitting on foot and pattern on instep till you have

41 shells knitted in all. Then slip 5 stitches from each end of the instep needle on to a foot needle, so that you now have 41 stitches on the instep and 41 stitches divided between the two foot needles. For the **Toe**—Beginning on the first foot needle, * knit 1, slip 1, knit 1, pass the slipped stitch over, knit plain to within 3 stitches of the end of the second foot needle, knit 2 together, knit 1; on the instep needle, knit 1, slip 1, knit 1, pass the slipped stitch over, knit plain to within 3 stitches of the end of the needle, knit 2 together, knit 1; knit 1 plain round. Repeat from * once; then decrease in every round till the toe is brought to 22 stitches. Slip the 11 foot stitches on to one needle, hold this level with the instep needle and cast off by knitting together a stitch from each needle.

Child's Fancy Knit Sock, Oak-Leaf Pattern.

CHILD'S FANCY SOCK.

THIS pretty sock should be knitted with Andalusian or soft white Merino wool, and four steel knitting needles, No. 16. Cast 30 stitches on the first needle, 18 on the second, and 18 on the third needle, 66 stitches in all. Purl 2 rounds. Then knit the pattern for the **edge. 1st round**—Make 1, knit 6, and repeat. **2nd round**—Knit 1, * purl 2 together, knit 5, and repeat from *; there will be 4 to knit at the end of the row. Repeat these 2 rounds four times Purl 2 rounds, and in the last of these purl the last 2 stitches together, to bring on the needles 65 stitches. **1st pattern round of the Leg**—Knit 1, purl 1, knit 1, purl 2, and repeat. **2nd round**—The same. **3rd round**—Knit 1, purl 2, knit 1, purl 1, and repeat. **4th round**—The same. Repeat these four rounds nine times, making 40 rounds of the pattern. **41st round**—Mark with a piece of cotton the 1 plain stitch that runs straight down the leg in the middle of the first needle, this stitch is to be considered as the seam stitch, and in this sock is always to be knitted plain unless otherwise directed; on the first needle knit in pattern as before till within 5 stitches of the seam stitch, then knit 1, purl 1, knit 2 together, purl 1, knit the seam stitch, purl 1, slip 1, knit 1, pass the slipped stitch over, purl 1, knit 1, and continue in pattern. **42nd round**—When 4 stitches before the seam stitch, knit 1, purl 1, knit 1, purl 1, knit the seam stitch, purl 1, knit 1, purl 1, knit 1, and continue in pattern. **43rd round**—When 4 before the seam stitch, knit 1, purl 3, knit the seam stitch, purl 3, knit 1, and continue in pattern. **44th round**—The same. **45th round**—When 4 before the seam stitch, knit 1, purl 1, knit 1, purl 1, knit the seam stitch, purl 1, knit 1, purl 1, knit 1, and continue in pattern. **46th round**—The same. **47th round**—Like the forty-third round. **48th round**—The same. **49th round**—When 4 before the seam stitch, knit 1, knit 2 together, purl 1, knit the seam stitch, purl 1, slip 1, knit 1, pass the slipped stitch over, knit 1, and continue in pattern. **50th round**—When 3 before the seam stitch, knit 2, purl 1, knit the seam stitch, purl 1, knit 2, and continue. **51st round**—When 3 before the seam stitch, knit 1, purl 2, knit the seam stitch, purl 2, knit 1, and continue. **52nd round**—The same. **53rd round**—When 3 before the seam stitch, knit 2, purl 1, knit the seam stitch, purl 1, knit 2, and continue. **54th round**—The same. **55th round**—Like the fifty-first round. **56th round**—The same. **57th round**—When 3 before the seam stitch, knit 1, knit 2 together, knit the seam stitch, slip 1, knit 1, pass the slipped stitch over, knit 1, and continue. **58th round**—When 2 before the seam stitch, knit 2, knit the seam stitch, knit 2, and continue. **59th round**—When 2 before the seam stitch, knit 1, purl 1, knit the seam stitch, purl 1, knit 1, and continue. **60th round**—The same. **61st round**—When 2 before the seam stitch, knit 2, knit the seam stitch, knit 2. **62nd round**—The same. **63rd round**—When 2 before the seam stitch, knit 1, purl 1, purl the seam stitch, purl 1, knit 1, and continue. **64th round**—The same. **65th round**—When 2 before the seam stitch, knit 2 together, purl the seam stitch, slip 1, knit 1, pass the slipped stitch over, and continue. **66th round**—When 1 before the seam stitch, knit 1, purl the seam stitch, knit 1, and continue. **67th and 68th rounds**—The same. **69th round**—When 1 before the seam stitch, slip 1, knit 2 together, pass the slipped stitch over, and continue. **70th, 71st, and 72nd rounds**—Knit in pattern all round, 55 stitches on the needles. Now continue the four pattern rounds straight on without any more decrease for 28 rounds, and there will be 100 rounds knitted, and 55 stitches on the needles. For the **Heel**—After knitting the seam stitch, purl 1, knit 1, purl 2, knit 1, purl 1, knit 1, purl 2, knit 1, purl 1, knit 1, purl 2; turn the work, slip the first stitch, knit 1, purl 1, knit 1, * purl 1, knit 2, purl 1, knit 1, and repeat from * till you have 29 stitches in all on the needle. Let the remaining 26 stitches remain equally divided on two needles for the instep. **3rd row of Heel**—Slip the first stitch, purl 1, knit 1, purl 1, knit 1, * knit 1, purl 2, knit 1, purl 1, repeat from * four times. **4th row**—Slip the first stitch, knit 1, purl 1, knit 2, * purl 1, knit 1, purl 1, knit 2, repeat from * four times. Proceed thus, knitting the 29 stitches forwards and backwards for 24 rows. **To turn the Heel**—Slip the first stitch, knit 14, slip 1, knit 1, pass the slipped stitch over, knit 1; turn the work, slip the first stitch, purl 2, purl 2 together, purl 1; turn, slip the first stitch, knit 3, slip 1, knit 1, pass the slipped stitch over, knit 1; turn, slip the first stitch, purl 4, purl 2 together, purl 1; turn, slip the first stitch, knit 5, slip 1, knit 1, pass the slipped stitch over, knit 1; turn, slip the first stitch, purl 6, purl 2 together, purl 1; turn, and continue thus till all the

side stitches are knitted in, and there will be 15 stitches on the needle for the top of the heel. Knit plain these 15 stitches, and on the same needle pick up and knit 15 stitches along the side of the flap, on another needle knit the 26 instep stitches in pattern, and on the next needle pick up and knit 15 stitches along the other side of the flap, and knit 7 stitches from off the top of the heel. You now have 70 stitches in the round. Knit plain along the foot needle, knit in pattern on the instep needle. For the **Gussets**— * On first foot needle, knit 1, slip 1, knit 1, pass the slipped stitch over, knit plain to within 3 stitches of the end of the second foot needle, knit 2 together, knit 1, knit pattern on the instep needle; knit 2 rounds plain on foot and pattern on instep; and repeat from * till reduced to 55 stitches in the round. Knit for the **Foot** upon these 55 stitches, still keeping the pattern down the instep, for 55 rounds. Then knit plain along the first foot needle, and knit the last stitch, together with the first stitch, from the second foot needle, so making an even number of stitches, 54, in the round. From this, divide the stitches equally, placing 18 stitches on each needle. For the **Toe**—Beginning on the second foot needle, knit 1, slip 1, knit 1, pass the slipped stitch over, knit to within 3 stitches of the end of the pin, knit 2 together, knit 1; do the same on each of the other needles; knit one plain round. Repeat these two rounds till the toe is reduced to 12 stitches. Then place 6 instep stitches on one needle, and 6 foot stitches on another needle; hold these level with each other, and cast off by knitting together a stitch from each needle.

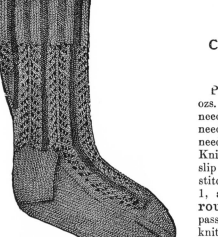

Open Knit Sock for Child of Two. Sprig Pattern.

CHILD'S SOCK. WITH FANCY KNIT FRONT.

Procure 3 balls of white Cocoon wool, or 2½ ozs. of white Andalusian, and four steel knitting needles, No. 16. Cast 30 stitches on the first needle, and 20 stitches on each of two other needles, 70 stitches in all. Purl 2 rounds. Knit 1 plain round. **4th round**—Knit 3, slip 1, knit 2 together, pass the slipped stitch over, knit 3, make 1, knit 1, make 1, and repeat. **5th round**—Plain. **6th round**—Knit 2, slip 1, knit 2 together, pass the slipped stitch over, knit 2, make 1, knit 3, make 1, and repeat. **7th round**—Plain. **8th round**—Knit 1, slip 1, knit 2 together, pass the slipped stitch over, knit 1, make 1, knit 5, make 1, and repeat. **9th round**—Plain. **10th round**—Knit 5, knit 2 together, * knit 8, knit 2 together, repeat from * and at the end of the third needle knit 1, knit 2 together. There are now 62 stitches in the round. Purl 2 rounds. Knit plain 1 round. This finishes the border. For the **Leg—1st round**—Beginning on the first needle, knit 10, purl the next stitch for the seam stitch (it should be the centre stitch of the three taken together in the pattern above), knit 20, purl 1, knit 1 and purl 1 ten times, knit 10. Knit 4 more rounds the same. **6th round**—Knit 10, purl the seam stitch, knit 21, purl 1, knit 1 and purl 1 nine times, knit 11. Knit 4 more rounds the same. Repeat these ten rounds. And now the pattern continues the same down the front of the sock but the leg has to be decreased, consequently, in the third, fourth, fifth, sixth, and seventh time of repeating the 1st round, before the seam stitch knit 2 together, knit 1, purl the seam stitch, knit 1, slip 1, knit 1, pass the slipped stitch over. This proceeding will bring the sock to 52 stitches in the round. Knit two repeats of the pattern (20 rounds) on these 52 stitches for the ankle. There are now 90 rounds of pattern knitted in all. For the **Heel**—Beginning on the first needle, knit to the seam stitch, purl that, knit 11, purl 1, knit 1; turn the work, slip the first stitch, knit 1, purl 11, knit the seam stitch, purl 11, knit 1, purl 1. Let the 25 stitches for the instep remain divided upon two needles till the heel is finished. **3rd row of the Heel**—Slip 1, purl 1, knit 11, purl the seam stitch, knit 11, purl 1, knit 1. **4th row**—Slip 1, knit 1, purl 11, knit the seam stitch, purl 11, knit 1, purl 1 Repeat these two rows fourteen times more. **To turn the Heel**—Slip 1, purl 1, knit 13 (the seam stitch is discontinued), slip 1, knit 1, pass the slipped stitch over; turn, slip the first stitch, purl 3, purl 2 together; * turn, slip 1, knit 3, slip 1, knit 1, pass the slipped stitch over; turn, slip 1, purl 3, purl 2 together; and repeat from * till all the side stitches are knitted in, and 5 stitches remain on the needle for the top of the heel. Knit plain these 5 stitches, and on the same needle pick up, and as you pick up knit 17 stitches along the side of the flap; knit the 25 instep stitches in pattern all on one needle; and on another needle pick up and knit 17 stitches along the opposite side of the flap, and knit 2 stitches from off the top of the heel. Thus there are 64 stitches arranged upon three needles. Knit plain the next needle. Knit pattern on the instep needle. For the **Gussets**—* Beginning on the first foot needle, knit 1, slip 1, knit 1, pass the slipped stitch over, knit plain to within 3 stitches of the end of the second foot needle, knit 2 together, knit 1; knit pattern on the instep needle. Knit 2 rounds plain on foot and pattern on instep. Repeat from * till reduced to 50 stitches in the round. Continue thence on the 50 stitches for 50 rounds. For the **Toe**—* Beginning on the first foot needle, knit 1, slip 1, knit 1, pass the slipped stitch over, knit plain to within 3 stitches of the end of the second foot needle, knit 2 together, knit 1; on the instep needle, knit 1, slip 1, knit 1, pass the slipped stitch over, knit plain to within 3 stitches of the end of the needle, knit 2 together, knit 1; knit 1 plain round; and repeat from * till reduced to 18 stitches. Place the pins together, and cast off.

CHILD'S FANCY KNIT SOCK.

OAK-LEAF PATTERN.

PROCURE 3 skeins of Strutt's crochet cotton No. 20, and four steel knitting needles No. 18 or No. 20. Cast 32 stitches on the first needle, 24 stitches on the second needle, and 24 stitches on the third needle, making a total of 80 stitches. Knit in ribbing 3 stitches purl, 5 stitches plain, for 30 rounds. **1st Pattern round**—Make 1, slip 1, knit 2 together, pass the slipped stitch over, make 1, knit 5, and repeat. **2nd round** — Plain. **3rd round** — Same as the first round. **4th round**—Plain. **5th round**—Same as the first round. **6th round**—Plain. **7th round**—Knit 3, make 1, slip 1, knit 1, pass the slipped stitch over, knit 1, knit 2 together, make 1, and repeat. **8th round**—Plain. **9th round**—Make 1, slip 1, knit 2 together, pass the slipped stitch over, make 1, knit 1, make 1, slip 1, knit 2 together, pass the slipped stitch over, make 1, knit 1, and repeat. **10th round**—Plain. Repeat these ten rounds. The first decrease occurs in the 45th round of the sock (in knitting the 5th round of the pattern). With a thread of cotton mark the line of straight stitches in the middle of the first needle, and keep that line for the back of the leg as if it were a seam stitch; on each side decreasings are to be made, as follows, till two patterns are entirely knitted out. In this round—the 45th round—when 9 stitches before the seam stitch, make 1, slip 1, knit 2 together, pass the slipped stitch over, make 1, knit 3, knit 2 together, make 1, slip 1, knit 2 together, pass the slipped stitch over, make 1, slip 1, knit 1, pass the slipped stitch over, knit 3, make 1, and continue the pattern as before. **47th round**—When 8 stitches before the seam stitch, make 1, knit 3, make 1, slip 1, knit 1, pass the slipped stitch over, knit 2 together, make 1, knit 3, make 1, slip 1, knit 1, pass the slipped stitch over, knit 2 together, make 1, knit 3, and continue in pattern. **49th round**—When 8 stitches before the seam stitch, make 1, slip 1, knit 2 together, pass the slipped stitch over, make 1, knit 1, make 1, slip 1, knit 2 together, pass the slipped stitch over, make 1, slip 1, knit 2 together, pass the slipped stitch over, make 1, knit 3 together, make 1, knit 1, make 1, slip 1, knit 2 together, pass the slipped stitch over, and continue in pattern. **51st round**—When 7 stitches before the seam stitch, make 1, slip 1, knit 2 together, pass the slipped stitch over, make 1, knit 3, make 1, slip 1, knit 2 together, pass the slipped stitch over, make 1,

Plain Knitted Sock for a Child of Three.

knit 3, make 1, slip 1, knit 2 together, pass the slipped stitch over and continue in pattern. **53rd round**—Same as the 51st round. **55th round**—The same. **57th round**—When 7 stitches before the seam stitch, make 1, knit 3, make 1, slip 1, knit 1, pass the slipped stitch over, knit 1, slip 1, knit 2 together, pass the slipped stitch over, knit 1, knit 2 together, make 1, knit 3, and continue in pattern. **59th round**—When 6 stitches before the seam stitch, make 1, slip 1, knit 2 together, pass the slipped stitch over, make 1, knit 1, make 1, slip 1, knit 1, pass the slipped stitch over, knit 1, knit 2 together, make 1, knit 1, make 1, slip 1, knit 2 together, pass the slipped stitch over, and continue in pattern. **61st round**—When 6 stitches before the seam stitch, make 1, slip 1, knit 2 together, pass the slipped stitch over, make 1, knit 2, slip 1, knit 2 together, pass the slipped stitch over, knit 2, make 1, slip 1, knit 2 together, pass the slipped stitch over, and continue in pattern. **63rd round**—When 5 stitches before the seam stitch, make 1, slip 1, knit 2 together, pass the slipped stitch over, make 1, knit 5, make 1, slip 1, knit 2 together, pass the slipped stitch over, and continue in pattern. **65th round**—The same. **67th round**—When 5 stitches before the seam stitch, make 1, knit 3, make 1, slip 1, knit 1, pass the slipped stitch over, knit 1, knit 2 together, make 1, knit 3, and continue in pattern. **69th round**—When 5 stitches before the seam stitch, make 1, slip 1, knit 2 together, pass the slipped stitch over, make 1, knit 1, slip 1, knit 2 together, pass the slipped stitch over, knit 1, make 1, slip 1, knit 2 together, pass the slipped stitch over, and continue in pattern. **71st round**—When 4 stitches before the seam stitch, make 1, slip 1, knit 2 together, pass the slipped stitch over, make 1, slip 1, knit 2 together, pass the slipped stitch over, make 1, slip 1, knit 2 together, pass the slipped stitch over, and continue in pattern. **73rd round**—When 3 stitches before the seam stitch, make 1, slip 1, knit 1, pass the slipped stitch over, knit 3, knit 2 together, make 1, and continue in pattern. **75th round**—The same. **77th round**—When 3 stitches before the seam stitch, make 1, knit 2, slip 1, knit 2 together, pass the slipped stitch over, knit 2, make 1, and continue in pattern. **79th round**—When 2 stitches before the seam stitch, make 1, slip 1, knit 2 together, pass the slipped stitch over, and over the 1 stitch so formed slip the two stitches on the left-hand side (reducing the 5 centre stitches to one stitch), make 1, and continue in pattern. Knit a plain round, 64 stitches in the round. Now the pattern comes in correctly as in the first round. Knit straight on in pattern on these 64 stitches for the ankle till you can count 12 leaves down the leg (120 rounds knitted). For the **Heel**—After knitting the seam stitch, knit 16 stitches plain; turn the work, slip the first stitch, purl 32; and continue a plain row and a purl row on these 33 stitches, slipping the first stitch in every row, till 18 little rows are done; the 31 instep stitches remain in the meanwhile upon two needles till again wanted. **To turn the Heel**—Knit 32, turn, purl 31; turn, knit 30; turn, purl 29; and so on one stitch less in each row (still always slipping the first stitch) till you come to purl 11; then in each succeeding row knit 1 stitch more, and with it pick up and knit in a thread of the sock to prevent a small hole being formed, till the original number, 33 stitches, appear: this is a Niantic heel. Knit plain along the 33 stitches, and on the same needle pick up, and as you pick up knit, 10 stitches along the side of the flap; on another needle knit all the instep stitches in pattern; and on another needle pick up and knit 10 stitches along the opposite side of the flap, and knit 16 stitches off the top of the heel: you now have 26 stitches on this, which is the first foot needle, 27 stitches on the second foot needle, and 31 stitches on the instep needle. Knit the second foot needle plain. Knit pattern along instep needle. For the **Gussets**— * On the first foot needle, knit 1, slip 1, knit 1, pass the slipped stitch over, knit plain to within 3 stitches of the end of the second foot needle, knit 2 together, knit 1; knit pattern on instep needle. Knit one round plain on foot and pattern on instep. Repeat from * till reduced to 62 stitches in the round; and then knit straight on till 7 leaves are knitted down the instep. For the **Toe**—You still have 31 stitches upon the instep needle, and 31 stitches are divided upon the two foot needles. * On the first foot needle, knit 2, slip 1, knit 1, pass the slipped stitch over, knit plain to within 4 stitches of the end of the second foot needle, knit 2 together, knit 2 ; on the instep needle, knit 2, slip 1, knit 1, pass the slipped stitch over, knit plain to within 4 stitches of the end of the needle, knit 2 together, knit 2 ; knit 1 plain round ; repeat from * till reduced to 22 stitches. Slip the 11 foot stitches on one needle, hold it parallel with the instep needle, and cast off by knitting together a stitch from each needle.

OPEN KNIT SOCK FOR CHILD OF TWO.
Sprig Pattern.

Procure 3 ozs. of Strutt's Knitting Cotton, No. 14 ; and four steel knitting needles, No. 16 or No. 17. Cast 22 stitches on each of three needles, making a total of 66 stitches. Knit in ribbing, 3 stitches plain and 3 stitches purl, for 24 rounds. **1st Pattern round**—Beginning on the first needle, the first stitch of which is to be considered as the seam stitch, and in this sock is knitted *plain*, not purled as usual—Knit 1, make 1, slip 1, knit 1, pass the slipped stitch over, make 1, slip 1, knit 1, passed the slipped stitch over, purl 2, knit 2 together, make 1, knit 2 together, make 1, and repeat to the end of the third needle. **2nd round**—Knit the plain stitches and purl the purled stitches of last round. **3rd round**—Knit 2, make 1, knit 1, slip 1, knit 1, pass the slipped stitch over, purl 2, knit 2 together, knit 1, make 1, knit 1, and repeat. **4th round**—Knit the plain stitches and purl the purled stitches of last round. Repeat these four rounds three times. **17th round**—Decreasings begin : Knit 1, knit 2 together, make 1, slip 1, knit 1, pass the slipped stitch over, * purl 2, knit 2 together, make 1, knit 2 together, make 1, knit 1, make 1, slip 1, knit 1, pass the slipped stitch over, make 1, slip 1, knit 1, pass the slipped stitch over, repeat from * four times, purl 2, knit 2 together, make 1, slip 1, knit 1, pass the slipped stitch over. **18th round**—Same as the second round. **19th round**—Knit 4, * purl 2, knit 2 together, knit 1, make 1, knit 3, make 1, knit 1, slip 1, knit 1, pass the slipped stitch over, repeat from * four times, purl 2, knit 3. **20th round**—Same as the fourth round. **21st round**—Knit 4, then purl 2, and continue in pattern, and knit 3 at the end of the round. **22nd round**—Same as the second round. **23rd round**—Knit 1, slip 1, knit 1, pass the slipped stitch over, knit 1, purl 2, continue in pattern, and knit 1, knit 2 together at the end of the round. **24th round**—Same as the fourth round. **25th round**—Knit 3, then purl 2, and continue in pattern, and knit 2 at the end of the round. **26th round**—Same as the second round. **27th round**—Knit 3, purl 2, continue in pattern, and knit 2 at the end of the round. **28th round**—Same as the fourth round. **29th round**—Knit 1, slip 1, knit 1, pass the slipped stitch over, purl 2, continue in pattern, and knit 2 together at the end of the round. **30th round**—Same as the second round. **31st round**—Knit 2, then purl 2, and continue in pattern, and knit 1 at the end of the round. **32nd round** - Same as the fourth round. **33rd round**—Knit 2 together, draw last stitch from third needle over these, purl 2, and continue in pattern to end of round. **34th round**—Same as the second round. **35th round**—Purl 3 together at beginning of round, purl 2 together at end, and work the intermediate stitches in pattern. **36th round**—Same as the fourth round. There are now 55 stitches in the round, and the pattern comes in evenly as at the beginning. Knit 16 rounds for the ankle. For the **Heel**—Beginning on the first needle, knit plain 15 stitches ; turn the work, slip the first stitch, purl 28. Leave the 26 instep stitches standing as they are upon two needles, as they are not required till the heel is finished. On the 29 heel stitches knit a row and purl a row, always slipping the first stitch in every row, till 26 rows are knitted. **To turn the Heel**—Slip the first stitch, knit 15, slip 1, knit 1, pass the slipped stitch over, knit 1 ; turn, slip the first stitch, purl 4, purl 2 together, purl 1 ; turn, slip the first stitch, knit 5, slip 1, knit 1, pass the slipped stitch over, knit 1 ; turn, slip the first stitch, purl 6, purl 2 together, purl 1 ; turn, and proceed thus widening the heel one stitch each time of turning, till all the side stitches are knitted in, and 17 stitches remain on the needle for the top of the heel. Knit plain these 17 stitches, and on the same needle pick up, and as you pick up knit, 13 stitches along the side of the flap ; knit the 26 instep stitches in pattern all on one needle ; and on another needle pick up and knit 13 stitches along the opposite side of the flap and knit 8 stitches from off the top of the heel. Now

there are 69 stitches arranged upon three needles. Knit plain along the next needle, and keep in pattern along the instep needle. For the **Gussets**—* Beginning on the first foot needle, knit 1, slip 1, knit 1, pass the slipped stitch over, knit plain to within 3 stitches of the end of the second foot needle, knit 2 together, knit 1 ; knit in pattern along the instep needle. Knit 1 round plain on foot and pattern on instep. Repeat from * till reduced to 55 stitches in the round. Continue on the 55 stitches till the foot is the required length. For the **Toe**—* On the first foot needle, knit 1, slip 1, knit 1, pass the slipped stitch over, knit plain to within 3 stitches of the end of the second foot needle, knit 2 together, knit 1 ; on the instep needle, knit 1, slip 1, knit 1, pass the slipped stitch over, knit plain to within 3 stitches of the end of the needle, knit 2 together, knit 1 ; knit 1 plain round ; repeat from * till reduced to 23 stitches. Slip the foot stitches on to one needle, hold this level with the instep needle, and cast off by knitting together a stitch from each needle, taking 3 together in the centre to bring the stitches in nicely.

PLAIN KNITTED SOCK FOR CHILD OF THREE.

For this nicely fitting sock 2½ ozs. of Victoria yarn or Andalusian wool will be required, and four steel knitting needles, No. 16. Cast 29 stitches on the first needle, and 24 stitches on each of two other needles, making a total of 77 stitches. **1st round**—Beginning on the first needle, knit 2 and purl 2 three times, knit 2, purl 1 (this stitch is the seam stitch), knit 2 and purl 2 to the end of the third needle. Knit 23 more rounds the same as this round. Then knit 16 plain rounds, remembering the seam stitch which is to be purled in *every* round. **17th round**—Decreasings begin : Knit plain to 3 stitches before the seam stitch, knit 2 together, knit 1, purl the seam stitch, knit 1, slip 1, knit 1, pass the slipped stitch over, knit plain to the end of the round. * Knit 5 plain rounds. **Next round**—Plain, and decrease in the same way on each side the seam stitch. Repeat from * four times, when there will be 65 stitches in the round, 17 stitches on the first needle, and 24 stitches on each of two other needles. Knit 20 plain rounds still keeping the seam stitch in the centre of the first needle. For the **Heel**—Beginning on the first needle, knit 8, purl the seam stitch, knit 8, knit 8 from the next needle ; turn the work, slip the first stitch, purl 15, knit the seam stitch, purl 16 ; this brings 33 stitches on one needle for the heel, and the remaining 32 stitches are to stand as they are for the present, till the heel is finished. On the 33 heel stitches knit a row and purl a row, always slipping the first stitch and keeping the seam stitch in every row, till 28 rows are knitted. **To turn the Heel**—Slip the first stitch, knit 6, then * make 1, knit 2 together, knit 4, knit 2 together, knit 1, purl the seam stitch, knit 1, slip 1, knit 1, pass the slipped stitch over, knit 4, slip 1, knit 1, pass the slipped stitch over ; turn, make 1, purl till 9 stitches past the seam stitch ; turn, and repeat from *, till all the side stitches are knitted in ; the last time of all do not make a stitch at the beginning of the purl row. When the heel is finished there should be 15 stitches on the needle for the top of the heel. Knit plain these 15 stitches, and on the same needle pick up and knit 15 stitches along the side of the flap ; knit the 32 instep stitches all off on one needle ; and on another needle pick up 15 stitches along the other side of the flap, and knit 7 stitches from the top of the heel. You now have the stitches again arranged upon three needles, 77 stitches in the round, ready for knitting the gussets. Knit plain along the next needle, knit along the instep needle. For the **Gussets**—* Beginning on the first foot needle, knit 1, slip 1, knit 1, pass the slipped stitch over, knit plain to within 3 stitches of the end of the second foot needle, knit 2 together, knit 1 ; knit plain along the instep needle. Knit 2 plain rounds. Repeat from * till reduced to 65 stitches in the round ; the 32 instep stitches should still be intact upon one needle, and 33 foot stitches divided on two needles. Knit 30 plain rounds. For the **Toe**—* On the first foot needle, knit 3, slip 1, knit 1, pass the slipped stitch over, knit plain to within 5 stitches of the end of the second foot needle, knit 2 together, knit 3 ; on the instep needle, knit 3, slip 1, knit 1, pass the slipped stitch over, knit to within 5 stitches of the end of the needle, knit 2 together, knit 3 ; knit 2 plain rounds ; repeat from * three times : then work a decrease round and a plain round alternately, till the toe is reduced to 25 stitches. Slip the 13 foot stitches all on one needle, hold this level with the instep needle, and cast off by knitting together a stitch from each needle taking 3 together in the centre to bring them in equally.

WELDON'S
PRACTICAL CROSS-STITCH.

(FIRST SERIES.)

New and Original Designs for all Purposes.

SEVENTY ILLUSTRATIONS.

The Yearly Subscription to this Mag zine. post free to any Part of the World, is 2s. 6d.
Subscriptions are payable in advance. and may commence from any date and for any period.

The Back Numbers are always in print. Nos. 1 to 232 *now ready, Price 2d. each, or bound in* 19 *Vols., price* **2s. 6d. each.**

CROSS-STITCH EMBROIDERY.

CROSS-STITCH work has now become so universal that we feel sure a book can well be devoted to this quickly executed and attractive decoration, for mats, antimacassars, bags, quilts, covers, valances, &c., are now to be had in cloth, canvas, &c., ready for adorning with cross-stitch in silk, wool, or cloth. Cross-stitch, which originated from Russia and Germany, where it is much employed for all household linen, as it washes and wears so well, was originally worked over canvas, tacked on to the material to be decorated, and when the design was finished the canvas threads were carefully pulled away, thus leaving the design on the materials; but this is now entirely superseded by the beautiful German linens woven in all widths and colours, and in many fanciful designs suited to every purpose of decoration. There are also various coloured felts so useful for tablecloths, piano-covers, mats, curtain borders, antimacassars, and many other purposes, arranged with perforated designs ready for cross-stitch decoration; and this reminds me of the New Machine Perforated Batswing Cloth, introduced by Messrs. Briggs, of Manchester, in numerous designs, and all the most fashionable colours. This most useful cloth being perforated by machinery in numerous artistic designs, quite obviates the tedious task of counting stitches, and it will be found far superior to that perforated by hand, which, not being done with such preciseness, gives unevenness and irregularity to the working.

Antimacassars, cosies, footstools, slippers, mantel borders, &c., can all be had; and while being a pleasant and easy work, cross-stitch is exceedingly durable, and always ornamental now that such lovely silks and cottons can be had. Hitherto red and blue were the principal colours used, but now most lovely shades can be had for this very fashionable and useful needlework. For decorating such articles as will permit of washing, Meig's Ingrain cottons, size 18, should be used, as they wear so beautifully, work so

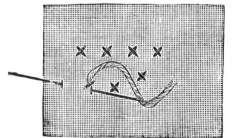

1.—The Manner of Working Cross-Stitch.

evenly, and always retain their brightness; but for articles to be sent to the cleaner's, silks or filoselles work up well, and they may be used for either cotton or woollen goods.

Cross-stitch is so extremely simple of execution that little instruction or practice is needed to do this work, the great thing being to cross all stitches one way and evenly, which can easily be managed with the lovely canvas materials now sold. These present quite a check or canvas-like surface of tiny squares, which have to be decorated with cross-stitch worked just as one does the ordinary Berlin wool stitch, or perforated cardboard work.

ILLUSTRATION 1 shows the manner of executing this most simple work which is done as follows: From the left-hand corner of one of the squares bring up the needle and cotton, then in a slanting direction, that is taking it across the square to the top of the right-hand side, you pass the needle down, this forming the first or under part of the stitch. Then comes the upper stitch, which gives it the form of a cross, from which it takes its

name, which you do thus: Bring the needle up the top left-hand corner of the square, and pass it down through the right-hand corner, when you will have formed the complete stitch, and this, through being repeated in designs and various coloured cottons, forms most attractive and quickly executed decorations for nearly everything.

In doing cross-stitch, each stitch can be at once perfected, as above described, or some prefer to do all the under stitches first, then cross all afterwards.

Holbein stitch, also called Italian or outline stitch, is often used in conjunction with cross-stitch, and is very useful for outlining a pattern.

ILLUSTRATIONS 21, 23, and 44 show exactly how Holbein stitch is used, and it must be worked with great regularity, and both sides are exactly alike.

All stitches must be perfectly horizontal and of equal length, and work in short stitches in satin stitch, and so arrange them that the outline be covered in straight lines, all of which must meet or join perfectly, turning if required at the end of each stitch.

Holbein work, which really dates from the time of Holbein, is most decorative and useful for tablecloths, towels, dresses, &c., worked in ingrain cottons, or for richer materials silks are used. Particularly useful for decorating children's dresses, &c., is cross-stitch, and every day makes it more and more fashionable, besides bringing us many pretty things to be further adorned with this fashionable needlework.

Cross-stitch is now worked in much greater variety than it originally was in Germany, and according to the purpose it is to be applied so can it be varied.

For quilts, and all such large articles, you can take four sections or squares of the canvas-like ground instead of one, and thus you get a bolder and more quickly executed design, for which you would use a coarse knitting cotton in deep red, blue, or brown. Red and navy blue cottons always form a happy combination, while two shades of brown, two of blue, and a good red can be used with good effect.

A little care and taste in the selection of the colours are as necessary in this simple work as in everything else, while the article to be decorated or the room it is to adorn must also form a guide.

There are so many pretty articles now to be had in white, brown, blue, pink, and various cream canvas and linen materials, arranged as antimacassars, nightdress cases, toilet mats, 5 o'clock tea cloths, sideboard and tray cloths, &c., for decorating with cross-stitch, and they are to be had in so many designs so as to meet all whims and fancies of the worker.

Some articles have alternate canvas and solid linen squares, diamonds, bands, &c., the canvas being for the cross-stitch, while others are entirely of fancy linen with just a band and centre for working the monogram, &c.; then such pretty coloured linen canvases can be had by the yard, and these are so useful for cutting into various width bands for antimacassars, &c., for cross-stitch embroidery suits every purpose, and especially is it to be recommended for household decoration

Coloured canvas is most useful for mantel valances, brackets, bookcovers, &c., worked in coloured cottons to match the room, while it is most durable work for children's dresses worked in blue or red cottons. Almost any design can be done in cross-stitch, while the same design worked in different colours and in different materials often presents quite another effect.

For quilts, cream and ecrue linen canvas of double width is to be had, and this decorated with a bold design worked in coarse red and blue knitting cotton, taking four squares to each stitch, is very artistic and most durable. The centre of the quilt can have a monogram worked in one or two colours, or a pretty star, diamond, &c., would look well.

No. 2.—Border in Cross-Stitch

A quilt ornamented with a deep border worked in red and blue could have a powdering of butterflies, birds, or cupids, worked in the two colours.

Antimacassars ornamented with butterflies, or tiny birds worked in various bright coloured cottons. or silks, always gain admiration, while interlaced rings in shades of green, red, pale blue, and brown, or faded leaves worked in reds and greens, are pretty for all purposes. French knots and the vein-like lines on the wings of butterflies can be done with a different shade of cotton to the cross-stitch foundation

ILLUSTRATION 29 shows leaves and acorns formed by filling in the canvas to form the design, while Illustration 39 shows exactly the reverse, since the leaves are filled in to form the design.

ILLUSTRATION 14 shows a really attractive design for two or more colours, forming a useful decoration for bordering purposes, or for antimacassars, bands, &c. The centre could even be used alone, as well as the border, which would form a quickly worked and pretty vandyke pattern for children's dresses. Our design is executed in two shades of brown, two of blue, and one red cotton, taking four squares for each stitch, using coarse cotton.

The centre pattern is worked with the centre of light brown, commencing with two stitches, then eight sets of three stitches, finishing with two. This is encircled with a moderately dark brown cotton, the outer stitches being in red cotton.

The vandyke border on either side is worked with light blue, dark blue, and red. The diamonds on either side of the vandyke are made with four stitches to each side in dark blue, and have a cross of five stitches in the centre in light blue, then either side of the vandyke is in dark blue, centred with two rows of red, another row of red being carried outside the vandyke as a finish. This design measures 7⅓ inches wide, or if only one square be taken to the stitch, it would be but half the width.

ILLUSTRATIONS 15, 54, and 55 give effective and quickly worked insertions, so useful for decorating children's dresses, antimacassars, mats, and every other purpose; the different stitches for each shade of cotton being clearly defined, or all one colour can be employed.

ILLUSTRATION 17 represents a handsome design to be used as a border, band, or an entire fill-in pattern, the design being formed with Italian or outline stitch in black, with the entire groundwork filled in with cross-stitch in a bright yellow or any other shade of cotton, taking four squares to each stitch. This worked on cloth would make serviceable stool covers, as it is so bold and quickly executed.

ILLUSTRATION 21 serves two purposes, for used in its entirety it forms an eleven-inch design for mantle borders, quilts, and large pieces of work. Then simply the insertion can be worked as a border or bands for any purpose desired, and it would measure 3½ inches wide. The greater part of the design is worked in Italian stitch, taking four squares to each stitch, blue knitting cotton being employed, and the close squares or dots in the large spray are done by first closing in a square of four, then working a cross-stitch from point to point, thus giving a kind of solid raised spot. The narrow insertion on either side of the deep band is worked in faded green and red cotton alternately, that is, every other pattern of nine cross-stitches are in red and then green.

ILLUSTRATION 22 represents a star filling in pattern, or all over design, suitable for any purpose, taking one or four squares to the stitch. Two colours are employed for the pattern, which can easily be followed by the clear illustration. The border is quickly worked, and very

effective, and can be used for dresses, aprons, bibs, towels, and other articles.

ILLUSTRATION 23 is a particularly effective and quickly executed design for any two shades of cotton desired, blue and red always forming an attractive bordering for teacloths or sideboard cloths as well as towels and such articles as are required to be washed.

The lighter stitches show where red cotton should be employed, and the darker stitches are made with blue cotton, worked principally in Italian stitch. It measures 3½ inches when worked. The centre of the red stars and the blue crosses consists of four cross-stitches each worked over one square of the canvas.

ILLUSTRATION 24 represents a bold design for large pieces of work, using one, two, or more shades of cotton as fancy may dictate. The design takes one square to each stitch, or four squares worked with knitting cotton would naturally make a larger and more effective piece of work. The branches of the upper part would look well in blue with the rest in red, while the narrow edge and slanting band in the border could be red, filling in the other stitches with blue.

ILLUSTRATION 25 represents a plush pillow ornamented with two bands of cross-stitch embroidery, worked on fine canvas. Any design one may desire can be introduced thus, and the border of Illustration 24, as well as just the diamonds of No. 32, or the pretty floral design 58, would be suitable.

ILLUSTRATIONS 2 to 6, and 38, show fancy borders which serve for any purpose. They can be worked in one, two, or more shades of cotton or silk, taking one or four squares of the canvas to each stitch, according to the purpose the design is intended. Naturally when four squares are taken to each stitch the design comes out very bold, and is suited to quilts, mantel borders, sofa covers, and such large articles.

ILLUSTRATIONS 7a and 8 represent effective insertions and borders worked in two or three colours, as clearly shown in the engravings. Two stitches are employed, cross-stitch forming the greater portion of the designs, with the small cross, and outlining to the diamonds done in Leviathan stitch, worked thus: Take four squares to each stitch, and first do a cross-stitch, then bring the needle up one of the between holes, and make a long cross-stitch which will fill in the holes between the cross, then repeat from side to side, thus making like a Maltese cross over a cross-stitch. The illustrations clearly define the stitches for each shade of cotton.

ILLUSTRATION 9 shows a teacloth decorated with Italian or outline stitch, the full-size working design of which is shown by Illustration 10. Two coloured cottons are employed, and the pattern can be easily copied. Drawn-work ornaments this design, the inferior edge having stars worked in Leviathan stitch as shown by Illustration 8, finished with a fringe.

ILLUSTRATION 29 shows a leaf and two acorns worked in Italian stitch, the entire groundwork being filled in with cross-stitch.

ILLUSTRATION 30, cross-stitch centre, has just a few Italian stitches introduced, and the canvas ground is so clearly given that no difficulty can possibly be experienced in copying this design, which is useful for centres of mats, &c.

ILLUSTRATION 31 is also very clearly engraved, and consists of a pretty floral design for its border, the leaves of which would look well worked in three shades of green, with the berries in deep red; the border and

No. 4.—Border for Towels, etc.

centre also being in red, with the tiny crosses and dots filled in in green.

ILLUSTRATIONS 32 and 33 give a handsome teacloth border and full working design, which is carried out in Italian stitch, worked in two colours. So clearly can the stitches be counted from the engraving that little directions will be necessary. A drawn-work border is arranged on either side of thi embroidery, then the cloth finished with a coarse lace.

ILLUSTRATIONS 34 and 36 are very effective and quickly worked designs, finished with simple borders, which will be found handy for many purposes.

ILLUSTRATION 39 will be found so attractive for antimacassars, bands and bordering purposes, if worked in three shades of green, the stem of the leaves being worked in a deep brown, and the border in the darkest shade of green.

No. 3.—Fancy Border

ILLUSTRATIONS 40 and 49 are so useful for bordering purposes, and are quickly worked, taking one or four squares to the stitch. Two shades of cotton are employed for the former design, and three shades for No. 49.

ILLUSTRATION 41 shows an effective centre and border for cross-stitch, while ILLUSTRATION 44 shows a border and corner entirely in Italian stitch, with the canvas ground so clearly represented as to enable any one to follow the pattern without the slightest difficulty.

ILLUSTRATION 45 gives an idea how canvas materials can be arranged as antimacassars, ornamented with bands of cross-stitch divided by drawn-work. Floral designs always come out so well for antimacassars worked in three shades of pink, and three of faded green, thus representing autumn leaves.

ILLUSTRATION 50 represents a corner and border, the pattern of which is formed by filling in the ground with cross-stitch. All red or any one colour could be used, or a second colour could well be introduced as a centre to the diamond parts.

ILLUSTRATIONS 51, 52, and 57 represent butterflies, which are so pretty worked in different shades of silk, such as two mauves and yellow, two pinks, and pale blue, brown, gold, and blue, the veins of the wings being long stitches over the cross stitch foundation, while the dots are worked in French knots.

These dotted over antimacassars are particularly pretty.

ILLUSTRATION 58, floral border and insertion, has the pattern formed by filling in the ground, and this is useful for all purposes. Our illustrations are so clearly drawn that description of same is really superfluous, as any one can follow the pattern without the slightest difficulty, while the colours of the cottons they employ are of course ruled by each individual fancy.

No. 7.—Border Worked with Peacocks.

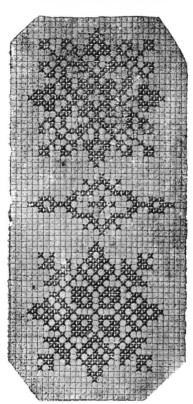

No. 5.—Cross-Stitch Design.

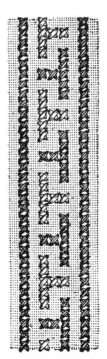

No. 6.—Border or Insertion for Dresses.

No. 7a.—Handsome Design for Cross-Stitch and Leviathan Stitch.

Nos. 8 and 8a.—Handsome Border for Quilts, Table Cloths, etc., and Butterflies for Cross-Stitch.

No. 9.—Five O'Clock Tea-Cloth.

No. 11.—Initial M.

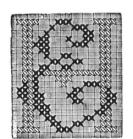

No. 12.—Initials E. H.

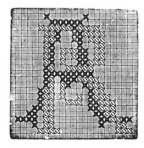

No. 13.—Initials A. R.

No. 10.—Working Design for No. 9.

No. 15.—Cross-stitch Insertion.

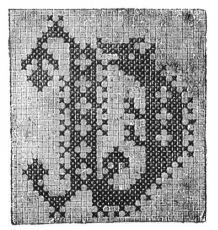

No. 16.—Initial D.

No. 14.—Insertion or Border worked in Five Colours.

No. 17.—Handsome Border, or Band in Cross-Stitch and Holbein Stitch

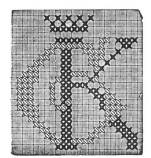

No. 18.—Initials G. K.

No. 19.—Initials O. F.

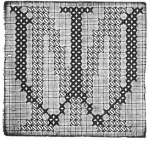

No. 20.—Initials M. W.

No. 21.—Mantel Border in Cross-Stitch and Italian or Holbein Stitch.

No. 22.—Star Pattern with Fancy Border.

No. 23.—Tea-Cloth Border.

No 25.— Plush Pillow, ornamented with
Cross-Stitch Bands.

No. 24.—Border for Side-board Cloths, Towels, &c

No. 26.—Initials R. E.

No. 27.—Initials R. D.

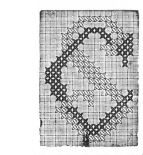

No. 28.—Initials S. C.

No. 29.—Acorn Spray.

No 30.—Cross-Stitch Centre for Mats or Book-Covers.

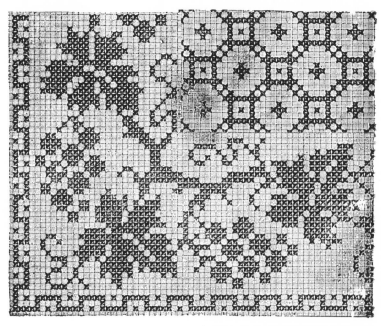

No. 31.—Floral Border with Fancy Centre.

No. 32.—Working Design for No. 33.

No. 33.—Tea or Tray Cloth.

No. 34.—Book Cover, Antimacassar Centre, or for Mats.

No. 35.—Initials A. P.

No. 36.—Square or Border.

No. 37.—Initials I. E.

No. 38.—Stag Border for Decorative Purposes.

No. 39.—Floral Border and Corner.

No. 39a —Sideboard and Tray Cloths in Italian and Cross-Stitches.   Worked in Red and Navy Blue.
Bordered with Drawn Work and Linen Fringe.

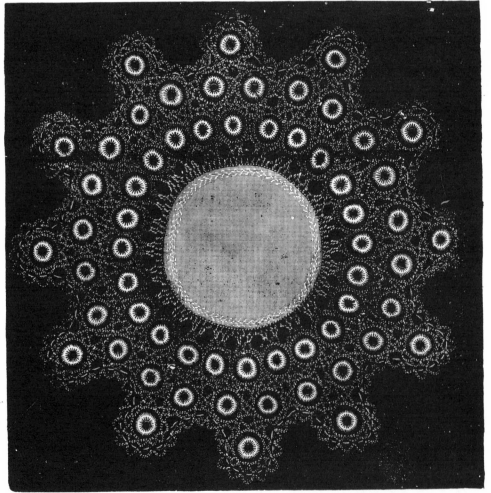

No. 40.—Border for Cloths and Towels.

No. 41.—Effective Border and Centre.

No. 42.—Initials P. H.

No. 43.—Initials G. U.

No. 44.—Border in Italian Stitch.

No. 45.—Antimacassar Worked in Cross-Stitch

No. 46.—Initials I. F.

No. 47.—Initials I. G.

No. 48.—Initials A. O.

No. 49.—Cross-Stitch Border for Working in Three Colours.

No. 50.—Corner in Cross-Stitch.

No. 51.—Butterfly.

No. 52.—Butterfly.

No. 53.—Initials B L.

No. 54.—Insertion in Cross-Stitch and Italian Stitch.

No. 55.—Insertion Worked in Two Colours.

No. 57.—Butterfly.

No. 53—Centre and Border Worked in Two Colours.

No. 58.—Floral Border and Insertion.

WELDON'S
PRACTICAL CREWEL WORK

(FIRST SERIES.)

With Full Directions of the Various Stitches, New and Artistic Designs, &c.

SEVENTY ILLUSTRATIONS.

The Yearly Subscription to this Magazine, post free to any part of the World, is 2s. 6d.
Subscriptions are payable in advance, and may commence from any date and for any period.

The Back Numbers are always in print. Nos. 1 to 231 now ready, Price 2d. each, or bound in 19 Vols., price 2s. 6d. each.

CREWEL WORK.

CREWEL, or Art Needlework, with which may be ranked silk embroidery, is represented each year in a newer and more artistic style; and one no longer sees the crude and inartistic attempts of a few years since, when crewel work was revived and became so fashionable; for like everything else, it improves with the age, and will continue to do so until absolute perfection is arrived at. Crewel work is of ancient origin and came from the East, where, as we all know, the Oriental embroideries are most exquisitely wrought, though not in the subdued and high-class tone and colouring one can boast of in this country. Much the same kind of work, under the name of "tapestry," was in vogue in the 16th and 17th centuries, when ladies of rank spent hours over their embroidery frames, working elaborate ornamentations for the walls of their habitations, besides curtains, coverlets, and raiment for their knights to wear over their armour; and many are well worth studying attentively, for they are still to be seen in ancestral halls and exhibitions.

Crewel and silk embroidery depend for good effect entirely upon the correct taste of the worker, as the manner in which the stitches are set in is of less importance than the effect produced by the skilful blending of shades. It requires, like painting, talent and original ideas, or at any rate one who can carry out the ideas of others. But there are some branches of the work I shall come to presently (I allude particularly to outline and darned embroidery) which would more befit the less gifted ones than vain attempts at crewel work, which requires such skill, taste, and even practice, as well as common sense and great observation. It is useless copying from nature, as some people so obstinately insist upon; what flower thus produced could be anything but crude and unnatural? For it is impossible to do nature justice, and this idea is entirely superseded by the high art and æsthetic colouring one sees at the Royal School of Art, and other good work societies, where the work is so perfectly rendered, according to the high-class style of the present age. Then, again, a great deal depends upon the design. No one would dream of selecting otherwise than what is of bold and handsome persuasion, or in conventional style—so complete a change from the cramped and inartistic productions of a few years back.

The best materials must likewise be chosen. The materials to work upon should be as follows: For crewels, use oatmeal cloth in cream or colours, white linen, twill linen sheeting, cross-stitch linens, huckaback towelling, coloured or cream Bolton sheeting, and diagonal serges, which are so remarkable for their great suppleness. Crewel wools must only be used for linen and woollen materials; and even house flannel is a good material for working bold designs.

For silks, plush is always attractive; also velvet, Roman sheeting, satin, &c. Use crewel embroidery needles, with short lengths of crewel or silk for working, and be sure to work loosely, in order not to pucker the work any more than can be avoided; and always commence at the bottom of a leaf or stem, and work upwards.

A piece of crewel work, when completed, should be laid right side downwards upon flannel or a thin blanket, and ironed on the wrong side—a damp cloth between the work and the iron may be necessary to remove all puckers and creases. Hem the work all round, and edge it with lace, which is newer than fringe, or a silk ball fringe if it be a satin or wool material.

To clean work it is best to send it to a really good cleaner's, if it be anything of a delicate nature, but work on washing materials can be washed at home with care, using lukewarm water, *without soda*, and the addition of a little bran in the water. Do not wring the work, but rinse well in cold water afterwards. If soap be used it should be a good toilet soap.

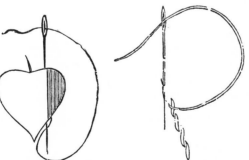
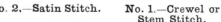

No. 2.—Satin Stitch. No. 1.—Crewel or Stem Stitch. No. 3.—A Padded Leaf worked in Satin Stitch.

In a screen in crewel work the four panels look well suggesting spring, summer, autumn, and winter: irises, white lilies, sunflowers, and chrysanthemums. Pomegranates, tiger lilies, and all large handsome flowers look well for this purpose, as well as storks and bulrushes, or swans and water.

The blinds of a house are now decorated with a strip of work at the bottom, and edged with lace, and this is really a very novel idea, and deserves to be carried into execution by all good workers, as it adds greatly to the attraction of one's windows. Clematis looks well as a design, or any bold flower, different coloured tulips, &c. Portières, if arranged on one of those convenient brass rods, serve much to add to the comfort and appearance of a house, besides being useful to keep out draughts.

The striped Austrian blankets are economical, and look well in a third sitting-room, or a bedroom, or any pretty crimson curtain. but of course nothing has the rich appearance of plush, and so handsome a material it seems a waste of time to decorate. But serges or satin sheeting are very suitable, the former for crewel and the latter for silks; and the design should be a bold one, such as huge lilies, poppies, or tulips, or a powdering of poppies, large daisies, or sunflowers is effective. When the curtain is completed line it with coloured twill or bolton sheeting, and edge with silk cord or ball fringe.

Outline Embroidery, as shown by illustration 45, which now finds so much favour, being effective and yet so easily done that any beginner may attempt this work, depends a great deal upon the design, which should be closer and with more work in it than one intended for darning afterwards. A conventional style looks best, or of the Arabesque order, whereas in darned embroidery even flowers are most effective. Outline embroidery consists of merely outlining the design in crewel or outline stitch, in either one or two shades, or more. Work neatly and carefully, keeping well upon the line of tracing, the design to be most accurately drawn. If one shade only is used, dark peacock blue crewel is effective, either in single or double thread; or washing or crewel silks, or four or five threads of a strand of filoselle. Ingrain cottons give the appearance of silk, and wash well. The materials should be linen, twill linen sheeting, Bolton sheeting, or any material preferred.

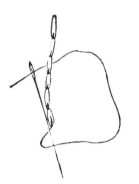

No. 5.—Split Stitch.

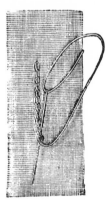

No. 6.—Chain or Tambour Stitch.

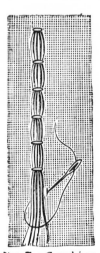

No. 7.—Couching

No. 4.—French Knots.

Outline and Darned Embroidery, as shown by illustrations Nos. 8 and 42, is done in the outline stitch, outlining the design, as in outline work, in one or two shades, and the leaves to be veined and the centres of flowers (with or without French knots) on huckaback towelling or cross-stitch linen—the most suitable material for darning upon, or outline the design in two shades with a double line, which gives effect. Then in a third or fourth contrasting shade darn the groundwork of the material, taking up the two or four threads in huckaback, or every other or every second stitch in cross-stitch material, in 6 threads of a strand of filoselle: nothing else looks so well for the darning unless ingrain cottons; but double crewels can be used.

Chain Stitch, as illustration 6, looks well as an outline stitch instead of the crewel stitch, as illustration 1; and then *honeycomb* stitch, as illustration 17, for a darned background stitch; but the veinings must be done in outline stitch. Chain stitch, No. 6, with couching, No. 7, all round it, also looks well. Or use any of the background stitches given as illustrations 17, 18, 19, 21, and 23 with either outline stitch or chain stitch for the outline work. The designs should be bold and handsome for this work, but not too straggling, and well traced upon the material, or it spoils the effect.

Two or three shades of terra-cotta filoselles look well for the outline, and the background to be a rich gold colour or peacock-blue; or a red outline with navy-blue ground always looks well.

An antimacassar can be darned all over or filled in with the groundwork stitch chosen, if the design be an "all over" one, extending over nearly all the surface of the material. If the design should be in the form of a deep border, half or three-quarters of a yard deep, trace it at the bottom of the antimacassar, leaving a margin of one or two inches; and then darn as far as the usual border or straight lines, which generally run along the top and bottom of such a border, and if not must be added as a finishing point for the darning. A monogram a little way above this line, on the unworked material, sets off the antimacassar, and is very generally employed, monograms being now so fashionable on almost everything. They can be designed either for working on cross-stitch material in cross stitch, or in outline stitch for any material Hem the antimacassar, and edge it with lace when completed. A mantel border or table border also look well in this work, worked in red or blue cottons, particularly if the design be an effective one, such as large griffins or large flowers, old work, or a conventional design.

Splash-backs, night-dress cases, comb-bags, ottoman and toilet covers, table-cloths, can all be executed in this pretty and easy work, which requires so little thought and study that it can be taken up at any time; and nothing improves a house so much as good fancy work, no matter how commonplace the furniture may be; and it is certainly very enlivening to have one's surroundings as charming as possible, with everything ornamented in a tasteful style; and we can transform everything about us in a most wonderful way, with a little thought and skill and at very little expense.

Squares for quilts in white linen are fashionable, and the design can be outlined in red cottons and darned in blue, and afterwards joined. They look well with a square of coarse guipure lace over Turkey red twill between each, and with handsome furniture lace all round. It is well to cover the joins with feather stitch if necessary.

A border or antimacassar strip, with a wide poppy border, as illustration 46, or any other bold design, can be treated as follows: Procure the coarse four-thread huckaback, outline the poppies rather coarsely and loosely with five or six threads of filoselle, in two or three shades of terra-cotta, in crewel stitch, the darkest shades to be on the furthermost petals of the poppy, and the centre to be worked in black for the pollen, and a green seed-vessel; for the leaves a light and a darker shade of sage green, darn in old gold six threads of filoselle. If for an antimacassar strip lengthways, edge with broad pieces of plush or wide furniture lace.

For crewel work, a design can also be treated in a conventional manner, and looks well filled in in crewel stitch, with two or three shades of peacock blue or green crewels, after the design is outlined with the darkest shade chosen.

Old Work, which generally consists of old lilies and impossible birds and flowers in the old style of centuries ago, can be worked in silks or crewels in the many bright shades as then used; or if required more subdued in tone, the flowers outlined in brown and filled in with dull pinks and blues, and the leaves outlined and varied in brown and filled in with shades of fawn colour or dull sage green. The centres of the flowers can be fawn-coloured French knots, as illustration 4, and if a blue flower a rim of pink in the centre, or if a pink flower a rim of blue.

Church Work.—For this work conventional designs are the

most suitable (when the work is not carried out in appliqué and couching), or anything quaint or symbolical, such as one sees in old churches. The design can either be filled in with different shades, as in "Old work," or merely outlined in crewel or chain stitches, as illustrations 1 and 6, with gold cord all round as in couching, as illustration 7, or strands of filoselle; or the spaces can be filled in

No. 8.—Spray Outlined in Ruby Silk and Filled in with Darned Stitch in Deep Gold.

with different stitches, such as Brick stitch (see illustration 19), a very useful stitch, and much used in Church work; or a space can be filled in with couching in strands of filoselle or gold cord, and is very effective, the couching being carried up and down the space until it is filled All the filling-in stitches given elsewhere will also be found useful, and in working a design for Church work, no regard is taken as to the natural colours of the design, and the brightest shades may be used.

The newest style of producing darned work, as shown by illustration 9, is to treat it as follows: Work round the edges of the flowers and leaves with filoselle in satin stitch, in uneven stitches close together, the flowers to be shades of terra cotta, and the leaves in greens, in a conventional colour. Only the edges of the flowers and leaves are to be worked, unless a wheel or French knots be added for the centre of the flowers, and the leaves to be veined in crewel stitch. Darn the background in 5 or 6 threads of peacock blue filoselle, see Figs. 43 and 46, work in terra-cotta crewels for flowers, and greens for leaves. Darn in blue silk. Or for a bold pattern for curtain borders, bed-hangings, carriage rugs, &c., work in crewels in a bolder style, and do not darn the border. Large irises, daffodils, lilies, and poppies are suitable. For a border of irises, as illustration 50, use two shades of yellow, and two of rather light browns in crewels on Bolton sheeting or twill linen sheeting.

The leaves should only be outlined in crewel stitch, as illustration 1, with double crewels, in sage greens, and veined. This is an artistic and effective style, but greatly depends upon the taste of the worker as well as the colouring, and it must be done in bold, large stitches, and not in the finer style in silks of a smaller design that is to be darned.

Flowers may also be treated thus for a small piece of work or antimacassar—large white lilies (No. 56), arums (No. 43), poppies (No. 46), &c. For the lilies, use white filoselle shading to pale greens, a thick edge of the satin stitch in white round the flowers, the cups and lines of shading inside and out in greens shaded yellow pollen, and leaves only outlined and veined in crewel stitch with sage greens and browns. Darn the groundwork in blue or red in

ordinary darning or honeycomb stitch. Poppies should be produced thus in shades of red with black pollen.

Another mode of varying outline work is to outline the design in double crewels, which goes much to set off a handsome design, and then to fill in the design with different stitches, and part to be filled in thick in crewel stitch with double crewels, which is most effective. Lace stitches may be used, as well as the most useful stitches here given. For the centre of a flower work a wheel, or the useful French knot; a leaf looks well in small dotted darned stitches for a change, and I have seen a design in gold on black done in nothing else throughout except French knots, and the stems with small spike stitches, which stand out well (as illustrations 27 and 28). This work resembles the beautiful old Italian work, which is so superior in design and execution. Brick stitch is a useful and quick way of filling in large spaces, and is much seen in old Italian work. With brick stitch the outline may be chain stitch with couching all round if preferred, and honeycomb stitch is most useful for filling in. The design can also be only couched with strands of filoselle, and filled in with French knots only, in peacock blue, or with various stitches besides if preferred. Cross-stitch linen is a good material for this kind of work also. I have seen a counterpane arranged with a border on twill linen sheeting all round, outlined in double peacock blue crewels, and filled in with different stitches, as Figs. 47 and 52. A monogram in the centre, and wide furniture lace all round it.

This work can also be done in flourishing thread on white linen, in two shades of blue, or white, and pink shading to terra-cotta. but it then refers more to Irish Montmellick work, except that this latter work is mostly done in white. Or I have seen the outline in flourishing thread, or even gold cord, and filled in with different stitches in different coloured silks, which is very effective and novel. Then, again, Montmellick work can be outlined with cord used for lace work, which gives solidity, and filled in with different stitches.

Peacock Feathers. These are most attractive for powdering purposes, and quickly worked. Peacock's feathers, as in Figs. 38 to 41, for any purpose—teacloth, child's dress, &c.—are worked in three shades of China blue, two shades of red, or as a real feather, the eye brown, shading to peacock green, and centre eye peacock blue in three shades; and they are very attractive as a bordering, or for dotting over an antimacassar, centreing mats, &c.

A new and effective work is to procure the cream muslin with large spot, now so well known; tack it upon gold sateen; then turn

No. 9.—Spray with Darned Background.

the spots into daisies by working over them in gold crewel silk, in satin stitch (as Fig. 2) for the centres, and loops of white crewel silk all round the centres, to represent the petals.

Illustration 55 shows a piece of spotted muslin in its natural size thus embroidered, while illustration 54 shows a pincushion ornamented with same. This embroidered muslin is useful for mats, antis, aprons, &c.; or muslin dresses embroidered round the skirt, collars, and cuffs would be most effective.

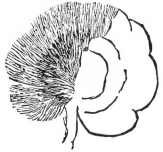

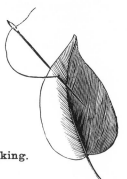

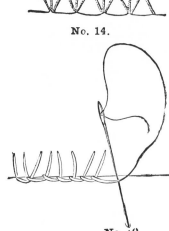

No. 10.—Twisted Chain or Rope Stitch   Nos. 11a & 11.—Feather Stitch, with Manner of Working.

No. 14.

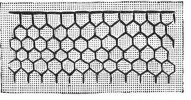

No. 17.—Honeycomb Stitch.

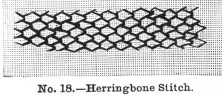

No. 18.—Herringbone Stitch.

No. 12.

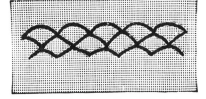

No. 19.—Brick Stitch.

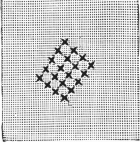

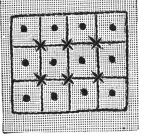

No. 16.

No. 25.—Cross Stitch.   No. 20.—Open Square Stitch.   No. 15.

No. 21.—Arch Pattern.

No. 13.—Various Blanket Stitches, with Manner of Working.

No. 26.—Spike Stitch.

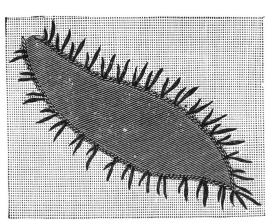

No. 27.—Spike Stitch.

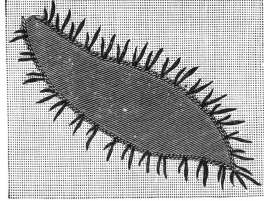

No. 30.—Spike and Chain Stitches.

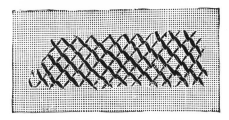

No. 23.—Small Diamond Pattern.

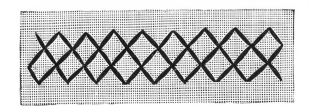

No. 24.—Large Diamond Pattern.

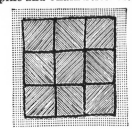

No. 22.—Dice Pattern.

Illustration 57, poppies and leaves to be outlined in silks or crewels, for an antimacassar, is a lovely bold design, which can be treated after illustration 45, with or without a darned background.

Illustrations 58 and 59 show artistic sprays for centreing the quilt design (No. 62), or for mats, panels, banners, &c., for outline crewel work.

Illustration 62 shows a new and attractive design for a quilt to be of linen with various designs worked on the centre or square in outline embroidery. Ingrain red and deep blue cotton will work up effectively, the border to the square be made of Turkey-red twill

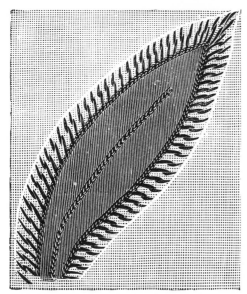

No. 28.—Spike Stitch.

und joined by feather stitching. The square measures 7 inches across, and the 4 pieces that form the border each measure $9\frac{1}{4}$ inches from point to point—that is, in length—and $2\frac{1}{4}$ inches across. Any design could be outlined on the square, such as cupids' heads, butterflies, birds, flowers, fruit, &c., just as one may fancy.

SHADING.

Shading is a matter of taste, and there is no rule for it. Use dark shades of green in olives, browns, and yellows, and do not select too many shades, as it is a mistake. A leaf can be filled in in all one shade, or in two halves with two shades of crewel, the upper half light, and the under half dark, but a good worker will find it better to shade a leaf as in painting, taking care to let the stitches blend, and melt into each other imperceptibly from one shade to the next, working from the top of the leaf or flower that is to be shaded, in this case the light at the top and shading darker. A naturalist's book with coloured prints is useful for reference, but the shades must be more subdued and toned down in the style of work of the present age.

STITCHES.

Crewel or Stem Stitch, also called Outline Stitch, is the chief and most-used stitch for crewel work. This, with Satin Stitch and the useful French Knot, are indeed the only stitches required for ordinary crewel work.

For Crewel Stitch, put the needle into the material, forward, in a slanting direction to the left, and keeping the thread upon the right-hand side of the needle, as in Fig. 1.

The stitches follow each other in succession, in an even line from left to right, and must not be drawn too tightly, as it causes the work to pucker. In working a leaf or flower, commence at the lower right-hand side, working towards the top, and taking care that the needle is drawn out to the left of the thread in going down the other side, and keeping the needle to the right of the thread instead of to the left. Work backwards and forwards, keeping the stitches close together in order that no portion of the surface of the material is to be seen between them. The outline of a leaf can be worked first if

preferred, and then filled in, working round and round until the centre is reached, the veining to be put in last.

In Outline Stitch, for purely outline work, take small neat stitches, and put the needle in exactly where it came out, so preserving a straight line as illustration 33.

Satin Stitch (Nos. 2 and 3) is mostly used for small flowers and for nearly all silk embroidery, and is taken in a diagonal direction across the material, bringing the needle each time almost back to the place from which it started, the length of the stitches to be according to the design, and lying closely side by side, without overlapping, or allowing the groundwork to be seen through them, and so producing a satiny smooth surface. As much thread should appear at the back as upon the surface, whereas in crewel stitch, which is more economical in the use of the thread, only small stitches can be seen at the back, and much less crewel or silk is used.

French Knots (see illustration No. 4), so useful for the centres of flowers, or to fill in spaces in outline embroidery, are worked by taking a stitch wherever the knot is to be, and without drawing it through; then wind the thread round and round the needle two or three times for a tiny knot, or many more times for a large one. Draw the needle through the winding quite tightly, forming a knot, which must then be secured to the material in the exact spot where it emanated from. The right hand should draw the thread underneath, while the left keeps the thread in its place until the knot is secured. French Knots make a pretty outline for a leaf or flower, by working them a little way apart, in a darker shade, outside the line of the outside edge, which should be in a lighter shade.

Split Stitch (Fig. 5).—This stitch is worked like crewel or stem stitch, except that the needle is brought up through the silk or crewel which splits it in passing through. This produces a more even line than crewel stitch, and is useful for the stem of a leaf or flower.

Chain Stitch or Tambour Stitch (see illustration 6).—This useful outline stitch, which takes the place of crewel or outline stitch for outlining a design, or can be used for filling in a space if

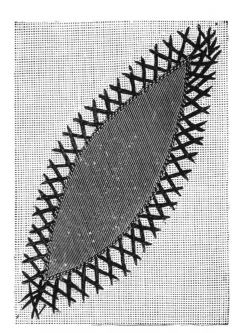

No. 29.—Spike Stitch.

the stitches are taken close together up and down, is worked as follows: Bring the needle from the back of the work to the spot the line is to be carried along, * hold the thread down with the left thumb, and take a stitch, bringing out the needle a little below where it was inserted, and over the thread held down, draw it up, and the stitch is formed. Put the needle down on the right side close to where it came out, and in the chain already made, and keep the thread down with the left thumb as before, and draw it through. Repeat from *

No. 42.—Outline Embroidery worked with Gold Silk in Stem Stitch, Outlined with Faded Green Silk in Vandyke Stitch.

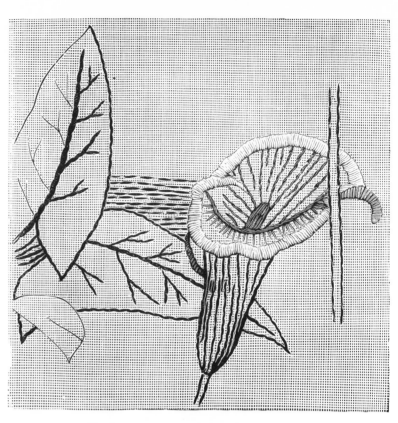

No. 43.—Arum Lily with Darned Ground.

No. 46.—Antimacassar Strip worked in Crewel Stitch on Coarse Huckaback Towelling, Darned with Old Gold Silk.

No. 47.—Design Outlined with Coarse Dark Blue Cotton in Stem Stitch, and Filled in with another Shade in Fancy Stitches.

No. 44.—Spray of Daisies.

No. 45.—Daisy and Foliage worked in Stem Stitch
as Outline Embroidery

No. 49.—Tulip worked in French Crewels.

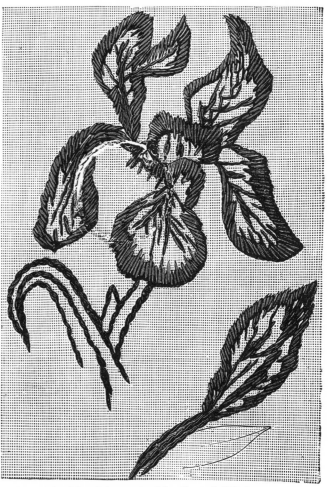

No. 50.—Iris worked in Crewel Stitch.

No. 38.

No. 39.
Peacock Feathers for Ornamental Purposes.

No. 40.

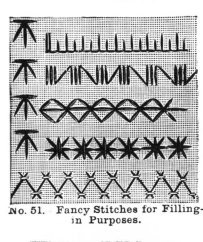

No. 51.—Fancy Stitches for Filling-in Purposes.

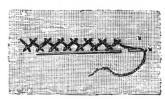

No. 31.—Outline Stitch.

No. 41.—Peacock Feathers for Crewel Work.

No. 34.—Herringbone Stitch.

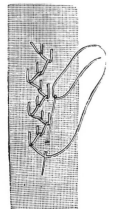

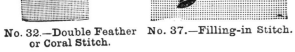

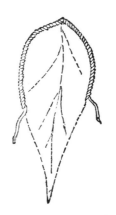

No. 32.—Double Feather or Coral Stitch.

No. 37.—Filling-in Stitch.

No. 33.—Outline Stitch for Bordering.

No. 36.—Outline Stitch for Leaves.

No. 35.—Single Feather or Coral Stitch.

No. 53.—Design Outlined in Stem Stitch.

No. 52.—Design Outlined with Crewel Stitch, and Filled in Fancy Stitches in One or more Colours.

No. 54.—Pincushion Ornamented with Spotted Muslin Embroidered as Daisies, after Illustration 55.

No. 55.—Spotted Muslin Embroidered as Daisies.

No. 56.—White Lily with Darned Ground.

Couching (Fig. 7).—Lay down a strand of filoselle or gold cord round the edge of the work, and putting in the end at the wrong side with a stiletto, secure it down at equal distances with small stitches as you proceed, brought from the back and taken back there again, which gives a rope-like appearance. Couching is most used with chain stitch, but can also be used for covering an outline without being preceded by another stitch.

Darned Stitch (Figs. 8 and 9).—The darned stitch consists of straight lines in and out of the groundwork like ordinary darning, in even stitches, taking up only a small portion of the material on the needle and missing double the length before putting in the needle again, so that the length of the stitch is longer on the right side than on the wrong. In huckaback towelling take up the two threads, or four threads, found on this, the most suitable material for darning upon, or on cross-stitch material, taking up one stitch and missing two. Use six threads of filoselle or ingrain cotton for the darning of a piece of work, whereas it can be outlined in crewel silk if preferred to filoselle, but the latter is best for the darning. This is the easiest, most useful and effective stitch for the darned background of an outline design. It can also be used as a filling-in stitch of a leaf

No. 57.—Poppies and Leaves to be Outlined in Silks or Crewels for an Antimacassar.

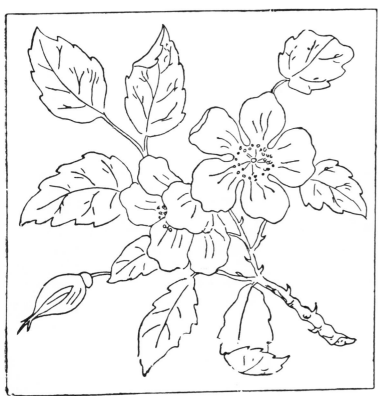

No. 58.—Spray of Wild Roses for Quilt. *See Illustration 62.*

No. 59.—Spray of Lilies and Daisies for Quilt. *See Illustration 62.*

or flower, and is very effective. For variety, cross the darning again, darning straight across it in and out of the stitches taken before.

Twisted Chain or Rope Stitch (Fig. 10) is worked like the ordinary chain stitch, except that instead of starting the second stitch from the centre of the last loop, the needle should be taken back to half the distance *behind* it, and the loop is pushed on one side to allow for the needle to enter, on a line with the last stitch.

No. 60.—Working Design of Outline and Filling-in Stitches.

It is a very effective outline stitch on coarse material, and should be worked in double crewels or the French crewels which are coarse, and gives the appearance of a twisted rope.

Feather Stitch (Figs. 11 and 11A), or *Opus plumarium*, is thus named from its resemblance to the plumage of a bird. For working the petal of a flower the outer part is worked from the inside and the outside, with alternately long and short stitches, which should form an even edge on the outline, but a broken one towards the centre of the flower. The stitches that follow to fill in the petal are worked like an irregular stem stitch, and are worked between the uneven lengths of the edge stitches, in order to blend with them, and two shades should be used, it being a useful stitch for shading a flower, and the shades should melt into each other, as it were, so that they cannot be distinguished, which is the secret of all good shading.

Blanket Stitch (Figs. 12 to 16) is used for the edge of a piece of work or a cloth, and is merely buttonhole stitch, and may be varied, as in our illustrations, by sloping the stitches right and left.

Honeycomb Stitch (Fig. 17).—This stitch is so called from its resemblance to the honeycomb, and is worked thus: A line of buttonhole stitches at even distances, finish off, and then begin again from the beginning for the second row, putting in the needle between each space of the previous row, and only taking up two or three threads of the material. This is one of the best background stitches, and gives a beautiful effect. It looks well in gold, or peacock blue filoselle on cream satin sheeting, the design outlined in shades of brown filoselle.

Herringbone Stitch (Fig. 18).—Begin at the right hand of the piece of huckaback towelling for the ground-work or background, sew the first line entirely on one row of the raised threads, putting the needle under the raised threads, and then slanting to the next raised thread, and putting it under the same way, so forming a line of slanting stitches. Work the next line in the same manner, except that the line of stitches must slant in the opposite direction

Brick Stitch (Fig. 19).—A most useful stitch for filling in large spaces, and is likewise quickly done, and was much used in the old Italian work. Cover the space you wish to fill up with a line of long or horizontal stitches, taken straight across the material from one outline to another, in double crewels or three threads of filoselle, all the thread should be kept on the right side of the work if one does not wish to be wasteful. Then turn and make short perpendicular lines or stitches between each horizontal stitch, about a quarter of an inch apart at right angles with the first lines, each stitch beginning opposite the centre of the first line and ending opposite the centre of the next stitch, and sew them down with tiny stitches a quarter of an inch apart, the same as the other perpendicular stitches. Commence again from the first row. An outline of couching, chain stitch, or rope stitch looks well with this valuable filling-in stitch.

Open Square Stitch (Fig. 20).—Work the material with small squares, in one shade in outline stitch, then with another shade work a cross-stitch where the squares intersect each other, and in the same colour work a French knot in the centre of the little squares. Gold and blue looks well, or red and blue shades. This is a good background or filling-in stitch.

Arch Pattern (Fig. 21).—Draw with a pencil a row of little arches, and work them in stem stitch very neatly, turn and work a similar row, so that the arches intersect each other. This is a good stitch for filling in a space, and in Old work the arches were often back stitched.

Dice Pattern (Fig. 22).—Mark the material with small squares, and then outline them in crewel outline stitch, small neat stitches. Fill in the first square with long slanting stitches, the next square in the same manner, but the stitches to slant in an opposite direction. Or in the first instance it may be more effective to take long stitches from one angle of a square diagonally to the opposite corner. Fill in the squares afterwards, and then outline them evenly in stem stitch.

Diamond Pattern (Figs. 23 and 24).—This background stitch is easily worked on huckaback. Insert the needle under one raised thread in one row, and under a raised thread in another row, slanting

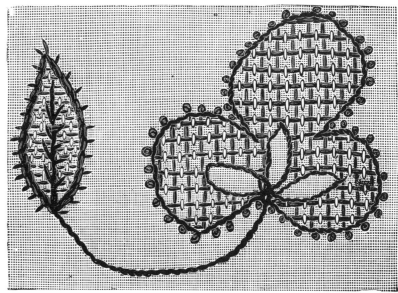

No. 61.—Example for Outlining in Stem Stitch and French Knots, with Filling-in of Fancy Stitches, in Two Shades of Blue Cotton.

Come back again slanting to the raised threads in the first row. The second row is the same as first, but commence on an entirely different line of raised threads, and slanting the thread upwards instead of downwards, as in previous row, so putting the thread in the same stitch as the row above.

Cross Stitch (Fig. 25).—For an ordinary cross stitch, take the first part of the stitch from the left-hand bottom side of the square across to the top right-hand side, and the second half from the right-hand bottom side to the left-hand top side, crossing over the first half. It is a useful background stitch, also worked in the depressed tiny squares of huckaback towelling. Or as a filling-in stitch of a flower or leaf, the stitches to be a little way apart.

Spike Stitches (Figs. 26 to 30).—For edging rope stitch in double crewels, three long stitches taken together in a tuft, leave a space and repeat. Or with chain stitch the long spike stitches look well, and are merely a long cross stitch. Another stitch is a edge of an antimacassar. Herringbone stitch resembles a series of small crosses, and is worked from left to right, taking up alternately three threads at the top and three threads at the bottom. It likewise comes in as a filling-in stitch for a small passage or space.

Single Feather or Coral Stitch (Fig. 35).—This stitch is very extensively used in embroidery. A central line is marked, and from this the stitches branch out on either side. The needle is set in slanting from the outside towards the centre, and the silk is always passed under the point of the needle.

Double Feather Stitch (Fig. 32).—This stitch is worked in

No. 62.—Breast Plate Square for Quilt with Embroidered Centre.
See also Illustrations 58 and 59.

straight long stitch and a short one, side by side. These stitches should emanate from the chain stitch outline edge.

Outline Stitch (Figs. 31, 33, 36).—This stitch is like a back stitch, taking short slanting stitches all along, through to the front, and out again at the back. An outline design looks well worked thus, in gold on black, and is quickly done.

Herringbone Stitch (Fig. 34).—This stitch is a very useful one for embroidery, also for a background or darned stitch on huckaback for an outline design. It is also much used in flannel work, being valuable as a means of keeping a hem down without making a double fold in the material. It can also be used for the the same manner as feather stitch, but has two stitches on either side.

Filling-in Stitch (Fig. 37).—This stitch is a good one for filling in a leaf, petal, or space. Outline the space or leaf in double crewels, and then in single threads cross over from side to side, in a slanting direction, in long stitches to the end of the leaf. Come back again thus in slanting stitches from one side to the other, crossing the first lines in the opposite direction and forming a diamond network. Wherever the lines cross each other work a single cross stitch, which sets it off and keeps all firm and secure. It is quickly done and is most effective.

WELDON'S
PRACTICAL BAZAAR ARTICLES

(FIRST SERIES.)

NEW AND ARTISTIC DESIGNS FOR

PINCUSHIONS, PENWIPERS, BAGS, TIDIES, &c.

62 ILLUSTRATIONS.

The Yearly Subscription to this Magazine, post free to any part of the World, is 2s. 6d.
Subscriptions are payable in advance, and may commence from any date and for any period.

The Back Numbers are always in print. Nos. 1 to 232 *now ready, Price 2d. each, or bound in 19 Vols., price 2s. 6d. each.*

TRANSFERRING DESIGNS TO MATERIALS.

BEFORE proceeding to describe the various little objects contained in this number of our Needlework Series, which are to be adorned with decorative needlework, it may not be out of place to give a few practical directions for transferring the various designs to the materials selected for working them upon.

There are several methods of doing this. One of the easiest for any white or light-coloured material is the following:—Take, on tissue paper, an accurate tracing of the required design, then having first by the aid of drawing pins tightly stretched the material upon a drawing board or deal table, pin the design in its destined position. Slip below it a piece of carbonic paper, and carefully go over the whole design with a fine pointed knitting needle, agate burnisher, or piece of hard wood sharpened to a point. Before removing the design, gently lift a portion of it up to see if every line has been accurately reproduced; if not, go over the missing parts.

POUNCING is another method of transferring the design; it is the one adopted by most decorative needle-workers, and is certainly preferable to the use of carbonic paper, when several copies of a design are required. To make a pounce, take a tracing on tissue paper, as described above, reverse it, and place it upon a second sheet of white paper, in order to render it opaque and show the line on the other side; lay this upon a blanket or some soft substance, and then with a medium-sized needle, which should for comfort sake be fastened into a slit cut into a paint brush stick, carefully prick pretty closely all along the lines of the design, reverse it, and fasten upon the material. Take a narrow strip of old flannel, roll it tightly up, and tie or sew it round; straighten with a pair of scissors the ends, and dip one of them in powdered charcoal; rub this well over the perforated design, and a good impression will be found below. This must then, to fix it, be traced over with vandyke brown—either oil or water colour will do. Charcoal is only suitable for use upon white materials, and any smudges left by it can be removed with dry bread.

To transfer designs to dark materials, finely powdered and very dry pipe-clay must be substituted for the charcoal, and the after-tracing must be executed in flake or Chinese white. The superfluous pipe-clay may easily be shaken or knocked off the material, and before using the pounce a second time it must be well tapped to clear the powder out of the perforation. Rough materials, such as flannel, serge, &c., should be pressed with a hot iron before attempting to transfer the designs to them; plush must be pressed down as smoothly as possible by the hand. With patience and a little practice the work of transferring may easily be accomplished, and it may frequently be made remunerative—either by tracing for friends or for fancy workshops, who are sometimes glad to give work of this kind to ladies residing in the neighbourhood.

To transfer to cardboard, china, &c., *black lead* transfer paper should be used instead of carbonic paper, the black lead being effaceable with bread or indiarubber; or a fairly good substitute may be made by rubbing some ordinary black lead evenly over a piece of thin paper. In all cases it should be a rule to use *three* drawing pins or other means of securing the design to the article it is to be reproduced upon. The reason is obvious: should one pin accidentally fall out, the design will remain securely in position held by the two remaining pins; if only one point of fixture were left, it would slip, and the design be spoilt.

PINCUSHIONS.

AMONGST articles that, if well made, generally meet with a ready sale at fancy fairs, and that also commend themselves to skilful needleworkers who have more leisure for manufacture than spare cash for the purchase of little tokens of affection, are the many varieties of pincushions that have from time to time been invented. Everyone knows what extremely handsome ones may be made out of cigar boxes, by neatly covering them inside and out with silk, satin, or even glazed calico; stuffing the lid with bran, and decorating the whole with muslin and delicate lace quillings and bows of ribbons. Circular toilet cushions made of two circles of calico, joined together by a straight band of the same, about an inch in width, and very firmly stuffed with bran, are a very useful shape, and may be covered

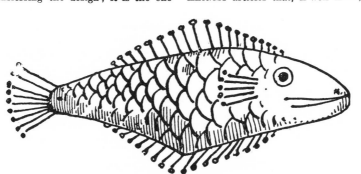

No. 1.—Fish Pincushion.

in various ways, either with satin first, and then with lace or embroidered muslin, or with satin or other opaque material itself, more or less elaborately embroidered. For this purpose little Cupids, or Kate Greenaway figures outlined on satin, finished off with two or three rows of iridescent spangles, cord, and Edelweiss lace, are extremely effective and quickly made up. Square pincushions may be decorated in the same way; the foundations of these are made of two squares of calico sewn together, and do not require the narrow band of material to connect them, as directed for the circular shape. The square toilet cushions may be covered entirely with lace over a coloured foundation; or with a square or circular loose top, fixed at the corners. The three descriptions of pincushions given represent the principal ones in use for toilet purposes; but of those destined for general use in the work-basket, sitting-room, &c., the variety both of design and shape is almost without limit. Of late the most fashionable

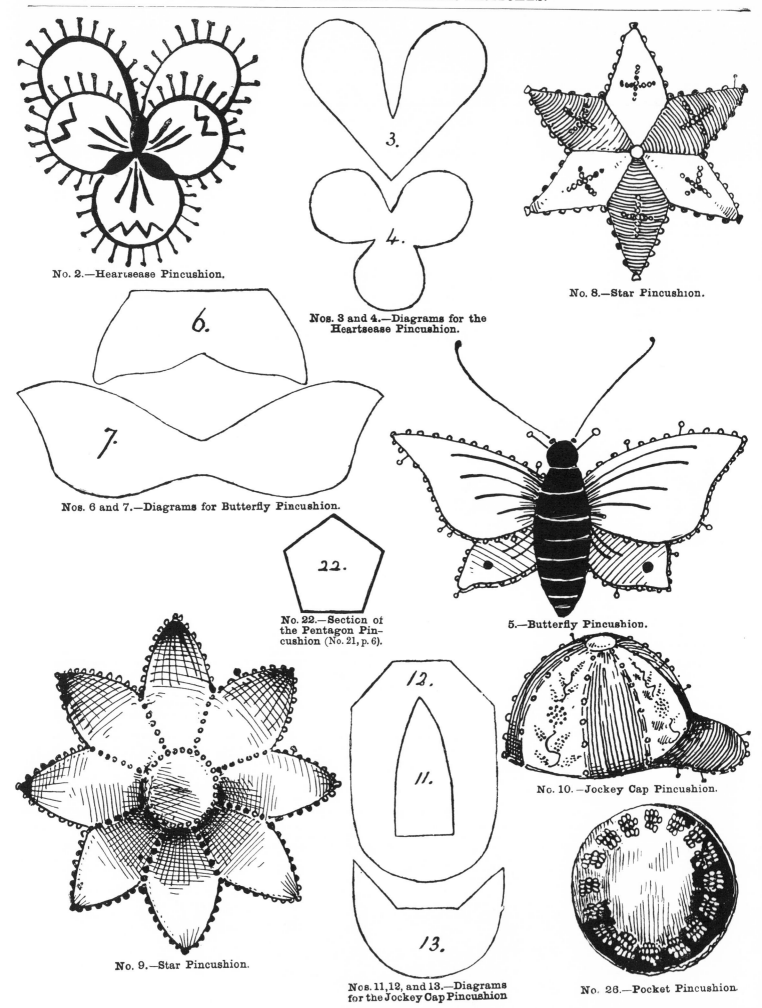

No. 2.—Heartsease Pincushion.

Nos. 3 and 4.—Diagrams for the
Heartsease Pincushion.

No. 8.—Star Pincushion.

Nos. 6 and 7.—Diagrams for Butterfly Pincushion.

No. 22.—Section of
the Pentagon Pin-
cushion (No. 21, p. 6).

5.—Butterfly Pincushion.

No. 10.—Jockey Cap Pincushion.

No. 9.—Star Pincushion.

Nos. 11, 12, and 13.—Diagrams
for the Jockey Cap Pincushion.

No. 26.—Pocket Pincushion.

pincushions have been elaborate and tastefully-made representations of water-lilies, sunflowers, fruit and vegetables of all kinds, not forgetting even the familiar toadstool, the latter being turned out in most realistic style by the aid of tinted velvet, with tiny Japanese frogs affixed to them. Mandolines, guitars, quivers with hearts attached to them, bellows, shoes, &c., most people have heard of, if not seen; and the designs for many of them may be traced back for several generations. Some years ago, when turning over the relics of work left by a lady who lived early in the last century, a bag containing many pretty and quaint forms of pincushions made upon card-board foundations came to light, the descriptions and patterns of which may perhaps be of service to readers of this paper; they may any of them be made with the greatest ease, if a few general rules are observed. In the first place, all the shapes must be accurately and smoothly cut out—jagged or uneven edges being quite fatal to perfection in the manufacture of these little oddments; secondly, it is advisable to cover the larger shapes, such as fish, butterflies, &c., with muslin or thin calico, as well as silk, as this makes the stitching together of the various portions a little easier; thirdly, the cardboard shapes must be very neatly and smoothly covered with whatever material has been selected for use. This is generally done by means of long threads drawn from side to side on the reverse side, but in many shapes a little embroidery paste may be made to serve the purpose; rye flour, with sufficient boiling water stirred with it to make a stiff paste, answers very well, but if paste instead of a needle and thread is used for covering, great care must be taken not to soil the materials used—only experienced workers should attempt to use it; fourthly, fine needles and strong sewing silk must be used, and the tiniest and most regular of over-cast stitches be made when joining the various portions of the pincushion together; nothing looks worse than cobbled edges and uneven stitches. As a simple form will be best to start with for those who are not experienced in this particular kind of work, we will first describe—

Fig. 1.—The **Fish Pincushion** has to be cut out in thin cardboard (visiting cards answer the purpose admirably), two pieces the shape and

diamond a few seed beads should be sewn on. The portion forming the stars should be joined on the reverse side, and the two stars afterwards be fastened together in the usual way by over-cast stitching; and whilst doing this a little wadding should be pushed up into the angle of each diamond, by aid of a bodkin or a pointed pair of scissors. When the pincushion is well stuffed it must be fastened off and finished by a few stitches drawn firmly through the centre, which will cause a depression in it; the stitches may be concealed by a gilt bead on either side of the star.

Fig. 9—**Eight Star Pincushion.**—This variety of the star requires 16 pieces for the border and two circles; they may easily be cut out from the illustration, and are to be made up as directed for fig. 8.

Fig. 10.—The **Jockey Cap** is composed of eleven pieces - 8 sections shape of fig. 11, and one each of diagrams 12 and 13. The eight pieces forming the cap should be covered in prettily contrasting silk, and four of them may have a little design worked upon them in seed beads; they should then be joined together, and have the flap (previously covered with silk) fastened on; lastly, the foundation piece (diagram 12) is to be joined on, filling the cap with bran before closing it up finally. In the event of the cap not being very neatly joined together, a small circle may be added to cover the centre of top, as shown in the engraving.

Fig. 14.—The **Coal Scuttle** is the quaintest and most uncommon of all the patterns given; it is a little more difficult to construct, but well worth the trouble, being really quite unique in appearance, and I have never come across it except in the collection of antique pincushions pre-viously mentioned. To make it, diagram 15 must be cut out and very neatly covered with amber, rose or blue satin, and the little design shown be worked on in the tiniest opal or crystal seed beads; it must then be very neatly lined (leaving a little space open on either side for the insertion of the handles), and the two short ends marked c c be joined together. The circle 16, covered with satin and embroidered with beads, should then be

No. 14.—Coal Scuttle Pincushion.

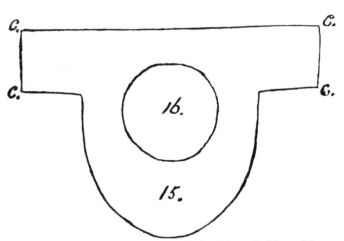

Nos. 15 and 16.—Diagrams for Coal Scuttle Pincushion.

size of the illustration; cover them with amber or pale blue satin, or, if neither of these are at hand, with any scraps of pretty silk or beads, and if the covering material has no pattern on it, the scales shown may be painted or worked on; or the whole may be covered with fine white net. Join the two sides together, commencing at the tail, and before closing this up insert just enough wadding into the body of the fish to give it a slightly round appearance; the mouth must now be worked in rather thick embroidery or sewing silk, and pins arranged all round the fish, and also where the fins are shown.

Fig. 2.—The **Heartsease** is a rather more complicated pattern, the pieces of card being a little more difficult to cover; four are required, two each of diagrams 3 and 4. The first are to be covered with purple silk, and the second pair with yellow or deep gold silk. It is not advisable to use satin for this pattern, on account of its liability to fray out. A few stitches may be embroidered in floss silk upon the trefoil-shaped portion, to simulate the markings of a pansy, and the four pieces must then be respectively joined together, and afterwards fastened together as shown in fig. 2, the connecting triangular links being formed of narrow pieces of silk or velvet, folded together and caught in the centre by a few stitches. The pins are to be placed round as shown.

Fig. 5.—The **Butterfly** consists of six pieces, four for the wings (see diagrams 6 and 7) and two for the body, which is of the shape shown in the made-up example, fig. 5. The wings should be covered in yellow, purple, white or brown silk; and the upper portions of them may be embroidered with silk, or have some spangles fixed on to them. The body should be covered with black velvet, crossed with silk or gold thread, and antennæ of the latter be added before joining all the various portions together as shown.

Fig. 8.—The **Star** consists of twelve diamond-shaped pieces, covered alternately with contrasting coloured silk, and in the centre of each

neatly sewn into the back of the scuttle, and a small support, stuffed with emery powder and formed of narrow ribbon and two tiny circles of card, be fastened below it, as shown in the illustration; the handle, composed of a narrow strip of card covered with ribbon, should then be fixed in position; and to hold needles a small piece of flannel neatly notched round may be laid on the inside of the scuttle; a bodkin and tiny thimble may be added to simulate a shovel.

Fig. 17.—A **Lady's Boot** is composed of two pieces of card the shape and size of diagram 18, covered with black silk; they are joined together by sarcenet ribbon, which should not exceed a quarter of an inch in width; and this, just above and below the top of the toe, must be gradually narrowed until both tips meet. The boot should be stuffed with either bran or wadding, and be finished off with a tiny ribbon bow, and tassel made of sewing silk.

Fig. 19.—**Pocket Pincushion.**—This is a very simple and easily made little pincushion. It is simply composed of two wooden button moulds covered with silk or satin, and laced over, as shown in the engraving, by thick purse silk. The button moulds are jointed together by sarcenet ribbon, the width usually sold at a penny a yard being the best kind to use; the filling should be of bran, and the little loops for suspension be made of the same ribbon as the edges. A somewhat similar pincushion may be made in imitation of a biscuit, by cutting out two rounds of biscuit-coloured leather, and edging them as above described by narrow biscuit-coloured ribbon, but instead of bran, the stuffing should consist of several rounds of flannel, and the pincushion should be quilted down to simulate the prickings of a biscuit.

Fig. 20.—The **Granny Cushion** is in quite a different style to the old-fashioned pincushions described above, it is probably of French manu-facture originally. To make it, two fairly large circles of satin of contrasting shades are required, the centre of one of these, which is to form the lining, must be cut out (it may be utilised for the stuffed portion of another cushion), and the two pieces of satin should then be joined together on the wrong side, and turned inside out. A little round ball-like pincushion stuffed with bran and covered on the top with satin, the same shade as that used for the exterior circle, must then be prepared and placed in the centre of the lined satin circles, which should then be drawn up around it, and tied into shape by ribbon of the same shade as the lining. It may, perhaps, be advisable to insert a circle of card and a little wadding round the pincushion, inside the cover, to keep it well set out. Any pretty contrasting shades of colour may be used for these Granny pincushions: a charming combination is effected by an exterior and cushion of olive green satin, lining and ribbon of pale salmon; or by exterior and centre of cardinal, lining and ribbon of pale salmon. Ditto, ditto, pearl grey and rose, or rose and turquoise blue.

Fig. 21.—Pentagon Pincushion.—A pretty form of pincushion is that composed of 12 pentagons. To make it, cut them out of cardboard, and cover them with different coloured pieces of silk. Then join them together as shown in our illustration. A little design may be painted in the centre

their being bent over as shown in fig. 23. At the base of each petal, two little plaits must be made when fixing it on to the foundation. The centre of the rose, which serves the purpose of a pincushion, is composed of a semi-circular ball, stuffed with wadding or bran, the top of it being covered with the same material as the petals are composed of. Finally, a double loop of ribbon finished off with a bow (want of space forbids this latter being shown in fig. 23) is to be added to the back of the rose, by which it may be suspended upon the wall or to the side of the toilet-table. Rose-coloured satin has been named for the pincushion, but of course any other shade of satin may be substituted, and it would really have a very pretty effect if composed of sateen or merino.

Fig. 26.—Pocket Pincushion.—A little pincushion which sells readily at bazaars, and is most useful for the pocket, may be made out of two circles of card and a little wadding round the pincushion, inside the cover, to keep it well set out. Any pretty contrasting shades worked upon it in chalk or crystal beads; four beads are taken up at each stitch, so the work is quickly done, and if strong cotton is used, the bead-work will outlast the pile of the velvet. The second circle of card should be covered with velvet or a piece of silk, and

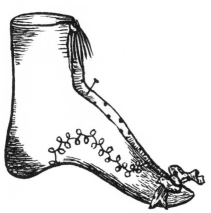

No. 17.—Lady's Boot Pincushion.

No. 19.—Pocket Pincushion.

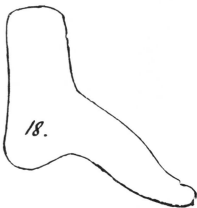

No. 18.—Diagram for Lady's Boot Pincushion.

No. 27.—Hassock Pincushion.

No. 20.—Granny's Cap Pincushion

No. 21.—The Pentagon Pincushion.

of each piece. Pins are to be inserted along the seams; no filling of bran or wool is required for this pincushion; it may be made of various sizes, that of our diagram 22 is a good proportion for ordinary pins.

Fig. 23.—Rose Pincushion.—This is one of the latest and most effective of the floral pincushions now so fashionable, it is not at all difficult to make, and would be a most attractive addition to a bazaar stall. To make it, cut a circular piece of card three inches in diameter, cover this on one side with olive green cambric, and upon this, on the uncovered side, fix, for the calyx of the rose, six leaves, see fig. 24, cut out of green plush lined with green cambric. This can be done by running round the edges on the wrong side with a sewing machine, and then turning the leaves inside out; two small plaits must be made to each one before fixing it on to the foundation; 36 pieces of rose-colour satin are now to be cut out after fig. 25: these are to be joined together on the reverse side round the edges, and turned inside out, and a piece of round bonnet wire is to be fixed round the inside of each of the 18 petals thus formed; this will keep them in shape, and permit of

both pieces be neatly sewn together; the pins are, as usual in this class of pincushion, inserted round the edges.

Fig. 27.—Hassock Pincushion.—A capital little pincushion, always useful and saleable, is the tiny hassock, fig. 27. It is simply composed of four pieces of cloth joined together to form a circle, and sewn round the edges to a narrow strip of the same material. Little handles are to be fixed at the sides, and a plain circle of cloth is sewn on for the bottom of the hassock. Before closing this up, sufficient bran must be pressed in, to make the pincushion very hard and firm. It may be made to any size, and in any colour, and narrow worsted braid may be sewn round the edge if this has not been joined together quite as neatly as might be desired.

Fig. 28.—Fish Needlebook and Pincushion.—To make this, cut two pieces of card the size and shape of illustration, and two the shape of head and body as far as the end of the last set of pins is shown. Cover the former pieces of card with amber or other coloured satin, fix the spangles on the tail where shown, and a large one for the eye (the place of these spangles, if none are at hand, may be supplied by a few stitches in filoselle silk, in which the mouth is also worked). Cover the smaller pieces of card with white silk or satin, and join them to the others very neatly round the edges ; fasten to one side a couple of pieces of flannel to hold needles, then join the two sides of the tail of the fish together, and overcast the edges with chalk or crystal beads set rather closely together. The beads round the open mouth of the fish are to be sewn on at a greater distance from each other in order to admit of a pin being inserted between each one. Or the pins may be passed through a bead, as shown in illustration ; but this is not such a good plan as sewing them on, as they naturally drop off on the removal of the pins for use. Pins must also be placed where shown for the fins.

Space forbids the description of many other varieties of pincushions, both with and without cardboard foundations, but those described may all be made at little or no cost, save that of the time and trouble involved. If for sale at bazaars, the minor varieties should be contributed in quantities of at least six or twelve of each pattern, as they attract so much more attention than when shown singly. An attractive method of display and disposal might be to fasten eight or ten different patterns together, and sell the collection in its entirety. The jockey caps as a rule fetch from 1s. to 1s. 6d. each ; the shoes, 6d. to 1s. ; the coal-scuttle is well worth 1s. 6d. or 2s. ; whilst the fish, being quickly made, may be remuneratively disposed of at from 3d. to 4d. apiece.

Fig. 29 —Toilet Tidy, in needlework, beads, and spangles. Our illustration, fig. 29, and its accompanying working designs, represents a familiar and most useful form of tidy, which, as a rule, is carried out in perforated cardboard, with some more or less trifling adornment in Berlin wool. By the aid of our design, a receptacle may be made more durable, and certainly far more pleasing to the eye, than those of the material alluded to. It is capable of being carried out by the aid of needlework or painting, but having been specially arranged with a view to the former, we will first give directions for that purpose. In the first place the design must be accurately transferred to some suitable material, such as satin, fine serge, or merino, and with silk or crewel wool ; the stems must then be outlined,

No. 23.—The Rose Pincushion.

together as shown in illustration 29 ; fine silk cord or beads may be sewn along the edges to conceal the seams, and give a finish to the tidy. A loop of cord for the purpose of suspension, as well as a loose white paper pocket to prevent the tidy being soiled whilst in use, will complete it

For a painted tidy, sketch the designs or transfer them to cardboard by means of blacklead paper, carbonic paper not being advisable for this purpose, as the marks it leaves are generally too heavy and quite indelible. Paint the design in water colour according to taste, edge the card with narrow silk ribbon, and make up as previously directed, or paint the design on gold American cloth with oil colours, mount on a card foundation, and make up. Velvet with lustra colours would also make a lovely tidy. In this, as in the other patterns we publish, there is practically unlimited scope for the individual taste and ingenuity of the worker.

Fig. 32.—A French Knot.—This stitch, so useful for centres of flowers, fillings of conventional designs, &c., is a very simple one. It is simply worked as follows: Draw the needle and silk through the material, twist the silk several times round the needle (see fig. 32), replace the point of the needle precisely in the same spot through which it has been drawn up, and keeping the silk firmly pressed down on the material by the thumb of the left hand, draw it through to the back of the material. A little practice will soon ensure perfection in this useful and effective stitch. It will be well to practise it in crewel wool before attempting to execute it in silk.

Penwipers.—Penwipers of various shapes and forms have from time immemorial formed part of the general stock-in-trade of a bazaar stall. If well made, and of really serviceable form, they generally command a ready sale. They are useful, also, for making up the contents of a bran pie, as scraps of cloth may generally be begged from the family tailor, consequently the expense of material has not to be taken into consideration. A very useful penwiper may be made by the following directions : Cut out three or four circles of black cloth about the size of the top of a wineglass or small tumbler; notch the edges very neatly, and join the pieces in the centre, one above the other. This forms the foundation. To decorate it, cut four circles, of precisely similar size, out of scarlet cloth, or pretty coloured flannel. Notch the edges, or overcast them with button-

and the leaves executed in satin stitch (see illustration 53). The flowers will look pretty either in gilt, chalk, or crystal beads, or failing these in French knots (see illustration 32), a detailed description of which will be found on this page. The spangles must be firmly sewn on, gilt or coloured ones may be used, or their place may be supplied by dots of double satin stitch, see illustration 52; the second row of stitches as shown, the reverse way to the under ones, will be found to be a great improvement to the dots as ordinarily executed in decorative embroidery. The letters and bow will look well in satin or ordinary stem (crewel) stitch. The work being completed, tack it smoothly over cardboard foundations cut to the exact proportions of illustrations Nos. 30 and 31 ; cover also a piece of card for the base, line all neatly, and join

hole stitch, using for the latter purpose silk of a contrasting colour to that of the cloth or flannel. Fold each of the circles in four, and fasten them by the point thus formed to the pieces joined together for the foundation, which is really the penwiper proper. A pretty metal button, little china figure, or one of the tiny Japanese green tree-frogs now so fashionable, fixed to the centre to conceal the joins, will make a pretty finish to this kind of penwiper. A variation of the same form is effected by fixing on six coloured circles instead of four, arranging them in such a way that they set up after the fashion of a semicircular rosette.

Fig. 33.—Umbrella Penwiper.—A more elaborate penwiper is the

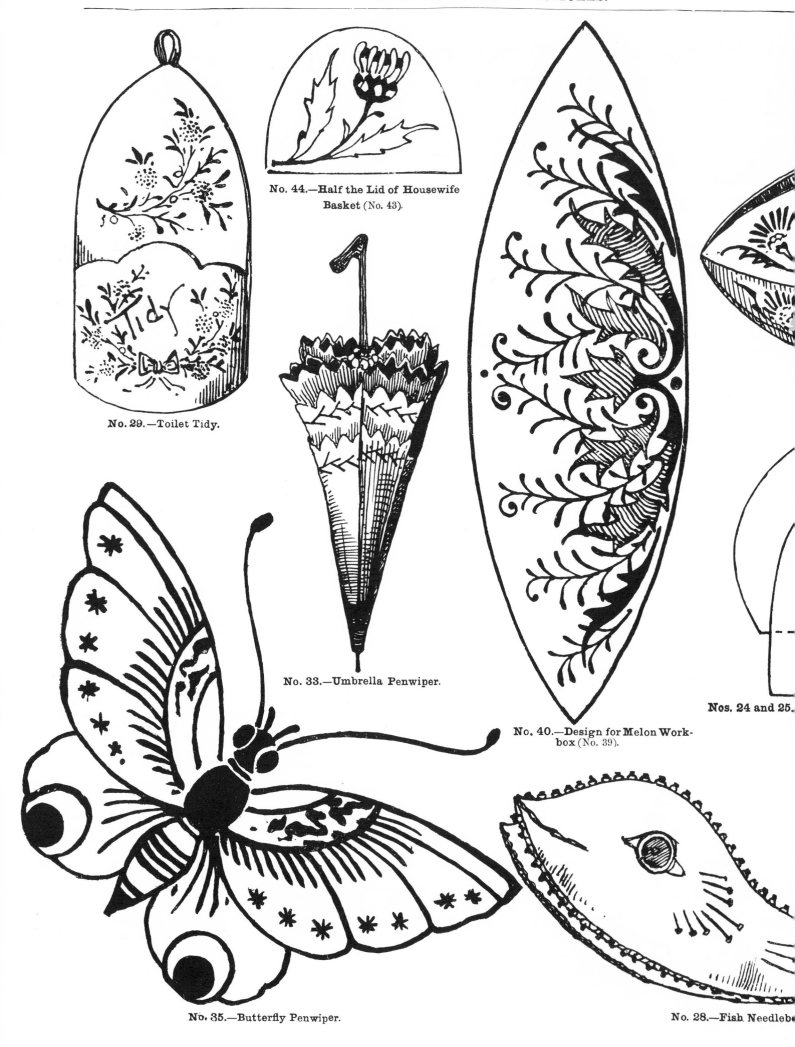

No. 44.—**Half the Lid of Housewife Basket** (No. 43).

No. 29.—Toilet Tidy.

No. 33.—**Umbrella Penwiper.**

No. 40.—**Design for Melon Work-box** (No. 39).

Nos. 24 and 25.

No. 35.—**Butterfly Penwiper.**

No. 28.—Fish Needleb

Workbox.

tal Diagrams for Rose Pin-
No. 23).

No. 32.—Manner of
Working French
Knots.

hion.

No. 41.—Design for Melon Workbox
(No. 39)

No. 34.—Diagram for Umbrella
Penwiper (No 33).

No. 37.—Orange Ball.

No. 36.—Star Penwiper.

No. 42.—Bolster Housewife.

Umbrella, the construction of which is clearly shown by diagram 32. The handle is formed of wire covered with sealing-wax, and the cover is composed of twelve pieces of cloth alternately scarlet and black. The long pieces for the lower ends (see diagram A) have the shorter but rather wider upper pieces (B and C) joined on by rows of feather stitch executed in some pretty shade of silk. The four sections thus joined are neatly seamed together, and a narrow piece of notched black cloth upon which to wipe the pens should be fixed under (fig. C), and after reversing the cover it must be slipped over the handle, and be fixed to it at the top by a row of small white or gilt beads ; the lower end should be finished off by a piece of leather or portion of an old kid glove gummed rather than sewn on.

Fig. 35. — Butterfly Pen-wiper.—The Butterfly, as shown by illustration 35, is an exceptionally handsome form of penwiper; it may be carried out in various colourings and in various materials, but preferably cloth should be selected for the foundation. To make it, cut it full size as shown out of one piece of scarlet, brown, or any self-coloured cloth, and overcast the edges with filoselle, purse-silk, or twist. Appliqué to the lower wing the small circles shown. They may be of velvet on cachemire, and sewn on either by couching or button-stitch. The markings of the wings are then to be worked in filoselle, and where on the latter the stars are shown, spangles may be placed, or the stars may be executed by silk-stitches crossing over each other. The butterfly's wings being completed, two or three pieces of black cloth of similar form, but just a trifle smaller, must be cut out and fixed below them, and the body must then be proceeded with. This should be cut out of cardboard, and covered with black velvet, stuffing it with a little wadding to give it a slightly raised appearance; the lines crossing the body are formed by silk or Japan gold thread; the eyes may be black beads or little dots of satin stitch in yellow filoselle, and the antennæ are made out of bonnet wire, with tiny morsels of plush or velvet gummed over the ends. When the body is firmly sewn on to the wings and under pieces of cloth forming the penwiper, the result cannot fail to give satisfaction. This butterfly design may be adapted for a pincushion, by cutting it out in cardboard, either all in one piece or in two sections as directed for the smaller butterfly, illustration 6, and according to the taste and skill of the worker any amount of decoration may be bestowed upon it. A pretty ornament for a Zulu hat basket might be made by cutting the butterfly's upper and under wings separately out of buckram (procurable from most linen-drapers, as it is used by them for their tickets of prices). The wings should be edged round with narrow bonnet wire, covered with plush, velvet, or satin, then neatly lined and finished off by a plush or velvet body. By bending the wire-bound wings the butterfly might be poised on the basket as though it had just alighted there.

Fig. 36.—Star Penwiper. -A capital way of using up tiny pieces of scarlet, blue, orange, and green cloth is to cut out a number of tiny stars, the size of those shown in our engraving. Six leaves of green cloth must also be cut out, then must be sewn on by the aid of feather stitch (which will simulate the veinings of the leaves) to a circular piece of white or light grey cloth carefully notched round the edges, and the stars must then be arranged on the top, sewing each one on by a stitch passed through a tiny circle of cloth of a contrasting colour to that of the star. Some circles of black cloth must be fastened under the top thus prepared, and a very effective and useful little penwiper will be the result

No. 30.—**Full-size Design for Back and Base of Toilet Tidy No. 29.**

Fig. 37.—Orange Ball, for knitting or crochet wool. One of the prettiest and most uncommon shaped bags for balls of cotton or wool may be made as follows in the form of an orange : Cut out of the buckram used by drapers twelve pieces of the shape and size of one-half of illustration 38 (two sections are given, on account of the double design required for decorating them). Cover them with orange satin or merino, upon which the little sprays shown have been embroidered. The little oranges should be represented as unripe, and worked in green. Line the twelve sections neatly with white satin or silk, and join them together in the centre where the dotted lines are shown. Between the lining and the outer cover of the twelve sections small loops of cord are inserted; the lower ones are drawn together by a small piece of cord forming a ring, and through the upper ones a yard of cord or ribbon is to be passed and joined together; a second yard is to be similarly passed through the reverse way, and also joined together, after which the ball of wool or silk may be placed inside, and the double strings be drawn up as shown in fig. 37 before suspending the bag over the arm or looping it on to the bar of a chair. We have mentioned orange satin as the covering for this little article, but any other colour or material may be selected. A pretty little bridal gift would be one of these bags, made of white satin, with ripe oranges worked upon it ; a lovely combination colouring would be pale blue satin lined with white ; and for a quiet, really useful bag for an elderly lady deep olive green might be selected. Then small sprays of orange blossom and fruit will be very serviceable for the decoration of various objects of fancy work, such as pincushions, &c., they could also easily be enlarged and used as powderings for chair-backs, footstools, children's dresses, &c.

Figs 39, 40, and 41.—Melon Workbox.—To make this useful and elegant box transfer either of the designs No. 40 or 41 to satin, fine serge, or merino. Five pieces will be required; these must be embroidered in crewel or silk, according to the taste of the worker; Japanese gold thread may appropriately be introduced into the design if at hand. Strain the four pieces of needlework over cardboard cut to the exact size of the outer line of the designs, and cover a fifth piece of cardboard of similar size with plain material (this is to form the under-part of the box); line them all neatly, and join together as shown in illustration 39. It will be an improvement to edge the seams with silk cord or to overcast them with beads. Handles of cord must be inserted between the lining and the exterior cover as shown, and if liked, a loop and button may be added to keep the box securely closed. The designs may be enlarged if a very capacious workbox is required. An extremely useful size is for each section to be eleven inches long by three-and-a-half inches across the widest part of the centre.

Fig. 42. — Bolster House-wife.--A serviceable little housewife may be made out of a piece of ribbon, satin, or silk, measuring two and a half or three inches in width, by ten inches in length. To make it, make a tiny roll of flannel the same length as the width of the ribbon, cover the two ends with a piece of the material selected for the housewife, and roll one end of the ribbon over it, sew it up, and also sew very neatly round the two ends. Hem the other end of the ribbon, and work a double row of feather stitch along it, then double it over, bringing it to within about half an inch of the little bolster pincushion. Fasten two tiny little pieces of flannel or pure white cloth upon the pocket, and to the lower end of it attach half a yard of narrow ribbon doubled in two ; the two strings thus formed are to tie the housewife, when it is rolled up as shown in the illustration. Our

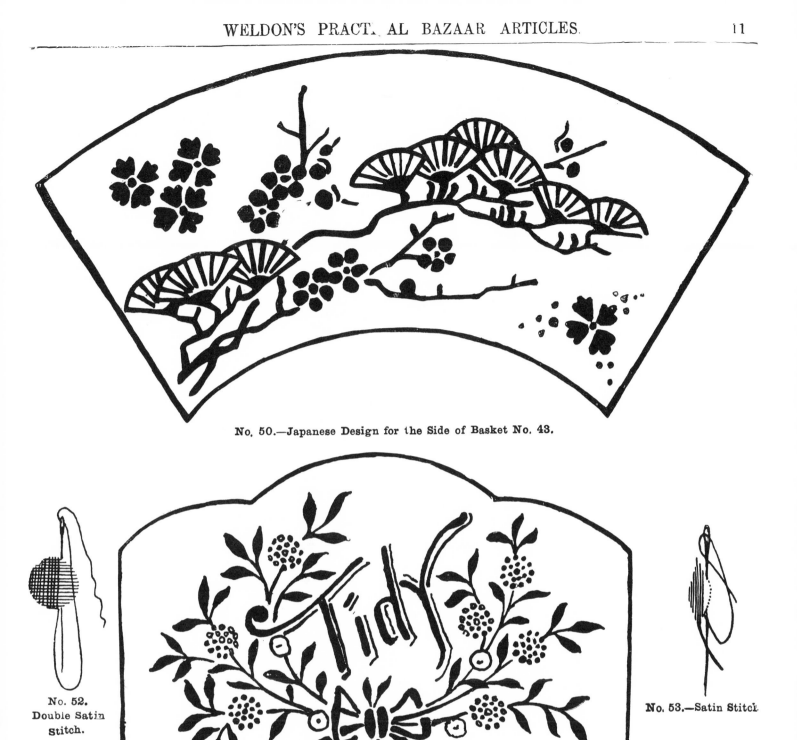

No. 50.—Japanese Design for the Side of Basket No. 43.

No. 52.
Double Satin
Stitch.

No. 31.—Full-size Design for Front of Toilet Tidy No. 29.

No. 53.—Satin Stitch

No. 38.—Diagram for Cutting out Orange Ball as Illustration No. 37.

model was made of rose-coloured satin, with feather stitching in black silk, but any kind of ribbon, plain or figured, may be used.

Fig. 43.—Housewife Basket.—This handy little receptacle for reels of cotton, buttons, tapes, &c., may be made in several sizes, and decorated in various ways, either by painting or needlework. The designs we give are suitable for either purpose. The basket is composed of five pieces, each of which must be cut out of thin cardboard, in duplicate, two of illustration 46 (the base), and four each of illustrations 44 and 45. These pieces must then be covered, half of them with the material selected for the exterior of the basket, and the remainder with something suitable for lining. The various portions must then be sewn together very neatly round the edges, and afterwards they must be joined together as shown by illustration 43 ; a handle, composed of strips of cardboard, strengthened with flat bonnet wire, twisted over with ribbon or velvet, and bows to match being added in their proper position. The edges of the two lids of the basket, which are fastened to it at the corners concealed by the bows of ribbon, and open upwards against the handle, may have pins inserted round the edges. Our smallest design may be worked or painted with the marguerite as shown ; or a basket cut to this size, and covered with satin, looks very pretty with a little border of beads round the sides, and rosettes of pearls and beads on the lid, as shown in illustration 43. The larger sized boxes (illustrations 47, 48, 49, 50 and 51) are made in precisely the same way, the width of handle and ribbon for bows being, of course, in proportion to the increased size of them. The Japanese design of fir will work out admirably in silk or gold thread. The butterflies may be painted or worked in natural colours. The lids of either of these larger designs are well suited for the decoration of tobacco pouches, purses, &c., and the side pieces might easily be enlarged for fan painting.

Fig. 54.—Quill Pen.—A very pretty fancy pen can easily be made by shaving off the feather from a long quill pen, then joining to the tip of it a piece of white purse silk, upon which has been threaded gilt or blue beads as follows : 1 blue, 4 gold, 1 blue, 8 gold, repeat these until a good number of beads have been threaded. Then commence twisting the silk round the pen, leaving the beads on the upper side as shown in illustration, the blue ones forming the centre of the gilt lozenges. Finish off neatly, and add a little tassel to the end of the pen. To make the pens more durable, a small gilt penholder might be fastened to the end of them.

Fig. 55.—Eighteenth Century Work Satchel.—This useful workbag or satchel, as such articles were called in olden times, is cut to the exact size of one decorated with braiding which was made in the last century. To make it, four sections are required of the size of illustration ; upon these the design shown is to be worked. The following schemes of colouring would be very beautiful : Olive green satin or grey blue satin, leaves green, flowers white with dull gold centres, gilt spangles; or white satin, leaves green, flowers light purple (to simulate the Michaelmas daisy), green spangles ; or white satin, green leaves, yellow daisies, crimson

No. 43.—Housewife Basket.

No. 45.—Side of Housewife Basket No. 43.

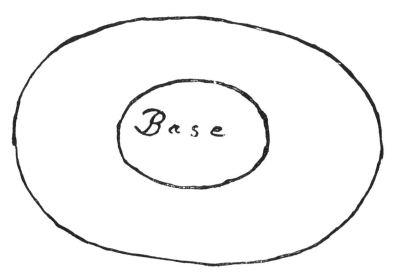

No. 46.—Base for Housewife Basket No. 43.

spangles. The embroidered needlework being completed, join the four pieces together, and place inside them a loose lining, formed of a similar number of pieces of white silk. Sew a narrow silk cord round the upper edge of the bag, forming it into loops as shown. A double length of silk cord is then to be passed through these loops, by which to draw the bag up, and it can then be suspended from the arm, or in any convenient position for use.

—◄✦►—

TRIFLES TURNED TO ACCOUNT.

Two wooden slippers—one for fresh and the other for burnt matches—fastened upon a square of white wood, is one of the novelties in the way of match safes. The legend, "It takes two to make a match," should be painted across the top.

Butterfly Slipper Case.—The foundation is a piece of wood or cardboard covered with calico or chintz; embroider the butterfly on holland lined with buckram; unite the wings by a body made of black velvet ; make the antennæ with wire, and the whole large enough for the slippers to lie in the bag attached behind the wooden foundation, hidden by the butterfly, the whole to be hung against the wall.

The newest way of trimming serge tablecloths is to put a corner of plush (half a square) at each corner of the cloth ; embroider on it a spray of flowers, and edge the whole with cord.

The Japanese and palm fans are turned to all kinds of uses in the way of wall ornaments, work bags, &c. The paper fans have satin bags over the lower part of the ribs, and two fastened together make a circle of colour admirable for wall decoration. One joined round, and the end sticks cut off, covers a flowerpot well. The last use for a palm fan is to cover it with plush, bordered with gold braid, and in the centre to fasten a photograph edged with the gold braid. It should be laid on cornerwise.

An old square washing stand, the top covered with millboard, and this and the bottom shelf with plush, a strip of plush bordered with fringe round, makes a music-stand ; and one of the old round-shaped washing-stands holds a flower-pot well. This should be painted with some of Aspinal's excellent enamel paints. A piece of wood with a cigar box at one end, having a place cut for the face of a shabby clock, the shelf and the box covered with plush or velvet, makes a presentable ornament at a small cost.

Some women have a mania for covering the walls of their sitting-rooms with trifling ornaments, and the last idea is pattens, the veritable wooden pattens which country-women wear, and certainly find in them the best protection to the feet as far as damp is concerned. But they are vastly transmogrified ; the wood is painted one colour, the leather another ; they are fastened with bright-coloured laces, and a flower-pot put within the strap after they are hung against the wall. Butter pats, too, are deemed suitable wall ornaments, painted with a landscape or a bunch of flowers the handles crossed, and a bow of ribbon uniting them. So much that we have hitherto considered rubbish is now made a thing of beauty, whether of perpetual beauty remains to be seen.

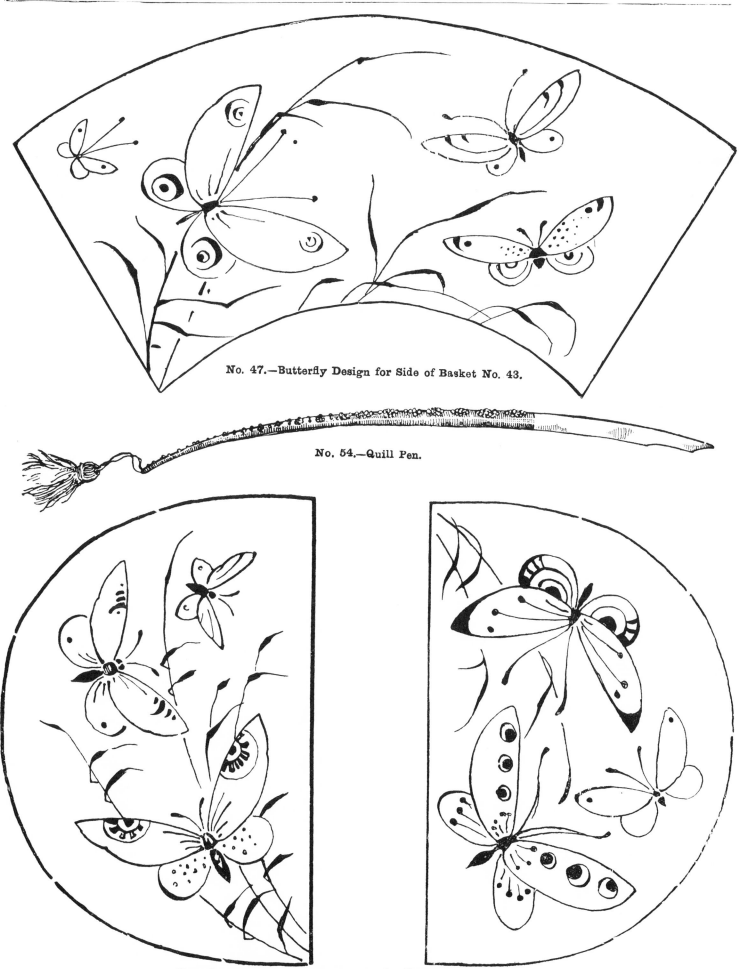

No. 47.—Butterfly Design for Side of Basket No. 43.

No. 54.—Quill Pen.

Nos. 48 and 49.—Butterfly Designs for the Lid of Basket No. 43.

No. 51.—Japanese Design for the Lid of Basket No. 43.

Very inexpensive screens can be made at home by covering an ordinary clothes-horse, or common wooden frame, with dark felt or plush, upon which Chinese crape pictures can be mounted. If the cloth is fastened within the margin of the wood, the latter can be ebonised, and a nice finish given to the screen by a heading of chenille where the cloth is nailed on.

A homely article, but a useful one, can be made from the legs or uppers of discarded stockings. Sew the uppers all together, just as you would prepare carpet rags. Then double once. Take three different lengths, and, as you double, plait or braid them together. It is impossible to braid evenly unless the lengths are secured firmly to some solid object. When braiding is done, then begin with strong twine and needle, and sew in whatever shape mat you wish. Such a mat is ver serviceable and durable for board floors.

Most people have seen the flour-tubs painted and lined with silk, to be used for work; but a newer idea is to get a small oyster or mustard barrel, stain it with oak or walnut stain, paint some rather large and effective flowers on it (yellow iris, single dahlias, or a long spray of blackberry leaves, all look well), line it with sateen, either the colour of the wood or some harmonising tint, finishing off with a little gimp or fringe at the top; tie on the lid, which of course must match, with ribbon (by means of holes made with a red-hot skewer, or knitting needle, in both lid and barrel), and you have a splendid receptacle for work, waste paper, or anything that is wanted to be out of sight, as well as a decidedly novel adornment for your room.

Milkmaids' pails are extremely pretty and ornamental, but of these the lining should be silk or satin, as there is no lid, only a thick knotted cord tied across to serve as a handle. Three-legged stools, which may be made by any carpenter, or bought for a trifle, and gipsy tables, look very pretty when stained or painted with Aspinal's enamel paints, which may be had in so many lovely shades; or if they are of nice wood they may be left the natural colour—walnut has a good grain, but fine deal when varnished has almost the appearance of a gilt background, and may be preferred by some to the darker surface, which for those who cannot do without drawing or tracing, the design is a little more difficult to manage, as pencil marks do not show well on the stained wood.

The little bottles of Italian wines, which are cased in a sort of reed or wicker basket, may be utilised in this way: Remove the bottle, then cut the case off below the neck, or deep enough to allow the basket to be good and open. On the outside paint some showy flowers. If not convenient to do this, then use artificial ones and a few bright ribbons. Line with strong fabric, suspend with three cords, and the housewife has a very handy basket for her keys. This same basket will also make a pretty ornament for Easter. Fill with white cotton and nestle a few eggs on top in the cotton.

A useful as well as ornamental umbrella holder for hanging on a wardrobe door can be made in this way: Take the unbleached linen canvas and cut a strip about one yard long (or length of umbrella) and ten inches wide. To this add or lay on top a similar sized piece. Stitch down through the centre. This gives two pockets or cases for umbrellas. Sew red or coloured braid loop on at top to hang by. They are pretty with appliquéd figures or monograms, worked in bright silks and bound to match.

A decorative catch-all, or receptacle for burnt matches, to hang in a corner, is made by taking the rivet out of a Japanese fan and running a cord in place of it to tie the sticks together over a tin or pasteboard cornucopia. Bright ribbons are woven in and out of the sticks, which should be black, and a bow with long loops hangs from the point, while a ruche of fringed silk or quilted satin ribbon finishes the top.

No. 55.—Eighteenth Century Work Satchel.

WELDON'S
PRACTICAL KNITTER.
(FIFTH SERIES).

How to Knit 38 Useful Articles for Ladies, Gentlemen, and Children.

THIRTY-ONE ILLUSTRATIONS.

The Yearly Subscription to this Magazine, post free to any part of the World, is 2s. 6d.
Subscriptions are payable in advance, and may commence from any date and for any period.

The Back Numbers are always in print. Nos. 1 to 232 now ready, Price 2d. each, or bound in 19 Vols., price 2s. 6d. each.

BABY'S OPEN KNIT SPENCER.

THIS exquisite little spencer is knitted in shell and feather pattern, with white Shetland wool, of which 2 ozs. will be required and a pair of No. 13 bone knitting needles. The spencer is not shaped, but being fine work and an open stitch, it fits any figure to perfection. **For the right front**—Cast on 57 stitches, and knit in ribbing of 3 stitches plain and 3 stitches purl for 30 rows. **31st row**—Slip 1, knit 2, * make 1, knit 2 together, knit 1 ; repeat from * to the end of the row. **32nd row**—Purl. This is the waist, and the small holes are to run a ribbon in. Now begin the body pattern. **1st row**—Slip 1, knit 1, * knit 2 together three times, make 1 and knit 1 five times, make 1, knit 2 together three times, knit 1; repeat from *; and there will be 1 more to knit at the end of the row. **2nd row**—Purl. **3rd row**—Plain. **4th row**—Purl. Repeat these four rows seventeen times, which will make eighteen patterns of shells. **Next row**—Cast off 20 for the neck, and knit the remaining thirty-seven stitches forwards and backwards in the pattern for six repeats, and then cast off all. **For the Left Front**—Cast on 57 stitches, and knit the same as above, but cast off 20 in the *last row* of the eighteenth shell pattern, and continue on the 37 stitches for the shoulder. **For the Back** — Cast on 90 stitches ; knit the same as directed for the fronts till you have a straight piece of twenty-four repeats of the pattern, then cast off all. Sew the shoulder-pieces to the back-piece ; it will be a straight seam, but the knitting is so elastic it will shape to the shoulder when on. Sew up the side seams, leaving space for the sleeves. **For the Sleeves**—Cast on 57 stitches. Knit 22 rows of ribbing, then knit the 31st and 32nd rows the same as the spencer fronts, and proceed to the shell pattern, working eighteen repeats of the pattern, and cast off. Knit the other sleeve the same. Sew the sleeves in the armholes. Work a crochet edging down the two fronts and along the neck of the spencer. **1st row**—1 treble in a stitch of the knitting, * 1 chain, miss one stitch of the knitting, 1 treble in the next, and repeat from *. **2nd row**—1 double crochet under one chain of last row *, 2 chain, 1 double crochet in the first of these chain, 3 treble in the next, miss the next chain stitch of last row. 1 double crochet under the next, and repeat from *. Run a ribbon in to tie round the waist, and place ribbon strings at the neck and in front of the spencer.

BABY'S HOOD.

THIS is a very simple hood and easy to make. It will require 2 ozs. of white Shetland wool, 1½ ozs. of white and 1 oz. of pale blue single Berlin, and two bone knitting needles No. 11. Cast on 14 stitches with the Shetland wool, and

work in plain knitting, increasing 1 stitch at the beginning of every row till you have 66 stitches on the needle, then decrease by knitting 2 stitches together at the end of every row till reduced to 14 stitches; cast off. Knit another piece exactly the same, and lay one over the other, as these pieces are for the crown and are to be used double. **For the Border**—Take the blue wool and pick up the stitches along two sides of the crown, and knit 8 plain rows, increasing 2 stitches in a row, that is increase a stitch at each corner of the fourteen straight stitches. Knit 1 plain row with white Berlin. **Next row**—Make 1, slip 1 (inserting the needle as if about to purl), knit 1, and repeat. **Next row**—Make 1, slip 1, knit 2 together, and repeat. Knit 13 more rows the same as the last row. **Next row**—Knit 1, knit 2 together, and repeat. Then with blue, knit 8 plain rows, and cast off. Pick up the stitches from corner to corner along the front of the hood and work in the same manner. With white wool crochet an edge all round the hood, 1 double crochet in a stitch of the knitting, 3 chain, 2 treble in the double crochet stitch just worked, miss two stitches of the knitting, 1 double crochet in the next, and repeat. Crochet two pieces of chain, and run one piece in at the back to confine the hood in shape, and the other at the front to tie under the chin; finish off the ends with tassels.

A PRETTY CUFF.

REQUIRED, 1½ ozs. of brown and 1 oz. of blue Scotch fingering. Two steel knitting needles, No. 14. With brown wool cast on 64 stitches. Knit 4 plain rows. **5th row**—With blue wool, plain. **6th row**—Knit 1, purl 1, and repeat. Knit 10 more rows the same as this row. **17th row**—With brown wool, plain. Knit 5 more plain rows. **23rd row**—Still with brown wool, knit 1, purl 1, and repeat. **24th row**—The same. **25th row**—Purl 1, knit 1, and repeat. **26th row**—The same. Repeat the last four rows three times. Then knit 6 plain rows. **45th row**—With blue wool, plain. **46th row**—Knit 1, purl 1, and repeat. Knit 10 more rows the same as this row. Then with brown wool, knit 4 plain rows, and cast off. Sew up.

UNDER-SLEEVE.

REQUIRED, 4 ozs. of brown Scotch fingering, and two steel knitting needles, No. 14. Cast on 85 stitches. **1st row**—Knit 3, purl 1, and repeat, end with knit 3. **2nd row**—Purl 3, knit 1, and repeat, end with purl 3. Repeat these two rows till 40 rows are done. * **Next row**—Knit 2 together at the beginning and end, working the other stitches in ribs the same. Knit 5 ribbed rows. Repeat from * till reduced to 61 stitches. Knit for the wrist 40 rows on these 61 stitches, and cast off. Knit the other sleeve the same, and join them both up

Baby's Open Knit Spencer.

YOUTH'S JERSEY STOCKING.

THIS nicely shaped stocking is knitted with German fingering, of which 8 ozs. will be required, and four steel knitting needles, No. 14 or No. 15. Cast 32 stitches on each of three needles, 96 stitches in all. Knit in ribbing, 3 stitches plain and 1 stitch purl, for 44 rounds. With a thread of cotton mark the 1 purl stitch in the centre of the first needle; it is to be the seam stitch of the stocking, and is to be purled in every round. **45th round**—Beginning on the first needle, rib to 1 stitch before the seam stitch, increase 1 (by picking up the thread that lies closely underneath the next stitch and knitting it), knit 1, purl

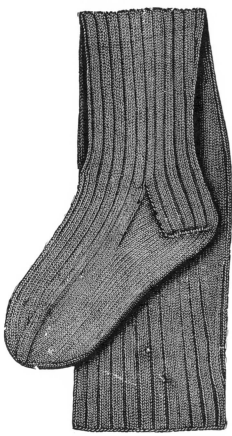

Youth's Jersey Stocking.

the seam stitch, knit 1, increase 1, and continue ribbing as before to the end of the third needle. * Rib 5 rounds, the only difference being that there is a stitch more to knit on each side the seam. **Next round**—Increase again in the same way, and repeat from * till there are 9 plain stitches to knit each side the seam stitch, 108 stitches in the round. Rib round and round till the stocking leg measures 8½ inches. **Next round**—Rib to 3 stitches before the seam stitch, knit 2 together, knit 1, purl the seam stitch, knit 1, slip 1, knit 1, pass the slipped stitch over, and continue ribbing to the end of the round. * Knit 7 ribbed rounds. **Next round**—Decrease again each side the seam stitch. Repeat from * till reduced to 80 stitches in the round, when the ribs come in quite evenly. Continue ribbing upon the 80 stitches for 44 rounds. **For the Heel**—Beginning on the first needle, rib to the seam stitch, and rib 19 stitches beyond; turn the work, slip the first stitch, and again rib 19 stitches beyond the seam stitch, thus getting 39 stitches on one needle, which rib forwards and backwards for 26 rows, slipping the first stitch in every row. Let the remaining 41 stitches stand as they are till required for knitting the instep. **To turn the Heel**—Slip the first stitch, knit plain 21, slip 1, knit 1, pass the slipped stitch over, knit 1; turn, slip the first stitch, purl 6, purl 2 together, purl 1; turn, slip the first stitch, knit 7, slip 1, knit 1, pass the slipped stitch over, knit 1; turn, slip the first stitch, purl 8, purl 2 together, purl 1; turn, and continue thus, each time working one more stitch upon the centre part of the heel, till all the side stitches are knitted in, and ending with a purl row, 23 stitches remain for the top of the heel. Knit plain these 23 stitches, and on the same needle pick up and knit 17 stitches along the side of the flap; rib the 41 instep stitches all or to one needle; and on another needle pick up and knit 17 stitches along the opposite side of the flap, and knit 11 stitches from the top of the heel. The stitches are now again arranged upon three needles, 98 stitches in the round. Knit plain the next needle. Rib along the instep needle. **For the Gussets**—* Beginning on the first foot needle—Knit 1, slip 1, knit 1, pass the slipped stitch over, knit plain to within 3 stitches of the end of the second foot needle, knit 2 together, knit 1; rib along the instep needle. Knit 1 round plain on foot and ribbed on instep. Repeat from * till reduced to 76 stitches in the round. Proceed on the 76 stitches till the foot is the length required, say about 6½ inches including heel. Leave off at the end of the first foot needle, knitting with the last stitch of that the first stitch from the second foot needle so as to equalise the stitches, and begin the toe exactly in the centre of the sole of the foot. From this centre re-arrange the stitches, placing 25 stitches on each needle. **For the Toe—1st round**—Knit 1, slip 1, knit 1, pass the slipped stitch over,

knit plain to within 3 stitches of the end of the needle, knit 2 together, knit 1; knit similarly on each of the other needles. **2nd round**—Plain. Repeat these two rounds till there are only 5 stitches on each needle. Break off the wool, and with a rug needle run the wool through the stitches and sew them up firmly.

BABY'S FIRST SOCK.

REQUIRED, 1½ ozs. of white Shetland wool, and four steel knitting needles, No. 18. Cast 29 stitches on the first needle, and 20 stitches on each of two other needles, 69 stitches in all. Knit in ribbing, 2 stitches plain and 1 stitch purl, for 30 rounds. **1st Pattern round**—Beginning on the first needle, knit 1, make 1, knit 2, slip 1, knit 1, pass the slipped stitch over, purl 1, knit 2 together, knit 2, make 1, and repeat six times, which will bring you to the end of the third needle; but as one extra stitch is required to bring the pattern in completely, pick up and work the last purl stitch from a thread of the knitting; there now are 70 stitches in the round. **2nd round**—Plain, excepting only the purled stitches of last round which must be purled again in this. Repeat these two rounds till 36 rounds are knitted. **For the Heel**—Beginning on the first needle, knit 5, purl 1, knit 18; turn the work, slip the first stitch, purl 17 knit the seam stitch, purl 18. Now continue on these 37 stitches forwards and backwards, and for strength it will be best to knit double in this manner. **3rd row of the Heel**—Slip 1, knit 1, slip 1, knit 1, and continue doing a slipped stitch after every knitted one, purl the seam stitch, and from that arrange so that the last stitch be knitted plain. **4th row**—Slip 1, purl 1, slip 1, purl 1, always purling the stitches that were slipped in last row. Repeat till 34 rows are done. **To turn the Heel**—Slip the first stitch knit 20, slip 1, knit 1, pass the slipped stitch over; turn, slip the first stitch, purl 5, purl 2 together; turn, and continue till all the side stitches are knitted in, and 7 stitches are on the needle for the top of the heel. Knit plain these 7 stitches, and on the same needle pick up and knit 18 stitches along the side of the flap; knit the 33 instep stitches in pattern all on to one needle; and on another needle pick up and knit 18 stitches along the opposite side of the flap, and knit 3 stitches from the top of the heel. Now the stitches are properly arranged on three needles, 76 stitches in the round. Knit plain along the next needle; keep in pattern along the instep needle. **For the Gusset**—* Beginning on the first foot needle,—knit 1, slip 1, knit 1, pass the slipped stitch over, knit plain to within 3 stitches of the end of the second foot needle, knit 2 together, knit 1; knit in pattern along the instep needle. Knit 1 round plain on foot, and keeping in pattern on instep. Repeat from * till reduced to 60 stitches in the round. Proceed on the 60 stitches till 36 rounds are done from the heel. Then knit 4 plain rounds. **For the Toe**—Beginning on the first foot needle, knit 4, knit 2 together, and repeat all round. Knit 4 plain rounds. **6th round**—Knit 4, knit 2 together, and repeat. Knit 4 plain rounds. **11th round**—Knit 3, knit 2 together, and repeat. Knit 3 plain rounds. **15th round**—Knit 3, knit 2 together, and repeat. Knit 3 plain rounds. **19th round**—Knit 2, knit 2 together, and repeat. Knit 2 plain rounds. **22nd round**—Knit 2, knit 2 together, and repeat. Knit 2 plain rounds. Then knit 2 together all round till only 4 stitches are left. Break off the wool, and sew these up securely.

KNEE-CAP.

REQUIRED, 3 ozs. of white Scotch fingering, and two bone knitting needles, No. 11. Cast on 47 stitches. **1st row**—Plain. **2nd row**—Purl 6, knit 35, purl 6. **3rd row**—Plain. **4th row**—Plain. **5th row**—Purl 6, knit 35, purl 6. **6th row**—Plain. Repeat these 6 rows three times. **25th row**—

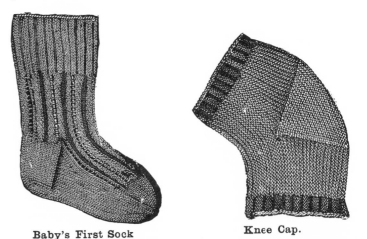

Baby's First Sock   Knee Cap.

Knit 23, increase 1 (by picking up the thread that lies directly under the next stitch and knitting it), knit 24. **26th row**—Purl 6, knit 17, increase 1, knit 19, purl 6. **27th row**—Knit 23, increase 1, knit 26. Now continue thus always increasing after the 23rd stitch, and keeping the edge in notches till you have 19 notches done; then knit 6 rows without any increase; and henceforward in every row knit 2 together after knitting the 23rd stitch, so as to decrease in the same ratio as you before increased, and when 47 stitches are attained knit 24 rows thereon to match the beginning, and cast off. Sew the cast off to the cast on stitches, and the knee cap is complete. Work the other one in the same manner.

GAITER FOR CHILD OF THREE.

REQUIRED, 3 ozs. of Fingering wool, and a pair of steel knitting needles, No. 13. Cast on 52 stitches, and knit in ribbing 2 stitches plain and 2 stitches purl for 14 rows. Knit 2 plain rows. **1st row of dice pattern**—Knit 2, purl 2, and repeat. **2nd row**—The same. **3rd row**—Purl 2, knit 2, and repeat. **4th row**—Same as the third row. Repeat these four rows seven times. In the next row decrease by knitting 2 together at the beginning and 2 together at the end of the row, and keep the dice knitting in pattern in the centre. Knit 7 rows. Next row decrease again. Knit 7 more rows. Now knit 2 plain rows, and decrease at the beginning and end of the second of these; there are now 45 stitches on the needle. **51st row**—Knit 3, purl 3, and repeat. **52nd row**—Purl 3, knit 3, and repeat. **53rd row**—Knit 3, purl 3, and repeat. **54th row**—Knit 3, purl 3, and repeat. **55th row**—Purl 3, knit 3, and repeat. **56th row**—Knit 3, purl 3, and repeat. Repeat these six rows, and also knit the 51st, 52nd, and 53rd rows once again. **For the 1st row of the Ankle**—Knit 6, purl 2, knit 4, purl 2, knit 17, purl 2, knit 4, purl 2,

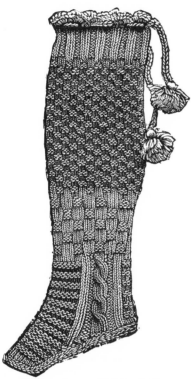

Gaiter for a Child of Three.

knit 6. **2nd row**—Purl 6, knit 2, purl 4, knit 2, purl 17, knit 2, purl 4, knit 2, purl 6. **3rd row**—Purl 4, knit 2, purl 2, slip the two next stitches on a spare pin, knit the 2 next, then replace the 2 slipped stitches on the left-hand pin and knit them, purl 2, knit 2, purl 13, knit 2, purl 2, slip the next 2 stitches on a spare pin, knit the 2 next, then replace the 2 slipped stitches and knit them, purl 2, knit 2, purl 4. **4th row**—Purl 4, knit 2, purl 2, knit 4, purl 2, knit 2, purl 13, knit 2, purl 2, knit 4, purl 2, knit 2, purl 4. **5th row**—Same as the first row. **6th row**—Same as the second row. **7th row**—Purl 4, knit 2, purl 2, knit 4, purl 2, knit 2, purl 13, knit 2, purl 2, knit 4, purl 2, knit 2, purl 4. **8th row**—Knit 4, purl 2, knit 2, purl 4, knit 2, purl 2, knit 13, purl 2, knit 2, purl 4, knit 2, purl 2, knit 4. **9th row**—Knit 6, purl 2, slip the 2 next stitches on a spare pin, knit the 2 next, replace the 2 slipped stitches on the left-hand pin and knit them, purl 2, knit 17, purl 2, slip the next 2 stitches on a spare pin, knit the 2 next, replace the 2 slipped stitches and knit them purl 2, knit 6. **10th row**—Purl 6, knit 2, purl 4, knit 2, purl 17, knit 2, purl 4, knit 2, purl 6. **11th row**—Purl 4, knit 2, purl 2, knit 4, purl 2, knit 2, purl 13, knit 2, purl 2, knit 4, purl 2, knit 2, purl 4. **12th row**—Knit 4, purl 2, knit 2, purl 4 knit 2, purl 2, knit 13, purl 2, knit 2, purl 4, knit 2, purl 2, knit 4. Repeat these twelve rows, and then knit the 1st, 2nd, 3rd, and 4th rows once again. Cast off 12, purl 1, knit 17, purl 2, turn, knit 2, purl 17, knit 2. Cast off 2, knit 1, purl 13, knit 2, turn, cast off 2, purl 1, knit 13, purl 2. Cast off 2, knit 14, turn, cast off 2, purl 12. Now knit in ridges on these 13 stitches for sixteen more rows and cast off. Cast off also the remaining side stitches. Sew up the leg of the gaiter, making the pattern meet nicely on each side the seam. Work 2 rows of single crochet to strengthen round the foot. Crochet an edge at the top of the gaiter, 1 double crochet in a stitch of the knitting, miss one stitch, 5 treble in the next, miss one stitch, and repeat. Work a crochet chain and run in at the top of the gaiter just under the crochet edge, make tassels at each end and tie in a bow. The other gaiter is worked in the same manner.

LADY'S PETTICOAT IN BASKET PATTERN KNITTING.

THIS petticoat has bands of basket-pattern knitting worked in grey and scarlet, the upper part being worked in a pretty close-ribbed stitch; it is gored and shaped to the waist, and will be found very comfortable fitting. Required, ½ lb. of scarlet, and 1 lb. of grey three-thread fleecy wool; a pair of long bone knitting needles, No. 8, and a pair No. 11. With scarlet wool cast on 167 stitches for the front breadth. **1st row**—Purl. **2nd row**—Plain. **3rd row**—Purl. **4th row**—Plain. **5th row**—Knit 1, * slip 1, knit 1, pass the slipped stitch over, knit 5, make 1, knit 1, make 1, knit 5, knit 2 together, repeat from *, and knit 1 stitch at the end of the row. **6th row**—Purl. **7th row**—Same as the fifth row. **8th row**—Purl. **9th row**—Same as the fifth. **10th row**—Purl. **11th row**—Purl. **12th row**—Plain. **13th row**—Same as the fifth. **14th row**—Purl. **15th row**—Same as the fifth. **16th row**—Purl. **17th row**—Purl. **18th row**—Plain. **19th row**—Purl. This completes the Border. Now with grey wool begin the Basket pattern by doing a purl row. **1st Pattern row**—Slip 1, purl 6, * knit 3, purl 7, repeat from * to the end of the row. **2nd row**—Slip 1, knit 6, * purl 3, knit 7, and repeat from *. **3rd row**—Same as the first. **4th row**—Purl. **5th row**—Slip 1, purl 1, * knit 3, purl 7; repeat from *. **6th row**—Slip 1, knit 6, * purl 3, knit 7, and repeat from *. **7th row**—Same as the fifth. **8th row**—Purl. **9th row**—Same as the first. **10th row**—Same as the second. **11th row**—Same as the first. Now take the scarlet wool and knit another basket pattern band of 12 rows, beginning at the 4th row of the pattern and work through to the 3rd row. Then with the grey wool knit another band the same as the first grey band, and then another scarlet band which should end with the third row of the pattern. Again take the grey wool and knit a purl row, knitting 2 together at the end of the row. There will be 166 stitches on the needle. The remainder of the petticoat is knitted with grey. **1st row**—Knit 2, purl 2, and repeat. **2nd row**—Purl 2, knit 2, and repeat. **3rd row**—Slip 1, knit 2 together, knit plain to within three stitches of the end, knit 2 together, knit 1. **4th row**—Purl. **5th row**—Slip 1, * purl 2, knit 2: repeat from *, and there will be 1 stitch to knit at the end of the row. **6th row**—Slip 1, * knit 2, purl 2: repeat from *, and there will be 1 stitch to purl at the end of the row. **7th row**—Same as the third row. **8th row**—Purl. This is the pattern. You decrease at the beginning, and at the end of every plain row till you have done 128 rows. Be careful to keep the stripes perpendicularly, as the decreasings cause an irregularity at the commencement of every pattern row. When the 128 rows are done there should be 102 stitches on the needle, and the front breadth is long enough. Slip the stitches on to a spare pin for the present. Re-commence for the back of the petticoat with 167 stitches, and knit exactly as described above till you have done 92 rows of the striped pattern and have 120 stitches on the needle. **Next row**—Knit 60 stitches in the pattern, turn, and knit back, and continue the pattern and the decreasing at the beginning of every plain row till you have 128 rows knitted and 51 stitches on the needle.

Lady's Petticoat in Basket Pattern Knitting.

Put these stitches on a spare pin while you knit the remaining 60 stitches the same, only decreasing at the end of the plain rows. Having completed the 128 rows on this side of the back breadth, and having 51 stitches on the needle, proceed to join the breadths together, at the same time reducing the stitches to the size of the waist—thus. on the side last worked knit 1, * knit 2 together, knit 3, repeat from * to the end; take the front breadth, holding it the right side towards you, and on to the same pin knit 5, * knit 2 together, knit 4, and repeat from * all along, knitting 5 at the end; then take the other half of the back breadth and * knit 3, knit 2 together, and repeat from *, knitting 1 stitch at the end. You now have 100 stitches on one needle with which to knit the waistband. Use the No. 11 needles, and knit plain knitting forwards and backwards for 15 rows, and cast off. And without breaking off the wool work double crochet round the placket-hole to strengthen it. Sew up the petticoat, the grey part with grey, and the scarlet bands with scarlet.

GENTLEMAN'S SILK SOCK.

REQUIRED, 5 ozs. of the best black spun silk, and four steel knitting needles, No. 17. Cast 42 stitches on the first needle, 34 stitches on the second needle, and 32 stitches on the third needle, 108 stitches in all. Knit in ribbing, 2 stitches plain and 2 stitches purl, for 70 rounds. The remainder of the sock is in plain knitting. With a thread of cotton mark the 2 purl stitches in the centre of the first needle, these are to be seam stitches, and are to be purled in one round and knitted in the next. Knit 24 rounds. In the 25th round begin the decreasing for the leg, thus—when 4 stitches before the seam stitches, knit 2 together, knit 2, purl the 2 seam stitches, knit 2, slip 1, knit 1, pass the slipped stitch over, and continue plain knitting to the end of the round * Knit 7 rounds. Next round decrease again in the same manner. Repeat

Gentleman's Silk Sock.

from * three times, and the stitches will be reduced to 98 stitches in the round. Knit 44 rounds for the ankle. For the heel—Beginning on the first needle—Knit plain to the seam stitches, purl those, knit 24 beyond; turn the work, slip the first stitch, purl 49. Let the other 48 stitches, which are for the instep, remain as they are for the present while you proceed with the heel, knitting a row and purling a row alternately on the 50 stitches, keeping the seam, and slipping the first stitch in every row, for 48 rows. To turn the Heel—Slip the first stitch, knit 23, purl 2 seam stitches, knit 1, slip 1, knit 1, pass the slipped stitch over, knit 1; turn, slip the first stitch, purl 5, purl 2 together, purl 1; turn, slip the first stitch, knit 2, purl 2 seam stitches, knit 2, slip 1, knit 1, pass the slipped stitch over, knit 1; turn, slip the first stitch, purl 7, purl 2 together, purl 1; turn, and continue thus widening the heel till all the side stitches are knitted in, and 28 stitches are formed on the needle for the top of the heel. Knit these 28 stitches, and on the same needle pick up and knit 24 stitches along the side of the flap; knit the 48 instep stitches all on one needle; and on another needle pick up and knit 24 stitches along the opposite side of the flap, and knit 13 stitches from off the top of the heel. Now there are 37 stitches on this needle, 37 stitches on the other foot needle, and 48 stitches on the instep needle. Knit along the next needle, and along the instep needle. For the Gusset—* Beginning on the first foot needle, knit 1, slip 1, knit 1, pass the slipped stitch over, knit to within 3 stitches of the end of the second foot needle, knit 2 together, knit 1; knit along the instep needle. Knit 2 plain rounds. Repeat from * till reduced to 96 stitches in the round. Then continue on the 96 stitches for 60 or more rounds, according to the length required for the foot, and leave off at the end of the first foot needle. For the Toe—Beginning in the centre of the sole; knit 10, knit 2 together, and repeat seven times more. Knit 6 plain rounds. 8th round—Knit 9, knit 2 together, and repeat. Knit 6 plain rounds. 15th round—Knit 8, knit 2 together. Knit 5 plain rounds. 21st round—Knit 7, knit 2 together. Knit 5 plain rounds. 27th round—Knit 6, knit 2 together.

Knit 4 plain rounds. 32nd round—Knit 5, knit 2 together. Knit 4 plain rounds 37th round—Knit 4, knit 2 together. Knit 3 plain rounds. 41st round—Knit 3, knit 2 together. Knit 2 plain rounds. 44th round—Knit 2, knit 2 together. Knit 1 plain round. 46th round—Knit 1, knit 2 together Knit 2 together all round. Break off the silk, and with a rug needle sew up the remaining stitches.

RIBBED SOCK FOR CHILD OF TWO.

PROCURE 1½ ozs. of white Andalusian wool, and four steel knitting needles, No. 17. Cast 28 stitches on the first needle, and 18 stitches on each of two other needles, 64 stitches in all. Knit in ribbing of 1 stitch plain and 1 stitch purl for 36 rounds. 37th round—Mark with a thread of cotton the purl stitch in the centre of the first needle, and consider it as a seam stitch, on either side of which decreasings are to be made; knit 1 and purl 1 till within 4 stitches of the seam stitch, then knit 2 together, purl 1, knit 1, purl the seam stitch, knit 1, purl 1, slip 1, knit 1, pass the slipped stitch over, knit 1, purl 1, and continue round. 38th round—Knit 1, purl 1, and when 4 stitches before the seam stitch, knit 2, purl 1, knit 1, purl the seam stitch, knit 1, purl 1, knit 2, purl 1, knit 1, purl 1, and continue round. Knit 4 more rounds the same as the last round. 43rd round —Knit 1, purl 1, and when 4 stitches before the seam stitch, knit 2 together purl 1, knit 1, purl the seam stitch, knit 1, purl 1, slip 1, knit 1, pass the slipped stitch over, purl 1, knit 1, purl 1, and continue round. 44th round—Knit 1, purl 1, all round. Knit 4 more rounds the same as the last round. Repeat from the thirty-seventh round. Now there are 56 stitches in the round. Rib 20 rounds for the ankle. For the Heel—Beginning on the first needle, rib to the seam stitch, and rib 15 stitches beyond; turn the work, slip the first stitch, and rib 30 stitches. Now there are 31 stitches on one needle for the heel, and the other 25 stitches are to remain as they are for the present. Rib forwards and backwards on the heel needle for 26 rows. To turn the Heel—Slip the first stitch, knit plain 18 stitches, slip 1, knit 1, pass the slipped stitch over; turn, slip the first stitch, purl 5, purl 2 together; turn, slip the first stitch, knit 5, slip 1, knit 1, pass the slipped stitch over; turn, slip the first stitch, purl 5, purl 2 together; turn, and work thus till all the side stitches are knitted in, and 7 stitches are on the needle for the top of the heel. Knit plain these 7 stitches, and on the same needle pick up, and as you pick up knit 15 stitches along the side of the flap; knit the 25 instep stitches in ribbing all on to one needle, and on another needle pick up and knit 15 stitches along the opposite side of the flap, and knit 3

Ribbed Sock for Child of Two.

stitches from the top of the heel. The stitches are now again arranged upon three needles, 62 stitches in the round. Knit plain along the next needle; rib the instep needle. For the Gusset—* Beginning on the first foot needle.— knit 1, slip 1, knit 1, pass the slipped stitch over, knit plain to within 3 stitches of the end of the second foot needle, knit 2 together, knit 1; rib along the instep needle. Knit 2 rounds plain on foot and ribbed on instep. Repeat from * till reduced to 54 stitches in the round, the 25 instep stitches being still intact upon one needle. Continue plain on foot and ribbed on instep for 38 rounds. For the Toe—Knit plain to the end of the first needle, that is to the centre of the foot, and from this re-arrange the stitches, placing 18 stitches on each needle. 1st round—Knit 1, slip 1, knit 1, pass the slipped stitch over, knit plain to within 3 stitches of the end of the needle, knit 2 together, knit 1; knit the same on each of the other needles. 2nd round—Plain Repeat these two rounds till there are only 4 stitches left on each needle. Break off the wool, and with a rug needle run the wool through the 12 stitches and sew them up securely

BIRD'S EYE PATTERN EDGING.

CAST on 18 stitches, and knit 1 plain row. **1st row**—Slip 1, knit 11, knit 2 together, make 1, knit 1, make 1, knit 2 together, knit 1. **2nd row** and every alternate row—Plain. **3rd row**—Slip 1, knit 10, knit 2 together, make 1, knit 3, make 1, knit 2. **5th row**—Slip 1, knit 9, knit 2 together, make 1, knit 2 together, make 1, knit 1, make 1, knit 2 together, make 1, knit 2. **7th row**—Slip 1, knit 8, knit 2 together, make 1, knit 2 together, make 1, knit 3, make 1, knit 2 together make 1, knit 2 **9th row**—Slip 1, knit 7, knit 2 together, make 1, knit 2 together, make 1, knit 5, make 1, knit 2 together, make 1, knit 2. **11th row**—Slip 1, knit 6, knit 2 together, make 1, knit 2 together, make 1 knit 7, make 1, knit 2 together, make 1, knit 2. **13th row**—Slip 1, knit 5

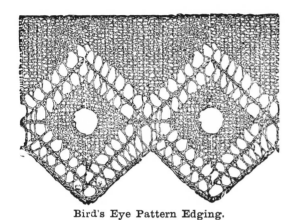

Bird's Eye Pattern Edging.

knit 2 together, make 1, knit 2 together, make 1, knit 9, make 1, knit 2 together, make 1 knit 2. **15th row**—Slip 1, knit 4, knit 2 together, make 1, knit 2 together, make 1, knit 11, make 1, knit 2 together, make 1, knit 2. **16th row**—Knit 8, knit 2 together, make 2, knit 2 together, knit 15. **17th row**—Slip 1, knit 5, make 1, knit 2 together, make 1, knit 2 together, knit 5, purl 1, knit 4, make 1, knit 2 together, make 1, knit 2 together, knit 1. **19th row**—Slip 1, knit 6, make 1, knit 2 together, make 1, knit 2 together, knit 7, knit 2 together, make 1, knit 2 together, make 1, knit 2 together, knit 1. **21st row**—Slip 1, knit 7, make 1, knit 2 together, make 1, knit 2 together, make 1, knit 5, knit 2 together, make 1, knit 2 together, make 1, knit 2 together, knit 1. **23rd row**—Slip 1, knit 8, make 1, knit 2 together, make 1, knit 2 together, knit 3, knit 2 together make 1, knit 2 together, make 1, knit 2 together, knit 1. **25th row**—Slip 1, knit 9, make 1, knit 2 together, make 1, knit 2 together, knit 1, knit 2 together, make 1, knit 2 together, make 1, knit 2 together, knit 1. **27th row**—Slip 1, knit 10, make 1, knit 2 together, make 1, slip 1, knit 2 together, pass the slipped stitch over, make 1, knit 2 together, make 1, knit 2 together, knit 1. **29th row**—Slip 1, knit 11, make 1, knit 2 together, make 1, knit 2 together, make 1, knit 2 together, knit 1. **31st row**—Slip 1, knit 12, make 1, slip 1, knit 2 together, pass the slipped stitch over, make 1, knit 2 together, knit 1. **32nd row**—Plain. Repeat from the first row for the length required.

BABY'S BOA.

THIS pretty boa is worked in looped knitting and will require nearly 2 ozs. of white single Berlin wool. A pair of bone knitting needles, No. 11. Cast on 10 stitches; knit 1 plain row. **1st row**—Slip the first stitch, insert the right hand needle in the next stitch as if going to knit it, pass the wool over the point and round the first and second fingers of the left hand three times, and then again over the point of the needle, and knit all four threads of wool in as you knit the stitch, knit 7 other stitches in the same manner, and knit the last stitch plain. **2nd row**—Slip the first stitch, knit the rest plain, taking every group of threads as one stitch and drawing in rather tightly. Repeat these two rows till the knitting measures 30 inches in length, when cast off. Sew the edges neatly together lengthways, and place a ribbon to tie in a bow at the neck.

REINS FOR CHILDREN.

THESE reins are quickly and easily knitted, and afford a great deal of amusement to children, be idea being capital exercise. Procure 3 ozs. of crimson double Berlin wool, 2 knitting needles No. 10, two ½ yard lengths of strong boxcord, a piece of wadding, a piece of crimson twill, 4 small fancy bells, and a few needlefuls of gold-coloured filoselle. For the piece that crosses the chest cast on 24 stitches; knit forwards and backwards all plain knitting, slipping the first stitch in every row to make a firm edge for 66 rows, and cast off; on this embroider five large stars with the gold-coloured filoselle, one star in the centre and two on each side, the bells also are arranged here, one bell above and one below the star in the centre and one to the right and one to the left.

For the armholes, join the pieces of cord in circles, cover them with wadding, making rings about 2 inches in thickness, and bind over neatly with the twill; cast on 12 stitches, knit a sufficient length to cover the foundation, and cast off; knit another length in the same way, and sew the knitting upon the wadded rings. Next sew on the front piece, the cast-on stitches to one ring, and the cast-off stitches to the other. For the reins, cast on 8 stitches, and knit a length of 2½ yards or 3 yards, and cast off; sew each end of this to the back of the armholes, and the reins are complete.

SLEEVE KNOTS FOR A BABY.

THESE are pretty to make for a small present or as a contribution to a Bazaar. Required ½ oz. of white Andalusian wool, and a little white and pink Shetland, knitting needles No. 18, and a crochet needle No. 14. With white Andalusian wool cast on 3 stitches. Knit 1 plain row. **2nd row**—Slip 1, increase 1 (by picking up the thread that lies directly under the next stitch and knitting it), knit 1, increase 1, knit 1. **3rd row**—Plain. **4th row**—Slip 1, increase 1, knit 3, increase 1, knit 1. Now continue plain knitting upon these 7 stitches, slipping the first stitch in every row, for 86 rows. Cast off; break off the wool and with the end crochet 8 chain stitches and join to the opposite side of the strip of knitting, to serve for a button-hole; place a small pearl button at the other end of the strip. On the **19th ridge** of the knitting work 7 treble stitches loosely with the white Shetland, turn, and work 7 treble stitches on the next ridge towards the centre, and catch the last of these trebles to the first, then proceed doing 7 treble stitches on each ridge successively, till you have worked upon 9 ridges, join the last stitch to the end of the nearest turning, and break off. Now use the pink Shetland for an edging, and with it work 1 double crochet and 3 chain between each treble stitch. The other sleeve knot is knitted in the same way.

KNITTED DRAWERS.

THESE drawers are for a child one year or a year-and-a-half old, and materials required, four ounces Saxony knitting yarn, Peacock quality, and four bone needles No. 3, ten inches long On one needle cast on 64 stitches. Knit plain 112 rows. On another needle cast on same number of stitches and knit same number of rows. You have now two pieces alike. To begin one of the legs take on a third needle 32 stitches from each of the two pieces, making 64. **1st row** of leg knit plain. Now narrow at the end of every alternate row, till you have but 50 stitches. **16th row**—Knit 2 plain, 2 purl, to end of needle. Repeat sixteenth row until you have 16 rows of ribbing. **32nd row**—Knit plain. **33rd row**—Knit 14 stitches plain. Slip 3 stitches on to a third needle, which you do nothing with till you have knitted 3 stitches plain, then carry the third needle over and knit the 3 slipped stitches. This makes the twist. Knit 10 plain, slip 3 on to the third needle, knit 3 plain Again knit the 3 slipped stitches as before; knit 14 plain. **34th row**—Knit 14 plain, 6 purl, 10 plain, 6 purl, 14 plain. **35th row**—Knit plain. **36th row**—Like thirty-fourth row. **37th row**—Like thirty-fifth. **38th row**—Like thirty-sixth. **39th row**—Like thirty-seventh. **40th row**—Like

Reins for Children.

thirty-third. **41st, 43rd, and 45th rows**—Like thirty-fourth row. **42nd and 44th rows**—Like thirty-fifth. You have now knitted the pattern twice, 6 rows for each pattern; repeat until you have 42 rows, and the pattern 7 times. **75th row**—Knit 20 stitches plain; take a third needle and knit the 10 plain stitches between the twisted stitches. Knit these 10 stitches plain, and purl 10 rows like the heel of a stocking. Pick up 8 stitches on each side, same as on a heel. You will now have 66 stitches Knit 10 rows plain. Narrow at the beginning and end of the needle each row for 6 rows. This completes one leg. Cast off and sew together. Take the remaining 64 stitches for the other leg and repeat directions from one-hundred and twelfth row, where the leg begins. Crochet a loose shell around the top through which to run the cord; finish with tassels

SMALL DIAMOND PATTERN.

A USEFUL pattern for handkerchiefs, shawls, tray covers, and other purposes. Cast on any number of stitches divisible by 8, with 3 additional stitches to keep the edge even. Purl a row. Knit a row. Purl a row. **1st Pattern row**—Slip 1, knit 3, * make 1, slip 1, knit 2 together, pass the slipped stitch over,

Small Diamond Pattern

make 1, knit 5, repeat from *, and knit 4 at the end of the row. **2nd row**—Slip 1, purl 3, slip the next stitch on the left-hand pin over the last of these purled stitches * make 1, purl 1, make 1, purl 2 together, purl 4, slip the next stitch on the left-hand pin over the last of these purled stitches, repeat from *, and end the row with purl 3. **3rd row**—Slip 1, knit 1, knit 2 together, * make 1, knit 3, make 1, slip 1, knit 1, pass the slipped stitch over, knit 1, knit 2 together, repeat from *, and at the end of the row slip 1, knit 1, pass the slipped stitch over, knit 2. **4th row**—Slip 1, purl 1, slip the next stitch on the left-hand pin over this purl stitch, * make 1, purl 5, make 1, purl 1, slip the 2 next stitches over this purl stitch, repeat from * and end the row with make 1, purl 1, slip the next stitch over this purled stitch, purl 1. **5th row**—Slip 1, knit 1, * make 1, slip 1, knit 1, pass the slipped stitch over, knit 3, knit 2 together, make 1, knit 1, repeat from *, and at the end of the row make 1, knit 2. **6th row**—Slip 1, purl 2, * make 1, purl 2 together, purl 2, slip next stitch on left-hand pin over the last of these two purl stitches, make 1, purl 3 and repeat from *. Repeat these six fancy rows for the length required. Finish with a plain row, a purl row, and a plain row, and cast off.

OPEN WORKED STOCKING FOR CHILD OF FOUR.

LOZENGE PATTERN.

REQUIRED, 4 skeins of Strutt's crochet cotton No. 20, and four steel knitting needles, No. 19 or No. 20. Cast 32 stitches on the first needle, and 28 stitches on each of the other two needles, 88 stitches in all. **1st round**—Knit 3, purl 3, knit 3, purl 3, knit 3, purl 1 for the seam stitch, then knit 3 and purl 3 alternately to the end of the round and till you come to the seam stitch. Knit 29 rounds of ribbing, counting the seam stitch (which is in the centre of the first needle), as the *first* stitch of each round. **1st Pattern round**—Purl the seam stitch, knit 8, * make 1, slip 1, knit 1, pass the slipped stitch over, knit 1, knit 2 together, make 1, knit 1, repeat from * ten times, make 1, slip 1, knit 1, pass the slipped stitch over, knit 1, knit 2 together, make 1, knit 8. **2nd round**—Plain. Repeat these two rounds four times. **11th round**—Purl the seam stitch, knit 9, * make 1, slip 1, knit 2 together, pass the slipped stitch over, make 1, knit 3, repeat from * ten times, make 1, slip 1, knit 2 together, pass the slipped stitch over, make 1, knit 9. **12th round**—Plain. **13th round**—Purl the seam stitch, knit 8, knit 2 together, * make 1, knit 1, make 1, slip 1, knit 1, pass the slipped stitch over, knit 1, knit 2 together, repeat from * ten times, make 1, knit 1, make 1, slip 1, knit 1, pass the slipped stitch over, knit 8. **14th round**—Plain. Repeat the last two rounds four times. **23rd round**—Purl the seam stitch, knit 7, knit 2 together, * make 1, knit 3, make 1, slip 1, knit 1, knit 2 together, pass the slipped stitch over, repeat from * ten times, make 1, knit 3, make 1, slip 1, knit 1, pass the slipped stitch over, knit 7. **24th round**—Plain. Repeat from the first pattern round. **49th round**—Here decreasings begin, take 2 stitches together on each side the seam stitch, doing 1 plain stitch between the decrease and the seam; the pattern is continued exactly the same, and decreasings are to occur in every sixth round till all the plain stitches are knitted out, and the pattern comes in evenly all round, 72 stitches in the round. Work till six complete patterns (144 rounds) are knitted; the seam stitch *here* will be as an ordinary stitch knitted plain because it belongs to the pattern. **For the Heel**—Purl the seam-stitch, knit plain 19 stitches, turn the work, slip the first stitch, purl 18, knit the seam stitch, purl 19; * turn, slip the first stitch, knit 18, purl the seam stitch, knit 19; turn, slip the first stitch, purl 18, knit the seam stitch, purl 19, and repeat from * till 32 little rows are knitted. While doing this the 33 instep stitches should remain divided upon two needles. **To turn the Heel**—Slip the first stitch, knit 21, slip 1, knit 1, pass the slipped stitch over, knit 1; turn, slip the

first stitch, purl 6, purl 2 together, purl 1; turn, slip the first stitch, knit 7, slip 1, knit 1, pass the slipped stitch over, knit 1; turn, slip the first stitch, purl 8, purl 2 together, purl 1; and continue working one more stitch each time of turning till all the side stitches are knitted in, and 23 stitches remain for the top of the heel. Knit plain along the 23 stitches, and on the same needle pick up and knit 17 stitches along the side of the flap; knit the 33 instep stitches in pattern all on to one needle, and on another needle pick up and knit 17 stitches along the opposite side of the flap, and knit 11 stitches from off the top of the heel. Now the stitches are arranged upon three needles. Knit plain along the next needle. Knit pattern along the instep needle. **For the Gussets**—* On the first foot needle knit 1, slip 1, knit 1, pass the slipped stitch over, knit plain to within 3 stitches of the end of the second foot needle, knit 2 together, knit 1; knit in pattern along the instep needle. Knit 1 plain round. Repeat from * till reduced to 66 stitches in the round. Continue knitting plain on the foot and pattern on instep till the foot is the length required. **For the Toe**—Knit to the end of the first foot needle, so that you may commence the toe exactly in the centre of the sole of the foot, from this arrange the stitches, 22 on each needle. **1st round**—Knit 1, slip 1, knit 1, pass the slipped stitch over, knit plain to within 3 stitches of the end of the needle, knit 2 together, knit 1; do the same on each of the other needles. **2nd round**—Plain. Repeat these two rounds till the toe is reduced to 4 stitches on each needle. Break off the wool, and with a rug needle run the wool through the stitches and sew them neatly together.

Open Worked Stocking for a Child of Four. Lozenge Pattern.

SMALL DIAMOND LATTICE PATTERN.

THIS is a pretty open pattern suitable for Shetland shawls, tray covers, looking-glass cloths, &c. Cast on as many stitches as required for the width of the article, in number divisible by 16, and 1 stitch additional to keep the pattern straight. Knit 1 plain row. **1st pattern row**—Knit 3, make 1, slip 1, knit 1, pass the slipped stitch over, make 1, slip 1, knit 1, pass the slipped stitch over, make 1, slip 1, knit 2 together, pass the slipped stitch over, make 1, knit 2 together, make 1, knit 2 together, make 1 knit 2, and repeat: knit the 1 extra stitch plain at the end of the row. **2nd row**—Purl. **3rd row**—Knit 1, knit 2 together, make 1, knit 2 together, make 1, knit 2 together, make 1, knit 3, make 1, slip 1, knit 1, pass the slipped stitch over, make 1, slip 1, knit 1, pass the slipped stitch over, make 1, slip 1, knit 1, pass the slipped stitch over, and repeat, knitting 1 at the end. **4th row**—Purl. **5th row**—Knit 2 together, * make 1, knit 2 together, make 1, knit 2 together, make 1, knit 5, make 1, slip 1, knit 1, pass the slipped stitch over, make 1, slip 1, knit 1, pass the slipped stitch over, make 1, slip 1, knit 2 together, pass the slipped stitch over, repeat from *, and at the end of the row knit 1 instead of knitting 2 together, and pass the slipped stitch over it, and knit the last. **6th row**—Purl. **7th row**—Knit 2, make 1, slip 1, knit 1, pass the slipped stitch over, make 1, slip 1, knit 1, pass the slipped stitch over, make 1, slip 1, knit 1, pass the slipped stitch over, knit 1, knit 2 together, make 1, knit 2 together, make 1, knit 2 together, make 1, knit 1, and repeat, knitting 1 at the end. **8th row**—Purl. Repeat from the first row of the pattern for the length required.

KNITTED "CATERPILLAR" STITCH.

THIS stitch is suitable for stripes for sofa pillows, &c., or made of cotton is very pretty for counterpanes. It should be combined with stripes of another pattern in pretty contrasting colours. Cast on 21 stitches, and knit 5 rows plain. **6th row**—Knit 8 plain, turn work, and purl the 4 stitches just knitted; knit these 4 stitches back and forth, purl and plain, 19 times. If you have followed directions carefully you will now have a long, narrow stripe with a right and wrong side, like a stocking. From the fullest needle - the one on which there are 13 stitches—slip four on to a third needle. Knit the remaining 9 plain. **7th row**—Knit 4, purl 9; bring the third needle containing the 4 stitches forward by slipping under the stripe already knitted; purl these 4 stitches, knit 4. **8th row**—Knit plain. **9th row**—Knit 4, purl 4; turn work, and knit plain the 4 just knitted; knit these 4 stitches

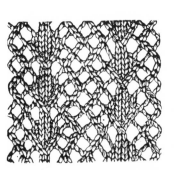

Small Diamond Lattice Pattern.

back and forward, purl and plain, 19 times, and slip off the 4 stitches same as in sixth row. When this is finished purl 5 and knit 4. **10th row**—Knit 13 stitches, and then bring third needle forward, same as in seventh row. Knit 8 stitches. **11th row**—Knit 4, purl 13, knit 4. Repeat pattern from sixth row until you have the desired length. Finish with 5 plain rows.

ELEGANT SILK SOCK.

This sock is knitted in longitudinal stripes of black and crimson, relieved at intervals with spots, crimson spots being on the black stripes and black spots on the crimson, and each spot encircled with a stitch of gold, thereby presenting a very unique, handsome appearance. The colours not in actual use are passed along the inside of the sock, which in this manner is rendered doubly thick and warm. When changing colours it is necessary to put the silk you have just been using *over* the silk you are going to knit with, on the *wrong side* of course, and close under the needle; thus both silks are twisted together and kept in place. An expert knitter may adopt this procedure with *every stitch*, and so work in the silk as to avoid the series of inner threads which are formed if a colour is simply left till it again wanted; either way be careful not to draw the silk so tightly as to pucker the knitting. Required—Imperial Knitting Silk, 3 ozs. of black, 2 ozs. of crimson, and 1½ ozs. of old gold. Four steel knitting needles, No. 17. With black silk cast 48 stitches on the first needle and 40 stitches on each of two other needles, 128 stitches in all. Knit in ribbing, 2 stitches plain and 2 stitches purl, for 36 rounds. Henceforward all plain knitting. **1st Pattern round**—Beginning on the first needle—Knit 8 stitches with crimson, 8 stitches with black, and repeat to the end of the third needle. **2nd round**—3 stitches with crimson, 2 with gold, 3 crimson, 8 black, and repeat. **3rd round**—2 stitches with crimson, 1 gold, 2 black, 1 gold, 2 crimson, 8 black, and repeat. **4th round**—1 stitch with crimson, 1 gold, 4 black, 1 gold, 1 crimson, 8 black, and repeat. **5th round**—Same as the fourth round. **6th round**—Same as the third round. **7th round**—Same as the second round. **8th round**—Knit 8 stitches with crimson, 3 stitches with black, and repeat. **9th round**—8 crimson, 3 black, 2 gold, 3 black, and repeat. **10th round**—8 crimson, 2 black, 1 gold, 2 crimson, 1 gold, 2 black, and repeat. **11th round**—8 crimson, 1 black, 1 gold, 4 crimson, 1 gold, 1 black, and repeat. **12th round**—Same as the eleventh round. **13th round**—Same as the tenth round. **14th round**—Same as the ninth round. Repeat these fourteen rounds till 35 rounds are done. **36th round**—Decreasings begin; on the first needle knit 8 crimson, 8 black, then with crimson knit 1, knit 2 together, knit 2, slip 1, knit 1, pass the slipped stitch over, knit 1, 8 black, 8 crimson, 8 black, and continue round to the end of the third needle. **37th round**—8 crimson, 3 black, 2 gold, 3 black, 6 crimson, 3 black, 2 gold, 3 black, 8 crimson, 3 black, 2 gold, 3 black, and continue. Knit 5 rounds with spot on the black stripes the same as before, crimson stripes plain, and there will be only 6 crimson stitches to knit at the seam. **43rd round**—8 crimson, 8 black, then with crimson knit 2 together, knit 2, slip 1, knit 1, pass the slipped stitch over, 8 black, 8 crimson, 8 black, and continue. **44th round**—3 crimson, 2 gold, 3 crimson, 8 black, 4 crimson, 8 black, 3 crimson, 2 gold, 3 crimson, 8 black, and continue. Knit 5 rounds with spot on the crimson stripes and plain black stripes, there will be 4 crimson stitches to knit plain at the seam. **50th round**—8 crimson, 8 black, then with crimson knit 2 together, slip 1, knit 1, pass the slipped stitch over, 8 black, 8 crimson, 8 black, and continue. **51st round**—8 crimson, 3 black, 2 gold, 3 black, 2 crimson, 3 black, 2 gold, 3 black, 8 crimson, 3 black, 2 gold, 3 black, and continue. Knit 5 rounds with spot on the black stripes, crimson stripes plain, only 2 crimson stitches to knit at the seam. **57th round**—8 crimson, 7 black, then with black slip 1, knit 1, pass the slipped stitch over, knit 2 together, knit 7, 8 crimson, 8 black, and continue. **58th round**—3 crimson, 2 gold, 3 crimson, 16 black, 3 crimson, 2 gold, 3 crimson, 8 black, and continue. Knit 5 rounds with spot on the crimson stripes, black stripes plain, 16 black stitches to knit at the seam. **64th round**—8 crimson, then with black knit 4, knit 2 together, knit 4, slip 1, knit 1, pass the slipped stitch over, knit 4, 8 crimson, 8 black, and continue. **65th round**—8 crimson, 6 black, 2 gold, 6 black, 8 crimson, 3 black, 2 gold, 3 black, and continue. Knit 5 rounds with spot on the black stripes, crimson stripes plain. **71st round**—8 crimson, then with black knit 3, knit 2 together, knit 4, slip 1, knit 1, pass the slipped stitch over, knit 3, 8 crimson, 8 black, and continue. **72nd round**—3 crimson, 2 gold, 3 crimson, 12 black, 3 crimson, 2 gold, 3 crimson, 8 black, and continue. Knit 5 rounds with spot on the crimson stripes, black stripes plain, 12 black stitches to knit at the seam. **78th round**—8 crimson, then with black knit 3, knit 2 together, knit 2, slip 1, knit 1, pass the slipped stitch over, knit 3, 8 crimson, 8 black, and continue. **79th round**—8 crimson, 4 black, 2 gold, 4 black, 8 crimson, 3 black, 2 gold, 3 black, and continue. Knit 5 rounds with spot on the black stripes, crimson stripes plain. **85th round**—8 crimson, then with black knit 2, knit 2 together, knit 2, slip 1 knit 1, pass the slipped stitch over, knit 2, 8 crimson, 8 black, and continue. **86th round**—3 crimson, 2 gold, 3 crimson, 8 black, 3 crimson, 2 gold, 3 crimson, 8 black, and continue. The pattern is now exactly as it was the beginning, though consequent upon the decreasings there are only 32 stitches on the first needle, the

other two needles holding 40 stitches each as at the commencement, so there are now 112 stitches in the round. Work on in pattern till you can count nine spots straight down the crimson stripes, and eight spots straight down the black stripes, ending with the round, 8 stitches crimson, 8 stitches black. **For the heel**—All black, beginning on the first needle; knit plain the 32 stitches, and also knit 8, purl 2, and knit 2 off the next needle; turn the work, slip the first stitch, purl 1, knit 2, purl 56, knit 2, purl 2; now 64 stitches are on the heel needle, and you let the other 48 stitches stand divided upon two needles till the heel is finished. On the heel needle, **3rd row**—Slip 1, knit 1, purl 2, knit 56, purl 2, knit 2. **4th row**—Slip 1, purl 1, knit 2, purl 56, knit 2, purl 2. Repeat these two rows till the flap is long enough, which it will be when 34 rows are knitted. **To turn the Heel**—Slip 1, purl 2, knit 36, slip 1, knit 1, pass the slipped stitch over; turn, slip 1, purl 16, purl 2 together; turn, slip 1, knit 16, slip 1, knit 1, pass the slipped stitch over; turn, slip 1, purl 16 purl 2 together; turn, and continue till all the side-stitches are knitted in, and 18 stitches remain on the needle for the top of the heel Knit plain the 18 stitches and on the same needle (still with black silk for all the sole) pick up and knit 24 stitches along the side of the flap; turn the work, slip 1, purl the 41 stitches, and pick up and purl 24 stitches along the opposite side of the flap: 66 stitches now on the needle. **For the Gussets**—* Slip 1, knit 1, slip 1, knit 1, pass the slipped stitch over, knit plain to within 4 stitches of the end of the needle, knit 2 together, knit 2; turn, and purl back; repeat from * till reduced to 48 stitches. Continue a plain row and a purl row for the foot for 36 rows Then **for the Toe**—* Slip 1, knit 2, slip 1, knit 1, pass the slipped stitch over, knit plain to within 5 stitches of the end of the needle, knit 2 together, knit 3; turn, and purl back; repeat from * till reduced to 14 stitches, and cast off.

For the Instep—Which is knitted on two needles, and kept in pattern the same as the leg. **1st row**—Knit 4 black, * 8 crimson, 3 black, 2 gold, 3 black, and repeat from *, and end with 8 crimson, 4 black. **2nd row**—Purl 4 black, * 8 crimson, 2 black, 1 gold, 2 crimson, 1 gold, 2 black, and repeat from *, and end with 8 crimson, 4 black. **3rd row**—Knit 4 black, * 8 crimson, 1 black, 1 gold, 4 crimson, 1 gold, 1 black, and repeat from *, and end with 8 crimson, 4 black. **4th row**—Purl 4 black, * 8 crimson, 1 black, 1 gold, 4 crimson, 1 gold, 1 black, and repeat from *, and end with 8 crimson, 4 black. **5th row**—Knit 4 black, * 8 crimson, 2 black, 1 gold, 2 crimson, 1 gold, 2 black, and repeat from *, and end with 8 crimson, 4 black. **6th row**—Purl 4 black, * 8 crimson, 3 black, 2 gold, 3 black, and repeat from *, and end with 8 crimson, 4 black. **7th row**—Knit 4 black, 8 crimson, 8 black, 8 crimson, 8 black, 8 crimson, 4 black. **8th row**—Purl 4 black, * 3 crimson, 2 gold, 3 crimson, 8 black, and repeat from *, ending with 4 black. **9th row**—Knit 4 black, * 2 crimson, 1 gold, 2 black 1 gold, 2 crimson, 8 black, and repeat from *, ending with 4 black. **10th row**—Purl 4 black, * 1 crimson, 1 gold, 4 black, 1 gold, 1 crimson, 8 black, and repeat from *, ending with 4 black **11th row**—Knit 4 black, * 1 crimson, 1 gold, 4 black, 1 gold, 1 crimson, 8 black, and repeat from *, ending with 4 black. **12th row**—Purl 4 black, * 2 crimson, 1 gold, 2 black, 1 gold, 2 crimson, 8 black, and repeat from *, ending with 4 black. **13th row**—Knit 4 black, * 3 crimson, 2 gold, 3 crimson, 8 black, and repeat from *, ending with 4 black. **14th row**—Purl 4 black, 8 crimson, 8 black, 8 crimson, 8 black, 8 crimson, 4 black. Repeat from the first row till you can count twelve spots on the crimson stripe and twelve spots on the black stripe from the top of the sock, ending with the row 8 crimson and 8 black. Knit the toe all black, the same as the toe on the sole. Sew together the instep and sole neatly.

Elegant Silk Sock.

CHILD'S KNITTED BIB.

Materials—Dewhurst's crochet cotton, No. 14, and 2 knitting pins, No. 11. Cast on 100 stitches. **1st row**—Plain. **2nd row**—Knit 48 stitches plain, narrow, narrow, 48 plain. **3rd row**—Slip 1, widen, purl entire row, widening 1 stitch before knitting the last. **4th row**—Like second row. **5th row**—Like third row. **6th row**—Like second row. **7th row**—Like third row. **8th row**—Slip 1 *, cotton forward, slip 1 as for purling, purl 1. Repeat from * till you reach the narrowing in the centre of the bib, narrow twice. Repeat from * to * to end of row. **9th row**—Slip 1, widen, knit plain the slipped stitch of preceding row and purl the purled stitches, remembering to widen before knitting the last stitch. Repeat the last 8 rows 12 times. Care must be taken to keep the narrow strip in the centre made by narrowing, plain on the right side, which is done by purling the two stitches every alternate row. It will be seen that the widening and narrowing come alternately, so as to keep the same number of stitches on the needle all the time. Cast off loosely and crochet 1 row of chain stitch entirely around the bib; finish with a tiny scallop of three long stitches into each loop, cord and tassels around the neck, and ribbons laced through the open-work.

GENTLEMAN'S SHOOTING STOCKING.
FLUTED PATTERN.

THIS stocking is much appreciated by sportsmen and bicyclists, as it is warm and gives a well-rounded appearance to the leg. If a full-sized stocking is required, procure 9 ozs. of 5-ply Scotch fingering and four steel knitting needles. No. 15; for a smaller size use German fingering or Alliance yarn. Cast 36 stitches on the first needle, and 30 stitches on each of two other needles, 96 stitches in all. Knit in ribbing, 3 stitches plain and 3 stitches purl, for 50 rounds. Then commence the pattern. **1st Pattern round**—Beginning on the first needle—Knit 1, purl 5, and repeat to the end of the third needle.

Gentleman's Shooting Stocking. Fluted Pattern.

2nd round—Knit 2, purl 4, and repeat. **3rd round**—Knit 3, purl 3, and repeat. **4th round**—Knit 4, purl 2, and repeat. **5th round**—Knit 5, purl 1, and repeat. Repeat these five rounds till 18 patterns are knitted, which will comprise 90 rounds. Mark with a thread of cotton the one purl stitch that runs straight down from the centre of the first needle, and consider it as a seam stitch, on each side of which decreasings are to be made. **91st round**—When 3 stitches before the seam stitch, purl 2 together, purl 1, purl the seam stitch, knit 1, slip 1, knit 1, pass the slipped stitch over, purl 3, work round in pattern as before. * Knit 4 pattern rounds, allowing for a stitch less on each side the seam. **Next round**—Decrease again. And repeat from * till reduced to 72 stitches for the ankle You will see that 4 patterns (24 stitches) are entirely knitted out, and the pattern comes in evenly as in the first five rounds. Knit 55 rounds in pattern for the ankle, so bringing 39 patterns down the leg. **For the Heel**—Beginning on the first needle—Knit in pattern to the seam stitch, purl that as usual and knit in pattern 18 stitches beyond; turn the work, knit in pattern 36 stitches; and continue forwards and backwards on these 36 stitches always slipping the first stitch in every row for 32 rows Meanwhile let the 36 instep stitches stand as they are, divided upon two needles. **To turn the Heel**—Slip the first stitch, knit plain 18 stitches, slip 1, knit 1, pass the slipped stitch over knit 1; turn, slip the first stitch, purl 3, purl 2 together, purl 1; turn, slip the first stitch, knit 4, slip 1, knit 1, pass the slipped stitch over, knit 1; turn, slip the first stitch, purl 5, purl 2 together, purl 1; turn, and continue thus widening a stitch in every little row, till all the side stitches are knitted in, and 20 stitches are brought on the needle for the top of the heel. Knit plain these 20 stitches, and on the same needle pick up and knit 18 stitches along the side of the flap; on another needle knit the 36 instep stitches in pattern, and on another needle pick up and knit 18 stitches along the opposite side of the flap, and knit 10 stitches from the top of the heel. The stitches are now arranged upon three needles, 92 stitches in the round. Knit plain along the foot needle. Knit in pattern on the instep needle. **For the Gussets**—* Beginning on the first foot needle —Knit 1, slip 1, knit 1, pass the slipped stitch over, knit plain to within 3 stitches of the end of the second foot needle, knit 2 together, knit 1; knit in pattern along the instep needle. Knit 2 rounds plain on foot and pattern on instep. Repeat from * till reduced to 70 stitches in the

round. Proceed without any further decreasing till 15 patterns can be counted down the foot; 54 patterns in all down the stocking. **For the Toe—1st round**—Beginning on the first foot needle—Knit 1, slip 1, knit 1, pass the slipped stitch over, knit plain to within 3 stitches of the end of the second foot needle, knit 2 together, knit 1; on instep needle, knit 1, slip 1, knit 1, pass the slipped stitch over, knit 7, knit 2 together, knit 10, knit 2 together, knit 9, knit 2 together, knit 1. **2nd round**—Plain. **3rd round**—Knit 1, slip 1, knit 1, pass the slipped stitch over, knit plain to within 3 stitches of the second foot needle, knit 2 together, knit 1; on instep needle, knit 1, slip 1, knit 1, pass the slipped stitch over, knit plain to within 3 stitches of the end of the needle, knit 2 together, knit 1. **4th round**—Plain. Repeat the last two rounds till the toe is reduced to 24 stitches. Slip the 12 foot stitches on to one needle, hold it parallel with the 12 instep stitches, and cast off by knitting together a stitch from each needle.

YOUTH'S SHORT STOCKING.

THIS is intended to garter below the knee, and is in size suitable for a boy aged from 13 to 15 years. Required: 8 ozs. of Allca wool, and four steel knitting needles, No. 14. Cast 28 stitches on the first needle, 28 stitches on the second needle, and 21 stitches on the third needle, 77 stitches in all. Knit round and round in ribbing, 5 stitches plain and 2 stitches purl, for 84 rounds. Now mark with a thread of cotton the 2 purl stitches in the middle of the first needle, and remember these are to be considered as seam stitches, and the decreasings of the leg are to be made on each side of them. **85th round**—Beginning on the first needle, rib to 3 stitches before the seam stitches, knit 2 together, knit 1, purl the 2 seam stitches, knit 1, slip 1, knit 1, pass the slipped stitch over, and continue ribbing as before to the end of the third needle. * Knit 7 ribbed rounds, the only difference being that there is a stitch less to knit on each side the seam stitches. **Next round**—Decrease again in the same manner. Repeat from * till reduced to 63 stitches And now the ribs come in evenly as in the first ribbed round, and you continue upon the 63 stitches for the ankle for 38 rounds. **For the Heel**—Beginning on the first needle, knit 5, which brings you to the seam, purl the 2 seam stitches, rib 16 stitches beyond; turn the work, slip the first stitch, rib 33 stitches. These 34 stitches on one needle are for the heel, let the other 29 stitches remain as they are till wanted for knitting the instep. Continue ribbing for the heel, always slipping the first stitch in every row for 28 rows. **To turn the Heel** - - Slip the first stitch, knit plain 15, knit 2 seam stitches together, knit 2, slip 1, knit 1, pass the slipped stitch over; turn, slip the first stitch, purl 5, purl 2 together; turn, slip the first stitch, knit 5, slip 1, knit 1, pass the slipped stitch over; turn, slip the first stitch, purl 5, purl 2 together, purl 1; turn, and continue thus till all the side stitches are knitted in, and 7 stitches are on the needle for the top of the heel. Knit these 7 stitches, and on the same needle pick up, and as you pick up knit, 16 stitches along the side of the flap; rib the 29 instep stitches all on one needle, and on another needle pick up and knit 16 stitches along the other side of the flap, and knit 3 stitches from

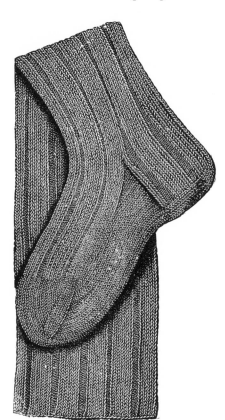

Youth's Short Stocking.

the top of the heel. There will be 68 stitches arranged upon three needles. Knit plain the next needle. Rib the instep needle. **For the Gussets**—* Beginning on the first foot needle—Knit 1, slip 1, knit 1, pass the slipped stitch over, knit to within 3 stitches of the end of the second foot needle, knit 2 together, knit 1; rib along the instep needle. Knit 2 rounds plain on foot and ribbed on instep. Repeat from * till reduced to 58 stitches in the round Continue for the foot on these 58 stitches for 44 rounds. **For the Toe**—* Beginning on the first foot needle—Knit 1, slip 1, knit 1, pass the slipped stitch over, knit to within 3 stitches of the end of the second foot needle, knit 2 together, knit 1; on the instep needle—Knit 1, slip 1, knit 1, pass the slipped stitch over, knit plain to within 3 stitches of the end of the needle, knit 2 together, knit 1; knit 1 plain round; repeat from * till reduced to 26 stitches. Slip the 13 foot stitches all on to one needle, hold it level with the instep needle, and cast off by knitting together a stitch from each needle.

CHILD'S CROSSOVER.

REQUIRED, 3 ozs of white single Berlin wool and a pair of bone knitting needles No. 11. Cast on 30 stitches. Knit 12 plain rows. **13th row**—Knit 3, make 1 and knit 2 together twelve times, knit 3 **14th row**—Plain. **15th row**—Knit 3, increase 1 (by picking up the thread that lies directly underneath the next stitch and knitting it), knit plain to the end. Every succeeding row is the same as the last row till you have 108 stitches on the needle; then knit 12 rows without increase, which brings you to the shoulder. Knit 54 stitches, turn, knit 3, knit 2 together, knit plain to the end. Knit 53 stitches turn. knit 3, knit 2 together, knit plain to the end; and continue thus till you have reduced to 40 stitches. You will see these decreasings are designed to

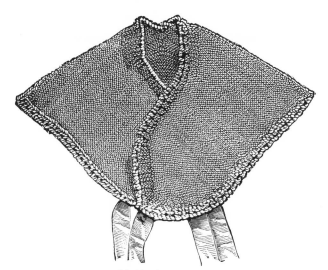

Child's Crossover.

shape the neck ; when 40 stitches are attained knit 36 plain rows: and afterwards decrease by knitting 2 together after the 3rd stitch in every row : bring the work to a point and fasten off. Knit the 54 stitches of the other shoulder to correspond. **For the Border**—With the same wool and pins cast on 4 stitches, and knit 1 row. **1st row**—Slip 1, knit 1, make 2, knit 2 together. **2nd row** Knit 2 purl 1, knit 2. **3rd row**—Plain. **4th row**—Cast off 1, knit 3. Repeat from the first row till sufficient is done to go all round the crossover, and sew it neatly on. Run a piece of white ribbon through the holes at the back of the crossover.

FANCY KNIT STOCKING FOR CHILD.

LAUREL-LEAF PATTERN.

THIS elegant little stocking is knitted with Evans' crochet cotton, No. 20, and four steel knitting needles, No. 19. Cast 36 stitches on the first needle, 30 stitches on the second needle, and 29 stitches on the third needle, 95 stitches in all. For the ribbing knit. **1st round**—Purl 2, knit 12, purl 2 for seam stitches, knit 12, purl 2, knit 4, purl 2, knit 4, purl 2, knit 4, purl 2, knit 4, purl 2, knit 17, purl 2, knit 4, purl 2, knit 4, purl 2, knit 4, purl 2, knit 4. Knit 35 more rounds the same as this round. For the **1st Pattern round**—Beginning on the first needle, purl 2, knit 12, purl 2 seam stitches, knit 12, purl 2, knit 4, purl 2, knit 4, purl 2, knit 4 ; then **Pattern**, purl 2, knit 2, make 1, knit 2 together, purl 2, slip 1, knit 1, pass the slipped stitch over, knit 5, make 1, knit 1, make 1, knit 1, make 1, knit 1, make 1, knit 5, knit 2 together, purl 2, knit 2, make 1, knit 2 together, purl 2, knit 4, purl 2, knit 4, purl 2, knit 4. **2nd round**—Purl 2, knit 12, purl 2 seam stitches, knit 12, purl 2, knit 4, purl 2, knit 4, purl 2, knit 4 ; then **Pattern**, purl 2, slip 1, knit 1, pass the slipped stitch over, make 1, knit 2, purl 2, slip 1, knit 1, pass the slipped stitch over, knit 15, knit 2 together, purl 2, slip 1, knit 1, pass the slipped stitch over, make 1, knit 2, purl 2, knit 4, purl 2, knit 4, purl 2, knit 4. **3rd round**—Purl 2, knit 12, purl 2 seam stitches, knit 12, purl 2, knit 4, purl 2, knit 4, purl 2, knit 4 ; then **Pattern**, purl 2, knit 2, make 1, knit 2 together, purl 2, slip 1, knit 1. pass the slipped stitch over, knit 4, make 1, knit 1, make 1, knit 3, make 1, knit 1, make 1, knit 4, knit 2 together, purl 2, knit 2, make 1, knit 2 together, purl 2, knit 4, purl 2, knit 4, purl 2, knit 4. **4th round**—Same as the second round. **5th round**—Rib 46 stitches as above ; then **Pattern**, purl 2, knit 2, make 1, knit 2 together, purl 2, slip 1, knit 1, pass the slipped stitch over, knit 3, make 1, knit 1, make 1, knit 5, make 1, knit 1, make 1, knit 3, knit 2 together, purl 2, make 1, knit 2, make 1, knit 2 together, purl 2, and rib as above the last 16 stitches on the third needle. **6th round**—Same as the second round. **7th round**—Rib 46 stitches ; then **Pattern**, purl 2, knit 2, make 1, knit 2 together, purl 2, slip 1, knit 1, pass the slipped stitch over, knit 2, make 1, knit 1, make 1, knit 7. make 1, knit 1, make 1, knit 2, knit 2 together, purl 2, knit 2, make 1, knit 2 together, purl 2, and rib 16 stitches to the end of the round. **8th round** — Same as the second round. **9th round**—Rib 46 stitches, then **Pattern**, purl 2, knit 2, make 1, knit 2 together, purl 2, slip 1, knit 1, pass the slipped stitch over, knit 1, make 1, knit 1, make 1, knit 9, make 1, knit 1, make 1, knit 1, knit 2 together, purl 2, knit 2, make 1, knit 2 together, purl 2, and rib 16 to

the end of the round. **10th round**—Same as the second round. **11th round**—Rib 46 stitches, then **Pattern**, purl 2, knit 2, make 1, knit 2 together, purl 2, slip 1, knit 1, pass the slipped stitch over, make 1, knit 1, make 1, knit 11, make 1, knit 1, make 1, knit 2 together, purl 2, knit 2, make 1, knit 2 together, purl 2, and rib 16 to the end of the round. **12th round**—Same as the second round. Repeat from the first pattern round till 60 rounds are knitted that is five repetitions of the pattern of twelve rounds. In the **61st round** (the sixth time of knitting the first pattern round) begin decreasing thus,—when 3 stitches before the seam stitches, knit 2 together, knit 1, purl the 2 seam stitches, knit 1, slip 1, knit 1, pass the slipped stitch over, and proceed as heretofore ; decrease in the same way in the seventh pattern round ; and continue thus decreasing every sixth round till 8 decreasings are done, when the stocking will be reduced to 79 stitches for the ankle. Proceed with ribbed knitting at the back and the fancy stripe in the front, till thirteen repetitions of the pattern are done (156 rounds) counting from the top. **For the Heel**—Beginning on the first needle, knit plain to the seam stitches, purl those, knit 16, purl 2, knit 2 ; turn the work, slip the first stitch, purl 1, knit 2, purl 16, knit the two seam stitches, purl 16, knit 2, purl 2. This brings 42 stitches on one needle for the heel ; the remaining 37 stitches are for the instep and must stand divided upon two needles till the heel is finished. **3rd row of the Heel**—Slip 1, knit 1, purl 2, knit 16, purl 2 seam stitches, knit 16, purl 2, knit 2. **4th row**—Slip 1, purl 1, knit 2, purl 16, knit the 2 seam stitches, purl 16, knit 2, purl 2. Repeat the third and fourth rows till 36 rows are knitted. **To turn the Heel**—Slip the first stitch, knit plain 24, slip 1, knit 1, pass the slipped stitch over ; turn, slip the first stitch. purl 8, purl 2 together ; turn. * slip the first stitch, knit 8, slip 1, knit 1, pass the slipped stitch over ; turn, slip the first stitch, purl 8, purl 2 together ; turn, and repeat from * till all the side stitches are knitted in, and 10 stitches remain on the needle for the top of the heel. Knit these 10 stitches, and on the same needle pick up 20 stitches along the side of the flap, knitting each stitch as you pick it up ; knit the 37 instep stitches in pattern all on one needle ; and on another needle pick up 20 stitches along the opposite side of the flap, and knit 5 stitches off the top of the heel. The stitches are now arranged upon three needles, 87 stitches in the round, ready for knitting the gussets. Knit plain along the next needle. Knit pattern on the instep needle. **For the Gussets**—* On the first foot needle knit 1, slip 1, knit 1, pass the slipped stitch over, knit plain to within 3 stitches of the end of the second foot needle, knit 2 together, knit 1 ; knit the instep needle in pattern. Knit plain on foot and pattern on instep for 2 rounds. Repeat from * till reduced to 75 stitches in the round. Knit plain on foot and pattern on instep for 54 rounds. **For the Toe**—Beginning on the first foot needle knit 2, slip 1, knit 1, pass the slipped stitch over, knit plain to within 4 stitches of the end of the second foot needle, knit 2 together, knit 2 ; on the instep needle knit 2, slip 1, knit 1, pass the slipped stitch over, knit plain to within 4 stitches of the end of the needle, knit 2 together, knit 2 ; knit 1 plain round ; and repeat from * till reduced to 23 stitches. Slip the 12 foot stitches on one needle, turn the sock inside out,

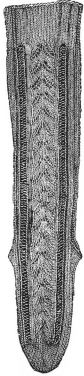

Fancy Knit Stocking for Child. Laurel Leaf Pattern.

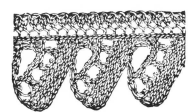

Gotto Edging.

hold the foot needle and the instep needle level with each other, and cast off by knitting together a stitch from each needle, taking 3 stitches together in the centre to bring them in evenly.

GOTTO EDGING.

CAST on 11 stitches, and knit 1 row plain. **1st row**—Slip 1, knit 2, make 1, knit 2 together, knit 3, cast on 4, knit 2 together, knit 1. **2nd row**—Knit 11. make 1, knit 2 together, knit 1. **3rd row**—Slip 1. knit 2, make 1, knit 2 together, knit 3, knit 1 and purl 1 in each of the next four stitches, knit the 2 last stitches. **4th row**—Knit 15, make 1, knit 2 together, knit 1 **5th row**—Slip 1, knit 2, make 1, knit 2 together, knit 1, make 2, knit 2 together, knit 1, make 2, knit 2 together, knit 1, make 2, knit 2 together, knit 1, make 2, knit 2 together, knit 1. **6th row**–Knit 3 and purl 1 four times, knit 3, make 1, knit 2 together, knit 1. **7th row**—Slip 1, knit 2, make 1. knit 2 together, knit 17. **8th row**—Knit 19, make 1, knit 2 together, knit 1. **9th row**—Slip 1, knit 2, make 1, knit 2 together, knit 17. **10th row**—Same as the eighth row. **11th row**—Same as the ninth row. **12th row**—Cast off 11, knit 7, make 1, knit 2 together, knit 1. Repeat from the first row for the length required.

NIGHTDRESS CASE.

FOR this useful and pretty case procure ½ lb. of Strutt's Knitting Cotton, No. 6 ; a pair of steel knitting needles, No. 12, and a yard of pink sateen for lining. Cast on 108 stitches. Knit 4 plain rows. **1st row**—Purl 2, * knit 1, make 1, slip 1, knit 1, pass the slipped stitch over, make 1, slip 1, knit 1, pass the slipped stitch over, make 1, slip 1, knit 1, pass the slipped stitch over, knit 3, purl 3, repeat from * ; and at the end of the row there will be 2 stitches to purl the same as at the beginning. **2nd row**—Knit 2, * purl 10 knit 3, repeat from *, and at the end of the row knit 2 to correspond with the beginning : every alternate row is the same as this row. **3rd row**—Purl 2, * knit 2, make 1, slip 1, knit 1, pass the slipped stitch over, make 1, slip 1, knit 1, pass the slipped stitch over, make 1, slip 1, knit 1, pass the slipped stitch over, knit 2,

Nightdress Case.

pur 3, repeat from * ; and purl 2 at the end of the row. **5th row**—Purl 2, * knit 3 make 1, slip 1, knit 1, pass the slipped stitch over, make 1, slip 1, knit 1, pass the slipped stitch over, make 1, slip 1, knit 1, pass the slipped stitch over, knit 1, purl 3, repeat from * ; and there will be 2 stitches to purl at the end. **7th row**—Purl 2, * knit 4, make 1, slip 1, knit 1, pass the slipped stitch over, make 1, slip 1, knit 1, pass the slipped stitch over, make 1, slip 1, knit 1, pass the slipped stitch over, purl 3, repeat from *, and purl 2 at the end of the row. **9th row**—Purl 2, * knit 2, knit 2 together, make 1, knit 2 together, make 1, knit 2 together, make 1, knit 2, purl 3, repeat from *, and purl 2 at the end. **11th row**—Purl 2, * knit 1, knit 2 together, make 1, knit 2 together, make 1, knit 3, purl 3, repeat from *, and purl 2 at the end. **13th row**—Purl 2, * knit 2 together, make 1, knit 2 together, make 1, knit 2 together, make 1, knit 4, purl 3, repeat from *, and purl 2 at the end **14th row**—Same as the second row. Repeat from the first row for the size you desire to make the case ; about six repeats of the pattern will be sufficient. Finish by knitting 4 plain rows, and cast off. **For the Edging**—Cast on 17 stitches, and knit 1 row plain. **1st row**—Slip 1, knit 2, make 1, knit 2 together, knit 1, make 1, knit 1, make 1, knit 1, make 1, knit 4, make 2, knit 2 together, make 2, knit 2 together, knit 1. **2nd row**—Knit 3, purl 1, knit 2, purl 1, knit 12, make 1, knit 2 together, knit 1. **3rd row**—Slip 1, knit 2, make 1, knit 2 together, knit 2 together, make 1, knit 2, make 1, knit 1, make 1, slip 1, knit 2 together, pass the slipped stitch over, knit 9. **4th row**—Knit 19, make 1, knit 2 together, knit 1. **5th row**—Slip 1, knit 2, make 1, knit 2 together, knit 2 together, make 1, knit 3, make 1, knit 1, make 1, slip 1, knit 2 together, pass the slipped stitch over, knit 3, make 2, knit 2 together, make 2, knit 2 together, knit 1. **6th row**—Knit 3, purl 1, knit 2, purl 1, knit 14 make 1, knit 2 together, knit 1. **7th row**—Slip 1, knit 2, make 1, knit 2 together, knit 2 together, make 1, knit 4, make 1, knit 1, make 1, slip 1, knit 2 together, pass the slipped stitch over, knit 9. **8th row**—Cast off 13, make 1, knit 2 together, knit 1. Repeat from the first row till you have knitted a length sufficient to go all round the piece of knitting, fulling it in nicely at the corners. Make up the pink sateen into a bag or case the size of the knitting measuring where the lace is sewn on, and attach the one to the other.

A COMB-BAG to match the nightdress case can be made by casting on 69 stitches and knitting in the same pattern, repeating the pattern about 11 times ; fold this in half and sew up the sides ; knit sufficient lace to go round, and make up pink sateen lining, with strings of pink ribbon to draw.

CHILD'S COMBINATION GARMENT.

REQUIRED, 8 ozs. of white peacock merino wool and two long bone knitting needles, No. 12. Commence at the bottom of the leg by casting on 56 stitches.

Knit in ribbing of 2 stitches plain and 2 stitches purl for 24 rows. **25th row**—Plain. **26th row**—Purl. Repeat the last two rows three times. **33rd row**—Slip 1, increase 1 by picking up the thread that lies close under the second stitch and knitting it, knit plain to within 1 stitch of the end of the row, where increase again by picking up the thread that lies under the last stitch and knitting it, then knit the last stitch plain. **34th row**—Purl **35th row**—Plain. **36th row**—Purl. Repeat the last four rows till in the 56th row you have 68 stitches on the needle. Then increase in every plain row till you have done 70 rows and have 82 stitches on the needle. Now still increase in every plain row, and in the purl rows knit first 1 plain stitch at beginning and end, then 2, then 3, then 4, and keep 4 plain stitches as an edge at beginning and end of each purl row, increasing in the plain rows *inside* these plain stitches till you have 100 stitches on the needle, and leaving off with the plain row, break off the wool, and slip the work on to a spare needle. Knit another leg exactly the same. And when this is done and you have purled along the 100 stitches, purl also on the same needle the 100 stitches of the first leg, and you will get 200 stitches all on one needle. **1st row**—Knit 4, knit 2 together, knit 90, which brings you to the 8 plain stitches in the centre of the needle, knit the first 2 of these together, knit 4, knit 2 together, knit 90, knit 2 together, knit 4. **2nd row**—Knit 4, purl 91, knit 6, purl 91, knit 4. **3rd row**—Plain. **4th row**—Same as the second. **5th row**—Plain. **6th row**—Same as the second **7th row**—Knit 4, knit 2 together, knit 89, knit 2 together, knit 2, knit 2 together, knit 89, knit 2 together, knit 4. **8th row**—Knit 4, purl 90, knit 4, purl 90, knit 4 **9th row**—Plain. **10th row**—Same as the eighth. **11th row**—Plain. **12th row**—Same as the eighth. **13th row**—Knit 4, knit 2 together, knit 43, knit 2 together, knit 43, knit 2 together, knit 2 together, knit 43, knit 2 together, knit 43, knit 2 together, knit 4. **14th row**—Knit 4, purl 88, knit 2, purl 88, knit 4. **15th row**—Plain. **16th row**—Same as the fourteenth. **17th row**—Plain. **18th row**—Same as the fourteenth. **19th row**—Knit 4, knit 2 together, knit 42, knit 2 together, knit 42, knit 2 together, knit 42, knit 2 together, knit 42, knit 2 together, knit 4. **20th row**—Knit 4, purl to within 4 stitches of the end, knit those. **21st row**—Plain **22nd row**—Same as the twentieth. **23rd row**—Plain. **24th row**—Same as the twentieth. **25th row**—Knit 4, knit 2 together, knit 38, knit 2 together, knit 25, knit 2

Child's Combination Garment.

together, knit 35, knit 2 together, knit 25, knit 2 together, knit 38, knit 2 together, knit 4.* Knit 5 intermediate rows. Decrease again six times in the next row following. Repeat from * twice. Now there are 164 stitches on. You may knit a few intermediate rows here, or not, as necessary to reach the child's waist. **Next row**—Knit 4, knit 2 together, * knit 5, knit 2 together ; repeat from *, and end with knit 4 ; 141 stitches on. **Next row**—Knit 4, purl to within 4 stitches of the end, knit those. **Next row**—Knit 4, knit 2 together, * knit 3, knit 2 together ; repeat from *, and end with knit 5 ; 116 stitches on. Knit 17 plain rows for the waistband, and in the 8th of these rows on the right-hand side of the garment make a button-hole three stitches from the edge by casting off 2 stitches, and replace them in the next row following. Having done the waistband, proceed with the body, which is worked in ribbed knitting 2 stitches plain and 2 stitches purl, with 4 edge stitches knitted plain on either side, and buttonholes formed on the right-hand side in every tenth row. Work from 30 to 40 rows to reach to the armholes. **Next row**—Knit 28 stitches only, turn, and knit back, and work 16 rows on these 28 stitches, and cast them off. Re-commence where you divided for the armhole, cast off 6, work on the next 48 stitches for 16 rows ; then for shoulder strap rib on the first 10 stitches for 30 rows and cast off ; cast off the 28 middle stitches and work another shoulder strap on the last 10 stitches, and cast off. Begin again at the division for the armhole, cast off 6, and work on 28 stitches for the other half of the back, doing 16 rows, and cast off. Sew the shoulder straps across. Crochet a little edge round the neck and armholes. **1st row**—Double crochet, contracting the neck into a nice shape. **2nd row**—1 double crochet on a stitch of last row, * 3 chain, 3 treble in the same place, miss 2 stitches, 1 double crochet on the next, and repeat from * Place buttons on the waistband and down the left-hand side of the back.

ENDYMION PATTERN.

THIS pretty pattern may be knitted either with cotton or wool according to the purpose for which it is required. Cast on any number of stitches divisible by twelve, and one extra stitch to keep the pattern straight, also it is well to have two or three additional stitches for edge stitches on each side the work, and these should be knitted plain in every row, and are not alluded to in the following directions. Knit 1 or 2 plain rows. **1st pattern row**—Knit 1, make

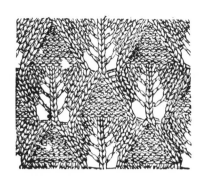

Endymion Pattern.

1, slip 1, knit 1, pass the slipped stitch over, purl 7, knit 2 together, make 1, and repeat: knit 1 at the end of the row. **2nd row**—Purl 3, * knit 7, purl 5, repeat from *, purl 3 at the end. **3rd row**—Knit 1, make 1, knit 1, slip 1, knit 1, pass the slipped stitch over, purl 5, knit 2 together, knit 1, make 1, and repeat; knit 1 at the end. **4th row**—Purl 4, * knit 5, purl 7, repeat from *, purl 4 at the end. **5th row**—Knit 1, make 1, knit 2, slip 1, knit 1, pass the slipped stitch over, purl 3, knit 2 together, knit 2, make 1, and repeat; knit 1 at the end. **6th row**—Purl 5, * knit 3, purl 9, repeat from *, purl 5 at the end. **7th row**—Knit 1, make 1, knit 3, slip 1, knit 1, pass the slipped stitch over, purl 1, knit 2 together, knit 3, make 1, and repeat; knit 1 at the end. **8th row**—Purl 6, * knit 1, purl 11, repeat from *, purl 6 at the end. **9th row**—Knit 1, make 1, knit 4, slip 1, knit 2 together, pass the slipped stitch over, knit 4, make 1, and repeat, knit 1 at the end. **10th row**—Purl. **11th row**—Purl 4, knit 2 together, make 1, knit 1, make 1, slip 1, knit 1, pass the slipped stitch over, purl 3, and repeat; purl 1 more at the end. **12th row**—Knit 4, * purl 5, knit 7, repeat from *, knit 4 at the end. **13th row**—Purl 3, knit 2 together, knit 1, make 1, knit 1, make 1, knit 1, slip 1, knit 1, pass the slipped stitch over, purl 2, and repeat; purl 1 at the end. **14th row**—Knit 3, * purl 7, knit 5, repeat from *, knit 3 at the end. **15th row**—Purl 2, knit 2 together, knit 2, make 1, knit 1, make 1, knit 2, slip 1, knit 1, pass the slipped stitch over, purl 1, and repeat; purl 1 more at the end. **16th row**—Knit 2, * purl 9, knit 3, repeat from *, knit 2 at the end. **17th row**—Purl 1, knit 2 together, knit 3, make 1, knit 1, make 1, knit 3, slip 1, knit 1, pass the slipped stitch over, and repeat, purl 1 at the end. **18th row**—Knit 1, * purl 11, knit 1, repeat from *, knit 1 at the end. **19th row**—Knit 2 together, * knit 4, make 1, knit 1, make 1, knit 4, slip 1, knit 2 together, pass the slipped stitch over, and repeat from *, at the end knit 1 instead of knitting two together and pass the slipped stitch over it. **20th row**—Purl. Repeat from the first pattern row for the length required.

BABY'S VEST KNITTED LENGTHWAYS.

THIS pretty little vest will require 3 balls of white Cocoon wool, and a pair of bone knitting needles, No. 11. It should measure about 11 inches in length. Commence for the sleeve by casting on 48 stitches. **1st row**—Knit 4, purl 4, and repeat. **2nd row**—The same. **3rd row**—Purl 4, knit 4, and repeat. **4th row**—The same. Repeat these four rows till 20 rows are knitted. The same pattern is continued throughout the vest. At the end of the twentieth row cast on 48 stitches for the front of the vest. **21st row**—Knit 12 stitches plain, then knit in pattern to the end of the needle, and cast on another 48 stitches for the back of the vest; there should now be 144 stitches on the needle. **22nd row**—Knit 12 stitches plain, then knit in pattern all along to the last 12 stitches which knit plain. Continue thus for 12 rows, taking care to knit the first 12 and the last 12 stitches plain, these being for the bottom edges of the vest, all the rest of the work to be in the pattern as already described. **33rd row**—Knit 64 stitches as before, cast off 16 for the neck, knit the remaining 64 stitches, and continue the knitting upon these last 64 stitches for 76 rows and break off.

slipping the stitches on to a spare pin. Resume by the cast-off stitches for the front of the vest, and knit 76 rows to correspond with the back piece. At the end of the 76th row cast on 16 stitches for the other shoulder, and knit the 64 stitches off the spare pin. You now again have 144 stitches on the needle. Knit 12 rows all along. Then cast off 48 stitches, knit to the end of the needle, cast off another 48 stitches. You now have 48 stitches remaining on which to knit 20 rows of the pattern for the other sleeve. Cast off all. Finish round the neck with a crochet edging as follows: **1st row**—1 treble, 1 chain, miss 1, repeat all round. **2nd row**—6 treble under the first chain stitch, 1 double crochet under the next chain stitch, and repeat. Run a narrow ribbon through the holes and tie in a small bow in front. Finish round the sleeves with just the second row of the edging.

Baby's Vest Knitted Lengthways.

BEADED CUFFS.

STAR PATTERN.

REQUIRED: 1 oz. of black Andalusian wool and gold beads, or black beads if preferred; knitting needles No. 17. Thread about 500 beads upon your wool, as it will take about that number to make one cuff; slip them down as far as they will go, and you afterwards bring up each bead as required, and push it close to the needle before knitting the stitch. Cast on 30 stitches, and knit one plain row without beads. **1st Pattern row**—Knit 6 stitches plain, 1 stitch with bead, 5 plain, 1 bead, 5 plain, 1 bead, 5 plain, 1 bead, 3 plain, 2 beads. **2nd row**—Plain. **3rd row**—5 plain, 3 beads, 3 plain, 3 beads, 3 plain, 3 beads, 3 plain, 3 beads, 2 plain, 2 beads. **4th row**—Plain. **5th row**—6 plain, 1 bead, 5 plain, 1 bead, 5 plain, 1 bead, 5 plain, 1 bead, 3 plain, 2 beads. **6th row**—Plain. **7th row**—3 plain, 1 bead, 5 plain, 1 bead 5 plain, 1 bead, 6 plain, 2 beads. **8th row**—Plain. **9th row**—2 plain, 1 bead, 3 plain, 3 beads, 3 plain, 3 beads, 3 plain, 3 beads, 5 plain, 2 beads. **10th row**—Plain. **11th row**—3 plain, 1 bead, 5 plain, 1 bead, 5 plain, 1 bead, 5 plain, 1 bead, 6 plain, 2 beads. **12th row**—Plain. Repeat from the first pattern row ten times. Cast off. Pick up the stitches along the plain side of the knitting, and knit in ribbed knitting, 2 stitches plain and 2 stitches purl, for 26 rows. Cast off. Work the other cuff in exactly the same manner, and sew them up.

LONG PURSE.

FOR this pretty purse 2 ozs. of Briggs' royal blue knitting silk will be required, and two steel needles, No. 16. Cast on 26 stitches. **1st row**—Plain. **2nd row**—Slip 1, * make 1, knit 1, make 1, knit 1, and repeat from *, knit the last stitch plain at the end of the row. There should now be 50 stitches on the needle. **3rd row**—Slip 1, * make 1, knit 2 together, repeat from *, end with knit 1: still 50 stitches on the needle. This third row is repeated throughout for the length of the purse, making a length of 8 or 9 inches. Cast off. Fold the work lengthways: gather up the ends and join together one-third of the length, leaving a space open in the centre for the reception of money. Finish off with gilt rings and tassels.

EDITH LACE.

CAST on 17 stitches. Knit a plain row. **1st row**—Slip 1, knit 3, make 1 and knit 2 together five times, cast on 4, knit 2 together, knit 1. **2nd row**—

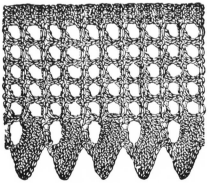

Edith Lace.

Knit 20. **3rd row**—Slip 1, knit 13, knit 1 and purl 1 in each of the next 4 stitches, knit the 2 last. **4th row**—Knit 24. **5th row**—Slip 1, knit 3, make 1 and knit 2 together five times, knit 10. **6th row**—Plain. **7th row**—Plain. **8th row**—Cast off 7, knit 16. Repeat from the first row for the length required.

INSERTION AND BORDER FOR A QUILT.

This is worked in two parts, the border being done separately and sewn on. Procure Strutt's knitting cotton, No. 6, and a pair of steel needles, No. 14. For the insertion cast on 32 stitches. **1st row**—Knit 3, make 1, knit 2 together, knit 1. **2nd row**—Purl 29, pass the cotton over the needle to make a stitch, knit 2 together, knit 1. **3rd row**—Knit 3, make 1, knit 2 together, purl 4, * pass the cotton over the needle to make a stitch, knit 1, pass the cotton twice round the needle to make a stitch, purl 5, repeat from * to the end of the row, where there will be 4 stitches to purl. **4th row**—Knit 4, * purl 3, knit 5, and repeat from * three times, purl 1, make 1, knit 2 together, knit 1. **5th row**—Knit 3, make 1, knit 2 together, purl 4, * make 1, knit 3, make 1, purl 5, repeat from * three times, there will be 4 to purl at the end. **6th row**—Knit 4, * purl 5, knit 5, repeat from * three times, purl 1, make 1, knit 2 together, knit 1. **7th row**—Knit 3, make 1, knit 2 together, purl 4, * make 1, knit 1, slip 1, knit 2 together, pass the slipped stitch over, knit 1, make 1, purl 5, repeat from * three times, there will be 4 to purl at the end. **8th row**—Knit 4, * purl 5, knit 5, repeat from * three times, purl 1, make 1, knit 2 together, knit 1. Repeat the last two rows five times. **19th row**—Knit 3, make 1, knit 2 together, purl 4, * knit 1, slip 1, knit 2 together, pass the slipped stitch over, knit 1, purl 5, repeat from * three times, purl 4 at the end. **20th row**—Knit 4, * purl 5, knit 5, repeat from * three times, purl 1, make 1, knit 2 together, knit 1. **21st row**—Knit 3, make 1, knit 2 together, purl 4, * slip 1, knit 2 together, pass the slipped stitch over, purl 5, repeat from * three times, purl 4 at the end. **22nd row**—Knit 4, * purl 1, knit 5, repeat from * three times, purl 1, make 1, knit 2 together, knit 1. **23rd row**—Knit 3, make 1, knit 2 together, knit 27. **24th row**—Purl 29, make 1, knit 2 together, knit 1. **25th row**—Knit 3, make 1, knit 2 together, purl 27. **26th row**—Knit 28, purl 1, make 1, knit 2 together, knit 1. **27th row**—Same as the twenty-fifth. **28th row**—Same as the twenty-sixth. **29th row**—Same as the twenty-third. **30th row**—Same as the twenty-fourth. **31st row**—Knit 3, make 1, knit 2 together, purl 1, * slip 1, inserting the needle as if about to purl, keep the cotton to the front of the work, purl 1, and repeat from * to the end **32nd row**—Purl 29, make 1, knit 2 together, knit 1 **33rd row**—Knit 3, make 1, knit 2 together, bring the cotton to the front of the work as if about to purl, slip a stitch, * purl 1, slip 1, and repeat from * to the end. **34th row**—Purl 29, make 1, knit 2 together, knit 1. Repeat the last four rows twice. **43rd row**—Knit 3, make 1, knit 2 together, purl 27. **44th row**—Knit 28, purl 1, make 1, knit 2 together, knit 1 **45th row**—Same as the forty-third row. **46th row**—Same as the forty-fourth row. **47th row**—Knit 3, make 1, knit 2 together, knit 27. **48th row**—Purl 29, make 1, knit 2 together, knit 1. Repeat from the third row for the length required. **For the Border**—Cast on 9 stitches. Knit a plain row to begin with. **1st row**—Slip 1, knit 2, make 1, knit 2 together, knit 1, make 2, knit 2 together, knit 1. **2nd row**—Knit 3, purl 1, knit 3, make 1, knit 2 together, knit 1. **3rd row**—Slip 1, knit 2, make 1, knit 2 together, knit 5. **4th row**—Knit 7, make 1, knit 2 together, knit 1. **5th row**—Slip 1, knit 2, make 1, knit 2 together, knit 1, make 2, knit 2 together, make 2, knit 2. **6th row**—Knit 3, purl 1, knit 2, purl 1, knit 3, make 1, knit 2 together, knit 1. **7th row**—Slip 1, knit 2, make 1, knit 2 together, knit 8. **8th row** Knit 10, make 1, knit 2 together, knit 1. **9th row**—Slip 1, knit 2, make 1, knit 2 together, knit 1 make 2, knit 2 together, make 2, knit 2 together, make 2, knit 2 together, knit 1. **10th row**—Knit 3, purl 1, knit 2, purl 1, knit 2, purl 1, knit 3, make 1, knit 2 together, knit 1. **11th row**—Slip 1, knit 2, make 1, knit 2 together, knit 11. **12th row**—Cast off 7, knit 5, make 1, knit 2 together, knit 1. Repeat from the first row till you have a sufficient length.

RECTANGULAR PATTERN FOR A TOILET TABLE COVER.

This also is suitable for spreading over a bedroom ottoman. Procure Strutt's knitting cotton, No. 8, and a pair of long steel needles, No. 12. Cast on 153 stitches, and knit 4 plain rows. **1st pattern row**—Knit 4, purl 1, * knit 2

together, make 1, knit 1, make 1, slip 1, knit 1, pass the slipped stitch over knit 3, purl 1, repeat from *, knit 4 at the end of the row. **2nd row**—Knit 5, * purl 8, knit 1, repeat from *, knit 5 at the end of the row. **3rd row**—Knit 4, purl 1, * knit 2 together, make 1, knit 2, make 1, slip 1, knit 1, pass the slipped stitch over, knit 2, purl 1, repeat from *, knit 4 at the end of the row. **4th row**—Same as the second row. **5th row**—Knit 4, purl 1, * knit 2 together, make 1, knit 3, make 1, slip 1, knit 1, pass the slipped stitch over, purl 1, repeat from *, knit 4 at the end of the row. **6th row**—Same as the second row. **7th row**—Knit 4, purl 1, * knit 2 together, make 1, knit 4, make 1, slip 1, knit 1, pass the slipped stitch over, purl 1, repeat from *, knit 4 at the end of the row. **8th row**—Same as the second row. Repeat from the first row for the length required. Then knit 4 plain rows, and cast off.

BORDER FOR TOILET TABLE COVER.

With the same cotton and needles cast on 13 stitches. **1st row**—Slip 1, knit 2, make 1, knit 2 together, knit 1, make 1, knit 2 together, make 1, knit 1, make 1, knit 1, make 1, knit 1, make 1, knit 2. **2nd row**—Purl. **3rd row**—Slip 1, knit 2, make 1, knit 2 together, knit 1, make 1, knit 3, make 1, knit 1, make 1, knit 3, make 1, knit 2. **4th row**—Purl. **5th row**—Slip 1, knit 2, make 1, knit 2 together, make 1, knit 1, make 1, slip 2, knit 3 together, pass the 2 slipped stitches over, make 1, knit 1, make 1, slip 2, knit 3 together, pass the 2 slipped stitches over, make 1, knit 2. **6th row**—Cast off 4, purl 12. Commence again at the first row, and continue till sufficient is knitted. Sew on to the toilet-table cover, fulling it in nicely at the corners.

GENTLEMAN'S SILK NECKTIE.

Procure 4 ozs. of Briggs' royal blue knitting silk and a pair of steel needles No. 13. Cast on 57 stitches, and begin by knitting a plain row. Slip the first stitch in every row. **1st Pattern row** — Knit 7, purl 3, and repeat, and end the row with knit 7, **2nd row** - Purl 7, knit 3, and repeat, and end the row with purl 7. **3rd row**—Knit 7, purl 3, and repeat, and end the row with knit 7. **4th row**—Plain knitting. **5th row**—Knit 2, * purl 3, knit 7, repeat from * and end with purl 3, knit 2. **6th row**—Purl 2 *, knit 3, purl 7, repeat from *, and end with knit 3, purl 2. **7th row**—Knit 2 *, purl 3, knit 7, repeat from *, and end with purl 3, knit 2 **8th row**—Plain knitting Repeat from the first row for the length required Cast off. Finish off the ends with a narrow fringe, cutting pieces of silk 2½ inches long, and knot two pieces together in every alternate stitch of the knitting, then separate the threads, and taking two threads from each strand knot them together about a quarter of an inch below the knitting.

Insertion and Border for Quilt.

WELDON'S
PRACTICAL
FOURTH SERIES.
CROCHET.
THIRTY=EIGHT ILLUSTRATIONS.

The Yearly Subscription to this Magazine. post free to any Part of the World, is 2s. 6d.
Subscriptions are payable in advance, and may commence from any date and for any period.

The Back Numbers are always in print. Nos. 1 to 232 now ready, Price 2d. each, or bound in 19 Vols., price 2s. 6d. each.

OUTDOOR PELISSE FOR A YOUNG CHILD.

FOR a walking pelisse for a child aged two or three years, nothing can surpass this in elegance and durability ; it measures about 24 inches in length, and is a perfect fit, shaped to figure. Every stitch of the working is here given, so that not the slightest difficulty can be experienced. The pelisse is worked in plain tricot, the trimming is looped knitting in imitation of astrachan. 1¼ lbs. of best white single Berlin or best white peacock wool will be required, a long wooden tricot needle No. 8, and a pair of steel knitting needles No. 12. Commence with 213 chain for the bottom of the pelisse above the trimming, and work 4 rows of plain tricot. 5th row—Raise 53 stitches, then raise 2 together, 22 stitches and then 2 together, 53 stitches and then 2 together, 22 stitches and then 2 together, and thence raise 54 stitches to the end, and draw back in the usual manner. Work 3 plain rows. 9th row—Raise 52 stitches, then raise 2 together, 22 stitches and then 2 together, 51 stitches and then 2 together, 22 stitches and then 2 together, and thence raise 53 stitches to the end. Work 3 plain rows. 13th row—Raise 51 stitches, then raise 2 together, 22 stitches and then 2 together, 49 stitches and then 2 together, 22 stitches and then 2 together, and thence raise 52 stitches to the end. Work 2 plain rows. 16th row—Raise 50 stitches, then raise 2 together, 22 stitches and then 2 together, 47 stitches and then 2 together, 22 stitches and then 2 together, and thence raise 51 stitches to the end. Work 2 plain rows. 19th row—Raise 49 stitches, then raise 2 together, 22 stitches and then 2 together, 45 stitches and then 2 together, 22 stitches and then 2 together, and thence raise 50 stitches to the end. Work 2 plain rows. 22nd row—Raise 48 stitches, then raise 2 together, 22 stitches and then 2 together, 43 stitches and then 2 together, 22 stitches and then 2 together, and thence raise 49 stitches to the end. Work 2 plain rows. 25th row—Raise 47 stitches, then raise 2 together, 22 stitches and then 2 together, 41 stitches and then 2 together, 22 stitches and then 2 together, and thence raise 48 stitches to the end. Work 2 plain rows. 28th row—Raise 46 stitches, then raise 2 together, 22 stitches and then 2 together, 39 stitches and then 2 together, 22 stitches and then 2 together, and thence raise 47 stitches to the end. Work 1 plain row. 30th row—Raise 45 stitches, then raise 2 together, 22 stitches and then 2 together, 37 stitches and then 2 together, 22 stitches and then 2 together, and thence raise 46 stitches to the end. Work 1 plain row. 32nd row—Raise 44 stitches, then raise 2 together, 22 stitches and then 2 together, 35 stitches and then 2 together, 22 stitches and then 2 together, and thence raise 45 stitches to the end. Work 1 plain row. Continue working in this manner, working one stitch less on each front and two stitches less across the back, keeping 22 stitches for each sidepiece, and doing one plain row between each row of decreasings, until you have completed 54 rows from the commencement, when there should be 34 stitches on each front, 13 stitches across the back, and 22 stitches on each sidepiece, which with the 4 seam stitches will make 129 stitches altogether. Work 5 plain rows. 60th row—Raise 57 stitches, increase 1 by raising a stitch in the chain before the next perpendicular thread, raise 13 stitches, increase 1 again, and thence raise 58 stitches to the end. Work 2 plain rows. Now for the First Front— 1st row—Raise 33 stitches (which with the stitch on the needle makes 34 in all), and work back. 2nd row—Raise 32 stitches, take up the last 2 together, and work back 3rd row—Raise 31 stitches, take up the last 2 together, and work back. Work 13 plain rows. Work 4 plain rows, increasing 1 stitch at the end of each row by raising a stitch in the chain before the last perpendicular thread. 21st row—Raise 34 stitches, and work back. 22nd row—Raise 31 stitches, then raise 3 together at the end, and work back. 23rd row—Raise 30 stitches, then 2 together at the end, and work back. 24th row—Raise 28 stitches, then 3 together at the end, and work back. 25th row—Raise 27 stitches, then 2 together at the end, and work back. 26th row—Raise 26 stitches, then 2 together at the end, and work back. 27th row—Cast off 8, then raise 2 together, raise 15, raise 2 together at the end, and work back. 28th row—Cast off 1, raise 2 together, raise 12, then 3 together at the end, and work back. 29th row—Cast off 1, raise 2 together, raise 8, then 2 together at the end, and work back. 30th row—Cast off 1, raise 2 together, raise 5, then 2 together at the end, and work back. 31st row—Cast off 1, raise 2 together, raise 2, then 2 together at the end, and work back. 32nd row—Cast off 1, raise 1 stitch, raise 2 together, and work back. 33rd row—Raise 2 stitches together, and finish off. For the other Front—1st row—Raise 34 stitches (counting them from the *end* of the row), and work back, drawing through the last 2 together. 2nd row—Raise 32 stitches, and work back, drawing through the last 2 together. Work 14 plain rows. Work 4 plain rows, increasing 1 stitch at the beginning of each row by raising a stitch in the chain in front of the first perpendicular thread, and work back. 21st row—Cast off 2 stitches, raise 33, and work back drawing through the last 2 together. 22nd row—Raise 32 stitches, and work back drawing through the last 2 together. 23rd row—Raise 31 stitches, and work back drawing through the last 2 together. 24th row—Cast off 1, raise 29, and work back drawing through the last 2 together. 25th row—Raise 28 stitches, and work back drawing through the last 2 together. 26th row—Cast off 1, raise 26, and work back drawing through the last 2 together. 27th row—Raise 17 stitches (leaving 8 unraised), and work back drawing through 2 together at the beginning, and 2 together at the end. 28th row—Cast off 1, raise 13, raise 2 together, and work back drawing through 2 together at the beginning, and 2 together at the end. 29th row—Raise 11 stitches, raise 2 together, and work back drawing through 2 together at the beginning, and 2 together at the end 30th row—Cast off 1, raise 3 together, and work back drawing through 2 together at the beginning, and 2 together at the end. 31st row—Raise 5 stitches, raise 2 together, and work back drawing through 2 together at the beginning, and 2 together at the end. 32nd row—Cast off 1, raise 2, raise 2 together. draw back through 2 together, and through 2 together, and finish with a row of slip stitches to shape round the neck. For the Back—1st row—Leave one perpendicular loop under the armhole, raise 23 stitches, increase 1, raise 15 stitches, increase 1, raise 23 stitches, and work back drawing through the last 2 together. 2nd row—Raise 59 stitches, raise the last 2 together, and work back drawing through the last 2 together. 3rd row—Raise 57 stitches, raise the last 2 together, and work back drawing through the last 2 together. 4th row—Raise 19 stitches, increase 1, raise 17, increase 1, raise 19, raise the last 2 together, and work back drawing through the last 2 together 5th row—Raise 55 stitches, raise the last 2 together, and work back drawing through the last 2 together. 6th row—Raise 17 stitches, increase 1, raise 19, raise 17, raise the last 2 together, and work back drawing through the last 2 together. 7th row—Raise 53 stitches, raise the last 2 together, and work back drawing through the last 2 together. 8th row—Raise 15 stitches, increase 1, raise 21, increase 1, raise 15, raise the last 2 together, and work back ; and *not* draw through 2 together at the end. Work 1 plain row. 10th row—Raise 15 stitches, increase 1, raise 23, increase 1, raise 15, and work back. Work 1 plain row. 12th row—Raise 15 stitches, increase 1, raise 25, increase 1, raise 16, and work back. Work 1 plain row. 14th row—Raise 15 stitches, increase 1, raise 27, increase 1, raise 16, and work back. Work 2 plain rows. Work 3 rows, increasing 1 stitch at the beginning, and 1 stitch at the end of each row. 20th row—Cast off 2, raise 61, raise 3 together at the end and work back drawing through the last 2 together. **21st row**—Raise 59 stitches, raise the last 2 together, and work back drawing through the last 3 together. **22nd row**—Raise 55 stitches, raise the last 2 together, and work back drawing through the last 2 together. **23rd row**—Raise 54 stitches, raise the last 2 together, and work back drawing through the last 2 together. **24th row**—Raise 51 stitches, raise the last 3 together, and work back drawing through the last 2 together. **25th row**—Raise 49 stitches, raise the last 2 together, and work back drawing through the last 3 together. **26th row**—Raise 45 stitches, raise the last 3 together, and work back drawing through the last 2 together. **27th row**—Raise 43 stitches, raise the last 2 together, and work back drawing through the last 2 together. **28th row**—Raise 41 stitches, raise the last 2 together, and work back drawing through the last 2 together. **29th row**—Raise 12 stitches, raise 2 together, and work back drawing through the last 2 together, this little piece is to heighten the shoulder. **30th row**—Raise 9 stitches, raise 3 together, and work back drawing through the last 3 together. **31st row**—Raise 5 stitches, raise 3 together, and work back drawing through the last 2 together. **32nd row**—Raise 2 stitches, raise 3 together and work back drawing through 2 together and 1 through 2 together; work a few slip stitches down the slope of the neck till you come within 15 stitches of the opposite shoulder, then raise 12 stitches, raise the last 3 together, and work back drawing through the last 2 together. **2nd little row**—Raise 9 stitches, raise 2 together, and work back drawing through the last 3 together. **3rd row**—Raise 5 stitches, raise 3 together, and work back drawing through the last 3 together. **4th row**—Raise 2 stitches, raise 2 together, and work back drawing through 2 together and 2 together, and fasten off. Sew up the sides and shoulders of the pelisse. **For the Sleeves**—Begin with 54 chain, and break off. **1st row**—Miss 20 chain, commence on the twenty-first and raise 14 stitches, work back; slip the wool stitch by stitch backwards along 4 of the commencing chain. **2nd row**—Raise 3 stitches in the 4 you have just slipped (which with the 1 on the needle makes 4 in all), raise 14 stitches above the fourteen of last row and 4 stitches in the chain on the opposite side, and work back; slip the wool along 4 more of the foundation chain. **3rd row**—Raise 3 stitches in the chain, raise 22 stitches above the 22 of last row, raise 4 in the chain on the opposite side, and work back; slip the wool along 4 more of the foundation chain. **4th row**—Raise 3 stitches in the chain, raise 30 stitches above the 30 of last row, raise 4 in the chain on the opposite side, and work back; slip the wool along 4 more of the foundation chain. **5th row**—Raise 3 stitches in the chain, raise 38 stitches, raise 4 in the chain on the opposite side, and work back; slip the wool along 4 more of the foundation chain. **6th row**—Raise 3 stitches in the chain, raise 46 stitches, raise 4 in the chain on the opposite side, 54 stitches in all, and work back. *Work 4 plain rows. In drawing back in the fourth row stop 6 stitches from the end, raise again to within 6 stitches of the other end, and draw back through all. Repeat from * 3 times more. Work 1 plain row. **24th row**—Raise 23 stitches, raise 2 together, raise 2 stitches, raise 2 together, raise 24 stitches, and work back. **25th row**—Plain, and in drawing back stop 6 stitches from the end, raise again to within 6 stitches of the other end, and draw back through all. **26th row**—Raise 22 stitches, raise 2 together, raise 2 stitches, raise 2 together, raise 23, and work back. Work 1 plain row. **28th row**—Raise 21 stitches, raise 2 together, raise 2, raise 2 together, raise 22, and in drawing back stop 6 stitches from the end, raise again to within 6 stitches of the other end, and draw back through all. Work 1 plain row. **30th row**—Raise 20 stitches, raise 2 together, raise 2, raise 2 together, raise 21, and work back. **31st row**—Plain, and in drawing back stop 6 stitches from the end, raise again to within 6 stitches of the other end, and draw back through all. **32nd row**—Raise 19 stitches, raise 2 together, raise 2, raise 2 together, raise 20, and work back. Work 1 plain row. **34th row**—Raise 18 stitches, raise 2 together, raise 2, raise 2 together, raise 19, and in drawing back stop 6 stitches from the end, raise again to within 6 stitches of the other end, and draw back through all. Work 1 plain row. **36th row**—Raise 17 stitches, raise 2 together, raise 2, raise 2 together, raise 18, and work back. **37th row**—Plain, and in drawing back stop 6 stitches from the end, raise again to within 6 stitches of the other end, and draw back through all. **38th row**—Raise 16 stitches, raise 2 together, raise 2, raise 2 together, raise 17, and work back. Work 1 plain row. Then work a row of crochet for edging, 1 double crochet in the first stitch of tricot, miss 1 stitch of tricot, 2 treble 1 long treble 2 treble all in the next, miss 1, and repeat, and fasten off. Make another sleeve similar to this one, sew them up, and sew them into the pelisse. **Now for the Border round the Bottom of the Pelisse**—With a No. 9 crochet needle work a chain of 215 stitches,

and do 4 rows of trebles, 213 trebles in a row, breaking off at the end of every row and keeping the work perfectly flat (you cannot see these four rows in the engraving; they are underneath the astrachan trimming, and are worked thus for the sake of lightness). **5th row**—Tricot, beginning on the second stitch, raise 11 stitches on consecutive stitches of the treble, and work back, drawing through the first 2 together and the last 2 together. **6th row**—Raise 8 stitches, taking up the small horizontal thread that lies at the *back* of previous row, and work back, drawing through the first 2 together and the last 2 together. **7th row**—Raise 6 stitches in the same way, and draw back as before. **8th row**—Raise 4 stitches in the same way, and work back, drawing through the first 3 together and the last 2 together. Do 1 double crochet in the middle of the stitches just drawn together, then slip along in four loose stitches down the side of the scallop so that the last of the four goes into the treble stitch, work 1 single crochet on the next treble, 1 single crochet on the next; raise 10 stitches (there will be 11 with the one on the needle), and work a second scallop like the first. There should be 17 scallops in all round the bottom of the pelisse. **9th row**—Begin again on the right-hand side, work 1 double crochet on the first stitch of the trebles, * 4 double crochet up the side of the scallop, 3 double crochet on the point of the scallop, 4 double crochet down the opposite side of the scallop, and 1 double crochet between the two single stitches of last row, and repeat from *. **10th row**—Re-commence on the right-hand side, and insert the hook always into the top and back thread of the stitches of last row, 1 double crochet on the first stitch, * miss 1, 1 double crochet on the next, 3 chain, another double crochet in the same place, miss 1, 1 double crochet on the next, 3 chain, another double crochet in the same place, miss 1, 1 double crochet on the centre stitch of the three double crochet of last row, 3 chain, another double crochet in the same place, miss 1, 1 double crochet on the next, 3 chain, another double crochet in the same place, miss 1, 1 double crochet on the next, 3 chain, another double crochet in the same place, miss 1, 1 double crochet on the double crochet between the scallops, and repeat from *, and fasten off at the end of the row. **For the Trimming**—Take the knitting needles, and cast on 12 stitches for the astrachan trimming round the bottom of the pelisse. **1st row**—Plain. **2nd row**—Slip the first stitch, insert the needle in the next stitch, put the wool over the point of the needle and round the first finger of the left hand twice, then wool over the needle, and knit the stitch in the usual manner drawing all 3 threads of wool through, knit 9 more stitches in the same way, knit the last stitch plain. Repeat these two rows for the length required, and cast off. Sew the border of treble stitches upon the pelisse and place this astrachan trimming over the 4 rows of treble and just above the scallops. Knit the trimming for the fronts of the pelisse and for the sleeves in the same way, but cast on only 6 stitches. Sew hooks and eyes to fasten down the front of the pelisse.

Outdoor Pelisse for a Young Child.

CUFFS FOR A LADY.

REQUIRED, 1 oz. of violet and ½ oz. of black single Berlin wool. A bone crochet needle, No. 9, will be a good size for the cuff itself, as the stitch looks better, and is more elastic if not worked too closely, and No. 12 needle for the border. Commence with the largest needle and violet wool, with 37 chain, turn, and work all along in single crochet, that is, insert the hook in a stitch and draw the wool through and also through the stitch on the needle. Turn the work, and now insert the hook so as to take up the one top thread of the single crochet stitches of the previous row drawing the wool through as before; turn the work, and again work single crochet, taking up the one back thread of the stitches of last row. Proceed in this manner, working one row on the top threads and the following row on the back threads till 19 rows are done. Fasten off, and sew up. The right side of the work is the side on which the ridges appear furthest apart, turn this side outside. Now for the **Frill round the Wrist**—With the fine crochet needle work first with violet wool round the margin of the commencing chain, 1 double crochet in the first stitch, * 5 chain, 1 double crochet in the third chain from the needle, 1 chain, miss two of the foundation, 1 double crochet in the next, and repeat from * to the end of the round, join to the first double crochet stitch and fasten off. Take the black wool and work a similar edge upon the ridge of single crochet just about half an inch from the margin. Then an edge with violet wool upon the ridge next above, and another edge with black wool upon the next ridge above. The colours used can of course be varied according to taste, as brown and gold, or red and fawn, and the result will be a pretty and useful pair of cuffs either for personal wear or for a present.

HOOD.

REQUIRED, 2 ozs. of white, and 1 oz. of pale blue single Berlin wool, and a bone crochet needle No. 8. With white wool make a chain of 68 stitches rather loosely for the front of the hood. 1st row—1 treble in the third stitch from the needle and treble to the end, making 65 treble in all. 2nd row—2 chain to turn, and work a treble on each stitch of previous row, inserting the hook in the small thread that lies below the top thread of every stitch, this is done that the two front threads of previous row may appear like a row of chain stitches on the right side of hood. 3rd row—2 chain to turn, and work 65 treble, inserting the hook in the two top threads of last row. 4th row—3 chain to turn, and work 65 long treble stitches (wool twice round the needle), taking up as described in the second row. 5th row—Same as the third row. 6th

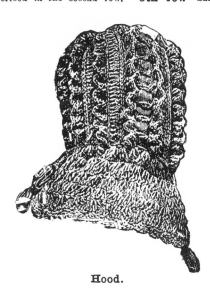

Hood.

row—Same as the second row. 7th row—Decrease on each side of the four centre stitches. And work 9 more rows in the same manner, decreasing in every row on each side the four centre stitches. Break off the wool, fold the work, and sew up the last row for the centre of the crown. The frill-like appearance is given by rows of double crochet worked with blue wool in zigzag across 2 rows of the treble. For the **Curtain**—Hold the hood the right side towards you, and beginning at the left corner of the front, work 64 treble along the neck of the hood. 2nd row—2 chain to turn, 2 treble, increase (by working 2 treble in the same stitch), 29 treble, increase, 29 treble, increase, 2 treble. Work 6 more rows increasing in the same way. Then with blue wool work a scallop border all round the hood and curtain, 1 double crochet, miss 2, 6 treble on the next, miss 2, and repeat. Run a ribbon in the row of long treble stitches and tie in a bow at the top. Crochet a chain with blue wool to tie at the back of the crown and also under the chin, finish all 4 ends of this with tassels, and place a tassel at each corner of the curtain.

TRICOT STRIPE FOR ANTI-MACASSAR.

IN PATTERN OF RAISED DIAMONDS.

THE quantity of wool required will of course depend upon the size the antimacassar is to be, 12 ozs. of white and 2 ozs. of blue single Berlin will make one sufficiently large for a sofa or small easy-chair; procure also a bone tricot needle No. 9, and two shades of blue filoselle for filling in the diamonds. With white wool make 26 chain, and work 2 rows of plain tricot. 3rd row—Pick up the stitches as usual, and coming back draw through 13, make 4 chain, draw through 13. 4th row—Pick up the stitches, and coming back draw through 12, 4 chain, through 2, 4 chain, through 12. 5th row—Pick up the stitches, and draw back through 11, 4 chain, through 2, 4 chain, through 2, 4 chain, through 11. 6th row—Pick up the stitches, and draw back through 10, 4 chain, through 2, 4 chain, through 2, 4 chain, through 2, 4 chain, through 10. 7th row—Pick up the stitches, and draw back through 9, 4 chain, through 2, 4 chain, through 4, 4 chain, through 2, 4 chain, through 9. 8th row—Pick up the stitches, and draw back through 8, 4 chain, through 2, 4 chain, through 6, 4 chain, through 2, 4 chain, through 8. Continue thus increasing the width of the raised diamonds till you have to draw through only 3 stitches at the beginning and 3 stitches at the end, when you will count 11 rows of raised tufts; now decrease the diamond till you bring it again to a single tuft. Repeat from the third row for the length required. With two shades of filoselle work a cross-stitch star to fill the centre of the diamonds. For the Edge—With blue wool—Holding the tricot the right side towards you work a row of double crochet along the side of the strip, turn, and work double crochet back. 3rd

row—1 double crochet on the first stitch of previous row, 1 treble inserting the hook down in the tricot in the place where a double crochet stitch is worked into, another treble in the same place, a double crochet on stitch of last row, 2 treble in the tricot, and repeat. Work a similar edge along the other side of the strip. Make as many more stripes as required, and join them together. Finish off the top and bottom of the antimacassar thus, with blue wool, 1 double crochet, * 5 chain, 1 treble on the top part of the double crochet just done, miss three tricot stitches, 1 double crochet in the next, and repeat from *. Fringe with white wool, 2 strands knotted in every loop of five chain, and again knotted together in itself.

Tricot Stripe for Antimacassar. In Pattern of Raised Diamonds.

THISTLE PATTERN.

THIS pattern is especially suitable for cotton crochet, for pincushion covers, insertion round quilts, or any purpose for which a close ground is required. Commence with a chain the necessary length. 1st row—12 consecutive double crochet, * 10 chain, 1 double crochet in the same place last double crochet is worked into, 10 chain and a double crochet twice more in the same place, 12 double crochet, and repeat from * to the end of the foundation. 2nd row—Plain double crochet working into the one top thread of the stitches of preceding row, and do one stitch only at the back of the thistle, holding down the loops of chain in the front of the work. 3rd row—Plain double crochet. 4th row —8 double crochet,* 1 double crochet on the next catching in the first loop of ten chain, 5 double crochet, 1 double crochet on the next catching in the third loop of ten chain, 5 double crochet, and repeat from *. 5th row—Double crochet. 6th row—11 double crochet, 6 treble on the next, catching down the middle loop of ten chain, and repeat. 7th row—6 double crochet, * 10 chain, 1 double crochet in the same place last double crochet is worked into, 10 chain and a double crochet twice more in the same place. 12 double crochet, and repeat from *. 8th row—Plain double crochet, same as the second row. 9th row—Double crochet. 10th row—2 double crochet, * 1 double crochet on the next catching in the first loop of ten chain, 5 double crochet, 1 double crochet on the next catching in the third loop of ten chain, 5 double crochet, and repeat from *. 11th row—Double crochet. 12th row—5 double crochet, * 6 treble on the next catching down the middle loop of ten chain, 11 double crochet, and repeat from *. Repeat from the first row for the length required.

SLEEVE HOLDER.

EVER since fashion demanded tight sleeves for wraps as well as for dresses, the feminine mind has been in a perturbed state regarding the donning of garments. An under-sleeve lodged half way to the elbow is a source of great annoyance, and anything to prevent this inconvenience is exceedingly welcome, especially if it be so simple a contrivance as a crocheted cord to each end of which a ring is attached. One ring is slipped on the first finger and the cord brought down and wound tightly around the sleeve near the wrist, leaving enough of the cord to allow the other ring to slip over the thumb, and the sleeve is drawn on without any difficulty and the holder removed. To make the cord, use worsted or zephyr of any colour you desire, olive, blue, pink, or brown are suitable, work 5 chain stitches, join them and make one single crochet in the back of each loop of the foundation; work on with single crochet in continuous rounds until your strip is 27 inches long. Fasten to each end a ring worked around with single crochet.

BEAN STITCH.

MAKE a loose chain for the foundation; in the third loop draw the thread through with an Afghan needle, as if to make a single crochet, put the thread over the needle, draw the thread through the

Thistle Pattern.

loop again; you have now 4 stitches, 1 remaining from foundation and the 3 made in this first loop. Leave them all on your needle and repeat the 3 stitches in each loop of the foundation chain until you reach the end and work a single crochet in the last foundation stitch. 2nd row—Work back as in Afghan stitch, only draw the thread each time through the 3 stitches made in each foundation stitch. 3rd row—Make 1 single crochet and between first and second group of stitches in the first row, work similar groups of three and continue to end of this row. The following rows are worked as described for second and third rows

BABY'S JACKET IN RUSSIAN CROCHET.

¹ HIS very pretty and comfortable little jacket is worked with white Andalusian wool, of which 4 ozs. will be required, and a bone crochet needle No. 12. Commence with 61 chain. **1st row**—Work 60 double crochet. **2nd, 3rd, and 4th rows**—The same, inserting the hook in the back thread of the stitches of preceding row, as the work is to form ridges. **5th row**—7 double crochet, a tuft, which is made by working 5 treble into the corresponding double crochet stitch of the next row below, and catch the last of the treble stitches into the first, double crochet to the end of the row, and work 2 double crochet in the last stitch to heighten for the neck. **6th row**—53 double crochet, 1 treble (worked into the second preceding row at the back of the tuft), 7 double crochet. **7th row**—5 double crochet, a tuft, 3 double crochet, a tuft, double crochet to the end of the row, and again work 2 double crochet in the last stitch. **8th row**—52 treble crochet, 1 treble, 3 double crochet, 1 treble, 5 double crochet. **9th**

Baby's Jacket in Russian Crochet.

row—3 double crochet, tuft, 3 double crochet, tuft, 3 double crochet, tuft, double crochet to the end of the row, and work 2 double crochet in the last stitch. **10th row**—51 double crochet, 1 treble, 3 double crochet, 1 treble, 3 double crochet, 1 treble, 3 double crochet. **11th row**—5 double crochet, tuft, 3 double crochet, tut, double crochet to the end of the row, and work 2 double crochet in the last stitch. **12th row**—54 double crochet, 1 treble, 3 double crochet, 1 treble, 5 double crochet. **13th row**—7 double crochet, tuft, double crochet to the end of the row, and work 3 double crochet in the last stitch. **14th row**—58 double crochet, 1 treble, 7 double crochet. **15th row**—Plain double crochet, working 2 double crochet in the last stitch, 67 double crochet in all. **16th row**—67 double crochet. **17th row**—Plain double crochet, working 3 double crochet in the last stitch. **18th row**—69 double crochet. **19th row**—7 double crochet, tuft, double crochet to the end of the row, doing 2 double crochet in the last stitch. **20th row**—62 double crochet, 1 treble, 7 double crochet. **21st row**—5 double crochet, tuft, 3 double crochet, tuft, double crochet to the end of the row, doing 3 double crochet at the end. **22nd row**—62 double crochet, 1 treble, 3 double crochet, 1 treble, 5 double crochet. **23rd row**—3 double crochet, tuft, 3 double crochet, tuft, 3 double crochet, tuft, double crochet to the end of the row, doing 2 double crochet in the last stitch. **24th row**—61 double crochet, 1 treble, 3 double crochet, 1 treble, 3 double crochet, 1 tr ble, 3 double crochet. Now proceed with tufts at bottom of jacket, and decrease at the shoulder every other row till reduced to 66 double crochet. Next row work 40 stitches, leave the remaining 26 stitches for the armhole, and turn, and work back. Work 15 stitches and back. Work 40 stitches and back. Work 15 stitches and back. Work 40 stitches, then do 26 chain to compensate for the 26 unworked stitches, and work back. Now increase every other row at the shoulder till 73 double crochet. Decrease every other row to 70 double crochet. Then do 10 rows on the 70 stitches, and this forms one-half the jacket: work the other half to correspond. **For the Sleeves**—Commence with 50 chain. Work ridged double crochet forwards and backwards, increasing 1 stitch at the end of every other row for 20 rows, then work 18 rows without increase or decrease, and afterwards decrease at the end of every other row till reduced to 50 stitches again. Sew up the sleeve, and round the edge work a scallop, 1 double crochet on a ridge of the sleeve, 5 treble on the next ridge, and repeat: turn this up about an inch to form a cuff. Work the other sleeve the same. Sew up the shoulders and sew in the sleeves. The little tufts are tiny bits of wool sewn on with a needle and cotton. Place strings of narrow ribbon to tie the jacket.

BABY'S BIB.

REQUIRED, Evans's crochet cotton No. 14, steel crochet hook No. 16. Begin for the **Neck** with 166 chain, and on both sides of this chain work 165 double crochet stitches; break off the cotton. **For the Front**—Hold the work the wrong side of the double crochet towards you, and work into the back thread of the stitches, so as to form ridges; leave the first 58 stitches, and, beginning on the 59th stitch, work 4 consecutive double crochet, 6 treble in the next, and catch the last of the treble stitches into the first to form a "tuft," 3 double crochet, another tuft, 15 consecutive double crochet, 3 double crochet in the next, which is the centre stitch, 15 consecutive double crochet, a tuft, 3 double crochet, a tuft, 4 double crochet, and leaving 58 stitches unworked, turn. **2nd row**—Miss the first double crochet of last row, and work 49 double crochet straight along, taking up the back thread of previous row. **3rd row**—Miss the first double crochet, work 24 consecutive double crochet, 3 double crochet in the centre stitch, 24 consecutive double crochet. **4th row**—Same as the second row, 49 double crochet. Repeat these four rows four times, keeping 49 stitches in a row. **21st row**—Not miss the first stitch, work 4 double crochet, a tuft, 3 double crochet, a tuft, 16 double crochet, 3 double crochet in the centre stitch, 16 double crochet, a tuft, 3 double crochet, a tuft, 4 double crochet. **22nd row**—Miss the first stitch, and work 51 double crochet. **23rd row**—Not miss the first stitch, work 25 double crochet, 3 double crochet in the centre stitch, 25 double crochet. **24th row**—Miss the first stitch, and work 53 double crochet. Now continue the four pattern rows, but not missing any more stitches at the beginning or end of the rows, so you will increase 2 stitches in every row, and in the 40th row you will work 85 double crochet. **41st row**—4 double crochet, a tuft, * 3 double crochet, a tuft, repeat from * eight times, 1 double crochet, 3 double crochet in the centre stitch, 1 double crochet, a tuft, * 3 double crochet, a tuft, repeat from * eight times, 4 double crochet. **42nd row**—Plain double crochet (87). **43rd row**—43 double crochet, 3 double crochet in the centre stitch, 43 double crochet. **44th row**—Plain double crochet (89). **45th row**—4 double crochet, a tuft, * 3 double crochet, a tuft, repeat from * eight times, 3 double crochet, 3 double crochet in the centre stitch, 3 double crochet, a tuft, * 3 double crochet, a tuft, repeat from * 8 times, 4 double crochet. **46th row**—Plain double crochet (91). **47th row**—45 double crochet, 3 double crochet in the centre stitch, 45 double crochet. **48th row**—Plain double crochet (93). **For the Border—1st row**—1 treble on a double crochet stitch of last row, * 1 chain, miss 1 stitch of the work, 1 treble in the next, and repeat from * all round the bib, and round both sides of the commencing rows of the neck; fasten off the cotton. **2nd row**—Begin with 1 double crochet at the extreme right hand of the neck band, 13 chain, miss 2 spaces of last row, 1 double crochet in the third, and continue round the bib and along the opposite side of the neck band, but not on the top of the neck. **3rd row**—1 double crochet over double crochet of last row, 13 chain, and repeat. **4th row**—The same. **5th row**—1 double crochet taking up the centre of all chains of last 3 rows, 7 chain, 1 double crochet taking up the centre of all next chains, and repeat. **6th row**—1 double crochet over double crochet of last row, 7 chain, and repeat. **7th row**—The same. **8th row**—1 double crochet over 2 last rows by inserting the hook in the double crochet of the fifth row, 13 chain, and repeat. **9th row**—1 double crochet over double crochet of last row, 13 chain, and repeat. **10th row**—The same. **11th row**—1 double crochet taking up the

Baby's Bib.

centre of all chains of last 3 rows, 7 chain, 1 double crochet taking up the centre of all next chains, and repeat. **12th row**—1 treble at the right-hand corner of the neck band, 1 chain, 1 treble 6 times along the beginning of the last 9 rows, 1 chain, miss 1, 1 treble all along the side of the neck band, round the bib, and along the opposite side of the neck band, 1 chain 1 treble 6 times along the ending of the 9 chain rows, and fasten off at the left-hand corner of the neck band. **13th row**—1 double crochet under first space of last row, * 1 double crochet, 4 treble, 1 double crochet, all under next space of last row, and repeat from * entirely round the bib and neck.

LADY'S BODICE IN RUSSIAN CROCHET.

THIS is intended to wear as a winter bodice under the dress. 8 ozs. of white Scotch fingering will be required, a No. 11 bone crochet needle, and nine white bone buttons. Commence with a chain of 96 stitches, and on this work double crochet forwards and backwards for 6 rows, inserting the hook so as to take up the back thread of each preceding row, as the work is to set in ridges. In the next row work only 18 double crochet, and turn, and double crochet back. This short row is to supply the necessary fulness round the hips, and though for the sake of brevity it is not again alluded to in the directions, it is to be worked after *every sixth* row. Work 10 full length rows. Then decrease 1 stitch at the shoulder end every other row till 33 rows in all are done. Now leave 30 stitches unworked at the shoulder end, and work on the other stitches for 6 rows. At the end of the next row make 30 chain to compensate for the thirty unworked

Lady's Bodice in Russian Crochet.

stitches, and afterwards increase at this end 1 stitch every other row till you work 95 double crochet. Then decrease 1 stitch every row at the same end till brought to 80 stitches. In the next row make buttonholes thus, 8 double crochet, * 3 chain, 6 double crochet, and repeat from * seven times ; then a row of double crochet all along as before, and fasten off. Work the other half of the bodice the same, and sew up the shoulders and back. **For the Neck-band** —Work 6 rows of double crochet along the top of the bodice, doing 60 double crochet in a row ; in the third row of this, on the button-hole side, make another buttonhole. **For the Sleeves**—Begin with 16 chain, and work in ridged double crochet, increasing 1 stitch at the end of every other row to 25 stitches, on these work 25 rows without either increase or decrease, and then decrease on the same side one stitch at the end of every other row to 15 stitches ; fasten off, and join the last row to the commencing chain. Work the other sleeve in the same way. Sew the sleeves in the armholes. **For the Border** round the Bodice and Sleeves—Work first a row of double crochet, and then this scallop, * 2 treble, 1 chain, 2 treble, all into one stitch of previous row, miss 1, 1 double crochet in the next, miss 1, and repeat from *. Sew the buttons down the other side of the front opposite the buttonholes.

CHILD'S JACKET WORKED IN CRAZY STITCH.

REQUIRED, 2 ozs. of white, 1 oz. of pink Shetland wool, and a bone crochet needle, No. 11. With white wool, commence with 50 chain, work 2 treble in the third chain from the needle, * miss one chain, 2 treble in the next, 1 treble in the next, and repeat from *, making 48 treble stitches in the row. The jacket is worked throughout in picots of crazy stitch, that is, each picot is composed of 1 double crochet, 3 chain, and 2 treble, *all* worked into the same stitch of previous row ; turn at the end of every row, beginning the next row with 3 chain and ending with a double crochet into the three chain. To increase, work two picots into the same place. **2nd row**—Work a picot upon every alternate treble stitch, 24 picots in all. **3rd row**—Again work 24 picots. **4th row**— 1 picot, increase, 22 picots, increase, 1 picot. **5th row**—26 picots. **6th row**—13 picots, increase, 13 picots. **7th row**—and every alternate row—to be worked in crazy picots all along, no increase. **8th row**—7 picots, increase, 13 picots, increase, 7 picots. **10th row**—7 picots, increase, 15 picots, increase, 7 picots. **12th row**—7 picots, increase, 7 picots, increase, 7 picots, increase, 7 picots. **14th row**—7 picots, increase, 10 picots, increase, 10 picots, increase, 7 picots. **16th row**—7 picots, increase, 12 picots, increase, 11 picots, increase, 7 picots **18th row**—7 picots, increase, 6 picots, increase, 7 picots, increase, 7 picots, increase, 6 picots, increase, 7 picots. **20th row**—7 picots, increase, 8 picots, increase, 8 picots, increase, 7 picots, increase, 8 picots, increase, 7

picots. **22nd row**—7 picots, increase, 10 picots, increase, 8 picots, increase, 8 picots, increase, 10 picots, increase, 7 picots. **24th row**—7 picots, increase, 12 picots, increase, 9 picots, increase, 8 picots, increase, 12 picots, increase, 7 picots. **26th row**—7 picots, increase, 14 picots, increase, 9 picots, increase, 9 picots, increase, 14 picots, increase, 7 picots. **28th row**—9 picots, miss 14 picots for the armhole, 10 picots, increase, 9 picots miss 14, 9 picots. Now work 13 more rows of the crazy stitch, increasing only in the centre of the back in every alternate row : continue the last of these rows all round the jacket. Then for a border, work with pink wool 4 rows of crazy stitch all round, and finish with one round of white, in all these rounds increasing a picot or two at the corners to keep the work flat. **For the Sleeves**—First work 3 rows of 2 or 3 picots under the arm in shape of a gusset, then work 10 rounds with 12 picots in a round ; take the pink wool and work 4 rounds, and finish with 1 round of white. Crochet a chain with one strand of white and one strand of pink wool together, and having turned down the border round the neck to simulate a collar, run this chain in through the treble stitches and through the collar, make tassels at the ends, and the jacket will be finished.

LADY'S VEST.
POINT DE CHANTILLY.

THIS is a warm, comfortable vest worked in tricot. the stitch being a pretty variation of the ordinary tricot stitch. Procure 12 ozs. of white Peacock fingering, and a No. 8 bone tricot needle. Begin for the bottom of the vest with a chain of 99 stitches. **1st row**—Insert the hook in the second chain from the needle, raise a loop, and work a chain stitch in it, then raise a loop in the next stitch and work a chain in that, and so on to the end of the row, keeping all the chain stitches on the needle ; to work back, draw the wool through the last stitch, and then through 2 stitches together, until all are worked off. **2nd row** —1 chain to begin, insert the hook in the first perpendicular loop and also in the thread at the back of it, raise a loop, and work a chain stitch in it, * insert the hook in the next perpendicular loop and also in the thread at the back of it, raise a loop, and work a chain stitch in it, repeat from *, keeping all the chain stitches on the needle, and work them off the same as before. Every succeeding row is worked the same as the second row. Decrease a stitch at the beginning and at the end of the seventh row. This is done by picking up 2 stitches together of the previous row. Repeat these 7 rows, decreasing again in the seventh row. Work 6 rows, and decrease again at the beginning and at the end

Lady's Vest. Point de Chantilly.

of the last of these Repeat these 6 rows, again decreasing in the sixth row Then work 5 rows four times, decreasing in every fifth row. Then 4 rows three times, decreasing in every fourth row. Then work 4 rows. There are now 62 rows done, and it is time to begin the sleeves, which are worked all in the piece. **63rd row**—Increase a stitch at the beginning and a stitch at the end of the row. In the next and following rows increase 2 stitches on each side until there are 114 stitches in the row. Then work 9 rows on these 114 stitches. Now for the shoulder work 49 stitches only, and draw back. Do 9 rows decreasing in each row at the neck end. Then do 5 rows without further decrease, and fasten off Leave 16 stitches in the middle for the neck. On the other side work 49 stitches to correspond for the other shoulder. This completes the front. Commence again with 99 chain, and work a similar piece for the back of the vest. Sew up the two sides and join the shoulder pieces together. Finish round the neck and sleeves with an edging ; thus, 1 double crochet in one stitch of the tricot, 5 treble in the next.

PETTICOAT WITH BODICE FOR CHILD OF TWO.

PROCURE 4 ozs. of white and 2 ozs. of ruby Scotch fingering wool, and a long tricot needle No. 7. With white wool commence with 200 chain for the bottom of the petticoat. Pick up each stitch of the chain as in ordinary tricot, and draw back in the usual manner. Work another row with white wool. Then 2 rows with ruby and 2 rows with white. 7th row—With ruby. 8th row—Also with ruby, pick up 20 stitches (with the first stitch already on the needle, this makes 21 stitches on now), pick up 2 together, 21 stitches, 2 together, 12 stitches, 2 together, 21 stitches, 2 together, 34 stitches, 2 together, 21 stitches, 2 together, 12 stitches, 2 together, 21 stitches, 2 together, 21 stitches, and draw back as usual. Work 2 rows with white, 192 stitches in each row. Then 2 rows with ruby. 13th row—With white. 14th row—Also with white, pick up 19 stitches, 2 together, 20 stitches, 2 together, 12 stitches, 2 together, 20 stitches, 2 together, 32 stitches, 2 together, 20 stitches, 2 together, 12 stitches, 2 together, 20 stitches, 2 together, 20 stitches, and draw back. Work 2 rows with ruby. 17th row—With white. 18th row—Also with white, pick up 18 stitches, 2 together, 19 stitches, 2 together, 12 stitches, 2 together, 19 stitches, 2 together, 30 stitches, 2 together, 19 stitches, 2 together, 12 stitches, 2 together, 19 stitches, 2 together, 19 stitches, and draw back. Work 2 rows with ruby. 21st row—With white. 22nd row—Also with white, pick up 17 stitches, 2 together, 18 stitches, 2 together, 12 stitches, 2 together, 18 stitches, 2 together, 28 stitches, 2 together, 18 stitches, 2 together, 12 stitches, 2 together, 18 stitches, 2 together, 18 stitches, and draw back. Work 2 rows with ruby. The remainder of the petticoat is worked entirely with white. In the 26th row decrease 8 times in the row in a straight line above the previous decreasings, and at the end of the drawing back work 8 chain to make a "lap"

row—5 chain to turn, 2 treble under each chain stitch of last row, 1 treble on the last of the long treble stitches, 1 treble on each of the two next treble stitches 2 treble under the 3 chain, 3 chain, 2 more treble in the same place. 4th row —5 chain to turn, 2 treble under the three chain of last row, 3 chain, 2 more treble in the same place, 1 double crochet on each stitch to the end of the row, making 21 double crochet in all. 5th row—1 chain to turn, double crochet on every double crochet of last row and on two treble stitches, inserting the hook so as to take up the back threads of last row, 2 treble under the three chain, 3 chain, 2 more treble in the same place. 6th row—5 chain to turn, 2 treble under the three chain of last row, 3 chain, 2 more treble in the same place, 3 chain, miss one stitch, 1 double crochet on the next, 5 chain and 1 double crochet on each alternate stitch to the end of the row. 7th row—6 chain to turn, 1 double crochet under first loop of five chain of last row, 5 chain, 1 double crochet under next loop of five chain, and continue 5 chain 1 double crochet under every loop round the scallop, then 3 chain, 2 treble under the three chain. 3 chain, 3 more treble in the same place. 8th row—5 chain to turn, 2 treble under the three chain of last row, 3 chain, 3 more treble in the same place. 9th row—5 chain to turn, 2 treble under the three chain of last row, 3 chain, 2 more treble in the same place. Repeat from the second row for the length required, and to make the scallops sit nicely catch at the end of the 2nd, 4th, and 6th rows by a single crochet stitch into a chain loop of preceding scallop. Twenty scallops will be a sufficient length to go round the neck of a chemise and eight scallops for each sleeve. The top is done when you have crocheted the length required, it is as follows: 1st row—2 treble under loop of five chain that turned, * 5 chain, 2 treble under the next loop, and repeat from *. 2nd row— 1 treble on the second treble of last row, 4 treble under the 5 chain and repeat to the end. 3rd row—1 treble on first treble stitch of last row, * 2 chain, miss 2 stitches, 1 treble on the next, and repeat from *. Run a narrow ribbon in and

Petticoat with Bodice for Child of Two.

Chemise Trimming.

Gentleman's Waistcoat.

underneath the placket hole. Beginning next row on the "lap," work 3 rows of plain tricot. Next row decrease again. Continue thus decreasing every fourth row till in the 46th row you pick up 12 stitches between each decrease, excepting in the front where there will be 16 stitches. Decrease again in the 48th row. Now the petticoat is reduced to 120 stitches for the waist. Work 30 rows on the 120 stitches; this brings you to the armhole. For the first half of the back, pick up 32 stitches, work 16 rows, and fasten off; pick up the last 12 stitches and work 8 rows thereon for a shoulder-strap, and fasten off. Miss six stitches from where you divided for the armhole, pick up 50 stitches for the front, and work 16 rows; then for the shoulder-strap pick up 11 stitches (one already on the needle makes 12), on which work 8 rows, and fasten off; pick up the last 12 stitches for another shoulder-strap, work 8 rows, and fasten off. Miss six stitches from the division for the armhole, pick up thence to the end, 26 stitches, and work 16 rows; then for the shoulder-strap pick up 11 stitches, on which work 8 rows, and fasten off. Sew up the shoulder pieces, and join the back of the skirt as far as the additional eight stitches for the "lap," sew these under the right-hand side. Work a row of single crochet round the neck and shoulders, and down the right-hand side of the placket hole, also round the armholes. And round the neck and armholes and bottom of the skirt work an edge thus: 1 double crochet into a stitch of the single crochet, * 2 chain, 2 treble on the double crochet, miss a stitch of the single, 1 double crochet on the next, and repeat from *. Sew five or six buttons down the back of the bodice, and on the opposite side work buttonholes with a rug needle.

CHEMISE TRIMMING.

THIS is worked with Evans' crochet cotton, No. 16, and a fine steel crochet needle. Commence with 7 chain, work 2 treble in the first of these chain stitches, 3 chain, 2 more treble in the same place. 2nd row—5 chain, turn the work, 2 treble under the three chain of last row, 3 chain, 2 more treble in the same place, then 9 long treble into the next hole with 1 chain between each. 3rd

out through the first row of this heading, tying it in a pretty bow in the front and on the top of the sleeves.

GENTLEMAN'S WAISTCOAT.

To make this warm, comfortably fitting waistcoat, procure 10 ozs. of double Berlin wool, brown, or any colour preferred, and a No. 7 bone crochet needle, or No. 8 for a small size. The work is plain double crochet forwards and backwards, turning at the end of every row, and inserting the hook so as to take up the two top threads of the stitches of the preceding row. Begin for the front with 46 chain, and work 3 rows of double crochet, 45 stitches in each row. 4th row—Which commences at the neck end—Increase a stitch at the beginning by working 2 double crochet in the first stitch. 5th row—Increase a stitch at the end. Repeat these two rows till 11 rows are done. 12th row— Decrease a stitch at the end. 13th row—Increase at the end. Repeat the last two rows till 22 rows are done. Then decrease at the end of every row till 31 rows are done. 32nd row—Work only 8 double crochet turn, and decrease a stitch at the end of each little row till all are worked off. Break off the wool And leaving 12 stitches for the armhole, double crochet thence on the remaining stitches for three rows; then work 14 stitches from the bottom, turn, and work back; next row work all up to the armhole. This completes one front. Commence with 46 chain for the other front, and in the second row of this make buttonholes thus: 4 double crochet, * 1 chain, miss 1, 5 double crochet, and repeat from *. Next row double crochet all along, and proceed, shaping the same as the front already done. For the Back—Work 60 chain, and do 5 rows of double crochet from end to end; then decrease at the end of the next row and every alternate row till 16 rows are done. Then decrease at the end of every row till 25 rows are done. Finish off the shoulder, and work the rows under the arm the same as directed for the front of the coat. Then re-commence on the 60 chain, and work the other half of the back to correspond. Sew up the shoulders, and sew under the arms, leaving about three inches open at the bottom. Bind the whole with mohair braid, and place two rows of buttons down the front.

HAND-BAG.

FOR this useful bag procure 6 ozs. of Macramé twine, a bone crochet needle, No. 8, and a yard of 2-inch wide dark green ribbon. Commence for the bottom of the bag with 4 chain, turn, and work 3 double crochet, and turn, and working into both top threads of the stitches of last row, do double crochet, increasing a stitch at the end of every row till 11 stitches are attained, then work 14 rows forwards and backwards on the 11 stitches, and afterwards decrease a stitch at the end of every row till brought to 3 double crochet again. This forms the base or foundation; fasten off. Now catch the thread into the tenth row of the foundation, and work for the sides in point neige stitch; beginning with 3 chain, raise a loop in the second of the chain stitches, raise a loop in the first chain stitch, another in the place you caught the thread into, and raise 2 more loops in the foundation. There will be 6 stitches on the needle, draw through all, 1 chain, * raise a loop in the thread that lies under the chain, another in the lower thread at the back of the group, another in the same stitch as the group is worked into, and 2 more along the foundation, draw the thread through all, 1 chain, and repeat from *. Continue this stitch round and round till 10 rounds are done. Then work 1 chain, 1 treble all round to make a series of holes in which to run the ribbon. Then finish off with a round of plain double crochet, and having joined the last double crochet stitch neatly to the first, make a length of 45 chain for a handle, catch the thread into a double crochet stitch on the same side of the bag, and an equal distance from the end, and crochet back on it 45 single crochet, and fasten off. Make a similar handle on the opposite side of the bag. Cut the ribbon in two pieces, and run it through the holes in such a manner that you can tie a nice bow on each side of the bag.

with a row of single crochet, inserting the hook below the margin of the treble stitches; also with a rug needle work a scarlet long stitch upon each of the treble stitches. Next sew up the back of the leg and the under part of the sole. With the rug needle and with scarlet wool work a row of cross stitches below the row of holes, and also do 3 rows of cross stitches down the front of the leg, stopping at the instep, where place a ribbon rosette with a steel ornament in the centre. Run ribbon through the holes round the leg, and tie in a pretty bow in front.

SOFA BLANKET.

THIS warm, useful sofa blanket is composed of squares of fancy tricot, worked with 2 good contrasting colours, the squares being joined together in process of working the open crochet that surrounds each square. Procure an equal quantity of fawn and of blue double Berlin wool, and a bone tricot needle No. 7. Begin with blue wool with 17 chain. **1st row**—Pick up each stitch of the chain as for ordinary tricot, and draw back in the usual manner. **2nd row**—Bring the wool to the right of the needle, pass it round the outer edge of the tricot, and along the front of the stitch on the needle, and under the hook towards the back and draw the wool through the stitch on the needle, * bring the wool to the front of the work, insert the hook in the next perpendicular tricot stitch of last row, pass the wool to the front and under the hook and draw the wool through the stitch, repeat from * to the end of the row, and draw back as usual. Work every row the same as the second row till the tricot forms a perfect square. Then do a row of single crochet all round the square, the same number of stitches

Hand-Bag.

Baby's Long Boots.

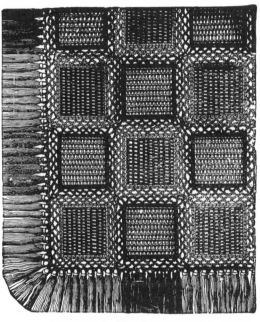

Sofa Blanket.

BABY'S LONG BOOTS.

REQUIRED, 2 ozs. of best white and ½ oz. of scarlet Scotch fingering, a bone tricot needle, No. 9, and 1½ yards of ¾-inch wide scarlet ribbon for trimming. Commence with white wool with 36 chain. **1st row**—Pick up all the stitches as in ordinary tricot and draw back. **2nd row**—Bring the wool in front under the needle, insert the hook in the perpendicular loop of tricot, put the wool back under the hook and draw wool through the stitch as usual, proceed to the end of the row in this manner, 36 stitches on the needle, and draw back. Work 6 rows thus. Then 3 rows, decreasing 1 stitch at the beginning and 1 stitch at the end of each row. Then 5 rows with 30 stitches in each row, always keeping to the fancy stitch as detailed in the second row. **Next row** work 12 stitches, increase 2 by pulling up two stitches before the next loop of tricot, work 6 stitches, increase 2, work 12 stitches, and draw back. Increase in this manner in every row, keeping always 6 stitches in the centre between the increasings, till you have 66 stitches on the needle, and draw back. **Next row** decrease a stitch at the beginning and a stitch at the end; and then to shape the sole of the foot do 3 rows decreasing at the beginning and end and also at each side of the 6 centre stitches, and break off the wool. For the **top** of the **Boot—1st row**—To make the row of holes in which to run a ribbon, insert the hook in the first stitch of the commencing chain, draw the wool through and * work 8 chain, miss 1 of the foundation, 1 single crochet in each of the 2 next stitches, and repeat from *; break off wool at end of the row. **2nd row**—Work same as the second row of the boot, picking up the 4 centre stitches of every loop of 8 chain, making in all 36 stitches on the needle, and draw back. Work 2 more rows. Then miss 3 stitches each side for 2 more rows. Next row work all 36 stitches again. Then for the last row work a scallop, 6 treble in the second stitch of tricot, miss 1, 1 double crochet in the next, and repeat. With scarlet wool edge this last row

on each side. **1st row** of the open border—Work 1 double crochet on the corner stitch of the square, 4 chain, another double crochet in the same place, * 4 chain, miss three, 1 double crochet on the next, and repeat from * to the corner, where work 2 double crochet with 4 chain between as at the first corner and proceed the same along each side of the square. **2nd row**—1 double crochet under the corner loop of four chain, 4 chain, another double crochet in the same place, 4 chain, 1 double crochet under the next loop of four chain, and continue the same all round, doing an extra loop of chain at each corner. Break off, and fasten off the wool. Work the next square in the same manner, but using fawn wool. When doing the last open round, place this square in proper position beside the square already done—by reference to the engraving it will be seen the tricot lies lengthways in one square and widthways in the next—where the squares touch catch from each 4 chain loop of this (when on the second chain of the four) to a corresponding loop of the other square.

WAISTCOAT IN TRICOTEE.

REQUIRED, 10 ozs. of black 3-thread fleecy wool or double Berlin, and a long bone tricot needle, No. 8. Commence with a chain of 66 stitches or as many as are required to make the width of one of the front pieces, measuring from a cloth waistcoat. Pick up each stitch in succession and work back in the ordinary manner, and continue in plain tricotee row by row till you have a length of 24 inches. Work the other front similarly. Send to a tailor to be made up. A pretty variation is to use wool of two colours, say black and violet, or brown and navy, and work alternately a row with each, not breaking off the wool at the completion of the rows, but carrying it on from one alternate row to the next.

ANTIMACASSAR STRIPE OF PLAIN AND TUFTED TRICOT.

With Cornflower Crewel Worked in the Centre.

Required, ½ lb of blue and ½ lb. of white single Berlin wool, a bone tricot needle No. 9, and a skein of white filoselle and two shades of b'ue. Use white wool for the centre stripe, beginning with 21 chain, and work all plain tricot, 21 stitches in every row, for the length desired ; on this embroider the cornflower spray as shown in the illustration. The narrow stripes are worked with blue wool, commencing with 10 chain, do 2 rows of plain tricot 10 stitches in a row. **3rd row**—Pick up the stitches as usual, and coming back draw through 3, work 4 chain draw through 2, 4 chain, draw through 5. **4th row**—Pick up as usual, and coming back draw through 4, work 4 chain, draw through 6. **5th row**—Same as the third row. **6th row**—Plain tricot. **7th row**—Pick up the stitches, and coming back draw through 6, work 4 chain, draw through 2, work 4 chain, draw through 2. **8th row**—Pick up as usual, and coming back draw through 7, work 4 chain, draw through 3. **9th row**—Same as the seventh row. **10th row**—Plain tricot. Repeat from the third row for the length required. In each space between the tufts work a leviathan cross stitch with white filoselle. Make another stripe of blue tricot and sew them stitch by stitch on each side of the white stripe. Then continue a white stripe and a blue one for the width of the antimacassar. Strengthen each outside edge with a row of chain stitches worked as single crochet on the margin of the tricot. Fringe each stripe with its own colour, two strands of wool together, and placing 3 fringes in each blue and 6 fringes in each white stripe, and make a heading of two rows of knots.

CURTAIN BAND.

The rosettes of this curtain band are graduated in size ; the largest, which is in the centre, has twelve points, the next ten and the other two have eight points each. Procure ecru or navy blue crochet cotton, Evans' No. 2, or corresponding size in any other make, and a steel crochet needle No. 18. Commence for the largest rosette with 12 chain, join round, and work 24 double crochet in the circle, join ; 13 chain, 1 treble in the fourth from the needle and 4 more treble in next consecutive stitches, 4 double crochet, 1 single crochet ; turn, 1 chain, 5 double crochet on five first stitches of last row, 2 treble in each of the next four stitches, 3 long treble in the last stitch ; turn, 1 chain, 1 double crochet on the first stitch, * 3 chain, 1 double crochet in the same stitch as last double crochet is worked into, 1 double crochet on each of the three next stitches, repeat from * four times, 1 single crochet on the last stitch, join to the next stitch but one on the circle, and work 11 more points like this point ; break off the cotton. To keep the points lying in place one over the other, work at the back of the rosette 1 double crochet under the chain stitch at the turn of the first row, 5 chain, 1 double crochet under the same chain stitch of the next point, and repeat; break off the cotton. Now outside the rosette work 1 double crochet under the loop of three chain at the corner of a point, 11 chain, 1 double crochet under the three chain at the corner of the next point, and so on, and join round ; next round, 1 double crochet in each stitch of previous round, and 3 double crochet in the centre stitch of the eleven chain. Work two rosettes commencing with 10 chain for the circle, in which work 20 double crochet, and finish off the same as the rosette already done, but making only ten points. Work four rosettes commencing with 8 chain, doing 16 double crochet in the circle, and making eight points ; two of these rosettes are edged the same as the large one, and two have 1 double crochet 9 chain worked from point to point on *five* points, leaving three points loose. Sew the rosettes together in a row, the largest in the centre, and the loose points at either end. **For the Border**—Begin on the middle one of the three loose points, work 3 treble, 4 chain, 3 treble, all under the three chain at the corner, 4 chain, 3 treble, all under the three chain at the corner of the next point, 9 chain 1 double crochet at the top of the rosette in the same double crochet where you began the chain that edges the rosette, 8 chain, 1 treble, 1 long treble, 1 double long treble, all on the stitch

at the top of the next point, 1 double long treble, 1 long treble, 1 treble, all on the seventeenth double crochet *before* the centre of the top of the next rosette, 4 chain, miss three, 3 treble on three next consecutive stitches, 8 chain, 1 double crochet on centre stitch of the rosette, 8 chain, miss twelve, 1 treble, 1 long treble, 1 double long treble on the next three consecutive stitches, and 1 double long treble, 1 long treble and 1 treble on three consecutive stitches of the third rosette, 8 chain, 1 double crochet on centre stitch of the three double crochet, 9 chain, 1 double crochet on centre stitch of the next three double crochet, 8 chain, miss eight, 1 long treble on the next, 4 chain, miss four, 1 double long treble on centre stitch of the next three double crochet, 1 treble long treble on centre stitch of three double crochet of next rosette, 5 chain, miss four, 1 double long treble on the next, 4 chain, 1 treble on centre stitch of next three double crochet, 9 chain, 1 double crochet on centre stitch of the next three double crochet ; this is the exact centre of the band, work to the end corresponding to this beginning, turn round the last rosette, and work the other side in the same way. **2nd row**—1 treble on every stitch of last row. **3rd row**—Begin with 20 chain for the button-hole loop at the end, 1 single crochet in the eighth from the needle, and work 2 double crochet in each stitch of the little circle and 12 treble along the remaining chain stitches ; then on to the previous row work 6 consecutive double crochet, 5 chain, and repeat all round ; when at the other end work another button-hole loop like that at the beginning.

BASSINETTE COVER.
Shell Pattern.

To be worked with white and pink single Berlin wool and rather fine bone crochet needle. Commence for the first shell with white wool, with 2 chain, turn, and do 3 double crochet in the first of the chain ; turn the work, and inserting the hook so as to take up the back thread of the stitches of preceding row that the shell may sit in ridges, work 1 double crochet in the first stitch, 3 double crochet in the centre stitch, and 1 double crochet in the last stitch; turn the work ; do 1 double crochet in each of the first two stitches, 3 double crochet in the centre stitch, 1 double crochet in each of the last two stitches ; turn the work, and now do 3 consecutive double crochet, 3 double crochet in the centre stitch, and 3 more consecutive double crochet ; and so on, always increasing in the centre stitch till you can count five ridges on each side of the shell. Then work a pink shell in the same manner. And proceed till you have done a sufficiency of each colour. Join the shells in such a way that the commencement of a shell comes always on the increased point of the shell beneath, pink above white, and white above pink. Half shells will be required to fit in round the outside. When the margin is straight border the cover with r pretty edging or knotted fringe.

CROCHET FRINGE.

This is intended to be produced with cotton to border quilts, toilet-covers, tray-cloths, &c., and it may either be worked round and round upon the article itself, or commenced on a foundation chain of the length required; if the latter break off at the end of every row and re-commence on the right-hand side. **1st row**—1 treble, * 2 chain, miss 2 stitches of the foundation, 1 treble in the next, and repeat from *. **2nd row**—3 treble under the first loop of two chain, * miss the next loop, 3 treble in the next, and repeat from *. **3rd row**—1 double crochet on the centre stitch of the first group of 3 treble of last row, * 3 chain, 1 treble on the first stitch of the next group of treble, 2 chain, another treble in the same place, 2 chain, 1 treble on the centre treble stitch, 2 chain, 1 treble on the third treble stitch, 2 chain, another treble in the same place, 3 chain, 1 double crochet on the centre stitch of the next group of three treble, and repeat from *. **4th row**—1 double crochet on the double crochet of last row, 3 chain, 1 treble under the first loop of two chain, 3 chain. 1 treble under the next loop, 3 chain, 1 treble on the centre treble stitch of last row, 3 chain, 1 treble under the next loop of two chain, 3 chain, 1 treble under the next loop, 3 chain, and repeat. **5th row**—1 double crochet under the second loop of three chain, * 5 chain, 1 double crochet under the next loop of three chain, do from * twice more, 3 chain, miss the next two loops of last row (those on each side of the double crochet stitch), 1 double crochet under the next, and repeat from *. Now cut a skein of cotton into lengths of 7 inches, and knot 7 threads together in each loop of five chain.

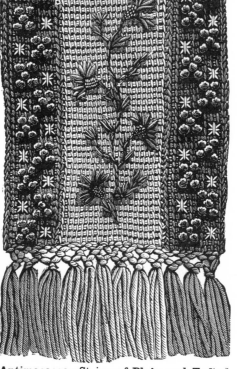

Antimacassar Stripe of Plain and Tufted Tricot.

Curtain Band.

INSERTION.

COMMENCE with chain sufficient for the length required. **1st row**—1 treble, * 2 chain, miss two of the foundation, 1 treble in the next, and repeat from * to the end of the row. **2nd row**—1 treble on the first chain stitch of last row, * 2 chain, 1 treble on the first of the next two chain stitches of last row, and repeat from *. **3rd row**—1 treble on the first chain stitch of last row, * 2 chain, 1 double crochet and 1 treble both on the treble just done, 1 treble on the first of the next two chain stitches, and repeat from *. Repeat the same three rows on the other side of the commencing chain

VENETIAN CAP.

REQUIRED, 1½ ozs. of rose colour and ½ oz. of white single Berlin wool. A bone crochet needle No. 8. Commence with rose colour with 84 chain; join round. **1st round**—3 chain to stand for a treble, * 1 chain, miss 1 stitch of the foundation, 1 treble in the next, and repeat from *; join at the end of this and every round, and *turn* the work so that the right side of the succeeding round comes to the wrong side of the round last done. **2nd round**—1 treble, 1 chain alternately, the trebles being over the treble stitches of last round. **3rd round**—The same. **4th round**—All treble, making 84 treble in the round. **5th round**—All treble, and decrease 6 times in the round, inserting the hook so as to take up every 13th and 14th stitch together, so working 1 treble over 2. **6th round**—Treble, and again decrease 6 times in the round between the decreasings of last round. **7th round**—The same, 66 treble. **8th round**—The same, 60 treble. **9th round**—The same, 54 treble. **10th round**—Decrease 8 times in the round. **11th round**—The same, 38 treble. **12th round**—The same, 30 treble. **13th round**—1 long treble on

of 7 loops, and repeat; join at end of the round and break off the wool. **6th round**—Take the white wool and work as described for the second round. **7th round**—With white wool, same as the third round, and this finishes the cap. Fold the Beehive pattern upon the cap like a band, and tack it in place; make a daisy tuft with strands of white wool and affix to the point of the cap bending this over the side of the cap to meet the band, just a stitch will keep it in place.

DRAPE FOR BRACKET, OR MANTEL BORDER.

REQUIRED, a ball of brown Macramé thread, a piece of inch-wide peacock-blue ribbon twice the length the piece of work is intended to be, and a No. 12 crochet needle. Commence with 20 chain. **1st row**—2 treble in the eighth chain from the needle, 3 chain, 2 more treble in the same place, 4 chain, miss four, 2 treble in the next, 3 chain, 2 more treble in the same place, 4 chain, miss four, 2 treble in the next, 3 chain, 2 more treble in the same place, 4 chain, turn the work. **2nd row**—2 treble under the three chain of last row, 3 chain, 2 more treble in the same place, 4 chain, 2 treble under the next three chain of last row, 3 chain 2 more treble in the same place, 4 chain, 2 treble under the next three chain of last row, 3 chain, 2 more treble in the same place, 4 chain. turn the work. **3rd row**—Same as the second row. **4th row**—Same as the second row. **5th row**—2 treble under the three chain of last row. 3 chain, 2 more treble in the same place, 4 chain, 1 double crochet over the bars of four chain of the last two rows, 4 chain, 2 treble under the next three chain of last row, 3 chain, 2 more treble in the same place, 4 chain, 1 double crochet over the bars of two previous rows, 4 chain, 2 treble under the next three chain of last row, 3 chain, 2 more treble in the same place, 4 chain, turn the work. Repeat from the second row till 10 rows are done. Then for the scallop, after doing 4 chain, work 1 double crochet under the loop of four chain along the *side* of the

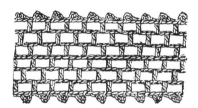

Insertion.

Full-size Working Design of Rosette for Curtain Band.

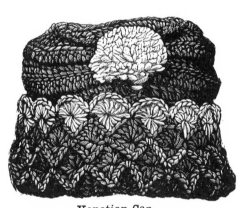

Venetian Cap.

Drape for Bracket, or Mantel Border.

every 2 treble of last round, making 15 long treble; break off the wool, and with a rug needle secure the top of the stitches together in a circle. Next, still with rose colour, work a round of treble stitches, 84, along the opposite side of the foundation chain. And for the Border, which is in Beehive stitch, work for the **1st round**—Holding the round of treble stitches the right side towards you, 1 double crochet on the first treble, miss 1 on the next, miss 1, and repeat, and join at the end of the round. **2nd round**—In this round each time of inserting the needle, put the hook in from back to front at the right-hand side of the treble stitch of last round, and bring it out from front to back at the left hand of the same treble stitch, so having the treble stitch itself upon the needle, draw the wool through in rather a loose loop or stitch; do 4 chain to stand for the first loop, then take up a loop as described in each of the 3 first treble stitches of last round, wool over the needle and draw through 4 stitches on the needle, 1 chain to tighten the group, 1 double crochet on the centre 1 of the 7 trebles of last round, raise 7 loops in the manner described above in the 7 next consecutive stitches, wool over the needle and draw through the 8 stitches on the needle, 1 chain, and repeat from *, and raise 3 loops at the end of the round to match the beginning, and join round. **3rd round**—Do 3 chain to stand for a treble, work 3 treble in chain stitch at junction of the round, 1 double crochet on double crochet of last round, * 7 treble on the chain stitch that unites the bunch of seven loops of last round, 1 double crochet on the next double crochet of last round, and repeat from *, do 3 treble at the end to correspond with the beginning, and join round. **4th round**—Work 1 double crochet on the chain stitch into which you have just joined, * raise 7 loops in the next 7 consecutive stitches, wool over the needle and draw through the 8 stitches on the needle, 1 chain, 1 double crochet on the centre 1 of the group of 7 trebles, and repeat from *, and join at the end of the round. **5th round**—1 double crochet on double crochet of last round 7 treble on the chain stitch that unites the bunch

work, 9 chain, 1 double crochet under the next loop of 4 chain, 9 chain, 1 double crochet under next loop of four chain, 9 chain, 1 double crochet under next loop of four chain, turn the work, 14 double crochet under the first loop of 9 chain, 7 double crochet under the next loop of nine chain. 9 chain, turn the hook in front of the work, and do a single crochet between the seventh and eighth double crochet stitches and 14 double crochet under this loop of nine chain, 7 double crochet in the same loop where seven double crochet are already worked, 7 double crochet under the next loop of nine chain, 9 chain, turn the hook in front of the work and do a single crochet between the seventh and eighth double crochet, then 7 double crochet under the nine chain just done, 9 chain, turn the hook in front of the work and do a single crochet between the seventh and eighth double crochet of last loop, then 14 double crochet under this loop of nine chain, 7 double crochet to fill up the next loop, and 7 more double crochet in the next loop; now 5 chain, turn the work, 1 treble on the third double crochet stitch, * 1 chain. miss one, 1 treble on the next, and repeat from * till 21 treble stitches are worked, 3 chain, 1 single crochet under the loop of four chain, turn the work, 5 chain, 1 single in the fourth chain from the needle, 1 chain, 1 treble on the first treble stitch of last row, * 5 chain, 1 single in the fourth chain from the needle, 1 chain, 1 treble on the next treble of last row, and repeat from *, making 22 treble stitches in all; 3 chain, 1 double crochet on the first treble stitch of the heading; 2 chain, 2 treble under the three chain of the tenth row. 3 chain two more treble in the same place, and continue the heading the same as before till another 10 rows are done, when you proceed with the working of the second scallop. Three scallops will be sufficient for a bracket; to make the commencement look the same as the last row work 1 row of the heading pattern reversely into the foundation chain. Cut the ribbon into two pieces and run it in and out through the heading in the manner shown in the illustration. sewing it firmly at the ends.

CHILD'S MUFF IN TUFTED TREBLE STITCH.

REQUIRED, 1½ ozs. of creamy-white Andalusian wool, a bone crochet needle No. 9, a piece of satin or fine flannel for lining, a layer of wadding, and 1 yard of cream satin ribbon for a bow. Commence with 32 chain, worked not too tightly, for the length of the muff; then 1 treble in the third chain from the needle, and 5 long treble (wool turned twice round the needle), and another treble in the same place; now take out the hook, insert it in the first treble, then take up again the stitch you have just let go, and draw it through the first treble stitch rather tightly, keeping the long treble stitches in a tuft to the front, 1 chain, miss one stitch of the foundation, in the next foundation chain work another tuft of 7 stitches in the same way, 1 chain, and continue to the end, making 15 tufts of trebles in all, with a chain stitch between each. Fasten off at the end of the row, and recommence on the right-hand side. The work is the same throughout, the tufts henceforward being under the chain stitch of preceding row. There should be 14 tufts in the second row, 15 tufts in the third row, and so on. Proceed till 19 rows are done. Then sew up the last row to the first. Put in the wadding and line the muff, and make a pretty wide bow to place over the join

LEWIS POINT PATTERN.

THIS stitch may be worked either in stripes or lengthways; if for an antimacassar the former is preferable, and the stripes should be of two good contrasting colours. Procure double Berlin wool, and a bone crochet needle No. 6, and com-

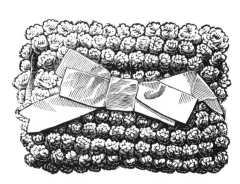

Child's Muff in Tufted Treble Stitch.

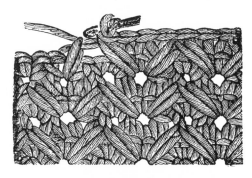

Lewis Point Pattern.

Bell-Pull.

mence with 13, 16, or 19 chain, in which work 1 row of plain double crochet: do not break off the wool, but *turn* at the end of this and every row. **2nd row**—2 double crochet, insert the hook in the first stitch of the commencing chain, and draw the wool up in a long loop loosely, insert the hook in the fourth stitch of the commencing chain, and draw up another long loop, wool over the needle, and draw through the 3 stitches on the needle, then 3 double crochet above three double crochet of last row, * insert the hook in the same place where the last looped stitch is worked and draw up the wool loosely, insert the hook in the fourth stitch of the commencing chain to the left hand and draw the wool up loosely, wool over the needle, and draw through the 3 stitches on the needle, 3 double crochet, and repeat from *, there will be 2 double crochet at the end of the row the same as at the beginning. **3rd row**—Plain double crochet. **4th row** is worked exactly the same as the second row, and to draw up the long loops which form the "points" you insert the hook in the double crochet stitches of the second row. **5th row**—Plain double crochet. Repeat thus for the length required, being careful to keep the "points" exactly in straight line one above the other.

BELL-PULL.

THIS is worked with medium-sized macramé thread, of which about two balls will be required if the pull is to be a long one. Use a No. 12 crochet needle, steel if procurable, if not a bone one will do. Begin with 16 chain. Work 3

treble in the sixth chain from the needle, 2 chain, 3 more treble in the same place, 3 chain, miss four, 3 treble in the next, 2 chain, 3 more treble in the same place, catch with a single crochet into the last stitch of foundation chain; * 5 chain, turn the work, 3 treble under the two chain of last row, 2 chain, 3 more treble in the same place, 3 chain, 3 treble under the next two chain of last row, 2 chain, 3 more treble in the same place; 5 chain, turn the work, 3 treble under the two chain of last row, 2 chain, 3 more treble in the same place, 3 chain, 3 treble under the next two chain of last row, 2 chain, 3 more treble in the same place; 5 chain, turn the work, 3 treble under the two chain of last row, 2 chain, 3 more treble in the same place, 3 chain, place hook under the three chain of the second row and work a double crochet, 3 chain, 3 treble under the next two chain of last row, 2 chain, 3 more treble in the same place; 5 chain, turn the work, 3 treble under the two chain of last row, 2 chain, 3 more treble in the same place, 3 chain, 2 treble under the next two chain of last row, 2 chain, 3 more treble in the same place; and repeat from * for the length required. Run an inch-wide ribbon in and out through the centre of the crochet, securing it at top and bottom. Cut eighteen threads ten inches long and knot three fringes in three holes of the foundation chain. The other end of the pull is to be fastened to the bell wire.

FASCINATOR.

THIS pretty fascinator is intended to be worn folded corner-ways, the corners to come on the top of the head to the front, the ends tie under the chin or pass round the neck. Procure 2½ ozs. of white Shetland wool, and a No. 10 bone

Fascinator.

crochet needle. Make a chain of 100 stitches, and work 3 treble into every third stitch. **Next row**—3 chain to turn, 3 treble in every space. Every succeeding row is the same as this last row. Continue till 52 rows are done or till your work forms a perfect square, then turn with three chain and work 3 groups of 3 treble stitches forwards and backwards for 36 rows, and break off wool. At the opposite corner in the chain stitches at the turning of the rows work 3 groups of 3 treble stitches, and complete another end of 36 rows to correspond. For **Border** all round the square and end, work **1st row**—4 treble into one space, 1 treble into the next space, and repeat, putting 6 treble at the corners. **2nd round**—4 treble in between the second and third trebles of last round, 1 treble on the previous one treble, and repeat, putting 8 treble at the corners. **3rd round**—8 treble in between the second and third trebles of last round, 1 chain, 1 treble on the previous one treble, 1 chain, and repeat, putting 10 treble at the corners. Now make little daisy tufts by winding wool about thirty times round a blacklead pencil, and sewing tightly with a needle and cotton, cut and trim to shape, and sew one tuft on the point of every scallop round the square, not round the ends.

LADY'S SHOULDER CAPE.

Point Battenberg.

THIS is a lovely raised pattern, and the cape is suitable either for wearing to the opera or for general use, according to the material employed. Our model is worked with white double Berlin wool, of which 1 lb. will be required, and a bone crochet needle, No. 8. Commence with 49 chain for the front of the cape. **1st row**—1 double crochet in the second chain from the needle ; insert the hook in the next stitch, draw the wool through, work 6 chain, wool over the needle, and draw through the two stitches on the needle, 1 double crochet on the next stitch of the foundation, a point on the next, and so on, and there will be 24 double crochet stitches, and 24 points in the row. Fasten off at the end of this and every row, and recommence on the right-hand side, which is the top of the cape. **2nd row**—1 double crochet on the first double crochet of last row, inserting the hook so as to take up the two top threads ; insert the hook under the loop of six chain and work a double crochet, and repeat. **3rd row**—1 double crochet on the first double crochet of last row, * 1 double crochet on the next, insert the

crochet under the first one chain of last row, * 1 chain, 1 double crochet under the next one chain of last row, and repeat from *, again making 40 double crochet in the row. Work 10 more rows like the second row. Then increase, by working an additional 1 chain, 1 double crochet at the beginning of every row, till in the 32nd row you do 60 double crochet. Then do 2 rows without increase, and 2 rows with increase till you have done 64 rows and have 76 double crochet in the row. Then increase 1 at the beginning of every row till you have done 90 rows. Do 2 rows without increase, 2 rows with increase ; 2 rows without increase, 2 rows with increase ; and 2 rows without increase, making 100 rows done, and 106 double crochet in the row. Now decrease 1 at the beginning of the next 2 rows, then 2 rows without decrease, and continue thus till the leg is nearly the length required—130 rows or thereabouts ; to slope the back, in the 131st row work 66 double crochet, turn, and work back ; work 48 double crochet, turn, and work back ; work 32 double crochet, turn, and work back ; work 16 double crochet, turn, and work back ; work forwards and back again the whole width of the leg ; break off the wool. This is the left leg. Work for the right leg in the same manner, only

Lady's Shoulder Cape. Point Battenberg.

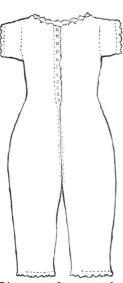

Diagram showing the Shape of Lady's Combination Garment.

hook in the next, draw the wool through, work 6 chain, wool over the needle and draw through the two stitches on the needle, and repeat from *. **4th row**—1 double crochet on each double crochet stitch of last row, and 1 double crochet under each loop of 6 chain. **5th row**—Begin on the double crochet that is worked in the fifth loop of 6 chain, and proceed as in the first row, and there will be 19 double crochet and 19 points in the row. **6th row**—Same as the fourth row. **7th row**—Begin on the double crochet that is worked in the fifth loop of 6 chain, and again work as in the first row, and there will be 15 double crochet and 14 points in the row. **8th row**—Same as the fourth row. **9th row**—Begin above the fifth point of the seventh row, and again work as in the first row, and there will be 10 double crochet and 10 points in the row. **10th row**—Same as the fourth row. **11th row**—Begin above the fifth point next ensuing, and again work as in the first row, and there will be 6 double crochet and 5 points in the row. **12th row**—Same as the fourth row. This finishes the gore. Repeat these twelve rows, and when the half of the cape is attained (which will be three gores for a small size, and four gores for full size), work four rows from the neck to the bottom, and for the rother half proceed reversely—that is, doing the shortest go e rows first. If the cape is for a thin person, the eleventh and twelfth rows may be omitted throughout, and only ten rows worked in a gore. **To finish the Cape**, work a row of plain double crochet up each front and round the neck ; then work a row of scallops thus—1 double crochet on the first stitch of last row, miss one, 5 treble in the next, miss one, and repeat. Cut the remainder of the wool into 6-inch lengths, and knot a fringe in every stitch along the botto n of the cape. Place ribbon strings at the neck, or a button, as preferred.

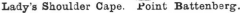

Full-size Working Design of Stitch used for Lady's Combination Garment.

LADY'S COMBINATION GARMENT.

REQUIRED, 1½ lbs. of best white Scotch fingering, and a bone crochet needle No. 13. Commence for the bottom of the leg with 81 chain. **1st row**—1 double crochet in the second stitch from the needle, * 1 chain, miss 1, 1 double crochet in the next, and repeat from *, making 40 double crochet stitches in the row : turn, with 1 chain at the end of this and every row. **2nd row**—1 double

remember the slope of the back has to come reversely to that already done. Now **for the Body**—Beginning at the right-hand front of the right leg. The legs have to be joined together at the back by overlapping 10 stitches of the right leg over 10 stitches of the left leg and crocheting both together. The decreasings are continued up each front, decreasing 1 at the beginning of the first 2 rows, then 2 rows without decrease, till you have done 168 rows in all, and you also decrease twice on the hips in every fourth row, but only *till* the work is the right dimensions for the waist. Begin and end the 168th row with 9 plain double crochet, that is, no chain stitch between these 9 edge stitches, but working a double crochet on the double crochet of last row. In the **169th row**, which should begin on the right-hand front, make a buttonhole thus—3 double crochet, 3 chain, miss 3, 3 double crochet, and proceed in stitch as before. Similar buttonholes are to be formed in every eighth successive row. In the **193rd row** increase twice on each side over the hip, also in the **197th** and **201st rows**. In the **203rd row** divide for the armholes, and work 2 front pieces and one back piece, each for 50 rows ; shape the shoulders in this way, working from the *shoulder* end, do 1 chain, 1 double crochet, thirteen times, turn, and work back : 1 chain, 1 double crochet, ten times, turn, and work back ; 1 chain, 1 double crochet, five times, turn, and work back : break off the wool. Sew up the shoulders. **The Sleeves** are worked in the armhole in the same pattern, 1 chain, 1 double crochet, and joined up afterwards. You begin under the armhole, decrease a stitch at the beginning of each of the first 12 rows, then do 10 rows without decrease. Sew up the round part of the legs, and work a row of double crochet to strengthen the edge along the open part. Work 3 rows of plain double crochet round the neck. **4th row**—For a scalloped edge, work 1 double crochet on double crochet of last row, miss 1, * 1 treble on the next, 1 chain and 1 treble three more times in the same place, miss one, 1 double crochet on the next, miss one, and repeat from *. **5th row**—1 double crochet on the double crochet of last row, 1 chain, 1 double crochet under one chain of last row, 3 chain, 1 double crochet under the next chain stitch, 3 chain, 1 double crochet under the next chain stitch, 1 chain, and repeat. Work these two scalloped rows round the sleeves and round the bottom of the drawers. Sew buttons down the left-hand front of the garment, one button will also be required at the back to keep the "over-lap" in its place.

POKE BONNET FOR A YOUNG CHILD.

THIS charming bonnet is not nearly so difficult of accomplishment as may appear at first sight, and if undertaken by a fairly good worker is sure to be very greatly admired. Materials required, a bonnet shape, 3 yards of pale blue satin ribbon for strings and trimming, a little fine muslin for head lining, 2 ozs. of white single Berlin wool, a crochet needle No. 8, and one No. 10. The brim is crocheted in a variety of Point Muscovite stitch, and the crown is Point Neige. Take the No. 10 crochet needle and begin with 57 chain, or so many as are sufficient to go from ear to ear round the outer rim at the back of the bonnet. **1st row**—1 single crochet in the first stitch from the needle, * insert the hook in the next stitch and do 3 chain, draw the wool through the last of the chain and through the stitch on the needle, 1 single crochet in the next stitch of the

Poke Bonnet for a Young Child.

foundation chain, and repeat from * ; break off the wool at the end of the row. **2nd row**—Re-commence on the right-hand side, work a point stitch over the single crochet and a single crochet over the point stitch of last row, and continue. Proceed in like manner till 5 rows are done, and fasten off. Begin again with 107 chain, or so many as will go round the front of the brim and meet the piece already done, the two pieces being afterwards joined together under the strings, do 9 rows, but at each end of the second and successive rows work one stitch less to decrease to shape. **For the Crown or Head-piece,** use the No 8 crochet needle, and begin with 42 chain for the back of the head. Point neige has already been described in these pages, so a repetition of the manner of procedure is unnecessary. Work as far as the top of the crown, 16 or 17 rows, increasing one stitch at the beginning and at the end of each row ; this done, work to *fit* your bonnet shape, 3 stitches in each row must be decreased on the top of the head, and other stitches decreased where necessary, till you have sufficient done to cover the head of the bonnet. Sew this piece on, stretching it to shape (if cleverly managed, it will fit without a wrinkle) ; sew the Muscovite strips on the brim, making the joins come by the ears. Neatly gather the satin for the lining of the brim, put head lining in in the usual way. Trim the bonnet with a nice looped bow in front ; the strings are brought to meet in a point on the head over the bow.

BABY'S GLOVES.

PROCURE 1 oz. of fawn and ½ oz. of red fingering wool and a bone crochet needle, No. 10. With red wool make a chain of 30 stitches, join round, and work 3 rounds of single crochet, taking up the back threads only. After this do 8 rounds with fawn colour. Then with the red wool again work 3 rounds, reducing 2 stitches in each round, and so bringing to 24 single crochet for the wrist. Now with fawn colour, and taking up the front threads of each preceding round, work 10 rounds, in the last three rounds of these increasing by 2 stitches in a round to 30 stitches. Next round work 9 single crochet and 3 chain for the thumb join round, and single crochet 8 rounds, 12 stitches in each round ; then do 2 rounds with red, and afterwards take 2 together till only three stitches are left sew these up with a rug needle. Proceed with the hand

on 24 stitches for 8 rounds, then do 6 rounds with red, and after this take 2 together all round, and sew up the top. For the little edge round the wrist crochet with red wool, 1 double crochet, 3 chain, alternately, and work the same edge 2 rounds above. At the back of the hand, on the red band round the wrist, sew a few loops of red wool in the form of a rosette.

Baby's Glove.

COUVREPIED.

THIS couvrepied may be worked with double Berlin wool or AA Peacock fleecy, and a bone crochet needle No. 6. The stripes are of good contrasting colours, say fawn and blue for the narrow, and black and amber for the wide stripes. Begin with fawn wool for the narrow stripe with 16 chain. **1st row**—Plain double crochet ; turn the work at the end of this and every row. **2nd row**—Double crochet, 15 stitches in the row, inserting the hook into both top threads of the stitches of preceding **row. 3rd row**—2 double crochet, take the blue wool over the needle, insert the hook on the right side to take up the second double crochet stitch of the second previous row, bringing it out to the left of the same stitch and draw the wool through, blue wool over the needle, insert the hook from the front to take up the next stitch of the second previous row and draw the wool through, blue wool over the needle, insert the hook to take up the next stitch of the second previous row and draw the wool through, blue wool over the needle and draw through 5 blue stitches on the needle, fawn wool over the needle and draw through the 2 stitches on the needle, 3 double crochet with fawn, then again raise blue loops in the second previous row, the first loop at distance of one stitch from the former group and the others in next two consecutive stitches, draw through as already described, work 3 fawn double crochet, another series of blue loops, and 4 double crochet at the end of the row ; break off the blue wool after doing the last tuft, and secure the t g ends with a rug needle. **4th row**—Same as the second row. **5th row**—4 double crochet, * blue wool over the needle in the manner described above, and raise loops in the three stitches between the group of loops raised in the third row, 3 double crochet with fawn, and repeat from *, and there will be 2 double crochet to work at the end of the row. **6th row**—Same as the second row. Repeat from the third row till the stripe is the length you wish it. The wide stripes are worked in the same manner, using black wool for the ground and amber for the raised loops, beginning with 24 chain to allow for five tufts in every pattern row. Work as many stripes as are required for the width of the couvrepied, and join them together with a row of double crochet. Finish off the top and bottom with a deep fringe.

WATCH GUARDS.

THESE guards are used by both ladies and gentlemen, and are especially appropriate for mourning. Procure 2 skeins of black purse silk and some small black beads. First of all thread the beads upon the silk. Then with a steel crochet needle commence with 6 or 8 chain, join round ; insert the hook in the first stitch of the chain, push a bead close to the work, draw the silk through, then silk round the needle and draw through the 2 stitches of the needle, so making a double crochet stitch ; continue in this way in each chain stitch of the foundation and go on round and round

Couvrepied.

putting a bead at every stitch until the guard is the required length. Attach a swivel at one end and a pendant at the other if the guard is an Albert. If a long chain affix a snap to secure the ends together.

WELDON'S
PRACTICAL SMOCKING.

(FIRST SERIES.)

How to Work Smocking, with Various Useful Designs for Ladies' and Children's Garments.

THIRTY-ONE ILLUSTRATIONS.

The Yearly Subscription to this Magazine, post free to any Part of the World, is 2s. 6d.
Subscriptions are payable in advance, and may commence from any date and for any period.

The Back Numbers are always in print. Nos. 1 to 232 now ready, Price 2d. each, or bound in 19 Vols., price 2s. 6d. each.

SMOCKING.

THE art of smocking is supposed to be of ancient origin, though little is really known of it until the thirteenth century, at which period it was usual for women and girls to wear loose garments called "smocs" or "smickets," the name being derived from the Anglo Saxon word "smocc," signifying "a garment to creep into." These smocs were made of fine linen richly ornamented with embroidery in gold and colours, and that they retained their distinctive name, though probably changing somewhat in character and material, is in evidence, from the fact that when in the reign of Queen Anne a fair was held annually in the locality now known as May-Fair, smock races figured conspicuously among the amusements, and young girls competed attired in their smocks, the prize being a new embroidered lace smock for each successful competitor.

Our grandmothers' acquaintance with smocking arose from its association with the loose, coarse garb adopted as an outdoor dress by countrymen, farm labourers, and others. These smock-frocks, as they were called, were made chiefly of jean or strong holland, the bodies and sleeves gathered and stitched in wonderfully quaint and elaborate devices, the skirt left loose and hanging. They had a picturesque effect, and must have been comfortable wear; it is therefore a matter of regret that they have now almost totally disappeared, and are only seen in remote districts.

When the rage for artistic dressing set in a few years ago, smocking was revived and brought into requisition for the ornamentation of ladies' and children's summer costumes, for lawn-tennis dresses, and holland blouses; and so greatly has it increased in favour that it is now a recognised style of fashionable dress, and forms an effective trimming, either in the form of a yoke or let in as a waistcoat; the sleeves also being smocked in similar pattern above the elbow and again at the wrist. A lovely costume for a little child can be made of cream-coloured cashmere, with a yoke worked with gold embroidery silk in diamond pattern, or basket pattern, the tops of the sleeves embroidered to match, left loose at the elbow, and again smocked at the wrist, a hem and three tucks round the bottom of the skirt (or a wide box-pleated flounce, with the centre of each pleat smocked at the top), and a wide gold silk sash below the waist tied in a large bow at the back; the bonnet also of cashmere, two box-pleats brought up over a high crown, and the front arranged in three "pokes" over the forehead, lined inside with cashmere in puckered gathers, and ornamented on the outside with similar gathers, gold smocking, lace, and a ribbon bow on the top. Pretty serviceable dresses are made of linen and cambric. the smocking done with pink, ruby, or blue; and strong useful overalls for children, made of holland smocked with Turkey red, are much admired.

Smocking is also used for afternoon tea-gowns, flannel dressing-gowns, muffs, hats, and other purposes.

Now, as the whole beauty of smocking depends upon the evenness and regularity of the gathering, means must be adopted to keep the lines of gathering threads perfectly straight, and also to regulate the distance of the stitches one from another: this it will be almost impossible to do without a chart or guide of some kind. One method of proceeding is to take a piece of perforated cardboard, about eighteen inches long, and six or seven inches wide, and in this, with a sharp penknife, cut a series of small holes as shown by illustration—thus: Commence three holes from one end, cut out the little square formed by the next four holes, leave six holes intact, cut out another little square of four holes, and so on along to the other end of the cardboard, six holes left between each square cut out; now, higher up on the cardboard, from the holes you have first cut, count four holes or five holes according to the width you desire to leave between your lines of gathering threads, and cut another row of holes exactly over and above the row already cut, and repeat this process for the width of the cardboard: this chart will appear like Figure 1: place it upon the material you intend smocking, taking care that it lies perfectly straight and even, and with a pencil (using black lead on light material and yellow lead on dark) make dots on the material through every hole of the card-

No. 1.—Chart of Perforated Cardboard.

board. If the card is not sufficiently large to mark the entire surface of material you intend smocking, you can lift it up and replace it in any desired position, taking care that it still lies evenly, which can be ensured by placing the top row of holes over the row last marked; be very careful not to let the cardboard slip whilst marking. The marking and the gathering had both preferably be done on the wrong side of the material, that is with the wrong side of the material uppermost, to keep the right side spotless and scrupulously clean. Thread a needle with cotton having a good knot at the end, and begin gathering by inserting the needle in the top dot on the right hand side, bring the point up half way between this dot

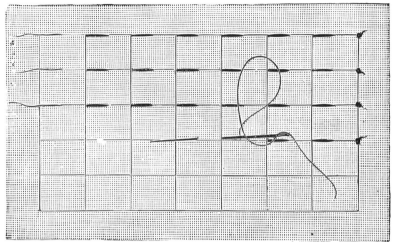

No. 3.—Showing Method of Drawing Lines on Material, and Gathering Commenced.

and the second dot in the same line, then in through the second dot and out half way between this and the third dot, and so on, till the gathering thread goes the whole way along, covering the row of dots. Again thread the needle, and now run along the second row of dots in the same manner, stitch under stitch, as see Figure 2. When as many rows are gathered as you require, draw up the threads, and keep the gathers in place by twisting the ends of the cotton round pins stuck in the material. If rightly done there will be no need of stroking the gathers down, they will lie in folds perfectly flat and even, as illustrations 2 and 3.

Quite lately, for convenience in smocking, Mr. Briggs has issued sheets of transfer papers imprinted with small dots at regular intervals; these sheets only require ironing on the material in the same manner as Briggs' well-known transfer designs for crewel work, and the dots immediately become apparent, and the gathering is done from one dot to the other in the manner described above.

Another and still handier guide than the perforated card, one more generally suited to beginners, and not to be despised by those proficient in the work, is made of a sheet of ordinary stout cardboard, from which cut a strip lengthways four or six inches in width; along each edge mark spaces with pen and ink, thus, | | |, half-an-inch apart along one edge, and three-eighths of an inch apart along the other edge; now put the half-inch edge of cardboard uppermost on the wrong side of the material and tick each mark, lift the cardboard as much lower down on the material as you anticipate the smocking will occupy, and tick other marks exactly below those already done; to be accurate, you will, of course, measure from the margin of the material; now draw lines from one tick to the other, the cardboard itself will serve as a ruler, and you will use a black lead for light material, and a yellow lead for dark, that the lines may be readily seen; these lines are to denote the *width* of the *stitches*, you use the three-eighth inch edge for gathering lines, ticking as many as required for the depth of the pattern on the right hand side and left hand side of the material, and drawing along from one side to the other; this will appear like a series of oblong squares, and is supposed to be for working the Honeycomb pattern to afford due depth to the cells. Other patterns may require some difference in the spacings; for instance, for the Diamond pattern the lines may be drawn three-eighths of an inch apart both ways, forming perfect squares. An expert worker may dispense with the drawing of lines, and just simply crease the material from tick to tick. Begin gathering on the top line, inserting the needle in on the right hand side where

the lines cross, bring up the point on the top line half way between the first and second perpendicular lines, then in at the crossing of the next lines, and out half way between the second and third perpendicular lines, and continue, till you have gathered all along to the end of the top line; leave the end of cotton: re-thread the needle, and proceed along each line in a similar manner, see Figure 3; and when all are done draw up the gathering threads and secure each by passing round a pin.

Before beginning any pattern ascertain how many rows and how many gathers will be required to bring the pattern in accurately, and mark the material to allow for just so many of each and no more; this is especially necessary with regard to Open Diamonds, Feather Stitch and Chevron, and other wide patterns. All gathering threads are pulled out when the work is completed. When working on striped material, a very pretty effect may be produced by reserving the white portion for the depth and bringing the coloured stripes up to form the front ridges of the gathers.

No. 4.—HONEYCOMB PATTERN.

THE engraving shows the real Honeycomb pattern of hollow cells caught together at the four angles by stitching. Having the gathering arranged and drawn up in the manner directed above, hold the material the right side towards you, thread your needle with coloured silk and bring it up from the back to the front at the left hand top corner in the first pleat and exactly over the gathering thread, catch the next pleat to this by a stitch from right to left through each, work another stitch through both pleats, then insert the needle in the same place but in the second pleat only, and bring it out in the same pleat over the second gathering thread, catch the third pleat to this by a stitch through each, work another stitch through both pleats, then insert the needle in the same place, but in the third pleat only, and bring it out in the same pleat over the first gathering thread, and proceed in this way all along, working a stitch alternately in each row; two pleats are taken together in every stitch, and the last pleat of one stitch becomes the first pleat of the next; in going from one line to the other, be careful always to slip the needle lengthways up and down, never across. Work the third and fourth lines as you have already worked the first and second, and continue till the requisite depth is attained.

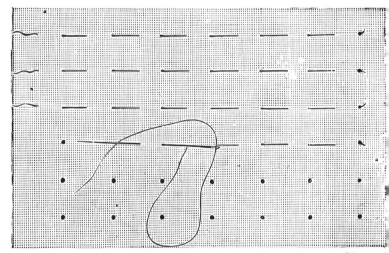

No. 2.—Piece of Material Dotted from the Chart showing Method of Gathering.

ANOTHER VARIETY OF HONEYCOMB.

A VARIETY of honeycomb, especially pretty for working round the necks of dresses, is done in the form of scallops. First of all, work a double line of honeycomb as described above. Then begin in the same pleat on the left hand side, do four stitches in one line and three stitches in the other, and fasten off. Begin again on the third pleat, and do two stitches in one line, and only one stitch intermediate in the second line, so bringing the scallop to a point. Arrange the size of the scallops so as to bring them in evenly upon the material. Larger scallops are made by beginning with six stitches instead of four, and reducing from the six to one only.

No. 5.—OUTLINE AND ROPE PATTERN.

THIS pattern is a combination of two kinds of stitches which together form a pretty, simple trimming, or either stitch may be used separately as a heading to a more elaborate pattern. The first line is outline stitch, so called from its resemblance to the outline stitch in crewel work. The needle being threaded with silk, or whatever you intend using for the smocking, begin at the top left-hand corner, bringing the needle up from the back into the first pleat over the

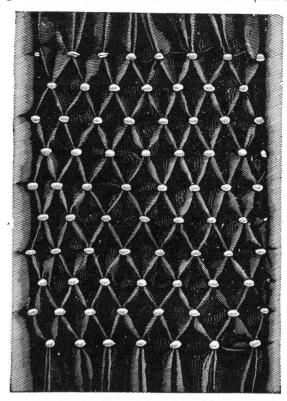

No. 4.—Honeycomb Smocking.

gathering thread, insert the needle from right to left to take up this pleat only, keep the silk well over the needle, and draw the needle out, take up the second pleat in the same way, then the third pleat, and so on, one pleat at a time, and always bringing the needle out below the stitch. The second and third lines are worked in rope stitch, begin on the left-hand side with the silk drawn up in front of the first pleat, take up the first pleat as described above, take up the second pleat in similar manner, but bring out the needle above the stitch, then take the third gather with the needle below the stitch, and take the fourth gather with the needle above the stitch, and continue; you will see this makes a pretty variation, and couples two gathers together in the working of every stitch.

No. 6.—HERRINGBONE PATTERN.

THIS pattern will require nine lines drawn across from right to left, three-eighths of an inch apart, and crossed by other lines half an inch apart for the width of the stitches. When the gathering is done, work a row of Outline stitch along the top and bottom lines. On the six centre threads three rows of Herringbone stitches are to be worked. Bring the needle out on the first of these threads in the first pleat, come down to the second thread and insert the needle from right to left through the third and second pleats, go up to the first thread and insert the needle from right to left through the fourth and third pleats, then down and through the fifth and fourth, and up and through the sixth and fifth, and proceed thus working a stitch on each line alternately to the end of the row. Work the other two rows of Herringbone in the same manner.

No. 7.—DIAMOND LATTICE PATTERN.

THIS very effective pattern is worked with double silk. The heading something resembles Honeycomb, but is not worked quite the same way, and in the centre or "Lattice" part of the pattern the silk is kept entirely in front of the work and passes across and across

diagonally from one line to the next. Fifteen gathering threads are required, and these should be drawn a quarter of an inch apart, excepting from heading to centre where half-an-inch is left, the cross lines giving the width of the stitches are three-eighths of an inch apart. For the heading, having the silk double, bring the needle up in the first pleat at the left hand top corner, insert it in the second pleat on the same line and bring it out in the same pleat on the second line, insert it in the same line of the third pleat and bring it out in the same pleat on the top line, insert it on the same line in the fourth pleat, and bring it out in the same pleat on the second line, insert it on the same line in the fifth pleat and bring it out in the same pleat on the top line, and so on up and down the two lines to the end of the row. Then work in the same manner from the third line to the second, which as you will see in the illustration brings a double set of stitches in the centre row, and completes the heading. The Lattice is worked on the nine centre gathering threads, taking only one pleat at a time. Bring the needle up in the second pleat of the first line (a stitch is to be formed below the stitch in the centre line of the heading), insert it on the same line to take up the third pleat only and draw the third and second pleats together with the silk below the stitch, insert needle on the second line to take up the fourth pleat only, then on the same line to take up the fifth pleat only and draw the fifth and fourth together with the silk above the stitch, insert needle on the top thread to take up the sixth pleat only, then on the same line to take up the seventh pleat only and draw the seventh and sixth pleats together with the silk below the stitch, continue to the end of the row. Then begin on the second pleat of the third line, take up the third pleat only and draw the third and second pleats together with the silk above the stitch, take up the fourth pleat on the second line, take up the fifth pleat on the same line, and draw these two pleats together in a stitch just close below the stitch that is there already, and with the silk below the stitch, insert needle on the third line to take up the sixth pleat only, then on the same line to take up the seventh pleat only, and draw these two pleats together with the silk above the stitch, and so on. Next, bring up the needle to work a stitch close under the first stitch of last row, and proceed as before till you complete the depth required. The pattern is finished with another heading like that with which it began.

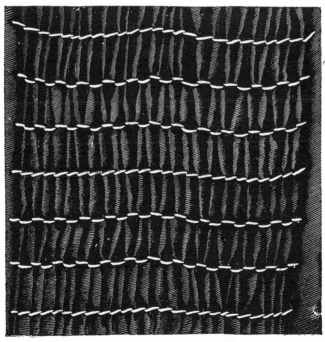

No. 5.—Outline and Rope Stitch.

No. 8.—BASKET PATTERN.

THIS will require ten lines drawn from right to left three-eighths of an inch apart, and cross lines the same width, or half an inch wide according as more or less fulness is desired. Run the gathers as previously directed. Then bring up the needle in the first pleat on the top line on the left-hand side, take up the second and first pleats together on the needle, take up the second pleat only on the needle in the same place, and, bringing out the needle below the stitch, take up the third and second pleats together on the needle, take up the third pleat only on the needle in the same place and bringing out the needle above the stitch; then work the fourth and third pleats similarly, then the fifth and fourth, and so on, bringing the needle out below the stitch and above the stitch alternately. On the space occupied by the three top lines you are to get in five lines of this basket smocking, then four single lines in the centre of the pattern, and again five lines close together to match the commencement.

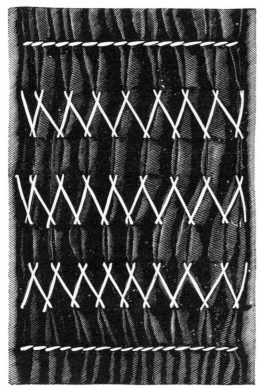

No. 6 —Herringbone Stitch.

No. 9.—DIAMOND PATTERN.

DRAW four lines from right to left three-eighths of an inch apart for the headings and other lines intermediary a quarter of an inch apart for the working of the diamonds, the perpendicular lines to cross these being three-eighths of an inch one from the other. The heading is of Outline stitch and Rope stitch as previously explained. For the diamonds, begin with a stitch on the first pleat just below the heading, next a stitch consecutively on the second, third, fourth, and fifth pleat, each stitch a little lower than the stitch previous, and so that the fifth stitch comes directly upon the next gathering thread, then work a stitch on each of the next four gathers in an upward direction, and you again come just under the heading, continue thus up and down to the end of the line. Recommence on the first pleat of the next gathering thread, and work successively upwards a stitch on each pleat till you come to the gathering thread already worked upon, when you will do a second stitch under the stitch already there, this is where the diamonds meet; go four stitches successively downwards and you will again be at the point of a diamond; again work upwards, then downwards, and so on for the width of the embroidery, always remembering that the double stitches which form the points of the diamonds are invariably to come upon a gathering thread, and that *three* stitches—neither more nor less— are to be on each side of every diamond.

DIAMOND PATTERN IN SCALLOPS.

A PRETTY variation in the Diamond pattern rendering it especially suitable for embroidering round the necks of children's dresses and overalls, is done in the form of scallops Commence with two lines worked according to the diamond pattern given above, then work three whole diamonds under five in the top line, two under the three, then one under the two, so bringing the scallop to a point of one diamond. This trimming can be worked wider or narrower as desired.

No. 10.—FEATHER STITCH AND ZIGZAG.

THIS is worked in the same manner as the ordinary Feather stitch on linen. Having the gathers in order, hold the material so that the pleats run from right to left instead of up and down. Begin in the second pleat a trifle above the gathering thread, and take up the first and second pleats with the silk round the point of the needle as if going to make a buttonhole stitch, then insert the needle to take up the second and third pleats a trifle below the gathering thread and wind silk round the point of the needle for another buttonhole stitch, and continue working alternately a stitch on each side of the gathering thread. The centre of the pattern is worked in the same way, only you do five stitches consecutively to the right and five stitches consecutively to the left, closely together, and in zigzag fashion

No. 11.—FEATHER STITCH AND CHEVRON.

DRAW lines at distances suitable for the pattern, and gather in the usual manner. Then commence by working the six straight lines of Outline stitch, after which do four lines of Feather stitch as shown in the engraving; for method of working see above The intermediate lines of Chevron are worked by taking up the pleats one by one in a slanting direction, doing first six stitches down and then six stitches up, in the same manner as the side stitches of the diamonds in Pattern No. 9.

No. 12.—SPANISH PATTERN.

THIS handsome pattern will require thirteen lines drawn from left to right, three-eighths of an inch apart, for gathering threads, and

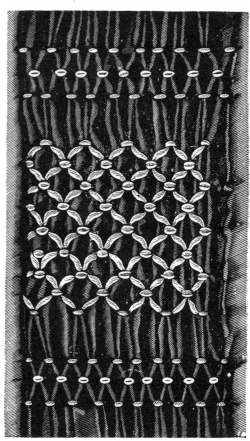

No. 7.—Diamond Lattice Pattern.

cross lines perpendicularly three-eighths of an inch apart, for gauging the size of the stitches. Work with double silk. In the centre pattern of diamonds, begin on the left-hand side on the fourth gathering thread, bring the silk up in the first pleat, sew the second and first pleats together, then a stitch in the second pleat only bringing out the silk below the stitch, do one stitch on the third pleat only half way between the gatherings, one on the fourth pleat only on the fifth gathering thread, one on the sixth pleat only half way between the fifth and sixth gathering threads, one in the same position on next pleat, and now bring out the silk above the stitch, work on three consecutive pleats upwards to the fourth gathering thread, catch the tenth and ninth pleats together, then a stitch through the tenth pleat only with silk brought out below the stitch, and continue to the end of the line. Re-commence on the left-hand side in the first pleat on the seventh gathering thread, sew the second and first pleats together, then a stitch in the second pleat only with silk out above the stitch, now work a stitch on each of three consecutive pleats upwards, and you come below the stitch already done, work on the sixth pleat bringing out the silk below the stitch, then do three stitches downwards, then three stitches upwards, and so on, to the end. Begin again below the first stitch on the seventh gathering thread, and work two more lines up and down, so making complete diamonds extending as far as the tenth gathering thread, where clench the bottom point of each diamond with an extra stitch, the same as the top points of the diamonds on the fourth gathering thread. Next do a line of Outline-stitch at top and bottom of the Diamond pattern, as nearly as possible over the fourth and tenth gathering threads. Then, for heading, bring silk out in the first pleat close above the top line of Outline-stitch, take the second and first pleats together, do another stitch through both, then take the second

second gathering thread, take the third and second pleats together, do another stitch through both pleats, insert the needle in the same place, but in the third pleat only, and slip it down the same pleat and bring it out above the third gathering thread, work a stitch here, and proceed in the same manner diagonally downwards till you reach the last gathering thread, where fasten off. Begin again at the top line, taking together the seventh and eighth pleats, and again work downwards. You miss four pleats between each slanting line of stitches. When you have accomplished the entire surface of the material from left to right, work across in the opposite direction, so forming diamonds.

No. 14.—BEADED HONEYCOMB.

A PARTICULARLY pleasing effect is imparted to Honeycomb by the introduction of a bead into every stitch, so giving the work a more than usually bright and attractive appearance. Our illustration shows white beads honeycombed on black sateen. Gold beads on black silk, satin, or cashmere would look remarkably pretty, as also would steel beads on grey beige or carmelite. Gather the material as directed for No. 4 Honeycomb. Then, being careful to select a needle large enough in the eye to be easily threaded, and yet sufficiently fine to pass through the beads, begin on the first gathering thread, and bringing up the needle in the first pleat, thread a bead, take up the second and first pleats together, pass the

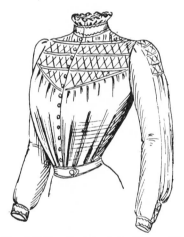

No. 3477.—Smocked Bodice with Pointed Yoke.

No. 3478.—Smocked Front and Sleeves.

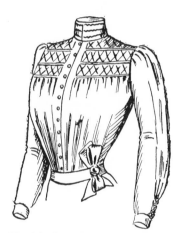

No. 3467.—Smocked Bodice with Full Sleeves.

Flat Patterns, each 6d.; Tacked up, including flat, 1s. 6d. each.

pleat only and slip the needle on the wrong side of the same pleat to the next gathering thread above, here do a stitch through the third and second pleat, then put needle in the third pleat and slip it on the wrong side of the same pleat to the gathering thread below, take up the fourth and third pleats together, do another stitch through both, then take the fourth pleat only and slip the needle to the gathering thread above, and repeat to the end. Recommence upon the second gathering thread, take the second and first pleats together, do another stitch through both, then take the second pleat only and slip needle down on the wrong side the same pleat to the stitch already done below, work another stitch directly over and above this stitch, then slip the needle to the second gathering thread and do a stitch there, and so on. Work a line of Outline-stitch on the first gathering thread. Work a similar heading on the opposite side of the Diamond pattern.

No. 13.—OPEN DIAMOND PATTERN.

FOR working this pattern, in which the diamonds are large and open, the gathering lines should be a quarter of an inch apart from left to right, and the cross-lines half an inch apart, so as to give a nice depth to the cells. Begin by bringing the needle out on the left-hand side in the first pleat on the first gathering thread, and take the second and first pleats together, do another stitch in the same place, insert the needle in the same place, but in the second pleat only, and slip it down the same pleat and bring it out above the

needle through the bead from left to right, and if possible make another stitch in the same place, and again pass the needle through the bead, then insert the needle in the second pleat only, and slip it down, bringing it out on the second gathering thread, where thread a bead and work a stitch taking up the third and second pleats together. Continue on these two lines to the end of the material. Then work along the third and fourth lines in a similar manner, and so on for the depth required.

No. 15.—EMPRESS PATTERN.

THIS is a wide and remarkably handsome pattern, and will require seventeen gathering lines half an inch apart from each other, crossed by perpendicular lines three-eighths of an inch apart. On the first gathering thread work a line of Rope-stitch as described in No. 5. Do Rope-stitch also upon the third, seventh, eleventh, fifteenth, and seventeenth gathering threads. This done, begin on the first pleat a trifle above the second gathering thread, take up in straight line the second pleat only, take up the third pleat exactly on the gathering thread, and in both these stitches bring out the silk below the needle. Now take up the fourth pleat exactly on the gathering thread, and with the silk above the stitch, take up the fifth pleat a trifle above the gathering thread and silk still above the stitch, then the sixth pleat in line with the stitch last done and silk below the stitch, then the seventh pleat just on the gathering thread and silk below the stitch, then the eighth pleat upon the gathering thread and silk above the stitch, and so on to the end. Begin again on the same gathering thread and work in the same manner, first *on* the gathering thread, and then just so far *below* the thread as you before went above. Next for the **Working of the Diamonds**—Bring the silk out in the first pleat, and on the fifth gathering thread, take up the second pleat a trifle above the fourth gathering thread, in the same place take up the third and second pleats together, then take third pleat only in the same place and bringing out the silk below the needle, take up the fourth pleat on the fifth gathering thread, take up the fifth pleat only on the same thread and with the silk above the stitch, then go up and make a double stitch, then down and make a single stitch, and so on. Begin again in the same place on the fifth gathering thread and work up and down to complete the lower half of the little diamonds. For the **Vandyke Pattern in the Centre**—Bring the silk out in the first pleat a trifle above the eighth gathering thread, then take up the second pleat on the same level, take up the third pleat upon the gathering thread, and do five more stitches on five successive pleats all in a slanting direction, the last of them coming exactly upon the tenth gathering thread and all with the silk brought out below the needle, take up the eighth pleat also upon the tenth gathering thread, but with the silk above the needle and work five stitches successively upwards to the level upon which you began, then take the fourteenth pleat on the same level with the last stitch but with the silk below the needle, and proceed downwards to the tenth gathering thread again, and proceed in the same manner to the end of the line. Next work another line of zig-zag stitches below this zig-zag. Work diamonds the same as before on threads twelve, thirteen, and fourteen. Work the little up-and-down pattern on the sixteenth gathering thread, similar to that on the second thread.

No. 16.—SMOCKING FOR A VEST, OR THE FRONT OF A BODICE.

THIS very handsome piece of work will require 14 inches of sateen, cambric, or other material, 30 inches wide. Draw nineteen lines for gathering threads the whole width of the material and three-eighths of an inch apart, excepting at the top and bottom of the Feather-stitch insertion, where a space of six-eighths of an inch is left, draw also another line an inch above the first of these, and another an inch below the last; cross these with perpendicular lines three-eighths of an inch apart for gauging the size of the stitches. Gather as directed in the preliminary instructions. Now, with embroidery silk, of colour to look well upon your material, work on the top gathering thread a line of Outline-stitch, and the same on the second, fifth, ninth, thirteenth, seventeenth, twentieth, and twenty-first gathering threads. By reference to the engraving you will see that these lines of Outline-stitch mark out the various insertions of which the pattern is composed. **For the Insertion**—Between the fifth and ninth gathering threads, work first in the exact centre four lines of Rope-stitch, taking care to have each line perfectly straight, and all the stitches the same degree of looseness exactly, not *too* loose. For the Feather-stitch, hold the work sideways towards you, and bring the needle up in the second pleat just above the top line of Rope-stitch, take up the first and second pleats together, bringing the silk round the point of the needle as if making a buttonhole stitch, take up the second and third pleats a trifle to the right and work another similar stitch, then a stitch on the third and fourth pleats, and another on the fourth and fifth, each a trifle to the right, now work in the same manner to the left three consecutive buttonhole stitches, bringing the last almost close to the line of Rope-stitch, then three stitches to the right, three to the left, and so on. And do another line of Feather-stitch on the opposite side of the Rope-stitches. **For the Diamond Insertion**—Begin close below the line of Outline-stitches on the fifth gathering thread, bringing the needle up in the first pleat, take up the second pleat only on the same level, take up the third pleat half way below this and the sixth gathering thread, take up the fourth pleat on the sixth gathering thread, all these with the silk brought out below the stitch, take up the fifth pleat on the sixth gathering thread and with the silk brought out above the stitch, take up the sixth pleat half

No. 18591.—Girl's Blouse.
In ages 10 to 16 years.
Flat Paper Pattern, 6d.; Tacked up, 1s. 6d.

No. 3468.—Fancy Smo
Flat Pattern, 6d.; Tac

No. 3436.—Smocked Dress.
Ages 6 to 14 years.

No. 3479.—Child's Smocke
Princess Dress.
Ages 2 to 8 years.
Flat Paper Patterns, each

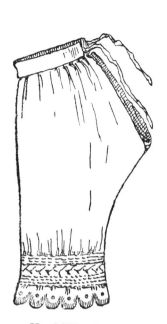

No. 3471.—Smocked Drawers.
Flat Pattern, 6d.; Tacked up, 1s. 4d.

No. 3469.—Smocked Bathing Suit.
Flat Pattern, 6d.; Tacked up, 1s. 6d.

way between this and the fifth gathering thread, take up the seventh pleat close below the line of outline stitches, take up the eighth pleat on the same level, work again downwards, then upwards, and continue to the end of the row. Note, that the top stitch marking the point of the half-diamond comes exactly in the centre of the vandyke of the feather stitch in the insertion above. Recommence on the left-hand side, bringing out the needle in the first pleat on the seventh gathering thread, take up the second pleat only on the same gathering thread, take up the third pleat half-way between this thread and the thread above, take up the fourth pleat on the sixth gathering thread just below the stitch that is formed already, take up the fifth pleat only on the same level and bring the silk out below the stitch, and continue along. Begin again on the seventh gathering thread, and work first in a downward direction, then upwards, in the same manner as before; also work from the line of Outline-stitches on the eighth gathering thread upwards to the seventh gathering thread to complete the insertion. The third insertion resembles the first, but has an additional line of Feather stitching on each side. Then work another Diamond insertion. And the fifth insertion is like the first. Make up the smocking on a piece of lining cut to whatever size you desire to fit into the dress bodice; of course there will not be such a width of smocking required at the bottom as across the chest, and therefore from the eighth gathering thread downwards you can omit a certain number of pleats on either side, and so proportionately diminish the width of the smocking to suit the size of the lining; also, to save doing more work than is absolutely necessary, you can omit smocking on a few pleats in the centre of the top where the neck is to be cut.

A MORE SIMPLE STYLE OF SMOCKING FOR THE FRONT OF A BODICE.

A PIECE of material about 30 inches wide and 14 inches long will be required. Prepare by drawing lines the whole width of the material from left to right at intervals of half an inch and a quarter of an inch alternately apart, and cross these with other lines three-quarters of an inch apart for gauging the size of the stitches. Gather. Then with embroidery silk of colour to suit the material work a line of Outline stitch on every one of the gathering threads. The intervals of a quarter of an inch space are left unfilled. In the intervals of half an inch space work a double line of Honeycomb stitch, as directed in No. 4 Honeycomb Smocking, page 5.

No. 17.—MUFF.

PROCURE ¾ of a yard of black, and ¼ of a yard of ruby satin, a piece of thin black silk for lining, a piece of wadding, a little chenille trimming, 1 yard of black silk lace, and 1¾ yards of silk cord. Cut the black silk to the size required for the lining and sew it up round. Tack upon it a layer or two of wadding, and on the side of this, which is to be the front of the muff, place a facing of black silk. About 12 inches *in width* of the ruby satin will suffice; do the Honeycomb work thereon with black embroidery silk; and when finished line the inside with silk or muslin, and frill the satin in a wide pleat 1½ inch deep at the top, arrange this over the black silk facing in front of the muff to use as a pocket. Pleat black satin fully round the openings on each side of the muff, overlapping the ruby pocket of course, and confined in its place by black silk cord. Trim the bottom of the muff with a little chenille trimming, and place a bow of the same on the top to hang over the opening of the pocket. Edge the openings of the muff with lace, and add a cord to pass round the neck.

No. 3477.—SMOCKED BODICE WITH POINTED YOKE.

THIS is a very becoming style of bodice, arranged so that the smocking forms a pointed yoke, buttoned down the entire front, while the waist part is gathered into a band of the required size, a fitted lining both back and front being given to secure the fulness to

No. 19460.—Smocked Frock.
Ages 2 to 10 years.
up, including flat, 1s. 6d.

No. 3473.—Smocked Princess Dress.
Ages 8 to 14 years.

evenly. The smocked yoke is made both back and front, and any of the designs given in this issue can be employed, the neck being put into a band collar. The sleeve, full on the outside, is smocked to correspond with the yoke, the fulness then being continued on the outside, and then again smocked at the wrist, where it is put into a narrow band. Quantity of 36-inch material, 4 yards; lining, 2 yards.

No. 3478.—SMOCKED FRONT AND SLEEVES.

HERE is given a particularly pretty bodice for two materials, our model showing for plush or velvet, with plastron and sleeves of soft silk ornamented with any of the pretty stitches here given for

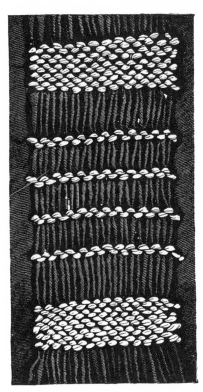

No. 8.—Basket Pattern.

smocking. The plastron when smocked is secured to a fitted lining, which keeps it nicely in shape, then it is sewn down the left side, while the right side of bodice hooks over it, finished with a shaped collar of velvet. The sleeve, full on the outside only, is smocked at the shoulder and wrist on to a fitted lining foundation, the wrist part being secured by a narrow band cuff. Quantity of plush, 2¼ yards; 30-inch silk, 2¼ yards.

No. 3467.—SMOCKED BODICE WITH FULL SLEEVE.

THIS smart bodice has the neck, back, and front honeycombed in a yoke form, the fulness beneath the yoke being gathered nicely into the waist, where it is put into a band of the required size. The neck is put into a band collar, while the pattern consists of fitted lining front and back, full front and back, collar, lining upper and under of sleeve, and full sleeve. This gathers on the outside of the arm into the shoulder, the fulness at the wrist being smocked, then put into a narrow band sufficiently large to permit the hand passing through, or else the size to fasten round the wrist with a button. The front of this bodice is smocked in two pieces, and the work reaches from the neck-band to within about an inch of the bottom of the arm-pits. Almost any of the designs illustrated in this number are suitable for working, arranging the depth of the insertions so as to get three lines of pattern in the allotted space. Or the depth worked

entirely in simple Honeycomb stitch will look very pretty. The sleeves are set in full at the top, and the wrist end is ornamented at the back with a little smocking to match that already done on the fronts. Quantity of 36-inch material, 4 yards; lining, 2 yards.

No. 3479.—CHILD'S SMOCKED PRINCESS DRESS.

THIS pretty little dress, suitable for children of two to eight years, can be reproduced in all soft materials, our model showing for washing silk cut quite *en princesse*, with the skirt part hemmed and set in tucks, each of which can be ornamented with a fancy stitching. The neck part, back and front, is smocked with any of the pretty stitches given in this issue, while the neck is finished with a roll collar ornamented with coral stitch. The yoke is gathered on to a fitted lining yoke for firmness, while the waist has its fulness confined by the soft silk sash which ties behind in loops and ends. The sleeve is particularly pretty, being smocked on to a fitted sleeve lining to regulate the fulness nicely, the shoulder part being several times gauged, with which the fulness of the wrist part corresponds, the cuff being turned back and ornamented with Feather-stitching. Quantity of 27-inch material, 4½, 5, and 5½ yards.

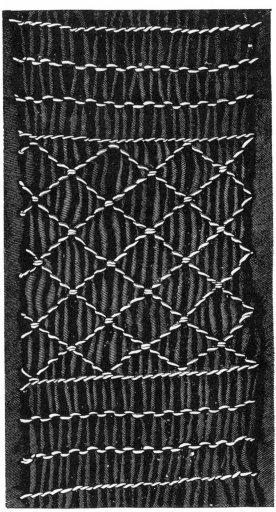

No. 9.—Diamond Pattern.

No. 3468.—SMOCKED APRON.

A DAINTY little apron for muslin, cambric, zephyr, alpaca, soft silk, &c., with its yoke and waist smocked, the pattern consisting of two pieces which are hemmed all round, then lace eased on, the left-hand corner of the apron being turned back with a small button. Three rows of Feather-stitching ornament the lower edge of this model, or tucks can be run in, in which case the turned-back corner must be cut off previous to running in the tucks, then put on. The waist part of the bib gathers into a narrow band, which also takes the apron. The smocking on the bib is supposed to be worked in Diamond pattern, No. 9, or the Diamond Lattice pattern, No. 7, is equally appropriate, and if these are considered too elaborate the Outline and Rope stitch, No. 5, will look neat and pretty. All these smockings are fully described under their respective headings, therefore the manner of working need not be again repeated here. The band is a straight piece of material. The smocking below is to correspond with that worked on the bib. The bottom of the apron is ornamented with three straight lines of Outline stitch alternated with three lines of Feather stitch worked in the method explained in No. 10, but *flatly* on the material, without gathers. Quantity of 36-inch material, 1½ yards; lace, 3 yards.

No. 3471.—SMOCKED DRAWERS.

THESE drawers are suitable for fine, soft calico or cambric, the legs of which are smocked, and the inferior edges scalloped and worked in buttonhole stitch centred with a raised satin spot. The

yoke, the fulness of the waist being confined by the belt fastened in the centre with a button. The pattern consists of the full front and back of blouse, fitted yoke to secure the smocking on to, sleeve, and belt. The yoke will look well smocked in a small Diamond pattern insertion like that shown in the centre of No. 9, but working two rows, and working three straight lines of Outline stitch above and below, and also between the two rows. The drawers are worked to correspond, but here only one row of diamond insertion is employed. Quantity of 27-inch serge, 10 yards.

No. 3436.—SMOCKED DRESS.

THIS style of dress is now much shown for children of 6 to 14 years, made principally in cachemire, washing silks, foulards, cambrics, &c. It consists of a smocked bodice and full skirt, this last named being finished with a deep hem, above which is worked a row of coral or Feather stitching in coloured silk, cotton, or wool.

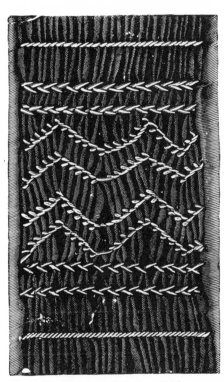

No. 10.—Feather Stitch and Zigzag.

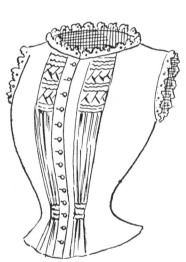

No. 3470.—Smocked Camisole.
Flat Pattern, 6d ; Tacked up, 1s. 4d.

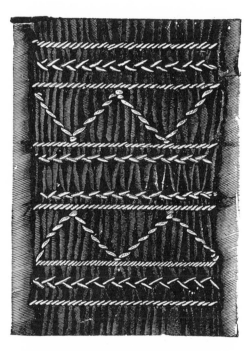

No. 11.—Feather Stitch and Chevron.

waist is evenly gathered into a band of the required size, at either end of which is a tape, or buttonhole and button can replace them. The legs must be run and felled, and the openings either hemmed, or turned down on the wrong side and tapes felled on for strength, then the two legs are joined down the centre a few inches from waist by a run and felled seam. The Feather and Zigzag, No. 10, or Feather and Chevron, No. 11, are suitable stitches for undergarments. Quantity of 36-inch material, 2¼ yards.

No. 3469.—SMOCKED BATHING SUIT.

IN soft serge or flannel this suit forms a pleasing change from the one usually worn, and navy blue smocked with red wool, silk, or ingrain cotton stands the sea-water better than any other colours. The entire edge of the blouse and drawers is scalloped and embroidered with Buttonhole stitch, each scallop being centred with a satin stitch spot; then the seams must be run and herringboned, and the drawers waist put into a band of the required size, the knees being smocked. The neck of the blouse is smocked to form a round

The waist part is gathered equally all round and sewn into a waist-band of the required size. The bodice is full, back and front, arranged across the front and back in yoke form, the Honeycomb stitch being worked in silk to match that employed for the skirt ornamentation. Those not requiring the Honeycomb stitching can run in several rows of gauging, from whence the fulness is brought down to the waist, and again very finely gauged to the required size. The neck is put into a band collar. A fitted lining foundation, front and back, are given, as well as a lining sleeve, on to which the full sleeve is gathered, being put full into the shoulder, while the wrist fulness is finely gauged to form a band to within an inch of the edge, which forms a frill over the hand. This pretty dress has an insertion of smocking round the neck, upon the shoulder seams, straight across the chest, and round the waist. The Basket pattern, No. 8; Diamond pattern, No. 9, and Spanish pattern, No. 12, are especially suitable. Full working instructions for these are given with each engraving, and therefore need not here be repeated. The sleeves are set in full at the top, and smocked round the wrists about an inch from the margin in pattern to correspond. Quantity of 27-inch silk, 5½, 6, 7, and 7½ yards.

No. 18591.—SMOCKED BLOUSE.

THIS pattern, obtainable in ages 10 to 16 years, is suited to flannel, cachemire, nun's veiling, silk, etc., smocked in diamond or any other stitch preferred, and further trimmed with insertion bands. The pattern has a fitted lining foundation for which sateen could be used, or for further warmth, use fine flannel or flannelette for the foundation. No. 29 of Weldon's Practical Needlework, price 2d. of all booksellers, or by post 2½d., gives a good selection of smocking designs and full descriptions. Quantity of 42-inch material, 1½, 1⅝, and 1¾ yards; trimming, 2 yards.

No. 19460.—SMOCKED FROCK.

PATTERN obtainable in ages 2 to 10 years, and it is suited to

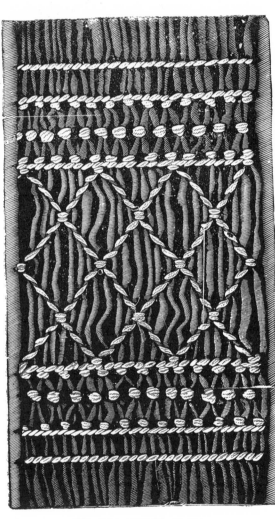

No. 12.—Spanish Pattern.

cambric, silk, nun's veiling, sateen, cachemire, art serge, velveteen, etc. The pattern is arranged with a lining bodice front and back, to be joined by the side seams and a seam avoided down centre front, to serve as a foundation for the dress, the backs having to be turned in and hemmed, and arranged to fasten with buttons and buttonholes, or hooks and eyes. For the dress join widths of material together by the selvedge edges to gain double the breadth of pattern, and form a round, which so fold that a seam is avoided down centre front; then cut to shape of pattern. Cut the back down a few inches to form the placket-hole, hemming the opening round, and at its termination making a single pleat towards the left, which stitch across to prevent it tearing further. The upper edge, back and front, also shoulders, and under portions of armholes, are then gathered, and

drawn up to corresponding widths of lining bodice, to which stitch dress, between the lines of round holes working the smocking in diamond or any other stitch preferred. Quantity of 32-inch material, 3, 3½, 4, and 4½ yards.

No. 3473.—CHILD'S SMOCKED PRINCESS DRESS.

HERE is given a pretty idea for a smocked princess dress, cut with a full front, back, and sleeves, the neck being put into a band collar. The full front and back are smocked on to a fitted lining in yoke form, the fulness of the waist being merely gathered to the lining, over which a full soft silk sash is arranged, tied in loops and ends behind, while the skirt part is hemmed, above which sm

No. 13.—Open Diamond Pattern.

tucks can be run in, if desired, ornamented with a fancy feather stitching. The sleeve is gathered into the shoulder and has the wrist part smocked, leaving an inch or so as a frill over the hand. Our illustration shows the front of the bodice smocked in yoke form from the neck-band to within an inch or two of the bottom of the armpits; this is done in Honeycomb stitch, intersected every six lines by two lines of Rope stitch worked an eighth of an inch apart. Or Diamond Lattice pattern, No. 7, may be employed, or Feather Stitch and Chevron, No. 11, or Spanish pattern, No. 12. The sleeves are set in full at the top, and smocked in pattern to match the yoke to a depth of about four inches round the wrists. In ages 8 to 14 years. Quantity of 36-inch material, 6½, 7½, and 8½ yards.

No. 3470.—SMOCKED CAMISOLE.

A SMOCKED camisole sets just as nicely as a gathered or pleated model, and very fine longcloth or, better still, cambric can be employed. This pattern is well-fitting, having a gore under the arm, round side-piece, and French back, all seams having to be neatly run and felled, the bottom part hemmed or piped, while the fronts, after being turned in, must be machine stitched close to the edge, then buttons and buttonholes arranged. The superfluous width of the fronts is taken up in the smocking at the neck, the waist being firmly gauged, then the neck and armholes are to be piped and trimmed with lace, &c., as fancy may dictate. Feather or coral stitching, worked in crochet cotton, is always a pretty finish to the neck and sleeves of undergarments. Each front is cut sufficiently large to allow of a strip of smocking about three inches in width being worked down each side. Almost any of the insertions illustrated on previous pages will be appropriate for the smocking, working a piece at the top to a depth of about five inches, and again doing a narrower insertion of the same pattern to confine the fulness at the waist;

straight material if fulness is not desired. Many of these designs, although shown for smocking, can be worked on flat material, and would form pretty insertions or borders to under garments, especially to flannel goods, such as petticoats, vests, dressing jackets, and dressing gowns, the edge being scalloped and worked with buttonhole stitch. A Princess dressing gown of cachemire with a plastron its entire length of soft silk, smocked from the neck to waist, after the style of No. 3478, smocked front and sleeves, would look particularly elegant, and beads can be introduced with excellent effect. The Empress pattern, No. 15, is such an effective design for the introduction of tiny gold, steel, pearl, or cut jet beads, which can be arranged at the top, centre, or bottom part of the diamond insertion in the pattern, the manner of picking up the beads being fully explained by No. 14, Beaded Honeycomb, on page 7. Grey cachemire smocked with grey silk and steel beads is always to be admired, or smocked simply with pale pink silk, or very pale blue, the effect is perfect. White flannel goods can be smocked with any colour, or for slight mourning black silk comes out very effectively, more especially when tiny jet beads are introduced. Illustration 7, Diamond Lattice, offers another opportunity for the

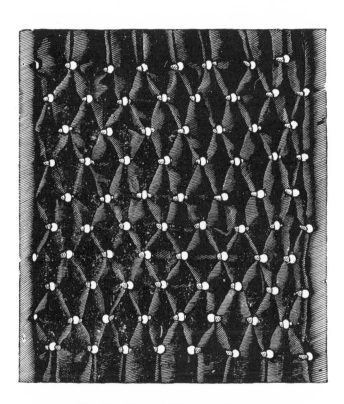

No. 14.—Beaded Honeycomb.

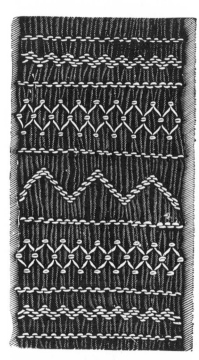

No. 15.—Empress Pattern.

of course just as many pleats are employed at the waist as at the top, but the gathers are drawn in closer, or, if preferred, they may be continued in well-pressed small pleats, and machine stitched across the waist, from whence they flow unconfined. This pattern camisole would also do for the ordinary pleated or gathered makes, by dispensing with the smocking; or it could even be employed for a pretty evening bodice in muslin, made over a silk foundation, while soft silk would smock splendidly. Very pale pink, blue, mauve, or cream washing silk is much used for undergarments, trimmed torchon lace, and our model is especially suited to such a material. A close and durable style of smocking for undergarments is shown by Illustration 11, Feather Stitch and Chevron, or Illustration 15, Empress pattern, is equally to be recommended, as it keeps the fulness even and flat to the figure, while it washes splendidly. Soft twill flannels make up nicely for underbodices for the winter season, and these smocked with white silk are most successful, or fine wool is sometimes used. If preferred, any ordinary shaped fitted underbodice could be made to resemble this illustration (No. 3470) by having two lengthway pieces or bretelles smocked and put on, or either pattern No. 10, 11, or 15 would look well worked on the plain

introduction of beads, and this is a quickly worked and very effective design. Children's dresses, and even infants' tiny clothes always look so pretty when nicely smocked. As a finish to smocked garments, fancy stitches can often be introduced with great success, and a great variety of stitches suitable for dresses and undergarments, as well as for decorative purposes, will be found in No. 5 of Weldon's Practical Needlework Series. Lace and muslin hats are even smocked, as well as fancy cushions, pockets, hand-bags; in fact, this needlework can be applied to so many purposes, and with such success, that we feel sure this issue will be much welcomed, as everything is so clearly illustrated and described, leaving no difficulty even for the inexperienced to encounter, for the various designs can be easily copied, and paper patterns of the various garments shown on pages 7, 8, 9, and 11 can be had at the prices quoted beneath each illustration. It must be clearly understood that the smocking is not done when a tacked or trimmed pattern is ordered, the tissue paper being too brittle to permit of such needlework, and for this very reason we have most carefully illustrated the various stitches, and described each so faithfully to avoid any little difficulty, or error. Quantity of 36-inch material. 1½ yards.

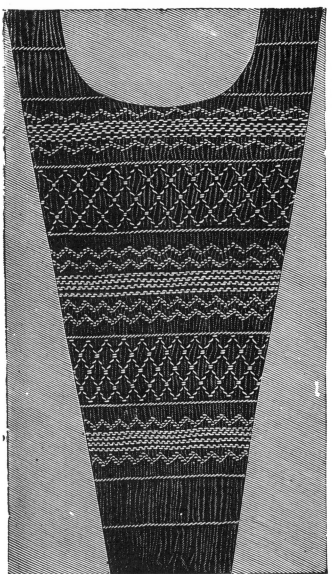

No. 16.—Vest or Front of Bodice.

No. 17.—Muff Honeycombed

WHAT OTHERS SAY OF
Weldon's Paper Patterns and Publications.

"I like 'Weldon's Home Milliner' very much; there is always something quite new in it, as well as good style."

"The cycling skirt I made from the pattern I had from you last year has been admired by all who have seen it, both friends and strangers."

"I have used your patterns for a number of years, and always found them very satisfactory."

"I have taken three of your papers for years past, and always find your paper patterns more accurate and thoroughly satisfactory than any others."

"I can honestly say your delightful Journal is truly worth the money; it seems to embrace everything. I shall certainly give my newsagent a standing order, and at the same time recommend it to my friends."

"Your patterns are a great boon to me."

"I really do not know what I should do without your useful needlework books."

"I made all my baby's long clothes so successfully from the patterns contained in 'Weldon's Home Dressmaker,' No. 67. When I started dressmaking a couple of years ago out in Java, I was absolutely inexperienced, not even knowing which way a sleeve ought to go in."

"I have taken 'Weldon's' for the last seven years, and like it better than any other paper. It is a most useful paper for people who live in the bush and small inland towns."

"Your patterns are certainly splendid; anyone can make from them, they are so plain and fully explained."

"I am passing specimen copy on to a friend. I think all your publications are very good, and the patterns very useful. I have used them for years, also the needlework books."

"I would not like to be without the 'Weldon's Journal,' for I think it always so charmingly interesting."

"Let me take this opportunity of saying how very useful I find your patterns, and what a very nice paper I think 'Weldon's Ladies' Journal' is. I have taken it in now for a year and shall always recommend it to my friends."

"Miss Shatton is writing to let Messrs. Weldons know that the pattern bodice made for her and the one made for her sister are perfect fits, and they are very pleased with them . . . the fitter took great pains over fitting the patterns."

"I received parcel of books and am delighted with them. I have made practical use of several of the free patterns enclosed and found them perfect. I most certainly will endeavour to persuade my friends to get your several magazines from their newsagent, as I intend in future to do myself."

"Success to your paper."

"I have taken your paper for years, and find it most satisfactory."

"Mrs. Jones wishes to say she has used Weldon's fashion books for many years, and has found them everything she could wish, and recommends them to all her friends."

"I know from personal experience that Weldon's patterns cannot be beaten."

"I am pleased to say I find Weldon's magazines and patterns splendid. By their help I am able to make my own and little one's dresses, and have done so for the last ten years."

"I may say I have taken 'Weldon's Ladies' Journal' for some time, and find your patterns excellent."

"I am very pleased with Weldon's publications, and will endeavour to introduce them to my friends, as they are most useful. I had no idea you issued so many."

"Many thanks for books and patterns safely received. I think they are wonderful value for money."

"I will do my best to introduce Weldons publications to my friends, as I have always found them to be most useful 'to me in dressmaking and household duties."

"I think your 'Weldon's Journal' a most helpful paper, and I prefer the patterns to any others I have tried. Wishing you continued success."

"I think Weldon's journals should be recommended everywhere, especially among families."

"I invariably take in Weldon's magazines, and I find them of great assistance."

"Being a dressmaker, I always buy Weldon's Fashion Books."

"I consider your books and patterns are the best one can get."

"I have always found Weldon's patterns excellent both for myself and my little daughter. My mother has also used them for years, and she thinks they are the best that can be obtained."

"In concluding I must add my little meed of praise for the excellent assistance your books give. I have been dressmaking in this little town of your Antipodes for nearly forty years, and have subscribed to various fashion periodicals, but as soon as 'Weldon's' were introduced here, I recognised their value, and have ever since been a subscriber to 'Weldon's Ladies' Journal,' 'Bazaar,' 'Illustrated Dressmaker,' and occasionally the 'Home Dressmaker,' and have watched with interest the progress of each. I can safely say that Weldon's patterns can *always* be relied upon; I could not truthfully say this of others. This is the first time I have applied for patterns, other than those supplied gratis with the Journals, but should they prove as satisfactory you will certainly hear again from me. With best wishes for the continued prosperity of your valuable journals."

"The Countess Guendi is very pleased with 'Weldon's Ladies' Journal. There is a great field in Italy for goods such as yours."

WELDON'S
PRACTICAL APPLIQUÉ WORK.

(FIRST SERIES.)

With New Designs of the Various Stitches Suitable for all Purposes.

FIFTY-TWO ILLUSTRATIONS.

The Yearly Subscription to this Magazine, post free to any Part of the World, is 2s. 6d.
Subscriptions are payable in advance, and may commence from any date and for any period.

The Back Numbers are always in print. Nos. 1 to 192 now ready. Price 2d. each, or bound in 16 Vols., price 2s. 6d. each.

APPLIQUÉ WORK.

THE word "appliqué" is from the French, and signifies the securing of one material on to another. It is a work which saves much labour in large pieces of work, and is quickly done, besides being most effective and handsome. Before going to the newer kind, I will commence with the ordinary and oldest kind of appliqué, which is generally composed of velvet, plush, satin, and silk laid according to the pattern chosen upon a handsome groundwork. Designs with large flowers or fruit look best, or griffins, or conventional designs. The tracing must be very accurate, and the design not so close a one as for crewel work, but bold and striking. First cut out the pattern, when traced, on, say plush, and paste it upon satin sheeting. When perfectly dry, couch it all round with gold cord, single or double, or a strand of filoselle.

Couching.—No. 24 consists of sewing down the gold cord or filoselle all round the design at equal distances, as clearly shown in our illustration, with stitches brought from the back of the work as you proceed, the ends to be put through to the back of the work with a stiletto, and firmly secured. In the newer appliqué work it is always worked round with chain or feather stitches before the couching, but in this case the pasting is not required, dut merely a few tacking threads to keep the work in its place. The veining of the leaves and flowers or small stalks, which are too qelioate for appliqué, should be worked in crewel or satin stitch

No. 1.—Square for a Quilt Bag, or Cushion in Appliqué.

with silks. Plush flowers and leaves look very well cut out singly and laid on the pattern, and the stalks and stems done in stem stitch with silks. But the newer patterns have wide stalks and stems, so that this mode is not necessary, and makes the work much easier.

When the work is completed it is as well to paste over the back in order to keep the ends tidy, or sew them down and line the work with coloured twill, Bolton sheeting, or a cheap silk or satin. There should never be too great a contrast between the groundwork and the design, nor too lavish a use of bright colours. Bright shades can be used, but must be toned down according to the present ideas, and intermingled with still more subdued ones.

For church work appliqué is very suitable, and brown plush on gold-coloured satin sheeting gives good effect, secured with gold or silver cord, either single or double. The veining can be done with gold, silver, or copper-coloured thread, which is now so much in use. It may be necessary to buttonhole down such materials as those which fray out readily. The couching then follows closely to it, and it is then perfectly firm and secure; or feather stitch, with or without couching, is effective.

I will now proceed to the newer kind of appliqué work, often called Baden Appliqué, which is an easy, effective, and useful work. In washing materials use oatmeal cloth and white linen for the backgrounds, or coloured Bolton sheeting looks well, particularly pale blue.

First trace the design with black carbonic paper (to be had at any stationer's) with a bone crochet hook upon the red twill, or navy blue or sage green twill are effective ; but with the green, silks go best. The designs should be stiff, upright, conventional flowers or fruits, such as pomegranates, lilies, poppies, tulips, irises, sunflowers, chesnuts, dahlias, &c., or an all-over design, such as a large spray of pomegranates or sunflowers, which is placed in the centre of the oatmeal cloth with tacking threads, while the stiff designs would be arranged three or four inches from the bottom of the antimacassar. Work all over the lines of the pattern in chain stitch (see illustration) with Dewhurst's Three Shell embroidery cotton, No. 18 ingrain-red or blue cottons, or Faudel and Phillips's excellent knitting cottons by the skein ; or crewels in dark sage greens for the leaves can be used, and colours for the flowers, two shades of brown-yellows for the tulips or irises, reds for the poppies, and light peacock-blues for the lilies in a conventional style, and so on. Filoselles can be used, but the foundation should then be olive green or crimson satin sheeting, and a couching (No. 24) instead of spike stitches (as illustrations 5, 6, and 7) ; besides, the cottons and crewels are best for washing pieces of work. Outline the veinings in crewel stitch or chain stitch (No. 34). Pomegranates require the centres cutting out, and a few French knots worked on the foundation where the centres are cut from (as No. 21). Now proceed with a sharp pair of scissors to cut out the twill all round the edge of the pattern on the outside edge, leaving a groundwork of the oatmeal cloth. Do not cut too closely to the chain stitch in case it frays out ; then work any of the spike stitches (shown by illustrations 5, 6, and 7) all round the outside edge, emanating from the chain stitches, and extending to the oatmeal groundwork, as these illustrations clearly show, which give a good variety of spike stitches.

Edge the antimacassar with lace, and it is completed. A pomegranate centre (No. 21), when the material is cut out for French knots (No. 35), will require spike stitches all round the inside edge, as clearly shown by illustrations 21 and 44. These antimacassars wash well with bran in the water, and no soda to be used. Holland is also as useful as the twill for the appliqué, but then flourishing thread to match is requisite, and a dark background, such as red serge. Holland also looks well on pale blue Bolton sheeting. A conventional pattern can also be worked in these materials.

This work can likewise be edged all round with short satin stitch, as in crewel work (see illustration 19). Two shades of red filoselles on Turkey-red twill look well, and besides satin sheeting for a background, linen can be used, but the combination is not so serviceable. Illustration 11 is of Turkey-red twill, the flower and top of the bud being worked in satin stitch in red silk, while the leaves,

stem, and inside decoration of the bud and flower are worked in a deeper shade, the contrast of red silk being excellent. Yellows and browns in silks go well with sage green twill for sunflowers, and browns and greens for the leaves, as shown by illustration 2, which is traced on faded green twill, which can be mounted on any foundation and colour desired. Our illustration shows for the entire sunflower to be worked with chain stitch in deep gold silk, round the outer edge of which is a couching of brown silk, done as clearly shown by illustration 24. The centre of the sunflower is worked in crewel stitch with brown silk, then the leaves and stalks are outlined with chain stitch in a faded green silk of a brighter shade to the twill, bordered with a couching of brown. This is very quickly worked, and is most effective for antis, pillows, bags, &c. Illustration 30 shows a pretty design for a corner, and would be worked about 17 inches long, while a useful square is shown by illustration 46.

No. 2.—Sunflower in Appliqué, Worked in Stem and Chain Stitches, Outlined with Couching.

Begonia leaves, of which a worked spray is shown by No. 20, and a lovely border by No. 31, make handsome mantel and bracket borders, as well as clusters for pillows, antis, table-cloth corners, &c., and have the advantage of being quickly worked. Procure a yellow-green twill, which tack upon peacock blue or olive green Bolton sheeting, veining and outlining the leaves with dark red silk ; then round the outer edge of the leaves and stems work a couching in deep gold silk.

If crimson plush be used for a foundation, a pale sea-green satin can be used for a border of dahlias or other flowers, a satin stitch edge all round the flowers in a light crimson filoselle ; then for the lines, veinings, and couching all round use a darker shade of crimson filoselle. The centres of the flowers to be yellow. For the leaves a dark green filoselle in satin stitch, and a couching of sea green filoselle to match the satin. This gives a really beautiful piece of work. If chesnuts are to be worked (see illustration 19), use sage green twill with a satin stitch edge (with or *without* couching beyond it) for the leaves and stalks, and dark green or brown veinings. The chesnuts to be *fully* worked in satin or crewel stitch in gold, shading to brown, and a darker brown for the French knots all over the chesnuts. Our illustration clearly shows the light part to be of the gold silk, with the dark shading round the chesnut to be of brown filoselle or silk. Sunflowers look well in red twill on peacock blue serge, as shown by illustration 22. The outline and veinings entirely in a dark red crewel, and the spike stitch edge worked with bright red soft Saxon knitting yarn, Faudel and Phillips's Peacock quality, which gives a very handsome effect. Cut out the centres of the sunflowers, work two rings of chain stitch all round, and then cross bars of chain stitch, forming a network of squares, in dark red crewel, over the centres of these little squares being worked with French knots, which

No. 3.—Spray for Quilt or Cushion.

No. 4.—Griffin Design

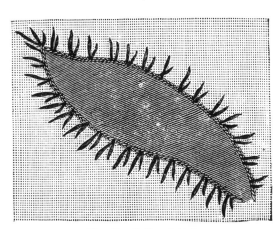

No. 5.—Spike Stitch.

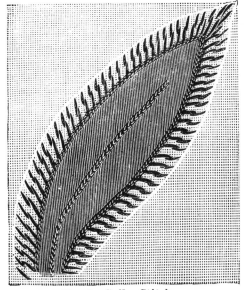

No. 6.—Spike Stitch.

No. 7.—Three-Spike Stitch.

No 8.—Spray of Thistles for Bag, Cushion, or Quilt.

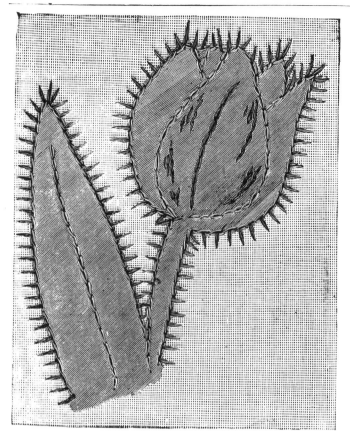

No. 9.—Tulip Outlined with Chain and Spike Stitches.

No. 10.—Spray of Lilies.

No. 11.—Passion Flower and Leaves Outlined in Satin Stitch.

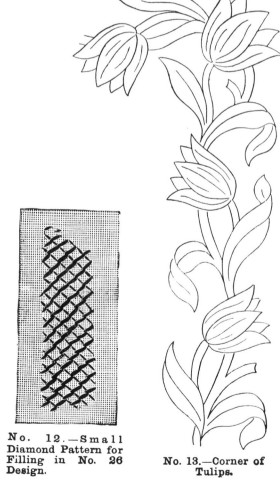

No. 12.—Small Diamond Pattern for Filling in No. 26 Design.

No. 13.—Corner of Tulips.

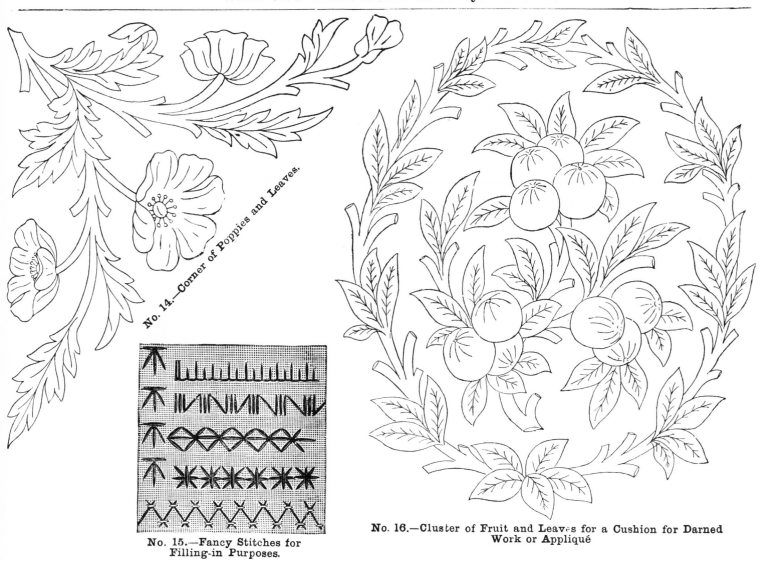

No. 14.—Corner of Poppies and Leaves.

No. 16.—Cluster of Fruit and Leaves for a Cushion for Darned
Work or Appliqué

No. 15.—Fancy Stitches for
Filling-in Purposes.

No. 17.—Pomegranate Spray for a Quilt, Bag, Cushion,
and other Purposes.

No. 18.—Design for Brush and Comb Bag in
Appliqué or Darned Work.

No. 19.—Chesnut and Leaves in Appliqué, Outlined with Satin Stitch.

No. 20 - Begonia Leaf for Appliqué, Out Stitch and Couching, with Veining done

No. 23.—Artistic Design for a Splash Back for Coarse Outline Work or Appliqué.

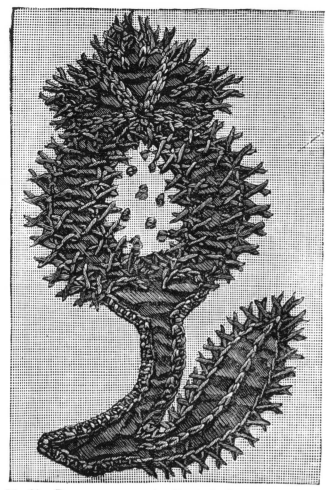

No. 21.— Pomegranate in Appliqué, Centred with French
Knots Outlined with Satin and Spike Stitches.

No. 22.-- Manner of Working a Sunflower in Appliqué, Outlined
with Chain and Spike Stitches.

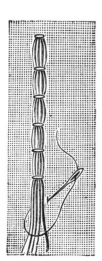

No. 24.—Manner of
Working Couching
for Designs 2 & 20

No. 25.—Design for Outline or Appliqué Work.

give a pretty effect, and illustration 22 clearly shows a sunflower and leaf worked with the rest of the material traced and tacked on the blue serge ready for working.

Another style is a white linen appliqué on red twill, worked in Dewhurst's embroidery cotton in red, No. 18, and white flourishing thread, which washes extremely well; or red twill on oatmeal worked in the same manner for a tea-cloth or mantel-border, griffins forming a most effective design for working. The edge can be buttonholed closely in white everywhere, and outlined *inside* all round, as well as the veinings, in the red cotton. Another way is to work the buttonhole stitches a little way apart in red, with the spike part of the stitches lying outside, beyond a chain stitch outline; or besides the chain stitch outline, this latter buttonhole edge both inside and outside it, one edge in red and the other in white.

Chain stitch, feather stitch, buttonhole stitch, French knots, cross stitch, coral stitch, satin stitch, outline stitch, couching, and spike stitches will all be found requisite for the different kinds of appliqué work, and give beautiful effect if applied with taste and skill, according to the design that is to be worked, and likewise according to the materials used, and our readers would find "Weldon's Practical Crewel Work," price 2d., post free 2½d., very useful for showing the various stitches, &c., for embroidery. One pattern would look best with only chain stitch or satin stitch, and couching beyond, with perhaps French knots for the centre of a flower for silk work, while in cottons buttonhole stitch, either close or the stitches worked a little way apart, for an edge would be suitable. Or with crewels the chain stitch and spike stitches, and so on. Feather stitch fills in a stem, as also coral stitch, and outline stitch for the lines and veinings if chain stitch is not used for the latter purpose.

Pomegranates, as shown by illustration 21, look well in dark blue twill on cream oatmeal or mummy cloth, the entire pattern being bordered with chain stitch; then when the superfluous twill is cut away, work on either side fancy spike stitches, dotting the centre with French knots all worked with Dewhurst's embroidery cotton in navy blue. Red twill worked with red cotton on a cream ground looks well; the illustration clearly shows the different stitches and manner of working this bold and effective design. Illustrations 17, 33 and 37 show pretty arrangements of pomegranates and leaves.

Illustration 9 shows a tulip in red twill worked on a linen foundation, the entire flower and leaves being outlined with pale blue crewel in chain stitch, the centre line of chain and little dashes in the centre of the tulip being worked in a darker blue to match the spike stitches, which entirely edge this design. The two shades of wool are clearly illustrated, so no difficulty need be experienced by even an amateur doing this effective and quickly executed work.

Lilies always work out effectively, and illustration 32 shows for red twill on a linen foundation, the entire flower being outlined and veined in chain stitch work with yellow crewels. The spike stitches round the flower are executed in yellow, while the stem and leaves are worked in dark faded green crewel. Of course, any colours can be chosen for these designs as well as materials, the great point being to make something artistic and pretty.

Illustration 26 shows another way of producing embroidery, the entire design being outlined with crewel or silk in chain stitch, No. 34, and the veining done in stem stitch. The entire groundwork is then worked with some fancy stitch, such as small diamond patterns, as illustration 12, and any two shades can be employed. The darkest shade would be used for the chain stitch and veining, and any material one may desire to employ can be thus ornamented.

Cretonne Work is a species of appliqué in a modern style, although not so fashionable as hitherto. A good pattern always looks well, and this work is useful for wall brackets, as well as being very effective and quickly done. Be careful to select a good bold design, sunflowers always look well. Cut out the sunflower cretonne sprays and arrange them on a satin or plush bracket in an effective manner with tacking threads. They can be button-holed all round if a quick way is desired, or a thick satin stitch in silks all round the edges, prevents them fraying. Use gold filoselle for the flowers and green for the leaves, matching the cretonne colouring as nearly as possible. This has a very pleasing effect when completed, and in the distance has the appearance of silk embroidery. A border looks well, if a good pattern, outlined everywhere on the cretonne with gold cord without cutting it out. In cretonne work the flowers and leaves need not be worked over in the centres and veinings, but some people prefer to touch them up a little with effective stitches here and there.

The Arabian Work is also a species of appliqué, and the chief material used is what is termed a "poor man's handkerchief" in England, or the coloured peasant's handkerchief to be had in France, where the best patterned ones are to be met with. The old-fashioned pine pattern gives the best effect, and can be obtained at some fancy-work or draper's shops, but everything depends upon the pattern of these cotton handkerchiefs, as well as taste in the worker. For a border or bracket, cut out the pines, and arrange them according to taste upon satin sheeting with tacking threads; place them in a row according to size and one's fancy, then feather stitch them all round, and edge with spike stitches—a short stitch and a long stitch look best. Inside these two rows on the pine, work a ring of cross stitches close together all round the circle, then work a straight line in crewel

No. 26.—Design for Outline Work in Chain Stitch, Groundwork Filled in with Small Diamond Stitch, No. 12.

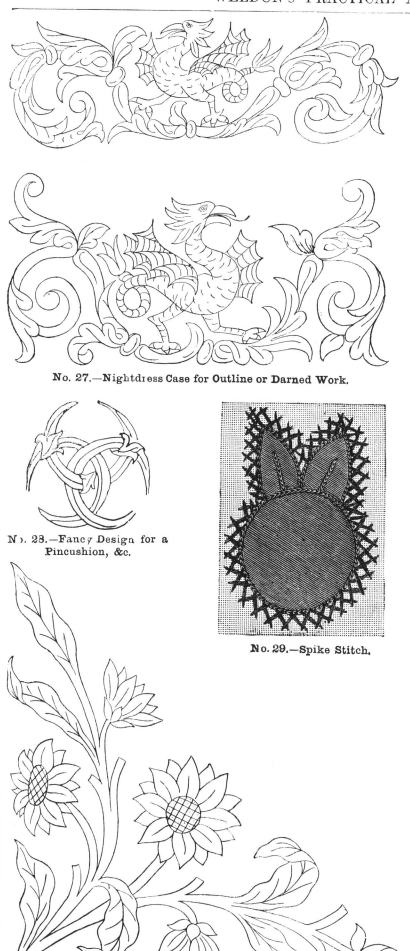

No. 27.—Nightdress Case for Outline or Darned Work.

No. 28.—Fancy Design for a Pincushion, &c.

No. 29.—Spike Stitch.

No. 30.—Sunflowers arranged as a Corner for Table Cloths, Cushions, &c.

No. 31.—Begonia Leaves for Mantel Border or Table Cloth.

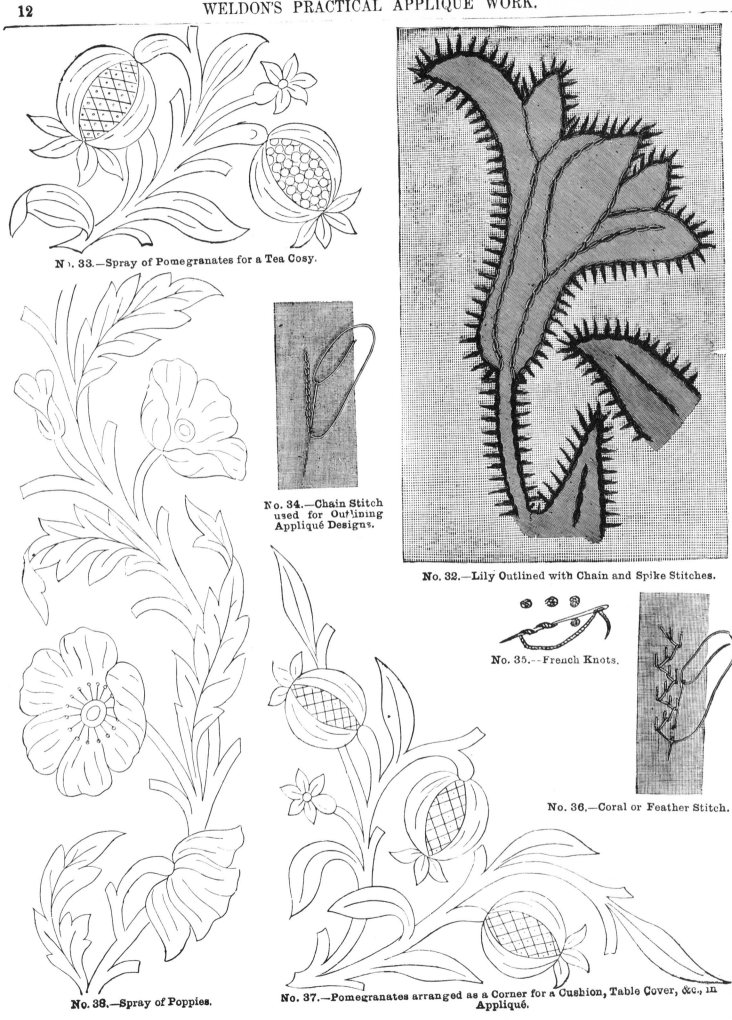

No. 33.—Spray of Pomegranates for a Tea Cosy.

No. 34.—Chain Stitch used for Outlining Appliqué Designs.

No. 32.—Lily Outlined with Chain and Spike Stitches.

No. 35.--French Knots.

No. 36.—Coral or Feather Stitch.

No. 38.—Spray of Poppies.

No. 37.—Pomegranates arranged as a Corner for a Cushion, Table Cover, &c., in Appliqué.

No. 39.—Design of Tulips for an Antimacassar in Appliqué.

No. 40.—Herringbone Stitch.

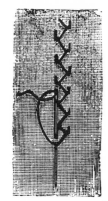

No. 41.—Single Coral or Feather Stitch.

No. 43.—Griffins for Outline or Appliqué Work for Antimacassar or Sofa Back.

No. 42—Corner of Pomegranates.

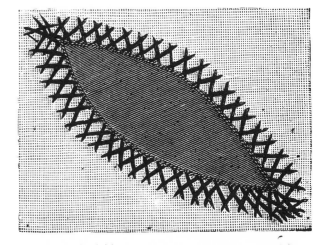

No. 44.—Herringbone Stitch for Appliqué Work.

No. 45.—Tulip Spray to be Worked after Design No. 9.

outline stitch on both sides of these, or only on the inside edge if thought sufficient. Then another row of cross stitches, and so on, and again feather stitch all round the circle, all in different coloured silks for each round until the centre is reached, then a line of gold braid is effective; the extreme centre to be worked in satin stitch in pretty shades according to the pattern (and the colouring of the pattern) which exists there.

For small tea-cloths a whole handkerchief can be used, with the centre cut out and a plush centre inserted in its place, the border of the handkerchief to be worked all over in satin stitch, or as the cut-out pines, according to the pattern it may be, as well as one's own ideas and taste, and any fancy stitches may be used. In some cases the centre of the handkerchief can be cut out and worked all over, and then a plush *border* added all round it. This work much resembles Indian embroidery, and any bright shades may be used, being a good way to use up odds and ends of silks, no matter how short the lengths. Crewels may be used if preferred, and I have seen a nightdress case look well done in this manner, giving a handsome and original effect.

A lace pattern handkerchief to work all over is a good pattern, the bars of the lace work to be worked in outline stitch, showing the usual black or red groundwork through. Gold cord all round the edge of pattern is an improvement, and fancy stitches to fill in look well, and give a variety in appearance. Tussore silk with patterns on it, designed especially for this purpose, is the newest kind of thing in this work, and may be had at Liberty's in Regent Street, who have a choice assortment of silks, materials, and muslins for decorative purposes.

No. 47.—Roman Appliqué.

No. 46.—Sunflower for a Quilt, Cushion, Square, &c., to be Worked after No. 22 Style.

Roman Work (as shown by illustration 47) is composed of holland appliqué, over red or blue twill, with a close buttonhole stitch all round the pattern, with or without bars between, like lace work. It is useful for nightdress cases and general purposes.

WELDON'S
PRACTICAL NETTING.

(FIRST SERIES.)

Full Details as to the Requisites for Netting, also Explanatory Notes and Illustrations. Stitches fully Explained and Illustrated.

The Yearly Subscription to this Magazine, post free to any Part of the World, is 2s. 6d.
Subscriptions are payable in advance, and may commence from any date and for any period.

The Back Numbers are always in print. Nos. 1 to 214 now ready, Price 2d. each, or bound in 17 Vols., price 2s. 6d. each.

NETTING.

NETTING is one of the prettiest kinds of Fancy Work, and has been fashionable from time immemorial. The materials are inexpensive and easily obtained, and the work possesses the advantage of great strength and durability, combined with extreme lightness and laciness of appearance. Every stitch is independent and distinct in itself, and cannot by any possibility become unravelled or undone ; netting, therefore, is a work that can be laid down at any moment, and taken up again, without fear of stitches running as they sometimes do in knitting and crochet.

Very many useful articles can be made in netting. A few years ago netted curtains were seen almost everywhere, and were especially nice for rooms with a north aspect, as they do not obscure the light. They have, however, been displaced by the cheapness of woven lace curtains; and now there is a rage for netted d'oyleys, or damask d'oyleys with a netted edge, also for lace of various widths for trimming dresses, and narrower lace for edging underlinen; fine netted collars and cuffs look well on little boys' knicker-bocker suits, and are pretty for ladies' morning wear ; netted fichus, neck-handkerchiefs, and shawls need only to be seen to be appreciated ; while netted gloves and mittens, caps, purses, antimacassars, &c., will always be found useful.

Plain netting can be much elaborated and improved by means of darning on the groundwork with a needle and cotton, and filling up certain holes of the netting so as to produce a pattern of stripes, diamonds, or other design. Almost any of the geometrical and conventional patterns arranged for cross-stitch can be adapted and reproduced in darned netting, and among these may be mentioned the borders No. 14, No. 31, No. 41, and No. 50, in our "Practical Cross-Stitch" paper, No. 14 of this series.

Another form of netting is the coarse work employed for hammocks, for lawn tennis nets, and fishing nets.

Then there is Guipure netting, or Guipure d'Art, consisting of squares of plain netting with a pattern embroidered thereon in point-lace stitches, in imitation of Cluny and point de Bruxelles ; but as it would occupy a great deal of space to explain and illustrate all the lace stitches that may be employed, this branch of the subject is not entered upon in the present paper, which is devoted solely to Fancy netting.

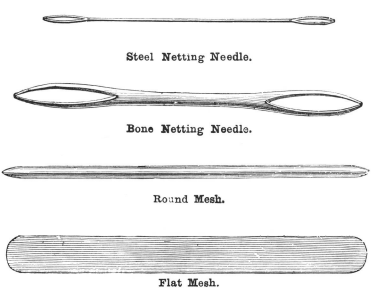

Steel Netting Needle.

Bone Netting Needle.

Round Mesh.

Flat Mesh.

NECESSARIES FOR NETTING.

REQUISITES FOR NETTING.

NETTING needles and meshes are made of steel for fine work, and of bone and wood for coarser work. Steel knitting needles are handy for meshes, and these and all other *round* meshes are gauged by Walker's Bell Gauge; a No. 14 knitting needle is equivalent to a flat mesh measuring an eighth of an inch wide, and a No. 7 knitting needle is equivalent to a flat mesh a quarter of an inch wide. Flat meshes are made of bone and wood, and are gauged by their width—a quarter of an inch, half an inch, and so on ; the larger the size of the stitch required, the wider must the mesh be, and the netting needle must be proportioned accordingly—not too large, or it will be difficult to push through the loop, and not too small, or it will hold only a scanty supply of thread, and so necessitate a number of joins. To fill a netting needle, pass the end of the thread through the little hole or eye, and tie it, then wind the thread through the prongs lengthways from end to end. A long darning needle may be employed for very fine netting, and is necessary when commencing a piece of work upon a linen or damask material which will not permit of a filled needle passing through. When copying from a worked pattern of netting, and wishing to estimate the size of the mesh used, measure by one side of a square, and select a mesh the exact size of it. Of course mesh and material must be suited to the work you are going to do. Strutt's best knitting cotton is used a good deal for netting, also Strutt's crochet cotton, Evans's crochet cotton, and Finlayson's Scotch linen crochet thread Any of the ordinary wools and silks may be used for netting.

It is essential that the foundation of the work be kept firm enough to offer sufficient resistance to enable the knots to be properly tightened, and for this purpose a heavily weighted cushion that may be placed upon a table is a most convenient apparatus; some ladies, however, who have been accustomed to a long stirrup to pass over the foot still prefer it. A stirrup may be made of a piece of ribbon, tape, or even string.

the stitch properly you must be careful to draw the thread tightly round the mesh by help of the loop still upon the little finger, and when it is as close as it can be release the loop from the little finger and draw the knot up tightly and securely. Repeat this process till you have as many stitches on the mesh as are necessary for the width of the work required. If more than will conveniently stand upon the mesh, you can let some drop off at the left-hand side. When the row is complete draw the mesh out, and a row of even loops will be found hanging from the stirrup string, attached thereto by knots, and sliding freely along it. Turn the work over so that the thread hangs at the left-hand side; place the mesh close to the lower edge of the row of loops, pass the thread round the fingers in the manner already described, and work another line of stitches, taking up in succession every loop of last row. Then turn again, and do a third row in the same way, and continue. All netting is worked from left to right, and it takes two rows to form a diamond. When the needle is emptied it must be refilled, and the new thread joined by a knot. It is advisable, if possible, to make all joins come at the end of a row. To save time, a piece of cotton netting, of sufficient width for a variety of purposes, may be kept

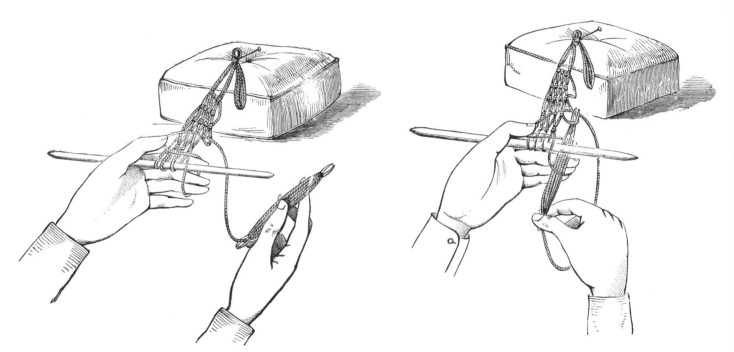

Fig. 1.—Showing the First Position.   Fig. 2.—Second Position.

METHOD OF WORKING.

THE STITCH OF NETTING.

HAVING your needle and mesh ready, and the stirrup secured to a cushion or passed round the foot, begin by tying the tag end of the thread to the string of the stirrup; then take the mesh in the left hand, and hold it firmly between the thumb and the first finger, under the thread, and close up to the knot you have just tied; take the needle in the right hand, and bring the thread from the knot down the front of the left hand and then round to the back, embracing the third and second fingers; pass it behind the mesh and *on* the first finger, and hold it there by pressure of the thumb, as see Figure 1; now carry the thread loosely towards the right over the foundation and behind the mesh and all the fingers, and then pass the needle upwards through the loop that encircles the third and second fingers, between the mesh and the first finger, under the stirrup string, and lastly over the part of the thread that proceeds backwards from under the thumb to the prong of the needle, see Figure 2, which, though representing a few rows of the work done, shows exactly the position of the hands. Now retain the mesh in just the same position as you have it while you draw the needle through and gradually tighten the thread in the form of a loop under the little finger, then (still drawing the needle) let go first the loop held in position under the thumb (see Figure 3), then the loop that embraces the third and second fingers; and now to form

upon the stirrup to use as a " foundation " for other netting; then when a piece of work is finished you cut the stitches of the last row of the foundation, and draw out the little ends of cotton from the stitches of the work.

No. 1.—PLAIN NETTING.

THIS is the ordinary netting stitch described above; it forms simple diamonds or lozenges, and is useful for a variety of purposes. Commence with the number of stitches necessary for the width required, and net as directed till you have sufficient rows for the length. When opened and spread out, plain netting should appear like the engraving No. 1. The plain netting stitch and the two stitches next following are the ones employed for darning upon.

No. 2.—SQUARE NETTING.

SQUARE netting is commenced at one angle or corner, and netted diagonally across the square to the opposite corner (see No. 2a). Begin by working two stitches on to the stirrup or into one loop of the piece of netting which serves as a foundation; withdraw the mesh, turn the work, and proceed as for plain netting but increase a stitch in every row by working *two* stitches in the *last* loop of the previous row. When you have the desired number of stitches on the mesh for the size of the half square, which will be one stitch *more* than the number of holes the finished square must contain along each side, do a row without increase; and then, to form the remaining half of the square, decrease by taking two loops together at the end of every row, and so reduce till two stitches only are on the mesh; break off the threads, and unite these two stitches together by knotting the end of the thread at the top of them. Release the work from the foundation, and draw the first corner up tightly with the tag-end of the thread. No. 2 shows a square finished. These squares are used for Guipure d'Art and for darning upon.

No. 3.—OBLONG NETTING

COMMENCE in the manner described for Square netting, and increase a stitch at the end of every row till there are *two* more stitches on the mesh than the number of holes the half square counts along each side, for so many holes as you have along the side of the half square, so wide will be the measurement of the oblong; this done, decrease at the end of the next row by taking

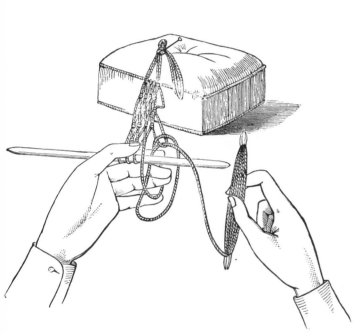

Fig. 3.—Third Position.

two loops together; and henceforth increase a stitch at the end of one row, and decrease a stitch at the end of the next row. Mark the decreasing side with a piece of coloured cotton, so that there may be no mistake. The side on which the increase is made is the longest side of the netting, and when this side is as long as you desire the oblong to be take two loops together at the end of every row, till the corner is brought to a point of two stitches only, when finish off as for the corners of Square netting. A piece of Oblong netting will appear as illustration No. 3. Lawn tennis nets are made in Oblong netting, it also is used for curtains, antimacassars, and various other articles.

No. 4.—DIAMOND NETTING.

AN uneven number of stitches are required for this pattern. Put on about 15 stitches to make a sample piece to get the stitch perfect. 1st row—Net 1 stitch in the ordinary manner, make the next stitch a long stitch by twisting the thread twice round the mesh, and repeat; the row will end with a plain stitch as it began. 2nd row—Plain netting, making even the stitches of last row. 3rd row—1 long stitch, 1 plain stitch, and repeat; end the row with a long stitch as it began. 4th row—Plain netting. Repeat these four rows for the length required.

No. 5.—SQUARE DIAMOND NETTING.

THIS is the same stitch as the pattern last described, only it is worked so as to form a series of squares instead of diamonds. Put on 2 stitches for the corner, and at the end of each row increase a stitch by working 2 stitches in the last stitch of last row. The pattern is formed by passing the thread once round the mesh for the small holes, and twice round the mesh for the large holes. In process of working be careful that a long stitch always comes under a short stitch, first one and then the other alternately. You can make a square suitable for Guipure d'Art, or carry the pattern on to form a piece of Oblong netting. Bring the last corner to a point by taking 2 loops together at the end of every row, and fasten off.

No. 6.—SWISS DIAMOND NETTING.

FOR this effective pattern put on any number of stitches divisible by five, and four stitches over at the end to make the edges correspond with each other. 1st row—Work 4 plain stitches, * work 1 long stitch by passing the thread twice round the mesh (to do this twist the thread once round the mesh before encircling the loops round the fingers; the other part of the stitch is made in the ordinary

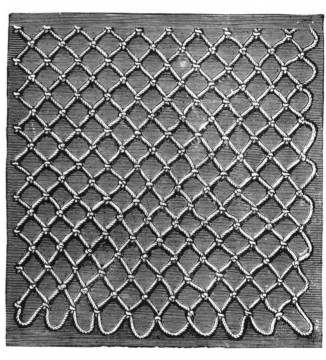

No. 1.—Plain Netting.

process of drawing up the knot), work 4 plain stitches, and repeat from * to the end of the row. 2nd row—1 long stitch, 3 plain stitches, * 1 long stitch into the centre of the long stitch of last row, 1 long stitch into the next plain stitch, 3 plain stitches, and repeat from *. 3rd row—1 long stitch, 2 plain stitches, * 1 long stitch into the next long stitch, 1 plain into the next long stitch, 1 long stitch into the next plain stitch, 2 plain stitches, and repeat from *, and end with 1 long stitch. 4th row—1 plain stitch, 1 long stitch, 1 plain stitch, 1 long stitch, * 2 plain stitches, 1 long stitch, 1 plain stitch, 1 long stitch, and repeat from *. 5th row—1 plain stitch, 2 long stitches, * 3 plain, 2 long, and repeat from *, and end with 1 plain stitch. 6th row—2 plain stitches, 1 long stitch, * 4 plain, 1 long, and repeat from *, and end with 1 plain stitch. 7th row—1 plain stitch, 2 long stitches, * 3 plain, 2 long, and repeat from *, and end with 1 plain stitch. 8th row—1 plain stitch, 1 long stitch, 1 plain stitch, 1 long stitch, * 2 plain, 1 long, 1 plain, 1 long, and repeat from * 9th row—1 long stitch, 2 plain stitches, 1 long stitch, * 1 plain, 1 long, 2 plain, 1 long, and repeat from *. 10th row—1 long stitch, 3 plain stitches, * 2 long, 3 plain, and repeat from *. This completes one pattern. Repeat the pattern from the first row.

No. 7.—ROUND NETTING.

ROUND netting much resembles plain netting in appearance and in manner of working, but by a trifling difference in the method of passing the needle through the loop the stitches are a little twisted, and a closer and more round-looking stitch is produced. It may be commenced with any number of stitches. When these are put on the stirrup string, and the mesh is withdrawn and placed in position ready for working the second row, proceed as follows :—Form the loop on your fingers in the usual manner, and pass the needle

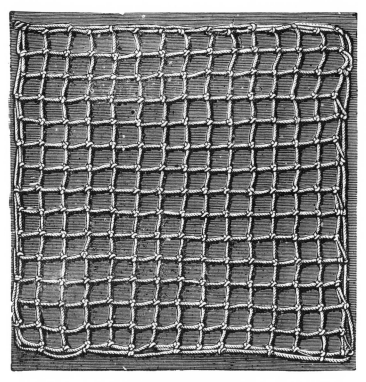

No. 2.—Square Netting.

upwards through the loop encircling the third and second fingers and between the mesh and the forefinger, but *not* taking up the netted stitch of last row; retain the position of the thumb and fingers, and loop while you draw the needle so far up as to bring the thread from it close under the little finger; turn the needle round, and insert it through the stitch of preceding row downwards over the mesh, the thread being to the right of the needle; draw it through, and now let the loops slip one by one from the fingers, and draw the knot in firmly; continue with every stitch in the same manner. Round netting is pretty and effective for purses.

No. 8.—LOOPED NETTING.

PUT on as many stitches as required for the width of the work. **1st row**—Thread twice round the mesh, and net one stitch, and with the thread once round the mesh net two more stitches in the same place; repeat this in every loop to the end of the row. Every succeeding row is the same, inserting the needle under the long loop of last row, and missing the two short loops. A very light, lacy-looking pattern is hereby produced.

No. 9.—SPOTTED NETTING.

COMMENCE by mounting any desirable number of stitches upon the stirrup string. **1st row**—Pass the thread twice round the mesh, and net 1 stitch, and in the same place net 2 more stitches with the thread once round the mesh. **2nd row**—With the thread passed twice round the mesh net 1 stitch in every long loop of last row, missing both the short loops. Repeat these two rows for the length required.

No. 10.—SPRIG NETTING.

THIS is a simple and pretty stitch, useful for any purpose for which a rather close pattern is preferred. Begin with any number of stitches. **1st row**—Net 3 stitches of ordinary plain netting in every loop. **2nd row**—Take up all 3 stitches together as one, be careful to draw the knot tightly, and repeat. Continue these two rows alternately.

No. 11.—SPIKE NETTING.

MOUNT any uneven number of stitches upon the stirrup string. **1st row**—Plain netting. **2nd row**—Work 4 stitches into the first loop, and 1 stitch in the next loop; 4 stitches in the next, and 1 stitch in the next, and so on alternately, and end with 4 stitches in the last loop of the row. **3rd row**—Plain netting, gathering together the group of increased stitches as one. **4th row**—1 plain stitch in the first loop, and a spike of 4 stitches in the next loop, and repeat. The spike stitches are to come between the groups of spike stitches in the second row. **5th row**—Plain, gathering the four spike stitches together as one. Repeat the pattern from the second row.

No. 12.—HONEYCOMB NETTING.

A PROPER combination of plain and twisted loops will produce the pretty Honeycomb pattern represented in the engraving No. 12 ; this is sometimes called "English" netting, and sometimes the "Box" pattern. It requires an even number of stitches. **1st row**—Plain netting. **2nd row**—Take up the second loop and net a stitch, then the first loop and net a stitch, next the fourth loop, then the third loop, and so on, doing alternately a stitch forward and a stitch backward to the end of the row. **3rd row**—Plain netting. **4th row**—Net a stitch in the first loop, next take up the third loop, then the second, next the fifth, then the fourth, and continue. Repeat the pattern from the first row. When a sufficiency is worked break off after doing the third row. This pattern is useful for a veil or a purse, also for window curtains and various other purposes.

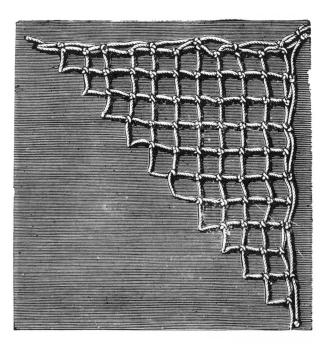

No. 2a.—Commencement of Square and Oblong Netting.

No. 13.—LEAF NETTING.

FOR Leaf netting, commence with any number of stitches divisible by four, and allow two stitches over at the end to bring the pattern in nicely. Net 2 plain rows. **3rd row**—Net 3 stitches in the first loop, 3 in the next, * 2 consecutive stitches plain, 3 in the next loop, and 3 in the next, and repeat from *. **4th row**—Gather together on the needle the first 5 loops of last row, picking them up in rotation from left to right ; these are the increased stitches of last row, and they form the "leaf ;" knot them together as 1 stitch, net 3 consecutive stitches plain, and repeat, ending with a "leaf" and 1 plain stitch **5th row**—Plain netting. **6th row**—Plain. **7th row**—Net the first 2 loops plain, * do 3 stitches in the next

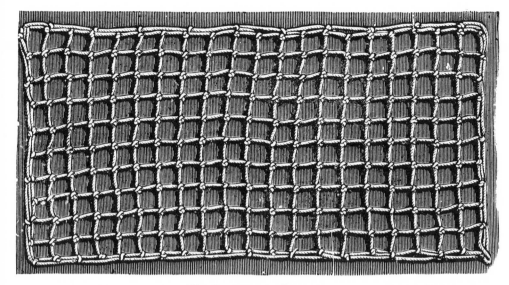

No. 3.—Oblong Netting.

loop, 3 in the next, then 2 stitches plain, and repeat from **8th row**—Net 2 stitches plain to begin, * pick up the next 5 loops on the needle and knot them together as 1 stitch, net 3 consecutive stitches plain, repeat from * to the end of the row, where there will be 2 stitches to net instead of 3. The "leaves" in this row are formed in intermediate position between those already done. **9th row**—Plain netting. **10th row**—Plain. Repeat from the third row for the length required, and leave off after doing the sixth row. Count the stitches in the plain row after every leaf, to ascertain that none have been increased or diminished. From its extreme lightness this pattern is pretty for a veil, for mittens, and a variety of purposes.

No. 14.—DOUBLE LEAF NETTING.

THIS much resembles the foregoing example, but the leaves are double, and therefore more distinct. Mount upon the stirrup string any number of stitches divisible by four, with two stitches over at the end to allow for uniformity of pattern. Work 2 rows of plain netting. **3rd row**—Net 3 stitches in the first loop, 3 in the next loop, * then do 2 consecutive stitches plain, 3 in the next loop, and 3 in the next, and repeat from *. **4th row**—Gather together on the needle the first 5 loops of last row, and knot them together as 1 stitch, net 3 stitches plain, * pick up the next 5 loops together and knot them as 1 stitch, net 3 stitches plain, and repeat from *, and end the row with a "leaf" and 1 plain stitch. **5th row**—Same as the third row. **6th row**—Same as the fourth row. **7th row**—Plain. **8th row**—Plain. **9th row**—Net 2 consecutive stitches plain to begin, * net 3 in the next loop, 3 in the next, then 2 stitches plain, and repeat from *. **10th row**—Net 2 stitches plain, * pick up on the needle the next 5 loops together, and knot them as 1 stitch, net 3 consecutive stitches plain, repeat from *, and at the end of the row there will be 2 stitches to net plain. **11th row**—Same as the ninth row. **12th row**—Same as the tenth row. **13th row**—Plain. **14th row**—Plain. Repeat the pattern from the third row. When a sufficient length is worked break off after doing the eighth row.

No. 15.—LEAF AND HONEYCOMB NETTING.

THIS pattern is formed by means of the Leaf netting and Honeycomb netting combined. Commence with any number of stitches

divisible by four, and 2 stitches over at the end to bring the pattern in nicely. Begin with the Leaf pattern, of which work 14 rows from the instructions already given ; then turn to the Honeycomb description, and work 10 rows ; and continue these two patterns alternately. If desired, the Honeycomb part may be netted with thread of a different colour from the Leaf pattern.

No. 16.—PERPENDICULAR NETTING.

ANY even number of stitches may be used for this pattern. **1st row**—Plain netting. **2nd row**—Miss the first loop of last row, take up the second loop and net a stitch, then net a stitch in the first loop, next take up the fourth loop, then the third, and so on alternately, a stitch forward and a stitch backward to the end of the row. These two rows constitute the pattern, and are to be repeated for the required length.

No. 17.—DIAGONAL NETTING.

COMMENCE with an even number of stitches. **1st row**—Insert the point of the needle in the first loop, and draw the second loop downwards through it ; net a stitch in the second loop, and then net a stitch in the first loop, not twisting the loops at all ; insert the point of the needle in the third loop, and draw the fourth loop downwards through it ; net a stitch in the fourth loop, and then a stitch in the third loop ; and continue crossing the loops and netting them to the end of the row. **2nd row**—Net the first loop plain, with the point of the needle pass the third loop downwards through the second loop, net a stitch in the third loop, and then net a stitch in the second loop ; pass the fifth loop downwards through the fourth

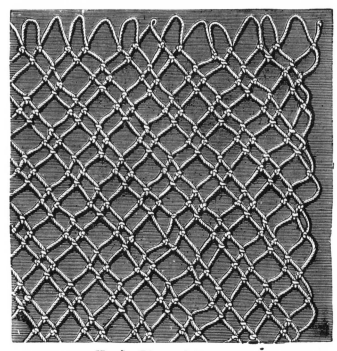

No. 4.—Diamond Netting.

loop, and net it, and then net the fourth loop, and proceed in like manner to the end of the row, where net the last stitch plain. **3rd row**—Same as the second row. **4th row**—Same as the first row. Repeat from the first row. You will observe the second and third rows have each an edge stitch, and the first and fourth rows have not. The pattern runs diagonally across from edge to edge.

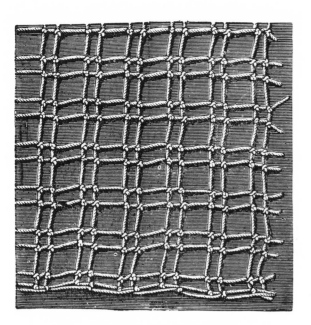

No. 5.—Square Diamond Netting.

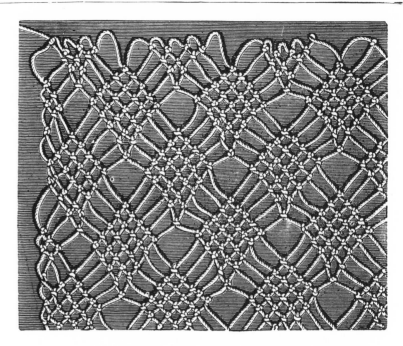

No. 6.—Swiss Diamond Netting.

No. 18.—GRECIAN NET, OR ROSE NETTING.

Two meshes of different size are necessary for the production of this pattern, which is one of the most charming designs in fancy netting. For the smaller of the two meshes select a steel knitting needle No. 9, and for the other a wooden needle No. 6, or what is better, a flat bone mesh, measuring about a third of an inch in width. Mount upon the stirrup string any even number of stitches. 1st row—Plain netting, with the large mesh. 2nd row—With the small mesh—draw the first loop of previous row upwards through the second loop of the same row, and net a stitch in it; then look through the first loop, the upper part of which is now secured in the knot you have just formed, and you will see a portion of the second loop crossing along just below; draw this part of the second loop up through the little opening under the knot, and net a stitch in it; entwine every two loops together in this manner to the end of the row. 3rd row—Plain netting, with the large mesh. 4th row—with the small mesh—net a plain stitch in the first loop of previous row, then draw the second loop upwards through the third loop, and net a stitch in it, and next bring the second loop up through the little opening under the knot, and net a stitch in it and continue, and finish with a plain stitch at the end of the row. 5th row—Plain netting, with the large mesh. Repeat from the second row. The pattern is complete upon the termination of the third row.

Another form of Grecian netting is a simple continuation of the first and second rows only, by which means the large holes are produced one over the other in a straight line. Whichever way it be done, Grecian netting is a favourite pattern for purses, mittens, neck-handkerchiefs, shawls, curtains, and numberless other articles.

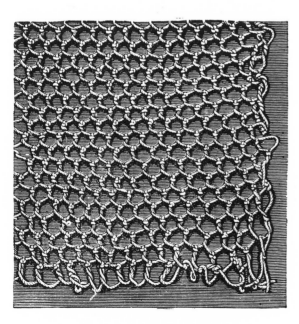

No. 7.—Round Netting.

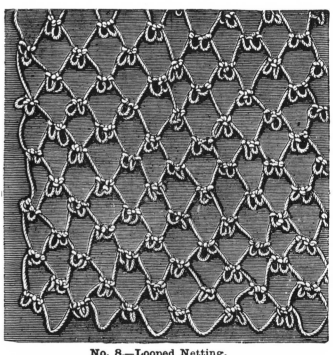

No. 8.—Looped Netting.

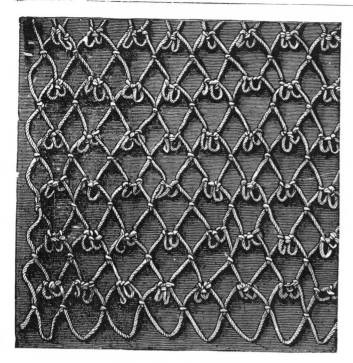

No. 9.—Spotted Netting.

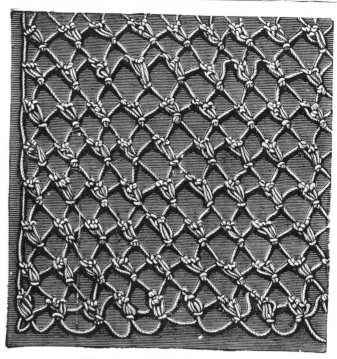

No. 10.—Sprig Netting.

No. 19.—MOSAIC NETTING.

(Otherwise called French Ground Net.)

MOUNT upon the stirrup string any even number of stitches. **1st row**—Net the first loop in the ordinary manner, make the next stitch a long stitch by twisting the thread twice round the mesh (to do this twist the thread once round the mesh before encircling the thread round the fingers; the other twist is given in process of drawing up the knot), and continue 1 plain stitch and one long stitch to the end of the row. **2nd row**—Plain netting. The stitches of last row being uneven in length, the stitches of this row will naturally draw uneven also. **3rd row**—Work alternately 1 long stitch and 1 plain stitch in this manner; draw the first loop of last row upwards through the first long loop of the first row, and net a long stitch in it; the pressure arising from this action causes the second loop of last row to come partially up in the same place; draw it up a little more prominently, and net a plain stitch in it, and proceed to the end of the row. **4th row**—Plain netting. **5th row**—Begin with 1 plain stitch in the first loop of last row, then continue 1 long stitch and 1 plain stitch alternately, drawing the loops of the fourth row up through the long loops of the third row, in the same manner as instructed for the working of the third row; end the row with 1 long stitch in the last loop. **6th row**—Plain netting. Repeat from the third row.

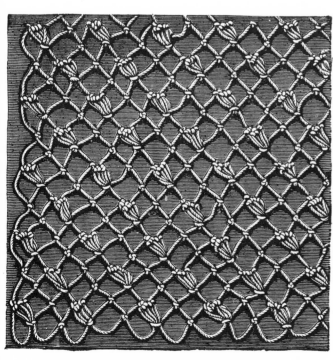

No. 11.—Spike Netting.

No. 12.—Honeycomb Netting.

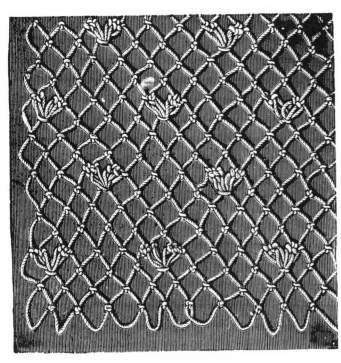

No. 13.—Leaf Netting.

No. 20.—ORIEL NETTING.

COMMENCE with any even number of stitches. **1st row**—Plain netting. **2nd row**—1 plain stitch and 1 long stitch alternately. **3rd row**—Long stitch netting, that is with thread twice round the mesh to every stitch. **4th row**—Draw the first loop of last row upwards through the first long loop of the second row, and net a plain stitch in it; draw the second loop of last row up in the same place, and net in it a plain stitch, and continue. Repeat the last two rows for the length desired.

No. 21.—VALENCIENNES NETTING.

PUT on any number of stitches divisible by four. Work **2** rows of plain netting. **3rd row**—Net two stitches plain,* thread over the mesh (*not* round the fingers), and insert the needle in the work below the knot immediately underneath in the last row but one, and draw the needle and thread through ; do this *twice* more, and you will have three loose loops (not stitches) on the mesh ; then pass the thread round the mesh and fingers in the usual way, and knot a plain stitch in each of the next 4 consecutive loops of last row, and repeat from * ; the row will end with 2 plain stitches. **4th row**— 1 stitch plain,* next gather 4 loops together on the needle, and knot them as 1 stitch ; net 3 consecutive stitches plain, and repeat from * ; there will be 2 plain stitches to net at the end of the row. **5th row**—Plain netting. **6th row**—Plain netting. **7th row**—Net 4 plain stitches to begin, then * below the knot immediately underneath, and in the last row but one make a group of loose loops as instructed in the third row ; knot a plain stitch in each of the next 4 consecutive loops of last row, and repeat from *. **8th row**—Plain netting. **9th row**—Plain netting, and repeat from the third row for the length required. The appearance of Valenciennes netting may be considerably altered by arranging the long loose loops in different positions, according to taste.

No. 22.—SPIDER NETTING.

TWO meshes are required for this, No. 12 and No. 3, or, instead of the latter, a flat bone mesh measuring half an inch in width. Commence with an even number of stitches, and

work 3 rows of plain netting with the smallest mesh. **4th row**—With the large mesh—net 1 stitch in each loop of last row. **5th row**—Also with the large mesh—take up the second loop, and net a stitch ; then the first loop, and net a stitch ; next the fourth loop, then the third loop, and so on, doing alternately a stitch forward and a stitch backward to the end of the row, and so crossing the stitches that they present the appearance shown in the engraving No. 22. Now work 3 rows of plain netting with the smallest mesh, and repeat the pattern from the fourth row.

No. 23.—OPEN TWISTED NETTING.

TWO meshes, No. 12 and No. 5, will be required. Mount an even number of stitches upon the stirrup string, and begin by doing 2 rows of plain netting with the smallest mesh. **3rd row**—With the largest mesh—net 1 stitch in each loop of the preceding row. **4th row**—With the small mesh—place the thread in position on the fingers as usual, and pass the needle upwards through the loop encircling the third and second fingers and between the mesh and the forefinger, and now draw the needle up, retaining the position of the thumb and fingers and loop, while you draw the needle so far up as to bring the thread from it close under the little finger ; insert the needle in the first loop of the preceding row, and to produce the coiled appearance shown in the engraving (No. 23), twist the loop twice from right to left round itself, then release the loops from the fingers and tighten the knot. Work to the end of the row similarly. **5th row**—Plain netting with the small mesh. **6th row**—Plain netting, with the large mesh. **7th row**—With the small mesh— draw the first loop of previous row upwards through the second loop of the same row, and net a stitch in it ; then look through the first loop, the upper part of which is now secured in the knot you have just formed, and you will see a portion of the second loop crossing along just below ; draw this part of the second loop up through the little opening under the knot, and net a stitch in it, and entwine every two loops together in this manner to the end of the row. **8th row**—Plain netting, with the small mesh. Repeat from the fourth row for the length required, and break off on the termination of the fifth row.

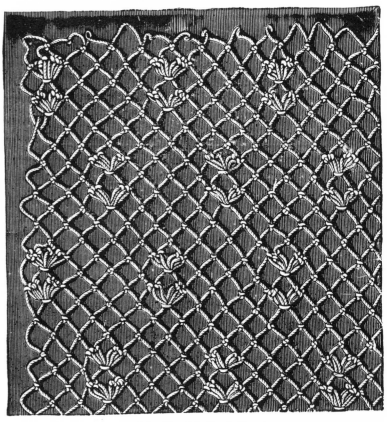

No. 14.—Double Leaf Netting.

nee lle, otherwise the needle cannot be passed through the loops of the netting. No loops whatever are entwined round the fingers. Hold the mesh and the needle in the usual manner; bring the thread over the mesh, and pass it round under the mesh (not round any of the fingers), and insert the needle from the back to the front of the work into the loop that is to be taken up (or in case of the first row under the stirrup string); draw the needle through in the direction of the left shoulder, and when the thread is strained close and tight round the mesh retain it there by pressure of the thumb; the loose thread from the prong of the needle should fall over the work from left to right; pass the needle from the back in an upward direction on the left-hand side of the thread forming this particular stitch, that is to say, not through any loop of the netting, but *between* the stitch you are now making and the next stitch to the left; now draw the thread tightly in a knot, and the stitch is complete.

HOW TO DARN UPON A NETTED FOUNDATION

THE size of the cotton used in netting the foundation must to a certain extent determine the selection of the cotton for darning. Supposing the foundation is worked with Strutt's knitting cotton, probably the same make and size will also be suitable to darn with, or a size coarser or finer may be used if preferred. Crochet cotton, though very strong for netting, is rather harsh for darning, and Strutt's knitting cotton, being softer, fills up the spaces better. Flourishing thread is nice to use upon fine cotton netting, to which it imparts a rich, shining appearance, owing to its glossy surface, so heightening the effect of the pattern. If any woollen article is to be darned, of course wool of the same texture will be selected for the

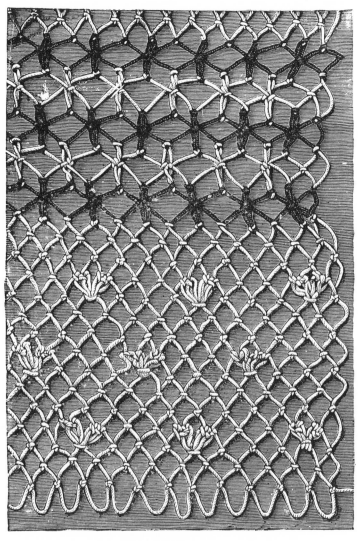

No. 15.—Leaf and Honeycomb Netting.

No. 24.—BUNCH NETTING.

PROCURE meshes of three different sizes, No. 14, No. 10, and No. 7. Begin with any number of stitches divisible by three, and allow two stitches over at the end of the row to bring the pattern in nicely. **1st row**—Plain netting, on mesh No. 10. **2nd row**—The same. **3rd row**—With the largest mesh—net 2 stitches plain, net 5 stitches in the next loop, and repeat, ending with 2 plain stitches. **4th row**—With the smallest mesh—net 1 stitch in every loop of the preceding row. **5th row**—Plain netting, with the smallest mesh. **6th row**—Plain netting, with the largest mesh. **7th row**—With mesh No. 10—net plain the 2 first loops of last row, * take up the 5 next loops, all on the needle, and net them together as 1 stitch (these are the 5 loops which were before increased), net the 2 next consecutive loops plain, and repeat from *. **8th row**—Plain netting, with the same mesh. Repeat the pattern from the third row.

A pleasing variation can be made in this pattern by working the second line of "bunches" in intermediate position between those made in the first line.

FISHERMAN'S NETTING.

SOMETIMES it is necessary to net with what is called a "fisherman's" knot; and as this is fashioned in rather a different manner from the ordinary knot used in working all the foregoing examples, it may be as well to explain the method of proceeding in case any one may wish to make trial of the same, though being chiefly adapted for coarse netting and for mending broken nets, it is not often required in ladies' work. The mesh must always be wider than the

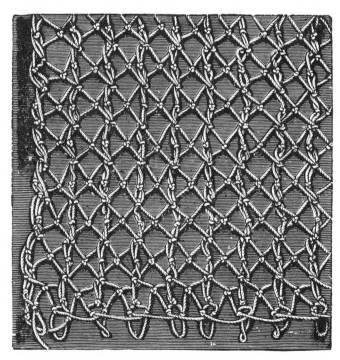

No. 16.—Perpendicular Netting.

darning, though it may be different in colour. An ordinary long darning needle will suffice to carry the cotton or wool. The patterns used for darning on Diamond netting are designed specially for the work, but most of the geometrical patterns applicable for square crochet and cross-stitch work are equally well suited for darning on Square or Oblong netting. The usual darning stitch is employed, inserting the needle over one thread of the netting and under the next; go as far as you can in a straight line, then turn, and put the needle over those threads it before went under, and *vice versâ*, till the space is filled. Do not on any account draw the darning but rather the reverse.   The stitches must all run in the same direction, either perpendicularly or from left to right, but not the two positions mixed in the same piece of work. If you wish to get from the filling of one hole to another hole close by you can twist the darning cotton almost invisibly round the intervening meshes of the netting, but if there be any distance to traverse it is neater to fasten off the darning cotton and begin again. Do not make any knots; turn all ends in neatly and securely.

needle again through the bead in an upward direction, so bringing on the knot; pick up another bead, and continue in like manner to the end of the row.

METHOD OF PUTTING ON BEADS TO FORM A PATTERN.

A LONG, fine darning needle is threaded with as long a needleful

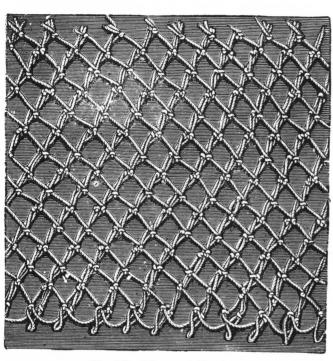

No. 17.—Diagonal Netting.

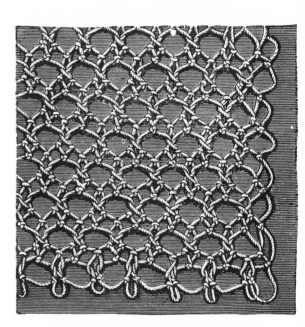

No. 18.—Grecian Net, or Rose Netting.

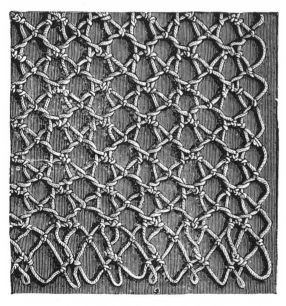

No 20 —Oriel Netting.

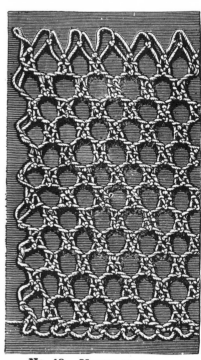

No. 19.—Mosaic Netting.

METHOD OF PUTTING ON BEADS SINGLY.

By this method the beads are brought *upon* the knot, and cannot slip about. Purses, mittens, and other articles can be considerably brightened in this way without being overweighted with beads. Take a fine long darning needle, and having threaded it with a sufficient length of silk, pick up a bead and slip it along close up to the mesh, net a stitch in the next loop as usual, and then pass the

of silk as is convenient to use, and the beads are picked up as required.   Usually 4 beads, or 6 beads, according to the size of the mesh, are picked up at a time; they are slipped down to the knot last made, and a stitch is netted in the next loop in the ordinary manner. In the succeeding row more beads are picked up, and the beads of last row are divided by the knot, so that 2 beads, or 3 beads, come on each side of the knot. Various designs of crosses, diamonds, and lozenges can be fashioned with beads.

NET FOR CATCHING MINNOWS.

REQUIRED a ball of fine green twine, and a netting needle, and No. 8 mesh. Commence with 16 stitches on a foundation thread of green twine. Draw out the mesh, and net a stitch in the first loop; tie the foundation thread round in a circle. Net 12 rounds plain and without increase. This makes a kind of little bag to hold a stone to sink the net into the water. **13th round**—Net 2 stitches in the first loop, net 1 stitch in the next loop, and repeat, which increases the number of stitches to 24. Net 2 plain rounds. **16th**

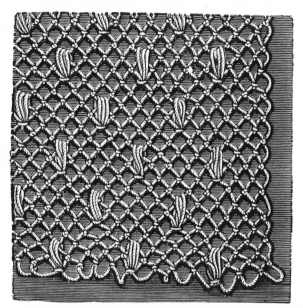

No. 21.—Valenciennes Netting.

round—Same as the thirteenth round, and thereby increasing to 36 stitches. Net 2 plain rounds. **19th round**—Net 2 stitches in the first loop, net 1 stitch in each of the next two loops, and repeat, which increases the number of stitches to 48. Net 2 plain rounds. **22nd round**—Net 2 stitches in the first loop, net 1 stitch in each of the next three loops, and repeat, so increasing to 60 stitches. Net 2 plain rounds. Now continue increasing 12 stitches in every third round, making these increase stitches *over* the stitch in which the last increase was made; the plain stitches between will, of course, augment one every time, and when there are 16 stitches between the increase stitches net 6 plain rounds, and finish with 2 rounds, turning the cotton twice round the mesh to make longer loops through which to pass a hoop. The number of stitches given will suit a hoop measuring two feet in diameter. If a larger net be wished for, a further number of rounds, increasing in every third round, will make it. Secure a stone in the little bag in the middle of the net, and tie thereon a few tufts of red wool to serve as a sort of bait.

HAIR-NETS.

THESE were formerly netted with black or brown silk for day wear, but have now fallen entirely out of use. Made with cotton, however, they are most comfortable things for keeping the hair tidy at night, and are particularly recommended to those who, not liking caps, still desire something close and yet light. Procure 2 reels of Dewhurst's crochet cotton No. 8, a steel netting needle, and meshes No. 8 and No. 5. Put 24 stitches on a foundation string, and work forwards and backwards in plain netting till you have made a perfect square. Now withdraw the foundation string, and replace it through the centre of the netted square. Net *round* the square, doing 1 stitch in each loop, 2 stitches in the corner loop in this first round, but afterwards no

increase whatever, only plain netting round and round till about 18 rounds are netted. Take No. 5 mesh, and net 1 plain round; in this round an elastic is afterwards to be run. Net for an edging— **1st round**—On No. 8 mesh, plain netting. **2nd round**—With No. 5 mesh—net 5 stitches in each loop of last round. **3rd round**—With No. 8 mesh—net 1 stitch in each of the 4 increased loops of last round, miss the intervening loop, and repeat. **4th round**—With the same mesh—net 1 stitch in each of the 3 loops of last round, miss the intervening loop, and repeat. **5th round**—With the same mesh—net 1 stitch in each of the 2 loops of last round, miss the intervening loop, and repeat. This finishes the net. Run an elastic or a piece of tape in the last round of the netting before the edging.

A GARTER.

THIS is a strip of plain netting, with a hole at one end similar to a button-hole. The strip is wound round and round the leg, and the other end is passed through the button-hole, turned back, and tucked securely underneath. Procure 1½ ozs. of strong black Scotch fingering, a netting needle, and No. 10 mesh. Begin with 22 stitches, and net 6 plain rows. Next work 10 stitches only, turn, and net back. Twice again net 10 stitches, and turn, and net back; break off the wool. Unite the wool to the last stitch on the opposite side, and net three times forwards and backwards 10 stitches only. Next row—Net 9 stitches; net 2 stitches in the next loop, which is the last loop before the button-hole; net 2 stitches in the first loop on the other side the button-hole; net 9 stitches to the end of the row; this restores 22 stitches in the row. Continue in plain netting till the garter is about 25 inches long; then reduce to a point by netting two loops together at the end of every row.

SILK PURSE, NETTED LENGTHWAYS.

THIS is a useful, strong purse, worked in rows of alternate colours.

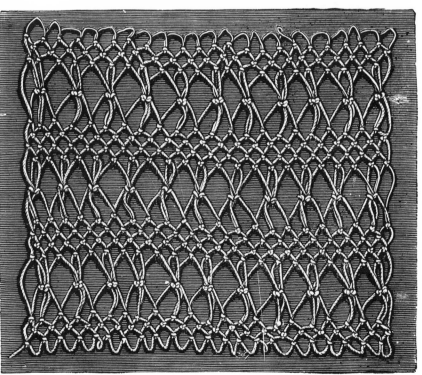

No. 22.—Spider Netting.

Black and amber make a pretty combination. Two skeins of purse silk of each colour will be required, and a steel netting needle, and No. 14 mesh. Begin with black silk by putting 70 stitches on a foundation. Break off the silk at the end of this and every row, and join on the other colour. **2nd row**—With amber silk, work in round netting to the end of the row. **3rd row**—Round netting with black silk. Continue thus till you have six inches netted; then draw up the ends, and join together 25 stitches each side, leaving the 20 centre stitches open for the admission of money. Add steel rings and tassels

LAWN TENNIS NETS.

THESE should be 8 or 9 yards long, and they are often made 5 feet high; in fact this is the height mentioned in the M.C.C. rules; but from 3 feet to 4 feet is amply high enough, as they are inconvenient when lying about on the ground, and by leaving space at

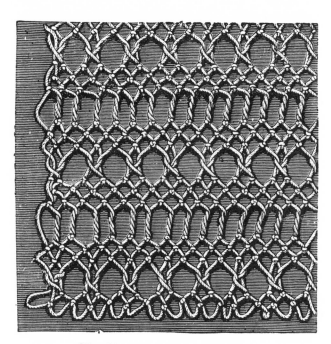

No. 23.—Open Twisted Netting.

the bottom one can roll the balls along the turf at the end of each game, instead of having to hit them over the net. Use coarse, strong twine, which may as well be a pretty colour as not. A net made with yellow twine, and having a piece of red and blue webbing run through the meshes at top and bottom and down the sides, will look remarkably effective. A mesh 1 inch or 1¼ inch wide will be required, and the work is done in the manner described for Oblong netting, viz., begin with 2 stitches, and increase a stitch at the end of every row till the half square of netting measures the same length along one of its sides as is desired for the width of the Tennis net; then mark the side upon which you intend to decrease, and at the termination of every row on *that* side take up two loops together, and net them as one stitch; increase as before in the rows which end on the *opposite* side, and when by this means the Tennis net is worked to its proper length bring it to a conclusion by taking two loops together at the end of every row. The "fisherman's knot" should be employed for this large netting, as no sawing of the twine is required to tighten the knot, nor are the fingers rubbed by the friction of the twine against them. If the Tennis net be made of common grey or brown string it should be soaked in tar before using, to make it durable and impervious to rain.

A HAMMOCK.

A HAMMOCK is generally used in the garden, and certainly is a very comfortable resting-place for those who like to sit much out of doors in sultry weather. It is made of a straight piece of netting

measuring about 2 yards long by 1½ yards wide. This netting is done in rows forwards and backwards, with coarse string or twine, upon a 2-in. wide wooden mesh. Instead of the ordinary knot, the "fisherman's knot" had better be employed, to save fraying the string and rubbing the fingers. Instructions for this knot are given on a previous page, and with a little practice it will be found quite as easy of accomplishment as the usual method. The hammock may be brightened by drawing slips of coloured cloth under the knots in process of tying them. When the piece of netting is finished slip a long round bar of wood into the meshes at that end of the netting which is to be the top of the hammock; the ends of this bar are to rest on branches of the trees. Run some thicker string through the edge stitches round the other three sides of the netting, drawing it in a little tightly; secure it round. Then with loops of string passed under this at the other two corners of the netting suspend the hammock in its place.

NETTED BEADED LONG PURSE.

THIS is worked in ordinary plain netting, and beads are introduced in every stitch. Procure 2 skeins of rather fine blue purse silk, 6 bunches of gold beads, a No. 14 mesh, and a fine long-eyed darning needle. The needle is to be threaded with as long a needleful of silk as is convenient to use, and the beads are picked up as required. Let the foundation consist of 40 stitches. On this net 1 plain row, and now to make it *round* draw out the mesh, and net a stitch in the first loop. **1st round**—Thread 4 beads on the needle, and slip them down to the knot just made; net a stitch in the next loop, and repeat to the end of the round. **2nd round**—Thread 4 beads on the needle, and net a stitch in the next loop, dividing the beads of last round so that they come 2 beads on each side of the knot, and repeat. Proceed in the manner directed for the second round till you have done three inches of the beaded netting; then for the opening of the purse

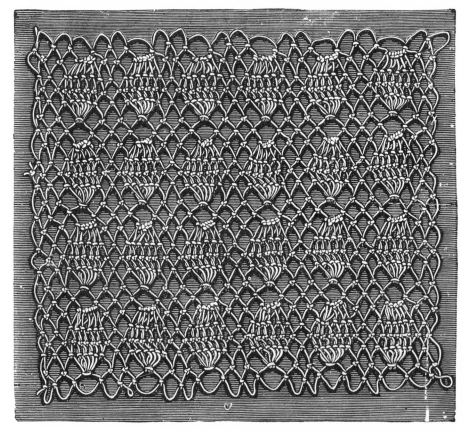

No. 24.—Bunch Netting.

work forwards and backwards in rows for two inches or a little over; and this done, again join, and work three more inches of round netting for the other end. Slip on two gold rings, and finish the purse with a fringe of gold beads at one end, and a long bead tassel at the other end.

WELDON'S
PRACTICAL MACRAMÉ LACE.

How to make Nightdress Cases,
Wall Pockets, Bags, Borders, Toilet Tidies, Cushions, Mats, &c.
EIGHTEEN ILLUSTRATIONS.
(THIRD SERIES.)

The Yearly Subscription to this Magazine, post free to any Part of the World, is 2s. 6d.
Subscriptions are payable in advance, and may commence from any date and for any period.

The Back Numbers are always in print.   Nos. 1 to 220 now ready, Price 2d. each, or bound in 18 Vols., price 2s. 6d. each.

No. 71.—TOILET TIDY.

THE model of this elegant tidy is worked in two separate pieces, one piece being for the front, the other for the back; it is executed with pink macramé thread, and the foundation is made of stout cardboard covered on both sides with dark crimson twill; the back is an oval piece measuring 8 inches long and 4¾ inches across at the widest part. First work the front piece, for which 26 threads, each measuring 2 yards in length, will be required; these threads are placed upon double foundation cords, as Figure 6 in "Weldon's Practical Macramé Lace," 1st Series, and so make 52 working threads. With the 4 centre threads work a Solomon's bar, as Figure 21, doing 24 knots or stitches: pin this up out of the way for the present. There are now 24 working threads on each side; with the 1st thread on the left-hand side work 14 buttonhole stitches upon the next 2 threads together, take the 24th thread in the left hand as leader slanting to the left, and work macramé knots on it with 23 threads to the left, take the 23rd thread as leader slanting closely underneath, and knot there on with 22 threads to the left; then with the 1st thread work 16 buttonhole stitches upon the next 2 threads together, now with the 21 threads towards the centre work 5 Solomon's knots close under the rib, using 5 threads to the 2nd knot and 4 threads to each of the others, leave 2 threads at each end, and work 4 Solomon's knots under the 5 knots, then leave 2 threads at the beginning (the side nearest the buttonhole stitches) and with the next 13 threads work 3 Solomon's knots, and leave 8 threads at the end; take the 24th thread in the left hand as leader to the left and on it work macramé knots with 23 threads to the left, take the 23rd thread as leader and knot on it with 22 threads; work 18 buttonhole stitches with the 1st thread over the 2nd and 3rd threads, then another line of double ribs; then 20 buttonhole stitches and a pattern of Solomon's knots worked as before, then

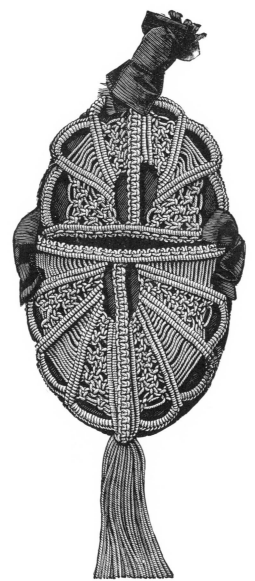

No. 71.—Toilet Tidy.

another line of double ribs, and this completes half the front of the tidy; work the other half to correspond; bring down all the threads smoothly and evenly in the centre as much as possible under the last two lines of ribs, let down the Solomon's knotted bar, and with the threads thereof tie all the threads of the scollop securely together in the form of a tassel, which should hang about 3 inches long. For the back of the tidy only 18 threads 1¾ yards long are required. Commence as described for the front, and work a bar of 19 Solomon's knots with the 4 centre threads. There are now 16 working threads on each side, with the 1st thread work 20 buttonhole stitches upon the 2nd and 3rd threads together, with the 13 threads towards the centre work 3 Solomon's knots, 4 threads in the first and last and 5 threads in the centre knot, leave 2 threads at each end and and work 2 Solomon's knots under these, then 3 knots, then 2 again, and then 1 knot, this last to be made with the 4 threads nearest the buttonhole stitches; take the 16th thread in the left hand as leader slanting to the left and work macramé knots on it with 15 threads to the left; take the 15th thread as leader and knot on it with 14 threads to the left; work 16 buttonhole stitches with the 1st thread on the 2nd and 3rd threads, then 2 more lines of ribs; now again do buttonhole stitches with the 1st thread upon the 2nd and 3rd threads making 14 stitches, and with the 13 threads to the centre work as before 3 Solomon's knots, leave 2 threads at each end and work 2 Solomon's knots under these, then 3 knots again, and finish the first half of the back by again working 2 lines of ribs; proceed with the other half to correspond; bring the ends down in the centre, lay the Solomon's bar in place, and after tying all securely together cut the ends even about 1 inch long. Make up the foundation for the tidy, sew on the macramé work, cover the ends of thread at the top with a bit of twill, and finish off with small ribbon bows on each side and at the top.

For references to Figures 1 to 152, see "Weldon's Macramé Lace," 1st Series, and for Figures 53 to 70, see "Weldon's Macramé Lace," 2nd Series

No. 72.—WATCH POCKET.

THIS useful little pocket is made with pink macramé thread, and is worked in two separate pieces, the front and back, in a pattern of small stars. The shape is formed of stout cardboard, covered on both sides with dark crimson sateen; the back measures 7 inches from point to point, and from 4 inches to 4½ inches in width. **For the Front**—Measure 24 threads from ½ a yard to 1 yard in length, and place them on foundation cords as Figure 6 in "Weldon's Practical Macramé Lace," 1st Series, the longest threads in the centre. This done, take the 1st thread as leader in the right hand, and on it work macramé knots with the 2nd, 3rd, and 4th threads; take the 2nd thread as leader in the same direction and work macramé knots on it with the 3rd, 4th, and 1st threads. Take the 8th thread as leader in the left hand, and work on it macramé knots with the 7th, 6th, and 5th threads, take the 7th thread as leader, slanting underneath, and knot upon it with the 6th, 5th, and 8th threads with the leader thread from the first point of the star, and with the next 3 threads to the left take the 4th thread from the end as leader in the same direction and knot upon it with 3 threads to the left, take the 5th thread as leader to the right and work macramé knots on it with 3 threads to the right; take the next thread as leader slanting closely underneath and knot upon it also with 3 threads to the right; thus the first star is complete; work 5 more stars in the row. Next, carry on the leader thread from the 3rd point of the second star, and on it work macramé knots with the leader thread from the 4th point of the first star, and with the 3 threads to the left, take the 8th thread as leader in the same direction, and knot upon it with 3 threads to the left; take the 9th thread as leader to the right and work macramé knots thereon with the 10th, 11th, and 12th threads, take the 10th thread as leader and knot upon it with the 11th, 12th, and 9th threads; then carry

No. 72.—Watch Pocket.

on the leader thread from the 3rd point of the third star, and work macramé knots on it with the leader thread from the 4th point of the second star, and with the next 3 threads to the left, take the 16th thread as leader in the same direction and knot upon it with the 15th, 14th, and 13th threads with the leader thread from the last made star and with the 3 threads to the left; take the 12th thread as leader slanting closely underneath and knot upon it with the 11th, 10th, and 9th threads; now recommence on the left hand side, turn the leader thread that hangs at the end and use it as leader thread to the right, working macramé knots on it with the 2nd, 3rd and 4th threads, take the end thread in the right hand as leader to the right, and work macramé knots on it with 3 threads to the right with the leader thread from the 3rd point of the star, and with the next 3 threads to the right; leave the first 4 threads hanging; take the 5th thread in the right hand as leader to the right, and work macramé knots on it with 3 threads to the right with the leader thread from the point of the next star, and with the next 3 threads to the right. Now proceed with the leader thread from the 3rd point of the fourth star, and work downwards in the same manner till the stars are brought to a point. Cut the ends of

threads level about 1 inch distant from the work, unravel, and comb out. **For the Back**—Measure 16 threads from ½ a yard to ¾ of a yard in length, and work exactly the same as the front piece. Sew the macramé work neatly upon the foundation in the manner shown in the engraving, and place a loop of ribbon at the top by which to hang the pocket up.

No. 73.—TIDY FOR TOILET TABLE.

THIS useful tidy is made on a foundation of cardboard; the outer cover, on which the macramé work is fastened, is a piece of stout cardboard 4¼ inches deep, bound round with narrow blue ribbon and sewn to a cardboard circle, also bound, measuring 4 inches in diameter, this is covered inside and outside with crimson sateen: the receptacle or tidy is a strip of cardboard 4 inches wide, bound with ribbon and sewn on a circle measuring *nearly* 4 inches in diameter, this circle is the bottom of the tidy and has a hole in the centre, bound with ribbon, and large enough for a finger to go through, being for the purpose of drawing this inner receptacle away from the outer covering. For the macramé covering procure a ball of nut-brown twine, and cut 50 threads measuring 1½ yards long. Take the threads 2 together and make double knotted picots. **1st row**—Work all threads in regular succession upon a foundation cord. **2nd row**—The same. **3rd row**—Leaves worked as directed in the fourth row of the Willow pattern, Figure 75. **4th row**—Foundation cord worked with macramé knots. **5th row**—Diamond bars with Solomon's knot in the centre as Figure 32, and Solomon's knots are worked also to fill up the spaces between the diamond bars. **6th row**—Foundation cord. **7th row**—The same. Cut the ends evenly about 1 inch from the last row, and unravel for fringe. Place the macramé work on the sateen covered foundation, joining the pattern nicely round. Finish with a bow of crimson ribbon on the top.

No. 73.—Tidy for Toilet Table.

No. 74.—SQUARE FOR CUSHION.

THIS square, the model of which is worked with dark brown macramé thread, makes a very handsome front for a sofa cushion or divan chair, and it may likewise be used as a centre for a gipsy table cloth on a foundation of peacock blue or old gold plush. Cut 6 threads, each measuring 3 yards in length, and knot them on a foundation cord, making 12 working threads. **1st row**—Work 3 Solomon's knots. **2nd row**—Leave the first and last 2 threads, and make 2 Solomon's knots with the 8 centre threads. **3rd row**—Same as the first row. **4th row**—Same as the second row. **5th row**—Same as the first row. Cut 18 more threads; knot 6 threads on each side of the square of Solomon's knots; carry the foundation cord round three sides, and work on it with macramé knots; now add 6 threads on the top foundation cord disposing them 1 between each of those originally put on and used for the Solomon's knots. You now have the 1st round done and 12 working threads on each side the square. **2nd round**—With the first 6 threads work 4 slanting ribs of macramé knots to the left, with the last 6 threads work the same slanting to the right; place 2 extra threads on the last leader thread each side, just passing them simply round the leader, not knotting them on; slant each leader thread the reverse way and work 4 more slanting ribs on each to correspond with those already done; with the 2 added threads work a simple Genoese bar of 20 stitches; do the same on each side. Now in the very centre of each side add 2 threads just laying them round the foundation cord, and work a Solomon's knotted bar of 12 stitches. At each corner add 2 threads in the same way and work a Genoese bar of 20 stitches, then take two more extra threads and lay them across the 2 centre threads and work a single Genoese bar of 20 stitches, using 2 extra threads as leaders and working each with 2 threads from the bar (the arrangement of this will be seen by refer-

it; you now have 52 threads on each side. **5th round**—Work 13 Solomon's knots in a line, work 12 Solomon's knots in the next line, then a line of 13 knots again. Do the same on each side; then at each corner add 1 thread on the foundation cord, 1 thread in each top loop of the first line of Solomon's knots, and 1 thread on each side on the two threads left in the second line of Solomon's knots; with the 2 centre threads as leaders and 1 thread on each side work a Solomon's knot, with the 2 side threads from this centre knot and the 2 next threads each side work other Solomon's knots, make a Solomon's knot with the 4 centre threads again, then again 1 knot

No. 74.—Square for Cushion.

ring to the engraving); add 2 additional threads at the back, and work a Solomon's bar of 7 stitches. Repeat thus on each side the square. **3rd round**—Place a foundation cord in perfect square and work macramé knots on it with all threads on each side; add 2 threads at each corner, 1 thread between the Solomon's bar and the Genoese bar, 1 thread between the two Genoese bars, 1 thread between the Genoese bar and the ribbed work, and the same to correspond on the opposite side. **4th round**—Carry a foundation cord round a second time and work all threads in macramé knots on

on each side, and now 1 with the 4 centre threads to form the point of the corner. **6th round**—Foundation cord worked with macramé knots. **7th round**—Place 1 additional thread at each corner and 1 thread between the two first Solomon's knots, so making 64 threads on each side and 4 threads for each corner; with the 4 corner threads work a Genoese bar of 12 stitches; with every 8 threads on each side work beaded diamonds of 4 ribs, producing 8 diamonds on each side. **8th round**—Foundation cord worked with macramé knots, and add 3 threads between the Genoese bar and the first diamond, and 1 thread at each corner. **9th round**—Carry a foundation cord round a second time, work all threads on it with macramé knots, and add 1 thread at each corner. Now cut off the ends of the threads evenly and unravel them for fringe, and the square is complete.

No. 75.—WILLOW PATTERN.

FOR this pattern, which is suitable for a bracket length or table border, measure threads each $3\frac{1}{2}$ yards in length, and in number divisible by 28; fold each 2 pieces together, and knot a heading of picots as instructed in Figure 37 in "Weldon's Practical

No. 75.—Willow Pattern.

Macramé Lace," 1st Series. **1st row**—Foundation cord worked with macramé knots. **2nd row**—With the 1st and 2nd threads work a single knotted bar of 7 stitches, with the 3rd and 4th threads work a single knotted bar of 5 stitches, with the 5th and 6th threads work a single knotted bar of 3 stitches, miss the next 2 threads, and with the 9th and 10th, the 11th and 12th, and the 13th and 14th threads, work single knotted bars of 3, 5, and 7 stitches respectively; for the large square take as leader in the left hand the 2nd thread of those missed, slant it vertically towards the left, and work macramé knots on it with the 1st missed thread and with the 3

threads belonging to the 3 knotted bars, take the 1st thread of the 4th knotted bar as leader slanting closely underneath, and on it work macramé knots with the same 7 threads as before, take the 2nd thread of the same knotted bar and knot upon it also with 7 threads, and so on each of the other threads in like manner, making vertical lines of macramé knots. You will see the square is to sit corner-ways, and all the leader threads hang to the left; with the 2 first of these leader threads work a single knotted bar of 7 stitches, with the 2 next leader threads work a single knotted bar of 5 stitches, and with the 2 next leader threads a bar of 3 stitches, leave the 2 next, and work on the right-hand side 3 more single knotted bars of 3, 5, and 7 stitches respectively, making the fancy beaded square complete. Work another beaded square with the next 14 threads, and so on to the end of the row. **3rd row**—Foundation cord. **4th row**—For the first leaf, take the 8th thread in the left hand as leader slanting to the left, and on it work macramé knots with the 7th, 6th, 5th, 4th, 3rd, 2nd, and 1st threads. Take the 7th thread as leader slanting underneath, and work macramé knots on it with the 6th, 5th, 4th, 3rd, 2nd, 1st, and 8th threads. For the second leaf use the 16th thread as 1st leader, and proceed in the same way, and so on to the end of the row. Begin again at the left-hand side, turn the 2nd leader thread slanting towards the right, and work macramé knots on it with the first 3 threads. Take the 1st thread as leader, slanting in the same direction, and knot on it with 2 threads; then take the 4th thread from the top of the first leaf as leader in the right hand, and work macramé knots thereon with the upper threads of the leaf with the leader thread of the second leaf and with the next 3 threads of the second leaf. Then take as leader the 1st thread that was knotted on to that leader, slant it under neath, and knot on it with the next 7 threads. Now take as leader the 4th thread from the top of the second leaf, and proceed in the same way. **5th row**—Foundation cord. **6th row** —For the triangular piece. Take the 10th thread as leader in the left hand slanting vertically towards the left, and on it work macramé knots with the 9 threads to the left. Take the 9th thread as leader, slanting closely under-neath, and work macramé knots on it with 8 threads to the left. Use the 8th thread as next leader, and knot it with 7 threads, and the 6 other threads successively as leaders, and gradually bring the knots to a point, working one knot less on each subsequent leader, and leaving all leader threads hanging. Then work the opposite side to correspond, beginning with the 11th thread, which take as leader thread to the right, and knot on it with the next 9 threads in succession, take the 12th thread as leader and work 8 knots, and so on to a point again. For the large beaded square, begin with a single knotted bar of 9 stitches, then a bar of 7 stitches, then 5, then 3, then 3 again, then 5, 7, and 9 stitches, so using 16 threads in all; take as leader slanting to the left the 1st thread in the second bar of 3 stitches, and proceed with a large beaded square, worked precisely like those in the second row, but having 8 vertical lines in it and 8 knots worked in each line, and finish with single knotted bars as it began. Then repeat a triangular piece and a beaded square alternately for the length required. **7th row**—Foundation cord. **8th row**—Work 6 button-hole stitches with the 1st thread upon the 2nd thread; take the 7th thread in the left hand as leader slanting to the left and on it work macramé knots with the 6th, 5th, 4th, 3rd, 2nd, and 1st threads; take the 6th thread as leader, slanting underneath, and work on it macramé knots with the 5th, 4th, 3rd, 2nd, and 1st threads, take the 5th thread as next leader and knot with 4 threads, and so on, reducing to a point as in the triangular piece above; next work 6 buttonhole stitches with the 14th thread upon the 13th thread, take the 8th thread as leader slanting to the right, and manipulate another pointed piece to correspond with the opposite side. Then with the 1 outside thread on each side work 12 buttonhole stitches upon the next thread adjoining; connect the angular pieces together by working a macramé knot with the last thread of the left-hand side on the last thread of the right-hand side, and carry on for the commencement of another triangular shaped piece the same thread for the 1st leader thread towards the left, and the thread from the left hand side as 1st leader thread towards the right. Work three patterns in depth, and finish off the third pattern by bringing the outside leader on each side towards the centre and working macramé knots thereon with each thread in succession to the centre, where knot the 1st leader thread to the 2nd, and tie tightly. The fringe is made by unravelling and combing out the ends.

No. 76.—DRAWING-ROOM WALL-POCKET.

THE engraving represents a new and very handsome wall-pocket which will be found most useful in a drawing room as a receptacle for odds and ends. Commence by preparing 88 threads, each measuring 3 yards in length, and with these make 44 picots as Figure 37, but tying 3 knots. **1st row**—Foundation cord, worked with macramé knots. **2nd row**—Stars. Take the first thread as leader in the right hand, and on it work macramé knots with the 2nd, 3rd, 4th, 5th, 6th, 7th, and 8th threads, take the 2nd thread as leader, slanting closely underneath, and knot upon it with the 3 u, 4th, 5th, 6th, 7th, and 8th threads; take the 16th thread as leader in the left hand, and work thereon macramé knots with the 15th, 14th, 13th, 12th, 11th, 10th, and 9th threads. also with the two leader threads from the first point, and with the next 6 threads to the left, take the 15th thread as leader in the same direction and knot on it with all threads to the left; take the 10th thread as leader in the right hand and knot upon it with 6 threads to the right, take the 9th thread as leader in the same direction and work thereon with 7 threads to the right. Repeat to the end, working 11 stars in the row. **3rd row**—Foundation cord. **4th row**—Diamond bars as Figure 32, making 2 diamonds in a bar.

No. 76.—Drawing-Room Wall-Pocket.

5th row—Foundation cord. **6th row**—Take the 1st thread as leader in the right hand, and on it work macramé knots with the 2nd, 3rd, and 4th threads. Take the 2nd thread, and work with the 3rd, 4th, and 1st threads. Take the 8th thread as leader in the left hand, and work macramé knots on it with the 7th, 6th, and 5th threads. Take the 7th thread and knot with the 6th, 5th, and 8th threads. Take the second leader thread and knot on it with the leader thread last used and the 3 threads to the right. Take the 5th thread in the same direction and knot on it with 3 threads to the right. Take the leader thread from the second point and work on it macramé knots with 3 threads to the left. Take the 4th thread and knot with 3 threads to the left; turn the leader thread in the right hand, and work on it macramé knots with the same 3 threads, but now to the right. Take the 1st thread as leader, and knot with the next 3 threads; leave this, and work another similar star from the foundation cord, then cross the leader as before, and knot with the 3 next threads. Take the next thread as leader, and work a second rib. Now work 2 ribs to the left, cross the last leader, and knot with 3 threads to the right, then work a second rib. Resume by the foundation cord, and, using from the 17th to the 32nd thread, work a double-pointed large star like those in the second row. Make a small star with the 8 centre threads from this large star, and then carry on the small star pattern from the points of the large star. There should be three whole small stars and a half star under each other to make a point under the centre of the large star. Then, with the 81st to the 96th threads (being the centre threads of the pocket), work 2 diamond bars as in the fourth row. On each side these work a large star; then carry on the pattern, making the right-hand side end the same as the left-hand side began, and finish by sloping off into points as shown in the illustration. Cut a piece of stout cardboard to the exact size and shape of the macramé work, and cover it with satin on both sides, sewing all ends of the macramé threads in between the cardboard and the lining. Cut a shaped piece of cardboard for the back of the pocket. It should be 14 inches high in the highest part, and about 11 inches wide. Quilt a piece of satin for the front of this, and put a plain piece at the back. Cut another cardboard to fit the bottom, which cover in the same way, and sew all in place. Finish off the front with a ruching of inch-wide satin-ribbon to match the lining. Place a loop at the top whereby to hang up the pocket.

No. 77.—D'OYLEY.

THIS d'oyley is worked with fine macramé twine on the same principle as the large square so fully detailed above. Commence with 16 threads 1¼ yards long on a foundation cord about 13 inches in length. **1st row**—Work 8 Solomon's knots. **2nd row**—leave the first 2 threads and the last 2 threads, and with those intermediate work 7 Solomon's knots. Continue these two rows till you have a perfect square of Solomon's knots. Cut 52 more threads; knot 16 threads on each side of the square, carry the foundation cord round all three sides and work all threads on it with macramé knots; place 16 threads on the top foundation cord between the original threads which now are formed into Solomon's knots, and add 2 extra threads at each corner; you now have the 1st round done, and there are 36 working threads on each side the square. **2nd round**—With every 4 threads work a Banister bar, making 9 Banister bars of 9 stitches on each side the square, add 2 threads at each corne , and work Banister bars of 12 stitches. **3rd**

1 yard of inch-wide ribbon to match. Cut a foundation cord 30 inches long. Begin by preparing 24 threads, each measuring 2½ yards in length, and place these on the foundation cord as in Figure 2 in "Weldon's Practical Macramé Lace," 1st Series. **1st row**—With every 4 threads work bars of Solomon's knots, 2 stitches in a bar, and 12 bars in the row. **2nd row**—Alternate the threads and work similarly, doing 11 bars in the row. Repeat these two rows till a perfect square is formed. Now knot 24 threads on each side of the square, and also along the top, attaching them in the manner shown in Figure 2, those at the top being placed between the threads already worked; pass the foundation cord round three sides of the square and work threads on it in macramé knots. Continue the foundation cord round a second time, working macramé knots with all threads, and put on two extra threads at each corner. Now flaps are to be worked to fold over the front of the square and meet in a point in the centre. Leave the corner threads for the present, and, with 48 threads on each side, work a pattern of diamonds, making 6 diamonds in the first row, 5 diamonds

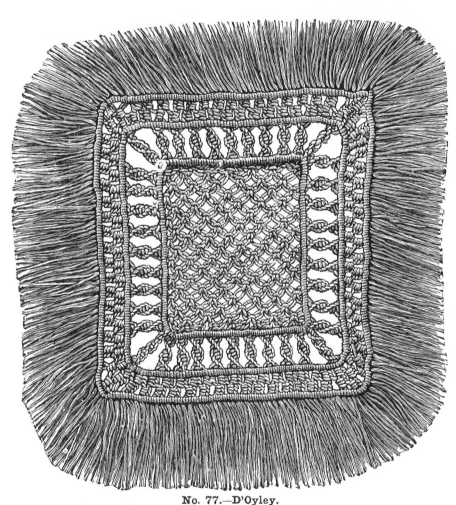

No. 77.—D'Oyley.

No. 78.—

round—Place a foundation cord in perfect square and work on it macramé knots with all threads, add 1 thread in the centre of the Banister bar at every corner and 2 threads between the corner bar and the next on every side. **4th round**—Buttonhole stitch, work 3 button-hole stitches with the 3rd thread over the 1st and 2nd threads, and with the 6th thread over the 4th and 5th threads, and so on. Do another round, making 3 button-hole stitches with the 5th thread over the 3rd and 4th threads, and with the 8th thread over the 6th and 7th threads, and so on. **5th round**—Foundation cord worked with macramé knots, and add 3 extra threads at each corner. Cut the ends evenly about an inch and a half from the cord and unravel for fringe.

No. 78.—HANDKERCHIEF CASE.

REQUIRED, two balls of primrose-coloured twine, a piece of pale blue sateen, about 22 inches by 11 inches, 1½ yards of silk cord, and

in the next, 4 in the next, then 3, then 2, then only 1 diamond, each diamond has a Solomon's knot in the centre and another Solomon's knot where the leader threads cross. Now use 2 threads on either side of the flap as foundation cords, knotting on all threads to form a strong double line of margin to the flap; cut off the ends about an inch from the edge, and unravel for fringe. Work three more flaps the same. Fold your sateen in a square the right size for lining, quilt it across and across, and, having arranged it to fit the macramé, edge it with silk cord. Fasten two opposite points of the flaps together with a loop, and on the other two points sew a ribbon to tie in a bow.

No. 79.—D'OYLEY.

THIS d'oyley is worked with a fine make of macramé thread. Begin by placing 18 threads on a foundation cord of about 15 inches in length. **1st row**—Take the first thread as leader in the right hand, and on it work macramé knots with the 2nd and 3rd threads, take the 6th thread as leader in the left hand and knot on it with the 5th and 4th threads, also with the first leader thread, and with the 2 threads to the left, take the 4th thread in the right hand and work macramé knots on it with the 5th and 6th threads, take the first leader thread and turn it to the right and knot on it with the 2nd and 3rd threads; take the 7th thread as leader in the right hand and on it work macramé knots with the 8th and 9th threads, take the 12th thread as leader in the left hand, and knot on it with all threads to the left. Proceed in this pattern till you have worked a perfect square. Cut 70 more threads; knot 18 threads on each side of the square; carry the foundation cord round all three sides, and work all threads in macramé knots upon it; place 18 threads on the top foundation cord between the original threads which are used in the diamond pattern, add 4 extra threads at each corner. The first round is now done, and there are 44 working threads on each side the square. **2nd round**—With every 4 threads work a Solomon's knot. **3rd round**—Foundation cord placed square and worked with macramé knots, add 2 extra threads at each corner. **4th round**—

manipulate picots of button-hole loops, thus, take 2 threads, fold both double to get the exact centre, and then work 9 buttonhole stitches with the centre of one thread to the centre of the other, and you will have a loop of buttonhole stitches and 4 ends of thread; work all the strands in this manner. **1st row**—Foundation cord working macramé knots with each thread in succession. **2nd row**—With every 4 threads make a Solomon's knot; recommence on the left-hand side, miss the first 2 threads, * take the next 4 threads, 2 from each Solomon's knot, and work a Banister bar of 6 stitches, with the next 4 threads work a single Solomon's bar of 3 stitches, and repeat from *; begin again on the left-hand side and with every 4 threads do another line of Solomon's knots. **3rd row**—Foundation cord. **4th row**—Take the first thread as leader in the right hand and work macramé knots on it with the 2nd, 3rd, 4th, 5th and 6th threads, take the 2nd thread as leader in the same direction and knot on it with the 3rd, 4th, 5th, 6th and 1st threads; take the 12th thread as leader in the left hand and on it work macramé knots with the 11th, 10th, 9th, 8th and 7th threads, take the 11th thread

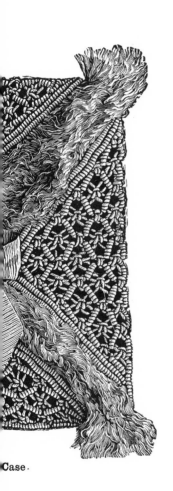

Case.

No. 79 —D Oyley.

With every 4 threads work bars of single Solomon's knots, making 5 stitches in every bar along the sides, and 6 stitches in each of the corner bars. **5th round**—Foundation cord worked with macramé knots, put on 1 additional thread in the centre of the Solomon's bar at every corner and 3 threads between the corner bar and the next bar on every side. **6th round**—With every 4 threads work a Solomon's knot. **7th round**—Foundation cord worked with macramé knots, and 3 extra threads put on at each corner. Cut the ends evenly, about an inch and a-half from the cord, and unravel for fringe.

No. 80.—NIGHT-DRESS CASE.

THIS night-dress case is made in the shape of a bolster, the macramé being a strip of insertion placed in the centre of a bolster bag made of a piece of ruby satin 26 inches long and 21 inches wide. Cut 84 threads, each measuring 2½ yards long. First of all,

as leader, and knot on it with the 10th, 9th, 8th, 7th, and 12th threads; with the 5th, 6th, 7th, and 8th threads work a single Solomon's knot. Continue thus with every 12 threads to the end of the row; then, with the 8 threads between the single Solomon's knots work a double Solomon's knot loosely: now, beginning again on the left-hand side, and using 2 threads of the first single Solomon's knot as leaders, work 2 ribs to the left, and with the other 2 threads of the same Solomon's knot as leaders, work 2 ribs to the right, and complete every star in the same manner. Now, with every 8 threads that lie below the single Solomon's knots work a double Solomon's bar of 5 stitches, and with every 4 threads where the leader threads meet work a Banister bar of 12 stitches Next do a line of stars to correspond exactly with those above. **5th row**—Foundation cord. **6th row**—Same as the second row. **7th row**—Foundation cord. Finish the insertion with a line of picots, to do which you take the 1st thread on the right-hand side of the work, and with it make 9 buttonhole stitches on the next thread; take the 5th thread, and with it work 9 buttonhole stitches over the next thread, and continue to the end. Turn all the ends of threads down on the wrong side, and secure them firmly with a needle and cotton, cutting off all bits which remain. Join the satin as if making a bolster, turn down a hem 2 inches deep on either side in such a way as to afford a kind of frill and a space for running in two pieces of silk cord to draw and tie in a bow. Join the macramé, making the foundation cords meet nicely, and bind together the loose threads between the foundation so as most nearly to resemble a knotting of the pattern.

No. 81.—WALL POCKET.

THIS elegant wall pocket can be worked any size required, and is a most useful receptacle for odds and ends, either in a drawing-room or bed-room. The one from which our illustration is taken is made with pink macramé thread on a foundation of ruby satin; it also would look well worked with brown thread and peacock-blue satin for foundation. 64 threads are employed, each thread measuring $2\frac{1}{2}$ yards long. Take 2 threads together, fold them in the middle, and knot in picots as Figure 37 in "Weldon's Practical Macramé Lace," 1st Series. **1st row**—Foundation cord worked with

the 7th thread work 7 buttonhole stitches upon the leader next it and *twist* these. Resume by the foundation cord, employing as far as to the 16th thread, thus—work 7 buttonhole stitches with the 16th thread upon the 15th thread, make 3 slanting ribs as in last pattern, and then work 8 buttonhole stitches with the 9th thread upon the 10th thread, work also 7 buttonhole stitches with the 12th thread upon the 11th thread, and *twist* these; take the 12th thread as leader in the left hand and work macramé knots on it with the 11th thread and with the 6 threads of the buttonhole bars, do 2 other slanting ribs under this rib, continue the last leader and on it with the next thread (these are the 5th and 6th threads as they now hang), work 6 buttonhole stitches and twist them round, work 8 buttonhole stitches with the 8th thread upon the 7th thread; next take the 1st thread as leader in the right hand and work macramé knots on it with the 7 threads to the right, do 2 other slanting ribs underneath, then work 7 buttonhole stitches with the 1st thread upon the 2nd thread; now take up the 9th thread and with it work 7 buttonhole stitches upon the 10th thread and twist these, take the 12th thread and work 8 buttonhole stitches upon the 11th thread; work 8 buttonhole stitches with the 13th thread upon the 14th thread, and 7 buttonhole stitches with the 15th thread upon the leader thread next it and twist these. Then proceed with each 8 threads of the foundation cord in succession, working downwards

No. 80.—Night-Dress Case.

macramé knots. **2nd row**—Begin by making 7 buttonhole stitches with the 8th thread upon the 7th thread, then take the 1st thread as leader in the right hand slanting vertically towards the right, and work macramé knots thereon with the 2nd, 3rd, 4th, 5th, 6th, 7th, and 8th threads, take the 2nd thread as leader, slanting closely underneath, and knot upon it with the 3rd, 4th, 5th, 6th, 7th, 8th, and 1st threads, now work 7 buttonhole stitches with the 1st thread upon the second thread, and the first pattern is complete; work the same pattern with every 8 threads along the row. **3rd row**—Foundation cord. **4th row**—Work 7 buttonhole stitches with the 8th thread upon the 7th thread, take the first thread as leader to the right and work macramé knots on it with 7 threads to the right, take the 2nd thread as next leader and knot upon it with 7 threads, take the 3rd thread as leader and again knot with 7 threads; then work 5 buttonhole stitches with the 1st thread upon the 2nd thread; take the 4th thread in the left hand and work on it macramé knots with the 3rd, 2nd, and 1st threads, take the 3rd thread and knot with the 2nd, 1st, and 4th threads, take the 2nd thread and knot with the 1st, 4th, and 3rd threads, work 5 buttonhole stitches with the 4th thread upon the 3rd thread; turn the last leader thread (now the 1st at the end) towards the right, and work macramé knots on it with 3 threads to the right, take the next thread as leader, and also knot with 3 threads, take the next thread as leader and again knot with 3 threads; with the 5th thread work 8 buttonhole stitches upon the 6th thread, and with

in the same manner; and finish off at the end of the row with half a pattern to match the beginning. **5th row**—Foundation cord. **6th row**—Same as the second row. **7th row**—Foundation cord. This finishes the macramé; cut the ends of thread about $1\frac{1}{2}$ inches deep, and unravel and comb it out. A shape of stout cardboard is covered with ruby satin, the back measures 10 inches by 5 inches, the front 15 inches by 5 inches, and the bottom is 10 inches long and $4\frac{1}{2}$ inches wide at its widest part, the front; the bottom is set in level with the last foundation cord of the macramé work; a long loose piece of satin gathered into a point at the bottom and finished off with a bow of ribbon hanging down in front, and loops of ribbon are sewn at the top to hang the pocket up by.

No. 82.—CARLOWITZ PATTERN.

THREADS for this pattern are required to be from 3 yards to $3\frac{1}{2}$ yards long, and 32 threads are needed for each pattern. Take 2 threads together, fold in half and make picots, as Figure 37 in "Weldon's Practical Macramé Lace," 1st Series. **1st row** —Foundation cord worked with macramé knots. **2nd row**—With every 4 threads work a double knotted bar of 4 stitches. **3rd row**—Foundation cord. **4th row**—Take the 8th thread as leader in the left hand and on it work macramé knots with the 7th, 6th, 5th, 4th, 3rd, 2nd, and 1st threads; take the 7th thread as leader in the same direction and knot upon it with the 6th, 5th, 4th.

3rd, 2nd, 1st, and 8th threads; take the 9th thread as leader in the right hand and work on it macramé knots with the 10th, 11th, 12th, 13th, 14th, 15th, and 16th threads; take the 10th thread as leader slanting underneath and knot upon it with the 11th, 12th, 13th, 14th, 15th, 16th, and 9th threads; then with the 4 centre threads of the half diamond work a double knotted bar of 6 stitches, and with the 4 threads on either side these work double knotted bars of 4 stitches; proceed thus with half diamonds and bars to the end of the row: then re-commencing on the left hand side, take the first leader thread in the right hand, slant it towards the right, and on it work macramé knots with the 2nd, 3rd, 4th, 5th, 6th, 7th, and 8th threads; take the next thread as leader in the same direction and knot upon it with the 3rd, 4th, 5th, 6th, 7th, 8th, and 1st threads; take the leader thread from the first point of the second diamond, carry it slanting further to the left, and on it work macramé knots with the leader thread from the point of the first diamond, and with the 15th, 14th, 13th, 12th, 11th, 10th, and 9th threads. Take the 16th thread as leader, slanting in the same direction, and knot upon it with 7 threads to the left. Finish off the other diamonds in the same way. **5th row**—Foundation cord. **6th row**—Same as the second row. **7th row**—Foundation cord. **8th row**—Scollop. Work a Solomon's knot with the 3rd, 4th, 5th, and 6th threads, the same with the 7th, 8th, 9th, and 10th threads, and also with the 11th, 12th, 13th, and 14th threads. Take the 1st thread as leader in the right hand, and work on it macramé knots with 7 threads to the right; do another rib slanting underneath. Take the 16th thread as leader in the left hand, and on it work macramé knots with 7 threads to the left. Work another rib in the same direction. Make 8 single knotted bars of 3 stitches with these 16 threads. Take the 1st thread as leader in the right hand, and macramé knot 7 threads upon it. Do a second leader in the same direction. Take the 16th thread as leader in the left hand and knot 7 threads upon it. Work another rib slanting underneath. Repeat this to the end of the row. Then take the 15th, 16th, 17th, and 18th threads, and make a Solomon's knot, then Solomon's knots with the 13th, 14th, 15th, and 16th, and with the 17th, 18th, 19th, and 20th threads. Under these work 3 Solomon's knots, and underneath again 4 Solomon's knots. Work similarly to fill up all the spaces between the ribs, then do 1 entire line of Solomon's knots from end to end. You now omit 2 threads on each side of the scollop, and continue working Solomon's knots till reduced to a point of 1 knot only. **For the Fringe**—Work with every 4 threads a Banister bar of 6 stitches, after which tie knots a third of an inch apart down every thread of the scollop, and finish by cutting off the ends evenly.

No. 83.—FIREFLY PATTERN.

FOR this elegant pattern, the original of which is worked with apple-green thread for a bracket, 20 threads are required, each 3¼ yards in length, and these are placed two at a time upon a first foundation cord. **1st row**—Foundation cord worked with macramé knots. **2nd row**—With every 4 threads work a Solomon's bar of 2 knots; then return to the beginning of the row, leave the first 2 threads, and with the last 2 threads from the first bar and the first 2 threads from the second bar work another bar of 2 Solomon's knots, and continue with every 4 threads along the row. **3rd row**—Foundation cord. **4th row**—Hold the 2nd and 3rd threads together in the right hand, and with the 1st thread in the left hand work thereon 5 buttonhole stitches, leave these, and take the 6th thread in the left hand as leader slanting to the left, and on it work macramé knots with the 5th, 4th, 3rd, 2nd and 1st threads, take the 5th thread as leader slanting in the same direction and knot on it with the 4th, 3rd, 2nd and 1st threads, then with the 1st leader thread work 5 buttonhole stitches over the 2 next threads,

take the 6th thread as leader holding it straight down and work macramé knots on it with 5 threads, take the next thread as leader and knot on it with 4 threads, this forms a "wing;" with the 4 next threads of the foundation cord work a Solomon's bar of 6 stitches; then

No. 81.— Wall Pocket.

with the next 6 threads manipulate a wing to correspond with that already done. Now, with the 19th, 20th, 21st and 22nd threads, which are the four centre threads of the pattern, work 1 Solomon's knot, and for the star take the 17th thread in the right hand as leader and work macramé knots on it with the 18th, 19th and 20th threads, take the 18th thread as leader slanting underneath, and knot upon it with the 19th, 20th and 17th threads, take the 24th thread as leader in the left hand and on it work macramé knots with the 23rd, 22nd and 21st threads, take the 23rd thread as next leader and knot upon it with the 22nd, 21st and 24th threads, also with the 2nd leader thread, and with the 3 threads to the left, take as leader the 4th thread from the left and knot upon it with 3 threads to the left, and then with the 4 threads to the right work the fourth point of the star; finish off the centre with 1 Solomon's knot as it began. Then with the remaining 16 threads repeat the winged pattern. **5th row**—Foundation cord with threads knotted thereon in regular order, the uppermost thread at the *back* of the wing is taken *first*, the leader threads of the wing come in 4th and 5th, and 12th and 13th, and so on. **6th row**—Solomon's bars, same as second row. **7th row**—Foundation cord. **8th row : For the Scollop**—Take the 5th thread in the left hand as leader slanting to the left and on it work macramé knots with the 4th, 3rd, 2nd and 1st threads, take the 6th thread as leader slanting closely underneath and on it work macramé knots with the same 4 threads, then the 7th thread, and then the 8th thread, in like manner, knotting each with the same 4 threads and leaving a little margin at the top so that the square sits cornerways ; work another square directly underneath using the same threads, and when this is done hold the 4 centre threads straight down and with the 2 threads together to the left and the 2 threads together to the right work a Solomon's knot. With the 4 next threads of the foundation cord make a Solomon's bar of 11 stitches. Now for the wing in the centre of the pattern, for which 16 threads are required, * hold the 2nd and 3rd threads straight down together in the right hand and with the 1st thread in the left hand work 5 buttonhole stitches over them, then take the 8th thread in the left hand as leader slanting towards the left and work on it macramé knots with the 7 threads to the left, take the 7th thread as leader slanting in the same direction, and knot upon it with 6 threads to the left, and repeat from * twice ; this is half the wing, work the other half to correspond ; turn the wing up to get to the wrong side, and taking the first string on each side, tie them tightly together, and so tie them all, leaving no parting down the centre of the wing. Then hold the 4 central and lowest strings of these straight down, and with 2 threads on each side (the two leader threads) work a double Solomon's bar of 4 knots, and with the strings at the back, 4 on each side, work a Solomon's bar of 7 knots. With the next 4 threads of the foundation cord make a Solomon's bar of 11 knots, and use the last 8 threads in working a bar similar to the one at the beginning of the row. Now, recommencing at the left-hand side, hold the 1st and 2nd threads together as leader, slanting vertically towards the centre of the scollop, and on them work macramé knots with 18 threads. Take the next thread as leader, slanting closely underneath, and knot upon it with 17 threads. Do the same on the right-hand side, then, with these 8 threads, work in the centre a double Solomon's bar of 12 knots, and pin this bar up out of the way for the present. Then * hold the 2nd and 3rd threads straight down together in the right hand, and, with the 1st thread in the left hand, work 13 buttonhole stitches over them. Take the 16th thread in the left hand as leader, slanting towards the left, and work on it macramé knots with the 15 threads to the left. Take the next thread as leader, slanting in the same direction, and knot on it with 14 threads to the left. Repeat from * till you have six of these divisional pieces, but in the three last divisions it will be best to work only 12, 11, and 10 buttonhole stitches respectively, instead of 13. Proceed with the opposite side to correspond. Then tie all the strings together two by two at the back, and bring the bar of Solomon's knots down over the joining ; tie the ends all firmly together to form a tassel, and one scollop is complete. Work more scollops in the same manner.

No. 84.—FANCY WORK-BAG.

THE model of this very pretty bag is worked with ecru macramé thread, which keeps its colour remarkably well, and looks very effective over a rich crimson sateen lining. The work is done in one piece, 56 threads being required, each 3 yards long. Place the threads upon double foundation cords as Figure 6 in "Weldon's Practical Macramé Lace," 1st Series. **2nd row**—Take the 1st thread in the right hand as leader, slanting to the right, and work macramé knots on it with the 2nd, 3rd, and 4th threads, take the 8th thread in the left hand as leader, slanting to the left, and on it work macramé knots with the 7th, 6th, and 5th

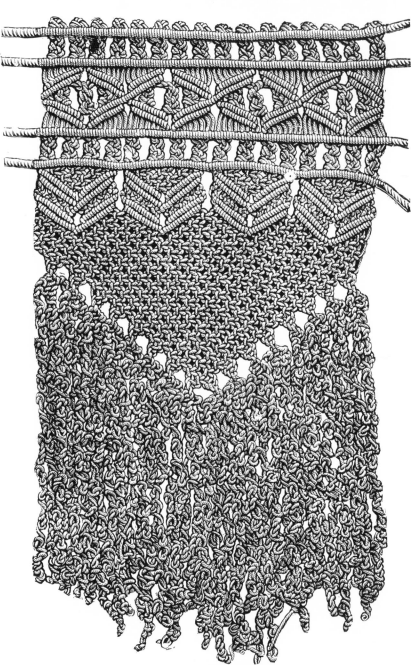

No. 82.—Carlowitz Pattern.

threads, also with the 1st leader thread and the 3 threads to the left, take the 5th thread as leader to the right and knot upon it with the 3 threads to the right. Work similar crosses with every 8 threads, making 14 crosses in the row. **3rd row**—Foundation cord. **4th row**—Take the 8th thread in the left hand as leader, slanting vertically towards the left, and on it work macramé knots with the 7th, 6th, 5th, 4th, 3rd, 2nd, and 1st threads, take the 7th thread as leader in the same direction and work on it macramé knots with the 6th, 5th, 4th, 3rd, 2nd, 1st, and 8th threads ; take the 9th thread in the right hand as leader, slanting vertically to the right, and work macramé knots on it with the 10th, 11th, 12th, 13th, 14th, 15th, and 16th threads, take the 10th thread as leader underneath and work on it macramé knots with the 11th, 12th, 13th, 14th, 15th, 16th, and 9th threads; then take the 4 centre threads, 2 from each side, and work a double knotted bar of 4 knots, take the four threads to the left hand and work a double knotted bar of 2 knots, and the same with the 4 threads to the right-hand; then take in the right-hand the 1st thread on the left-hand side, turn it as leader slanting to the right, and work macramé knots on it with the 7 next threads, take as leader the next thread on the left-hand side and knot it also with 7 threads; next take the thread on the right-hand side, turn it as leader slanting to the left, and work on it macramé

* With the 1st thread work 8 buttonhole stitches over the 2nd and 3rd threads together, and with the 4th thread work 7 buttonhole stitches over the 5th and 6th threads together. Take the 26th thread in the left hand as leader, slanting to the left, and work macramé knots on it with each of the threads (25) to the left. Take the 25th thread as leader, slanting closely underneath, and on it work macramé knots with 25 threads to the left. Repeat from * five times, which brings the scollop to its centre. Work the other half of the scollop to correspond. Turn up the scollop, and tie all the working threads together across and across on the wrong side of the work, and cut off the ends. Let down the Genoese bar, see that it comes as far down as the point of the scollop, and sew it invisibly

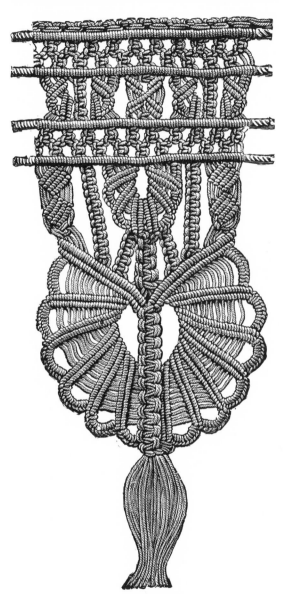

No. 83.—Firefly Pattern.

No. 84.—Fancy Work Bag.

knots with the 7 threads to the left. Take as leader the next thread on the right-hand side, and knot upon it with 7 threads. With the next 4 threads of the foundation, work a Genoese bar of 13 stitches. Then work another diamond, another Genoese bar, and another diamond. This uses 56 threads. Do the same with the other 56 threads for the reverse side of the bag. **5th row**—Foundation cord. **6th row**—Same as the second row. **7th row**—Foundation cord. **8th row**—Here begins the scollop which rounds into shape to form the lower part of the bag. With the 27th, 28th, 29th, and 30th threads (these being the 4 centre threads of the pattern), work a Genoese bar of about 32 stitches; pin this up out of the way, as it will not be required again till the scollop is made.

over the knotted join. Work a similar scollop for the opposite side of the bag. Fold the work together lengthways, sew the two scollops firmly together, and sew together the foundation cords of the insertion part. The tassels on each side the bag are made with 16 threads doubled through the top foundation cords and bound round tightly with an extra bit of thread; the ends are unravelled, and hang about 4 inches long. Make a shaped lining of crimson sateen with a ruching at the top. Sew on a ribbon handle, and place a bow in the centre thereof, and another bow at the bottom of the bag.

No. 85.—BAG FOR WORK OR BOOKS.

THIS handsome bag is made with ecru coloured macramé thread, lined with crimson sateen, it has a pocket pleated in the lining to hold cotton, needlecase, or purse, and is finished off round the top with a ruching of the same sateen; the work is done in one long straight piece, which is folded in half and joined as invisibly as possible. Cut 72 threads each measuring $2\frac{1}{2}$ yards in length. With every two threads knot a picot as instructed in Figure 37 in "Weldon's Practical Macramé Lace," 1st Series **1st row**—Foundation cord, every thread being worked thereupon with macramé knots. **2nd row**—With every 4 threads work a double knotted bar of 4 stitches. **3rd row**—Foundation cord. **4th row**—Take the 1st thread in the right hand as leader, slanting vertically to the right, and work macramé knots on it with the 2nd, 3rd, 4th, 5th, 6th, 7th, and 8th threads, take the 2nd thread as leader, slanting underneath, and on it work macramé knots with the 3rd, 4th, 5th, 6th, 7th, 8th, and 1st threads; take the 16th thread in the left hand as leader slanting to the left and work on it macramé

2nd, and 1st threads, take the 5th thread as leader in the right hand and work on it macramé knots with the 6th, 7th and 8th threads, and now with the 4 centre threads of this half diamond work 4 stitches of Genoese bar, take the 1st leader thread in the right hand, turn it as leader to the right and knot upon it with the next thread and with 2 threads of the Genoese bar. Take the 12th thread as leader in the left hand and work macramé knots on it with the 11th, 10th and 9th threads, with the 2nd leader thread and with the next 3 threads, also with the 1st leader thread and the 3 following threads; take the 13th thread as leader in the right hand and on it work macramé knots with the 14th, 15th and 16th threads, now work 4 stitches of Genoese bar with the 4 centre threads of this half diamond; carry on the 2nd leader thread further to the right and on it work macramé knots with 3 threads, and work 4 stitches of Genoese bar in the centre of this half diamond; carry on the 1st leader thread further to the right and work macramé knots on it with 3 threads, and also work 4 stitches of Genoese bar here again in the centre of the half diamond; turn the end leader thread to

No. 85.—Bag for Work or Books.

knots with the 15th, 14th, 13th, 12th, 11th, 10th, and 9th threads, take the 15th thread as leader in the same direction and knot upon it with the 14th, 13th, 12th, 11th, 10th, 9th, and 16th threads; hold the 2 centre threads straight down, and with the thread to the right and the thread to the left work an ornamental Genoese knot as described in Figure 41 in "Weldon's Practical Macramé Lace," 1st Series; next take the 8th thread in the left hand as leader slanting to the left and work macramé knots thereon with the 7th, 6th, 5th, 4th, 3rd, 2nd, and 1st threads, take the 7th thread as leader, slanting underneath, and knot with the 6th, 5th, 4th, 3rd, 2nd, 1st, and 8th threads; take the 9th thread as leader to the right and work on it macramé knots with the 10th, 11th, 12th, 13th, 14th, 15th, and 16th threads, take the 10th thread as leader and knot with the 11th, 12th, 13th, 14th, 15th, 16th, and 9th threads. With the next 8 threads work 2 Banister bars as Figure 26 in "Weldon's Practical Macramé Lace," 1st Series, then another star, 2 more Banister bars, and so on till all the threads are employed. **5th row**—Foundation cord. **6th row**—Same as second row. **7th row**—Foundation cord. **8th row**—Take the 4th thread as leader in the left hand and work macramé knots on it with the 3rd,

the right and knot upon it with 3 threads. Now take the 20th thread as leader in the left hand slanting to the left and work macramé knots on it with every thread in succession to the left, that is with 19 threads. Notice each diamond is composed of 8 threads, and work on as described, carrying the leader threads across and across, and making 4 diamonds in depth. **9th row**—Foundation cord. **10th row**—Same as the second row. **11th row**—Foundation cord. Now to make up the **Bag**—Fold the work in half lengthways the wrong side out and tie every 2 threads tightly together twice, cut off whatever ends there may be, turn the work the right side out, and join up the side securely and neatly, tying the loops together with an extra bit of thread to look as much like Genoese knots as possible. The **Handles** are made each of 5 macramé threads 1 yard in length, take the 5 threads together, fold them in the exact centre *below* the first foundation cord in the space *between* the double knotted bars above the Banister bars, work in double knotted bar stitch, and secure the ends of the threads in corresponding place below the first foundation cord in the space above the other Banister bars, as you will clearly see by the engraving. Put in the lining and the bag is complete.

How to Crochet 46 Useful Edgings and Insertions for all Purposes

The Yearly Subscription to this Magazine, post free to any Part of the World, is 2s. 6d.
Subscriptions are payable in advance, and may commence from any date and for any period.

The Back Numbers are always in print. Nos. 1 to 240 now ready. Price 2d. each, or bound in 20 Vols., price 2s. 6d. each.

No. 1.—MUSSEL-SHELL BORDER.

BEGIN with a foundation of chain the length required. **1st row**—1 treble in the fourth chain from the needle, 1 treble in the next, * 13 chain, miss thirteen of the foundation, work 16 consecutive treble, and repeat from *. **2nd row**—13 double crochet on the thirteen chain of last row, 5 chain, miss four, 8 treble on the centre eight of the sixteen treble of last row, 5 chain, miss four, and repeat. **3rd row**—11 double crochet beginning on the second double crochet of last row, 5 chain, 1 treble on the third treble stitch, 3 chain, another treble in the same place, 1 chain, miss 2, 1 treble on the next, 3 chain, another treble in the same place, 5 chain, and repeat. **4th row**— 9 double crochet beginning on the second double crochet of last row, 5 chain, 1 treble under the loop of three chain, 3 chain, another treble in the same place, 2 chain, 1 treble under the next loop of three chain, 3 chain, another treble in the same place, 5 chain, and repeat. **5th row**—9 double crochet on the nine double crochet of last row, 5 chain, 1 treble under the loop of three chain, 3 chain, another treble in the same place, 3 chain, 1 treble under the next loop of three chain, 3 chain, another treble in the same place, 5 chain, and repeat. **6th row**—7 double crochet beginning on the second double crochet of last row, 5 cnain, 1 treble under the loop of three chain, 3 chain, another treble in the same place, 2 chain, 1 treble under the next loop of three chain, 3 chain, another treble in the same place, 2 chain, 1 treble under the next loop of three chain, 3 chain, another treble in the same place, 5 chain, and repeat. **7th row**—Same as last row, working double crochet over the seven already worked. **8th row**—5 double crochet, beginning on the second double crochet of last row, 5 chain, 1 treble under the loop of three chain, 3 chain, another treble in the same place, 3 chain, 1 treble under the next loop of three chain, 3 chain, another treble in the same place, 3 chain, 1 treble under the next loop of three chain, 3 chain, another treble in the same place, 5 chain, and repeat. **9th row**—5 double crochet on the five double crochet of last row, 5 chain, * 1 treble under tne first loop of three chain, 3 chain, another treble in the same place, 1 chain, repeat from * four times do 4 more chain, and continue. **10th row**—3 double crochet beginning on the second double crochet of last row 5 chain, * 1 treble under the first loop of three chain, 3 chain, another treble in the same place, 2 chain, repeat from * four times, do 3 more chain, and continue. **11th row**—1 double crochet on the centre stitch of the three double crochet, 5 chain, * 1 treble under the first loop of three chain, 3 chain, another treble in the same place, 2 chain, repeat from * four times, and continue. **12th row**—1 double crochet under the loop of five chain, 1 chain, 6 treble under the first loop of three chain. * 1 chain, 1 double crochet under the two chain, 1 double crochet under the next loop of three chain, repeat from * three times, 1 chain, 1 double crochet under the loop of five chain, and continue. This completes the border. Finish by working a row of treble stitches along the opposite side of the foundation chain.

No. 2.—THE ELZY INSERTION.

COMMENCE with 22 chain. **1st row**—1 treble in the fifth chain from the needle, 1 chain, miss one, 1 treble in the next, 8 chain, miss ten, 1 treble in the

next, 1 chain, miss one, 1 treble in the next, 1 chain, miss one, 1 treble at the end. **2nd row**—4 chain to turn, 1 treble under the first one chain of last row, 1 chain, 1 treble under the next one chain, 8 chain, 1 treble in the last stitch of the eight chain of last row, 1 chain, 1 treble under the next loop of one chain, 1 chain, 1 treble in the loop at the end. **3rd row**—4 chain to turn, 1 treble under the first one chain, 1 chain, 1 treble under the next, 6 chain, 1 double crochet over the three last rows of chain stitches, 6 chain, 1 treble in the last stitch of the eight chain of last row, 1 chain, 1 treble under the next loop of one chain, 1 chain, 1 treble in the loop at the end. **4th row**—4 chain to turn, 1 treble under one chain of last row, 1 chain, 1 treble under next one chain, 8 chain, 1 treble in the last stitch of the second loop of six chain, 1 chain, 1 treble under the next loop of one chain, 1 chain, one treble in the loop at the end, 7 chain, 1 double crochet at the edge of the work in the third row from the needle, 3 chain, 1 double crochet at the edge of the next row. **5th row**—Turn, and work 1 treble under the loop of seven chain, 5 chain and 3 treble under the same loop five times, 3 chain, 1 treble under the first one chain, 1 chain, 1 treble under the next, 8 chain, 1 treble in the last stitch of the eight chain of last row, 1 chain, 1 treble under the next loop of one chain, 1 chain, 1 treble under the loop at the end, 7 chain, 1 double crochet at the edge of the work in the third row from the needle, 3 chain, 1 double crochet at the edge of the next row. **6th row**—Turn, work 1 treble under the loop of seven chain, 5 chain and 3 treble under the same loop five times. 3 chain, 1 treble under the first one chain, 1 chain, 1 treble under the next, 8 chain, 1 treble in the last stitch of the eight chain of last row, 1 chain, 1 treble under the next loop of 1 chain, 1 chain, 1 treble under the loop at the end. **7th row**—Same as the third row. **8th row**—Same as the fourth row. And continue the insertion, catching the centre loops together with a double crochet stitch in every fourth row, and working the scalloped edge on both sides at the end of every sixth row.

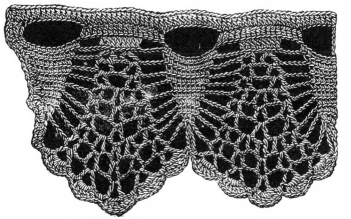

No. 1.—Mussel-Shell Border.

No. 3.—VICTORIA PATTERN.

IF fine white crochet cotton be used, this is a pretty pattern for edging drawers done with ingrain thread, it is suitable for bracket draping and other purposes. Begin with 10 chain. **1st row**—2 treble in the sixth stitch from the needle, 1 chain, 2 more treble in the same place, 3 chain, 2 treble in the last stitch, 1 chain, 2 more treble in the same place. **2nd row**—5 chain to turn. 2 treble under the first loop of one chain, 1 chain, 2 more treble in the same place, 3 chain, 2 treble under the next loop of one chain, 1 chain, 2 more treble in the same place. Repeat this last row till you have 9 little rows done Then to commence the scallop, work 4 chain, 1 double crochet under the first loop of five chain, 8 chain, 1 double crochet under the next loop of five chain, 8 chain, 1 double crochet under the next, 8 chain, 1 double crochet under the next. Turn the work, and make 12 double crochet in the two first of the loops of eight chain, and 6 double crochet in the third loop. Turn. 8 chain, 1 single crochet in between the sixth and seventh double crochet stitches of the first group, 8 chain, 1 single crochet in between the sixth and seventh double crochet stitches of the other group. Turn, and do 12 doubl.

crochet in the first loop of eight chain, and 6 double crochet in the second loop. Turn, 8 chain, 1 single crochet in between the sixth and seventh double crochet stitches of the first group. Turn again, and do 12 double crochet in the loop of eight chain, and 6 double crochet in each of the two half-finished loops of chain. Then 5 chain, turn the work, and go round the scallop doing 1 treble in every other double crochet stitch with 1 chain between each treble, shaping at the top with a treble in six successive stitches. Turn, 1 double crochet in the first space, 1 chain and 1 treble three times in the second space, 1 chain, and repeat nine times, ending with 1 double crochet; then 1 chain, 2 treble under the first loop of one chain of the ninth row, 1 chain, 2 more treble in the same place, 3 chain, 2 treble under the next loop of one chain, 1 chain, 2 more treble in the same place. Repeat from the second row. In working the successive scallops connect them by catching the first stitch of the last row into the last row of the preceding scallop. When a sufficient length is crocheted, work a row of heading along the top in this manner: 4 chain, 2 treble under loop of five chain, and repeat.

No. 4.—TRINITY EDGING.

PROCURE a piece of mignardese braid, a reel of Evans's crochet cotton No. 22, and a very fine steel crochet needle. Commence with two long treble stitches in the first piqué of the braid, * 8 chain, 1 single crochet in the fourth piqué of the braid, 1 chain to turn, and work 6 rows of double crochet forwards and backwards on the eight chain stitches, then 2 long treble in the fourth piqué from the one in which the single crochet is worked, and repeat from * for the length required; this will produce the series of little square diamonds as seen in the engraving. 2nd row—Begin on the right-hand side of the row of square diamonds, and along one side of the first diamond * work 4 treble with 1 chain between each; this brings you to the angle, where make 3 chain and another treble in the same place as the last treble stitch is worked into, then 1 chain 1 treble three times along the second side of the diamond, and repeat from * to the end of the row. 3rd row—1 treble under the first one chain of last row, * 1 chain, 1 double crochet under the next one chain, 5 chain, 1 double crochet under the next, 5 chain, 1 double crochet under the three chain, 5 chain, another double crochet in the same place, 5 chain, 1 double crochet under the

No. 2.—The Elzy Insertion.

next one chain, 5 chain, 1 double crochet under the next, 1 chain, 1 treble under the next, 5 chain, 1 double crochet under the first chain of the next square diamond, and repeat from * 4th row—1 treble under the one chain of last row, 1 chain, 1 double crochet under the first loop of five chain, 5 chain, 1 double crochet under the next loop of five chain, 5 chain, 1 double crochet under the five chain at the point, 5 chain, another double crochet in the same place, 5 chain, 1 double crochet under the next, 5 chain, 1 double crochet under the next, 1 chain, 1 treble under the one chain, and repeat. This completes the edging. On the other side of the braid work in each piqué a double crochet stitch with 1 chain between.

No. 5.—TORTOISE EDGING.

PROCURE a piece of fancy braid of the kind shown in the engraving. Evans's crochet cotton No. 18, and a fine steel crochet needle. On one side of the braid for the top of the edging, work 1 treble in the first picot, 3 chain, miss one picot, 1 double crochet in the next, 1 chain, 1 double crochet in the next, 3 chain, miss one picot, 1 treble in the next, and do the same in each tab of the braid for the length desired. Work on the opposite side of the braid for the Scallops—1st row—1 treble in the first picot, 1 chain and 2 treble in each of the next four picots, 1 chain, 1 treble in the last, and continue the same in each tab to the end of the braid. 2nd row—1 double crochet under the first one chain of last row, * 8 chain, 1 treble in the seventh chain from the needle, 1 chain, 1 double crochet under the next one chain of last row, and repeat from * three times; then 1 double crochet under the first one chain of the next scallop, and continue.

No. 6.—SPIDER-WEB EDGING.

THIS is a strong, pretty edging for underlinen. Use Evans's crochet cotton No. 24, and a very fine steel crochet needle. Commence with 22 chain. 1st row—1 treble in the fourth chain from the needle, 2 chain, miss two, 1 treble five times, 3 treble on the last three chain stitches. 2nd row—12 chain to turn, a treble in the tenth chain from the needle, 1 treble in each of the two next chain stitches, and 1 treble on the first of the four treble of last row, 4 chain, 1 treble on the last of the four treble 1 treble on each of the two chain, and 1 treble on

the treble stitch of last row, 2 chain and 1 treble three times, 2 chain. 2 treble at the end. 3rd row—3 chain to turn, 1 treble on the first treble stitch, 2 chain and 1 treble three times, 3 more successive treble, 4 chain, 1 long treble under the loop of one chain, 4 chain, 1 treble on the last treble stitch, and 3 treble on three chain at the end. 4th row—12 chain to turn, 1 treble in the tenth chain from the needle, 1 treble in each of the two next chain stitches, and 1 treble on the first of the four treble of last row, 4 chain, 3 double crochet, the centre one being over the long treble stitch, 4 chain, 1 treble on the last of the four treble stitches, 3 successive treble, 2 chain, 1 treble, 2 chain, 2 treble at the end. 5th row—3 chain to turn, 1 treble on the first treble stitch, 2 chain, 4 treble, the last being over the first of the four treble of last row, 8 chain, 5 double crochet, 8 chain, 1 treble on the last treble stitch, and 3 treble on three chain at the end. 6th row—6 chain to turn, 1 treble on the last stitch of four treble of last row, 3 successive treble, 7 chain, 3 double crochet on the centre of the five of last row, 7 chain, 3 treble on the last three stitches of the loop of chain, 1 treble on the first treble stitch, 2 chain, 1 treble, 2 chain, 1 treble 2 chain, 2 treble at the end. 7th row—3 chain to turn, 1 treble on the first, treble stitch, 2 chain, 1 treble, 2 chain, 1 treble, 2 chain, 4 treble, 3 chain, 1 long treble on the centre double crochet stitch, 3 chain, 3 treble on the last three stitches of the loop of chain, 1 treble on the first treble stitch. 8th row—6 chain to turn, 1 treble on the last stitch of the four treble of last row, 3 successive treble, 1 chain, 3 treble on three chain stitches and 1 treble on the first treble stitch, 2 chain, 1 treble, 2 chain, 1 treble, 2 chain, 1 treble, 2 chain, 2 treble at the end. 9th row—3 chain to turn, 1 treble on the first treble stitch, 2 chain and 1 treble four times, 2 chain, 1 treble on the last of the four treble or last row, 2 treble in the one chain stitch, and 1 treble on the first of the four treble stitches. This completes one scallop. Repeat from the second row for the length desired. Now bind round the scallops with a row of double crochet, doing 1 double crochet in the treble stitch at the end of the ninth row, and 5 double crochet under each loop of chain, with 1 double crochet between.

No. 7.—THISTLE BORDER.

PROCURE a piece of fancy braid of the kind shown in the illustration. Evans's crochet cotton No. 18, and a fine steel crochet needle. 1st row—3 treble in

No. 3.—Victoria Pattern.

the first picot of the braid, 2 chain, miss the next picot, 2 treble in the next working off both top loops together, 2 chain, miss the next picot, 2 treble in the next, working off both top loops together, 2 chain, miss the next picot, 3 treble in the next, and repeat the same in each tab of the braid for the length required; break off at the end of this and every row. 2nd row—1 treble, 2 chain, miss two, and repeat. 3rd row—1 double crochet on the first chain stitch of last row, * 6 chain, miss five stitches of last row, 3 long treble in the next, working off all three top loops together, 5 chain, 1 double crochet in the same stitch as the three long treble are worked into, and repeat from *. 4th row—1 chain, * 1 double crochet on the bunch of stitches of last row, 5 chain, and repeat from *. 5th row—1 treble, 2 chain, miss two, and repeat. Now work on the other side of the braid. 1st row—Same as the first row above. 2nd row—2 treble under the first loop of two chain, 5 chain, 1 double crochet on the top of the treble stitch just done, 1 chain, * 2 treble under the second loop of two chain, 5 chain, 1 double crochet on the top of the treble stitch just done, 1 chain, repeat from * twice more in the same place. 2 treble under the third loop of two chain, and repeat.

No. 8.—MIGNARDESE BORDER.

PROCURE a piece of mignardese braid and crochet cotton No. 18 or No 20. Commence with 1 treble in the first picot of the braid, 2 chain and 1 treble in six successive picots, * 8 chain, 1 long treble in the next picot, 5 chain, another long treble in the same place, 2 chain, 5 long treble in five successive picots, keeping the last loop of each stitch on the needle, and then drawing through all together and doing 1 chain stitch to tighten the group, 2 chain, 1 long treble in the next picot, 5 chain, another long treble in the same place, 5 chain, again another long treble in the same place, 2 chain, 5 long treble in five successive picots as a group, 3 long treble separate, 3 long treble as a group, 3 more long treble as a group, 3 long treble separate, 5 long treble as a group, 2 chain, 1 long treble in the next picot, 2 chain, catch by a single crochet to the five chain on the opposite side of the scallop, 2 chain, 1 long treble in the same picot last long treble is worked into 2 chain, catch by a single crochet to the other five chain on the opposite side of the scallop, 2 chain, 1 long treble in the same picot last long treble is worked into, 2 chain, 5 long treble in successive loops as a group, 2 chain, 1 long treble in the next picot, 2 chain, catch by a single crochet to th-corresponding loop of five chain, 2 chain, 1 long treble in the same picot last long treble is worked into, 3 chain, catch by a single crochet to the loop of eight chain, 5 chain, 1 treble in the next picot, 2 chain and 1 treble in 9 successive picots, and repeat from * till you have a sufficient length worked; end with 7 successive treble stitches as you began. **Now for the Heading—1st row—** 1 double crochet under first two chain of last row, 3 chain and 1 double crochet under next four spaces, * 3 chain, 1 long treble under the first loop of eight chain, 4 chain, 1 long treble under the next loop, 3 chain, miss the first space of two chain, 1 double crochet in the next, 3 chain and 1 double crochet six times in successive spaces, and repeat from *. **2nd row—**1 double crochet under the first space, 2 chain and 1 double crochet twice in successive spaces, * 2 chain, 4 long treble on the three chain of last row, 1 chain, 4 long treble on the four chain, 1 chain, 4 long treble on three chain, 2 chain, 1 double crochet under the second space of two chain, 2 chain and 1 double crochet under the next three spaces, and repeat from *. **For the Scallops—**Beginning on the opposite side of the braid in the picot just to the right of the seven treble stitches; * 3 long treble stitches in successive picots and drawn together as a group, 3 more long treble as a group, 3 long treble separate, 5 long treble as a group, 2 chain, 1 long treble in the next picot, 5 chain, another long treble in the same place, 5 chain, another long treble in the same place, 2 chain, 5 long treble as a group, 3 chain, 2 long treble in the next picot as a group, 7 chain, 1 long treble in the top thread of the long treble group just done, miss one picot, 2 long treble in the next as a group, 7 chain, 1 long treble in the top thread of the long treble group just done, repeat this till you have six groups of two long trebles, 3 chain, 5 long treble as a group, 2 chain, 1 long treble in the next picot, 5 chain, another long treble in the same place, 5 chain, another long treble in the same place, 2 chain, 5 long treble as a group, 2 chain, 4 long treble separate, and repeat from *: in course of working the following scallops catch with a single crochet into the loops of preceding scallop, as shown in the illustration

No. 9—JUBILEE BORDER.

THE centre of this handsome border is worked the short way, and the edging and heading are added afterwards. Commence with 24 chain. **1st row—** 1 treble in the sixth chain from the needle, 2 chain, another treble in the same place, 2 chain, miss two, 2 treble in the next, 2 chain, 2 more treble in the same

loop, and repeat from * twice, and fasten off. Work as many of these sectional pieces as will suffice for the length required, joining them in process of working by catching the third stitch of the last loop of five chain into the first loop of five chain of the preceding section. The side where a loop of seven chain of the second round is left vacant is the top of the border. Along this side work for the **1st row of the Heading—**3 double long treble in the first stitch of the group of double long treble stitches on the right-hand side, 4 chain, 3 treble under the loop of four chain, 4 chain, 5 long treble under the loop of five chain of the second round, 4 chain, 3 treble under the loop of four chain, 3 double long treble on the last double long treble stitch of the section, and continue the same to the end of the row. **2nd row—**Plain double crochet. **3rd row—**2 treble, 2 chain, miss two, and repeat. **4th row—**Double crochet. Work for the **Scallops** along the opposite side of the sections—**1st row—**1 double crochet on the first stitch, 5 chain, 1 double crochet on the centre stitch of the group of seven double long treble, 5 chain, 1 double crochet on the last stitch of the same group, 5 chain, 1 double crochet on the first stitch of the next group, 5 chain, 1 double crochet on the centre stitch of the group, 5 chain, 4 treble under the loop of five chain, 5 chain, 4 more treble in the same place, 5 chain and 1 double crochet five times along the opposite side of the section, and continue the same to the end of the row. **2nd row—**1 double crochet under the first loop of five chain of last row, * 5 chain, 1 double crochet in the next loop, 5 chain, another double crochet in the same place, repeat from * twice, then 5 chain, 6 treble under the loop of five chain in the centre of the scallop, 5 chain, 6 more treble in the same place, and crochet along the opposite side of the scallop to correspond. **3rd row—**1 double crochet under the first loop of five chain of last row, 6 chain, miss the next loop of five chain (the picot), 1 double crochet in the next, repeat twice, then 6 chain, 11 treble under the loop of five chain in the centre of the scallop, 6 chain and 1 double crochet three times along the side of the scallop. **4th row—**Same as the second row along both sides of the scallop, and 1 plain double crochet in each of the eleven treble at the point.

No. 11.—WILLOW PATTERN FOR SHAWL BORDER.

COMMENCE with chain sufficient for the length required, or, if preferred, the border may be crocheted upon the shawl itself. If worked in the length, break off at the end of every row, and begin again on the right-hand side. **1st row—**

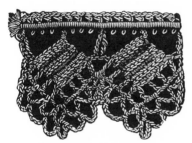

No. 4.—Trinity Border.

No. 5.—Tortoise Edging.

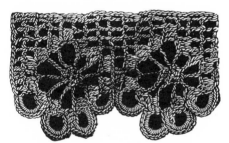

No. 6.—Spider-Web Edging.

place, 4 chain, miss five, 1 treble in the next, 2 chain and 1 treble three times in the same place, 4 chain, miss five, 2 treble in the next, 2 chain, 2 more treble in the same place, 2 chain, miss two, 1 treble in the next, 2 chain, another treble in the same place. **2nd row—**5 chain to turn, 1 treble under the first two chain of last row, 2 chain, another treble in the same place, 2 chain, 2 treble in the space between the two trebles of last row, 2 chain, 2 more treble in the same place, 2 chain, 1 double crochet in the third stitch of the loop of four chain, 5 treble in the first of the three centre loops, 3 treble 2 chain 3 treble in the next, 5 treble in the last of the three centre loops, 1 double crochet in the second stitch of the loop of four chain, 2 chain, 2 treble in the space between the two trebles, 2 chain, 2 more treble in the same place, 2 chain, 1 treble under the last loop of two chain, 2 chain, 1 more treble in the same place. **3rd row—**5 chain to turn, 1 treble under the first two chain of last row, 2 chain, another treble in the same place, 2 chain, 2 treble in the space between the two trebles of last row, 2 chain, 2 more treble in the same place, 4 chain, 1 treble under the centre loop of two chain, 2 chain and 1 treble three times in the same place, 4 chain, 2 treble in the space between the two trebles, 2 chain, 2 more treble in the same place, 2 chain, 1 treble under the last loop of two chain, 2 chain, 1 more treble in the same place. **4th row—**Same as the second row. Repeat these two rows for the length required. Now work along one side of the crochet for the Scalloped **Edging—1st row—**2 long treble, 3 chain, 2 long treble under every loop of five chain, and break off at the end of the row. **2nd row—**1 double crochet under the first three chain of last row, 1 chain and 1 treble six times under the next three chain, 1 chain, and repeat to the end. **3rd row—**1 double crochet under the first chain stitch of last row, * 5 chain, 1 double crochet under the next chain stitch, and repeat from * to the end; and this finishes the scallops. Work for the heading of the border, 3 treble under each loop of five chain, with 3 chain to divide the groups.

No. 10.—WATERFALL BORDER.

COMMENCE with 10 chain; join round, and work 24 treble in the circle, and join. **2nd round—**7 chain, miss two treble of last round, 1 double crochet in the next, and repeat, getting eight of these loops in the round, join. **3rd round—**3 single crochet under the first loop of seven chain, * 4 chain, 7 double long treble (cotton three times round the needle) in the next loop, 5 chain, 7 more double long treble in the same place, 4 chain, 1 double crochet in the next

Double crochet in every stitch of the foundation. **2nd row—**8 treble in the second stitch of double crochet, * wool over the needle, miss three double crochet, insert the hook in the next stitch of double crochet, draw the wool through and pull up a long stitch, wool over the needle, insert the hook in the same place and pull up another long stitch, wool over the needle, insert the hook in the same place and pull up a third long stitch, wool over the needle, insert the hook in the same place and pull up a fourth long stitch, wool over the needle and draw through all the long stitches and through the stitch on the needle, 1 chain, another bunch of long stitches in the same place, 1 chain, miss three double crochet, 8 treble in the next, and repeat from * to the end of the row. **3rd row—**1 treble on each of the six centre treble stitches of last row, * 1 chain, 1 bunch of long stitches (worked as already described) in the space between the bunches of last row, 1 chain, another bunch in the same place, 1 chain, 1 treble on each of the six centre trebles of last row, and repeat from *. **4th row—**1 treble on each of the four centre treble stitches of last row, 1 chain, 4 bunches of stitches with a chain stitch between each bunch in the space between the bunches of last row, 1 chain, and repeat. **5th row—**1 treble on each of the two centre treble stitches of last row, 1 chain, 2 bunches in the first space, 1 bunch in the next, 2 bunches in the next, 1 chain stitch being between each bunch, 1 chain, and repeat. **6th row—**1 double crochet on each treble stitch of last row, 1 chain, 2 bunches in each space between the bunches of last row, making 8 bunches in all, 1 chain between each bunch, 1 chain, and repeat. **7th row—**1 double crochet under the first one chain of last row, 2 chain, 1 double crochet in the first space between the bunches, 4 chain, 1 double crochet on the double crochet just worked, * 1 treble in the next space between the bunches, 4 chain, 1 double crochet on the treble just worked, repeat from * six times, 1 double crochet in the next space, 4 chain, 1 double crochet on the double crochet just worked, 2 chain, and work the same round the next succeeding scallops.

No. 12.—MARGUERITE BORDER.

PROCURE Evans's crochet cotton No. 24, and a very fine steel crochet needle. Commence with 30 chain. **1st row—**1 treble in the sixth chain from the needle, 2 chain, another treble in the same place, 1 chain, miss one, 1 double crochet in the next, 1 chain, miss one, 8 consecutive treble, 5 chain, miss one, 8 more consecutive treble, 1 chain, miss one, 1 double crochet in the next, 1 chain, miss one, 1 treble at the end, 2 chain, another treble in the same place. **2nd row—**

5 chain to turn. 1 treble under the two chain, 2 chain, another treble in the same place, 1 treble under the two chain, 2 chain, another treble in the same place, 4 treble on the first four treble of last row, 5 chain, 1 double crochet under the five chain of last row, 5 chain, 4 treble on the last four treble stitches, 2 chain, 1 treble under the two chain, 2 chain, another treble in the same place. **3rd row**—5 chain to turn, 1 treble under the two chain, 2 chain, another treble in the same place 1 chain, 1 double crochet under the two chain, 1 chain 2 treble on first two treble stitches, 4 chain, 1 double crochet under the five chain, 5 chain, 1 double crochet under the next five chain, 4 chain, 2 treble on last two treble stitches, 1 chain, 1 double crochet under the two chain, 1 chain, 1 treble under the two chain 2 chain, another treble in the same place **4th row**—5 chain to turn, 1 treble under the two chain, 2 chain, another treble in the same place, 2 chain, 4 consecutive treble beginning over the two treble of last row, 5 chain, 1 double crochet under the five chain, 5 chain, 4 consecutive treble ending over the two treble of last row, 2 chain, 1 treble under the 2 chain, 2 chain, another treble in the same place. **5th row**—5 chain to turn, and work same as the first row. And continue for the length required. **For the Scalloped Edge—1st row**—Work 2 long treble, 3 chain, 2 long treble, under each turn of five chain stitches; break off at the end of the row. **2nd row**—Beginning on the right-hand side, 1 double crochet under the first loop of three chain, 1 chain, 1 treble under the next loop of three chain, 1 chain and 1 treble six times in the same place, 1 chain, and repeat to the end of the row. **3rd row**—1 double crochet under the first one chain of last row, 5 chain, 1 double crochet under the next one chain, 5 chain and 1 double crochet six more times under successive one-chain stitches, and continue. To head the top, work a row of 3 treble under each turn of five chain stitches, doing 3 chain between each group of treble.

No. 13.—WIDE HANDSOME BORDER FOR FURNITURE.

To be worked with Strutt's knitting cotton No. 10, and a fine steel crochet needle, or with other material according to the purpose for which it is required. Begin with 30 chain, turn back, and work 29 double crochet. * Turn, work 27 double crochet, inserting the hook to take up the back thread of the stitches of last row, turn back, and again work 27 double crochet in the same manner. Turn, work 22 double crochet ; turn back, and again work 22 double crochet. Turn,

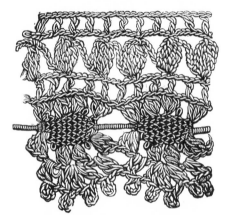

No. 7.—Thistle Border.

work 17 double crochet ; turn back, and again work 17 double crochet. Turn, work 10 double crochet ; turn back, and again work 10 double crochet. Now do 16 chain ; turn back, and work 10 double crochet, leaving five chain stitches unworked for the open part between the scallops. Turn, work 10 double crochet, 8 chain ; turn back, and work 17 double crochet. Turn, work 17 double crochet, 6 chain ; turn back, and work 22 double crochet. Turn, work 22 double crochet, 6 chain ; turn back, and work 27 double crochet. Turn, work 27 double crochet, 3 chain ; turn back, and work 29 double crochet. Repeat from * for the length required. Now to edge round these scallops, begin with 1 treble on the chain stitch at the tip of the first point, * 5 chain, another treble in the same place, 1 treble on the second double crochet stitch, 2 chain, 1 treble at the corner of the first ridge, 2 chain, miss two, 1 treble on the next, 2 chain, 1 treble at the corner of the next ridge, 2 chain, miss two, 1 treble on the next, 2 chain, 1 treble at the corner of the next ridge, 2 chain. miss two, 1 treble on the next, 2 chain, miss two, 1 treble on the next, 2 chain, 1 treble at the corner of the next ridge, 4 chain, miss two, 1 treble on the next, 4 chain, miss two, 1 treble on the next, 3 chain, 1 single crochet in the centre stitch of the five chain that connect the scallops, 3 chain, 1 treble in the third stitch of the next scallop, 2 chain, catch into the loop of four chain opposite, 2 chain, miss two, 1 treble in the next, 2 chain, catch into the four chain opposite, 2 chain, miss two, 1 treble at the corner, 2 chain and 1 treble nine times down the side to the point, and repeat from * and fasten off. Next the stars are to be made ; commence with 12 chain, join round in a circle ; work 4 chain to stand for a long treble stitch, 3 long treble in the same place, leaving the last loop of each on the needle, and drawing through all together when the tuft is completed, * 9 chain, miss one stitch of the circle, 4 long treble in the next, leaving the last loop of each on the needle, and then drawing through all together, repeat from * twice ; then 4 chain and catch on to the second space of two chain from the point of the second scallop, 4 chain, a tuft of long treble as before, 11 chain, catch on to the seventh space of two chain of the same scallop, 5 chain, catch on to the corresponding space of the first scallop, 6 chain, 1 single crochet in the fifth chain from the star, 4 chain, a tuft of long treble, 4 chain, catch on to the second space of two chain from the point of the first scallop, 4 chain, join to the first tuft of the star, and fasten off. Fill up all the spaces between the scallops with similar stars. Work for the lower edging. **1st row**—1 treble in the centre stitch of five chain at the

point of the scallop, * 4 chain, 1 treble in the centre stitch of the nine chain of the star, 13 chain, 1 treble in the centre stitch of the next loop of nine chain, 13 chain, 1 treble in the centre stitch of the next nine chain, 4 chain, 1 treble in the centre stitch of five chain at the point of the next scallop, and repeat from *. **2nd row**—1 treble in the fourth chain stitch of last row, * 2 chain, miss one, 1 treble in the next, 2 chain, miss seven over the point, 1 treble in the next, and repeat from *. **3rd row**—1 double crochet on the second treble stitch of last row, and work double crochet in every stitch, making 40 in all, which will bring you to the second treble from the point of the scallop, miss six, and repeat. **4th row**—Miss the first six double crochet stitches of last row, 1 treble on the next, * 5 chain, 1 single crochet in the fourth chain from the needle, 1 chain, miss two double crochet of last row, 1 treble on the next, repeat from * eight times, miss twelve double crochet at the point, 1 treble on the next, and repeat. This finishes the scallops. Now proceed for the heading. **1st row**—1 treble on the last row of the ridged double crochet, 2 chain and 1 treble three times, the last treble stitch being on the short row of the ridged crochet, * 2 chain 1 treble in the centre stitch of the 5 chain, 2 chain, 1 treble on the short row of the next lot of ridged crochet, 2 chain and 1 treble six times, the last of these treble stitches being on the other short row of the same lot of ridged crochet, and repeat from *. **2nd row**—1 double crochet on the first treble stitch of last row, 3 chain, 1 treble in the same place, * 1 chain, miss the next treble stitch of last row, 1 treble on the next, 3 chain, 1 double crochet in the same place, 3 chain, 1 treble in the same place, and repeat from *. **3rd row**—Same as the second row, working into each stitch of one chain. **4th row**—1 double crochet in each chain stitch of last row, with 5 chain between. **5th row**—1 treble, 2 chain, miss two, and repeat.

No. 14.—STAR EDGING.

COMMENCE with 18 chain. **1st row**—3 treble in the fifth chain from the needle, 1 chain, 3 treble in the next, 8 chain, miss seven, 3 treble in the next, 3 chain, 3 treble in the next, 1 treble in the last. **2nd row**—3 chain to turn, 3 treble under the loop of three chain, 3 chain, 3 more treble in the same place, 4 chain, 1 double crochet over the last row and into the foundation chain, 4 chain, 1 treble under the one chain, 3 chain, another treble in the same place. **3rd**

No. 8.—Mignardese Border.

row—4 chain to turn, 3 treble under the loop of three chain, 1 chain, 3 more treble in the same place, 3 chain, 1 treble on the one treble, 2 treble under the four chain, 2 treble under the next four chain, 1 treble on the first of the three treble stitches, 3 chain, 3 treble under the loop of three chain, 3 chain, 3 more treble in the same place, 1 treble on the chain that turned. **4th row**—3 chain to turn, 3 treble under the loop of three chain, 3 chain, 3 more treble in the same place, 2 long treble in between the six treble stitches of last row, 2 more long treble in the same place, 1 treble under the one chain, 3 chain, 1 more treble in the same place, 3 chain, 7 treble under the loop of four chain, 1 double crochet on the treble stitch at the end of the first row. **5th row**—4 chain and 1 double crochet under each one chain stitch of last row, 1 chain, 1 double crochet under the three chain, 3 chain, 3 treble under the loop of three chain, 1 chain, 3 more treble in the same place, 8 chain, 3 treble under the next loop of three chain, 3 chain, 3 more treble in the same place, 1 treble on the chain that turned **6th row**—3 chain to turn, 3 treble under the loop of three chain, 3 chain, 3 more treble in the same place, 8 chain, 1 treble under the one chain, 3 chain, 1 more treble in the same place. **7th row**—4 chain to turn, 3 treble under the loop of three chain, 1 chain, three more treble in the same place, 4 chain, 1 double crochet over the last three rows of eight chain, 4 chain, 3 treble under the loop of three chain, 3 chain, 3 more treble in the same place, 1 treble on the chain that turned. **8th row**—3 chain to turn, 3 treble under the loop of three chain, 3 chain, 3 more treble in one same place, 3 chain, 1 treble on the last of the three treble stitches, 2 treble under the loop of four chain, 2 treble under the next loop of four chain, 1 treble on the first of the three treble stitches, 3 chain, 1 treble under the one chain, 3 chain, 1 treble in the same place. 3 chain, 7 treble under the loop of four chain, 1 double crochet on the treble stitch at the end of the fifth row **9th row**—4 chain and 1 double crochet under each one chain stitch of last row, 4 chain, 1 double crochet under the three chain, 3 chain, 3 treble under the loop of three chain 1 chain, 3 more treble in the same place, 2 long treble in between the six treble stitches of last row, 8 chain, 2 more long treble in the same place, 3 treble under the loop of three chain, 3 chain, 3 more treble in the same place, 1 treble on the chain that turned. Work on in this manner, varying by one row in each pattern the position of the stars, and always catching together three rows of eight chain with a double crochet.

No. 15.—SHAMROCK PATTERN FOR SHAWL BORDER.

THIS may be commenced with chain for the length required or crocheted immediately upon the shawl; if the former, break off at the end of every row and begin anew on the right-hand side. **1st row**—Double crochet in every stitch of the foundation. **2nd row**—1 treble, 1 chain, miss one, and repeat. **3rd row**—Wool over the needle, insert the hook under the first one chain of last row, draw the wool through and pull up a long stitch, wool over the needle, insert the hook in the same place and pull up another long stitch, wool over the needle and make a third long stitch, wool over the needle and make a fourth long stitch, wool over the needle and draw through all the stitches on the needle, 1 chain, work another bunch of long stitches under the next one chain of last row, 1 chain, and repeat. **4th row**—1 treble under the one chain of last row, * 1 chain, 1 treble under the next one chain, and repeat from *. **5th row**—1 double crochet under the first one chain of last row, * 3 chain, miss the next space of one chain, 1 bunch of stitches in the next, 2 chain, another bunch in the same place, 3 chain, miss the next space of one chain, 1 double crochet in the next, and repeat from *. **6th row**—1 double crochet on the double crochet of last row, 3 chain, 1 bunch in the space between the bunches of last row, 2 chain, another bunch in the same place, 2 chain, another bunch in the same place, 3 chain, and repeat. **7th row**—1 double crochet on the double crochet of last row, 3 chain, 1 bunch in the first space between the bunches of last row, 2 chain, another bunch in the same place, 2 chain, 1 bunch in the second space between the bunches of last row, 2 chain, another bunch in the same place, 3 chain, and repeat. **8th row**—1 double crochet under the three chain of last row, 1 double crochet, 5 treble 1 double crochet all worked into each of the three spaces between the bunches of last row, 1 double crochet under the three chain, and repeat the same round every scallop of the border.

No. 16.—STAR-CROSS BORDER.

THIS handsome pattern may be worked with cotton for a quilt border or furniture trimming, and if done with wool it makes an elegant finish to a shawl.

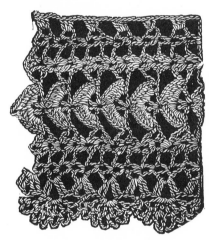

No. 9.—Jubilee Border.

Commence with 11 chain. **1st row**—1 treble in the fourth chain from the needle, 1 treble in the next, 3 chain, miss three, 1 treble in each of the three last foundation stitches. **2nd row**—6 chain to turn, 3 treble under the three chain, 3 chain, 1 treble on the chain that turned. **3rd row**—2 chain to turn, 2 treble under the three chain, 3 chain, 3 treble under the six chain, 6 chain 3 more treble in the same place. **4th row**—6 chain, 1 single in the sixth from the needle, 6 chain, 1 single in the sixth from the needle, 6 chain, 1 single in the sixth from the needle, 3 treble under the six chain of last row, 6 chain, 3 more treble in the same place, 3 chain, 3 treble, 3 chain, 1 treble on the chain that turned. **5th row**—2 chain, 2 treble under the three chain, 3 chain, 3 treble, 3 chain, 3 treble, 6 chain, 3 more treble in the same place. **6th row**—6 chain, 1 single in the sixth from the needle, 6 chain, 1 single in the sixth from the needle, 6 chain, 1 single in the sixth from the needle, 3 treble under the six chain of last row, 6 chain, 3 more treble in the same place, 3 chain, 3 treble, 3 chain, 3 treble, 3 chain, 1 treble in the chain that turned. **7th row**—2 chain, 2 treble under the three chain, 3 chain, 3 treble, 3 chain, 3 treble, 3 chain, 3 treble, 6 chain, 3 more treble in the same place. **8th row**—6 chain, 1 single in the sixth from the needle, 6 chain, 1 single in the sixth from the needle, 6 chain, 1 single in the sixth from the needle, 3 treble under the three chain, 3 chain, 3 treble, 3 chain, 3 treble under the six chain of last row, 6 chain, 1 single in the sixth from the needle, 6 chain, 1 single in the sixth from the needle, 6 chain, 1 single in the sixth from the needle, 3 treble under the same three chain as last three treble are worked under, 3 chain, 3 treble, 3 chain, 3 treble, 3 chain, 3 treble, 3 chain, 1 treble on the chain that turned. **9th row**—2 chain, 2 treble under the three chain, 3 chain, 3 treble, 3 chain, 3 treble, 3 chain, 3 treble. **10th row**—6 chain, 1 single in the sixth from the needle, 6 chain, 1 single in the sixth from the needle, 6 chain, 1 single in the sixth from the needle, 3 treble under the three chain of last row, 3 chain, 3 treble, 3 chain, 3 treble, 3 chain, 1 treble in the chain that turned. **11th row**—2 chain, 2 treble under the three chain, 3 chain, 3 treble, 3 chain, 3 treble. **12th row**—6 chain, 1 single in the sixth from the needle, 6 chain, 1 single in the sixth from the needle, 6 chain, 1 single in the sixth from the needle, 3 treble under the three chain of last row, 3 chain, 3 treble, 3 chain, 1 treble on the chain that turned. **13th row**—2 chain, 2 treble under the three chain, 3 chain, 3 treble under the next three chain. Repeat from the second row for the length

required. When a sufficient length is done work this heading along the straight side. **1st row**—1 double crochet and 1 chain alternately, and not too full; break off at the end of the row, and recommence on the right-hand side. **2nd row**—1 double crochet under the one chain of last row, 5 chain, 2 long treble in the same place, working off the top loops of both long trebles together with the chain stitch on the needle, miss two loops of one chain, 2 long treble in the third working off the top loops of both long trebles together, 4 chain, 1 double crochet in the same place, 11 chain, miss two loops of one chain, and repeat. **3rd row**—2 long treble stitches between the group of long trebles in previous row, working off the top loops of both long trebles together, 4 chain, 1 double crochet in the same place, 2 more long trebles in the same place, working off the top loops of both long trebles together with the chain stitch on the needle, 5 chain, 1 double crochet under the loop of eleven chain, 5 chain, and repeat; turn the work at the end of this row. **4th row**—1 double crochet on the first group of long treble stitches, 6 chain, 1 double crochet on the next group of long treble stitches, 6 chain, and repeat; turn the work at the end of the row. **5th row**—1 treble, 1 chain, miss one, alternately.

No. 17.—CORAL EDGING.

THIS is a pretty edging for underlinen if worked with Evans's crochet cotton No. 24 and a fine steel crochet needle. Begin with 11 chain; turn, and work 1 treble in the seventh chain from the needle, 2 chain, 1 treble in the next stitch of the foundation, 3 chain, another treble in the same place, 4 chain, 1 treble in the last of the foundation, 3 chain, another treble in the same place. **2nd row**—Turn with 3 chain, 5 treble under the loop of three chain of last row, 4 chain, 6 treble under the next loop of three chain, 2 chain, 1 treble under the loop that turned at the end, 2 chain, another treble in the same place. **3rd row**—5 chain to turn, 1 treble under the first two chain of last row, 2 chain, 1 treble under the next loop, 3 chain, another treble in the same place, 4 chain, 1 treble under the loop of four chain of last row, 3 chain, another treble in the same place. **4th row**—Same as the second row. Repeat the third and fourth rows for the length required.

No. 10.—Waterfall Border.

No. 18.—SCALLOPED EDGING WORKED ON PLAIN BRAID.

PROCURE a piece of plain braid, and with red ingrain cotton work thereon in cross-stitch the scroll pattern as shown in the engraving. With crochet cotton No. 20, work along one side of the braid for the Heading, 1 treble in two picots of the braid taken up together, * 3 chain, 1 treble in next two picots of the braid, and repeat from * to the end. Work for the Scallops on the opposite side—**1st row**—1 double crochet in two picots of the braid taken up together, 4 chain 1 double crochet in the two next picots, 7 chain, 1 double crochet in the two next picots, and repeat. **2nd row**—1 double crochet on the first double crochet of last row, * 1 long treble under the seven chain, 1 chain and 1 long treble six times in the same place, 1 double crochet on the double crochet stitch between the spaces of four chain, and repeat from *. **3rd row**—1 double crochet on the double crochet of last row, * 1 double crochet under the first one chain, 4 chain and 1 double crochet under the next one chain five times, 1 double crochet on the double crochet of last row, and repeat from

No. 19.—WIDE OPEN BORDER FOR FURNITURE TRIMMING.

THIS is worked with coarse ecru cotton or flax thread. Begin by working a hair-pin trimming four times the length required for the border. Hair-pin trimming is worked in this manner: having a stitch on the crochet needle, take the hair-pin (which should be a large one) in the left hand, the prongs upwards, hold the point of the crochet needle between the prongs of the hair-pin, the cotton falling from above to the right of the hair-pin, draw the cotton through the stitch on the needle, and * bring the needle out on the top of the hair-pin, turn the hair-pin over from right to left, at the same time slipping the needle again into position between the prongs with the cotton again to the right, draw the cotton through the stitch on the needle, and work a double crochet stitch in the loop that lies round the left-hand prong; repeat from *: when the hair pin is full you can drop off all the stitches, replace the last three or four, and continue. A sufficiency of the hair-pin trimming being worked, commence for

No. 11.—Willow Pattern for Shawl Border.

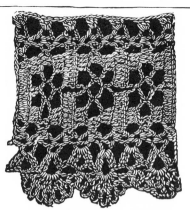

No. 12.—Marguerite Border.

No. 13.—Wide H..

No. 17.—Coral Edging.

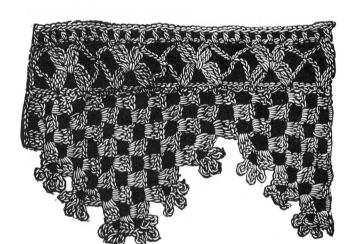

No. 16.—Star Cross Border.

No. 20.—Snowdrop Edging.

Ha..

No. 24.

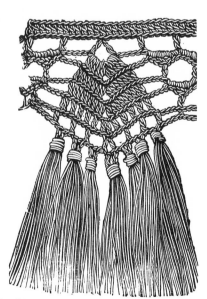

No. 22.—Fringe for Furniture Trimming.

No. 23.—Wide Scalloped Border.

No. 2

er for Furniture.

No. 14.—Star Edging.

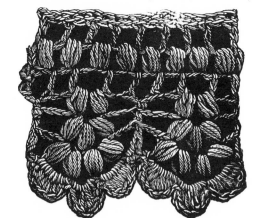

No. 15.—Shamrock Pattern for Shawl Border.

No. 18.—Scalloped Edging worked on Plain Braid.

ing.

ace Edging.

No. 21.—Narrow Wave Braid Edging

No. 19.—Wide Open Border for Furniture.

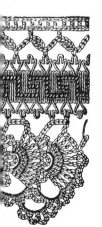

Edging.

No. 26.—Target Border.

No. 27.—Fringe for Quilts, Toilet Covers,

the border with 1 double crochet in each of the four first loops, * 9 chain, 1 double crochet in the next loop, 9 chain, miss one loop, 15 consecutive treble in next successive loops of the hair-pin trimming, 4 chain, 1 single crochet in the fifth stitch of the nine chain, 4 chain, miss one loop of hair-pin trimming, 1 double crochet in the next, 3 chain, 1 single crochet in the fourth stitch of the next nine chain, 5 chain, 1 double crochet in each of four successive loops; repeat from * to the end of the hair-pin trimming. **For the Heading of the Border,** work on this a row of 1 treble, 1 chain, miss one, and repeat. **For the Scallops,** work round the other side of the hair-pin trimming, thus: leave the first loop, work 1 double crochet in the next two loops taken together, 1 double crochet in each of six successive loops, * 6 chain, 1 double crochet in the fifth chain from the needle, 1 chain, 1 double crochet in the next loop, repeat from * nine times, 1 double crochet in five next successive loops, 1 double crochet in the next two loops taken together, 1 double crochet in each of six successive loops, catch with a single crochet into the corresponding stitch of the previous scallop, then repeat the picots, and continue.

No. 20.—SNOWDROP EDGING.

COMMENCE with 8 chain; work 1 double crochet in the second chain from the needle, 1 double crochet in the next, 4 consecutive treble stitches, and 1 long treble in the last of the foundation chain ; * then do 6 chain, 1 double crochet in the fifth chain from the needle, 8 chain, 1 double crochet in the second chain from the needle, 1 double crochet in the next, 4 consecutive treble, 1 long treble in the next; repeat from * till you have the length desired. Then, without breaking off, work **for the Scallops,** 1 double crochet on the long treble stitch just done, 6 chain, 1 single crochet in the sixth from the needle, 6 chain, 1 single crochet in the sixth from the needle, 6 chain, 1 single crochet in the sixth from the needle, 1 double crochet in the same chain-stitch that the long treble is worked into, 6 chain, 1 double crochet in the fifth from the needle, 1 chain, 1 double crochet at the top of the next long treble stitch, and continue to the end of

last row, 5 chain, and repeat from *. **5th row**—2 treble in the first chain stitch of last row, 1 double crochet on each of the other chain stitches, * 5 chain 9 consecutive treble stitches beginning over the seven treble of last row, 4 chain, 9 more consecutive treble, 5 chain, 2 double crochet 3 treble and 2 double crochet all under the centre loop of five chain of last row, and repeat from * **6th row**—1 treble on the first treble of last row, * 5 chain, 1 treble on the first of the nine treble, 1 chain, miss one, 1 treble on the next, and continue 1 chain 1 treble so as to get 12 treble stitches in all round the top of the scallop, then 5 chain, 1 treble on the centre stitch of the three trebles of last row, and repeat from *. **7th row**—1 double crochet on the treble stitch of last row, * 4 chain, 1 treble in the last stitch of the five chain of last row. 9 chain, 1 double crochet in the first of these chain stitches. miss three stitches of last row, 1 treble on the next, work round the top of the scallop 6 more picots of 9 chain ending with a treble on the first stitch of the five chain of last row, 4 chain, 1 double crochet on the treble stitch of last row, and repeat from *. ✓ This completes the heading. **For the Fringe,** cut the remainder of your thread or wool into lengths of 5 inches, and knot seven strands into each loop of the picoted edge.

No. 23.—WIDE SCALLOPED BORDER.

THIS is commenced with 21 chain. **1st row**—1 treble in the fourth chain from the needle, 5 chain, miss four, 1 treble in the next, 3 chain, another treble in the same place, 5 chain, miss five, 1 double crochet in the next, 5 chain and 1 double crochet three times in the same place, 5 chain, miss four, 1 treble in the next, 1 treble in the next. **2nd row**—4 chain to turn, 1 treble on the second treble stitch of last row, 5 chain, 1 treble in the centre loop of five chair of last row, 3 chain, another treble in the same place, 5 chain, 1 double crochet under the loop of three chain, 5 chain and 1 double crochet three times in the same place, 5 chain, 1 treble on the treble stitch of last row, 1 treble on the chain that turned. Repeat this last row till you have 12 rows done. Now begin for the scallop by making 8 chain and working 1 double crochet into the

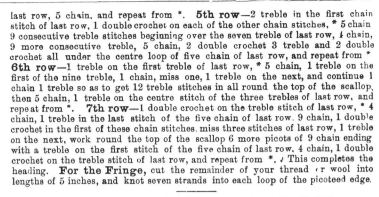

No. 28.—Picoteed Edging of Wave Braid.

No. 29.—Scalloped Edging of Wave Braid.

No. 30.—Neat Edging for Underlinen.

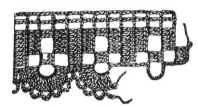

No. 31.—Polo Edging.

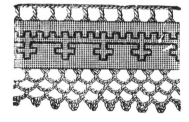

No. 32.—Simple Edging worked on Plain Braid.

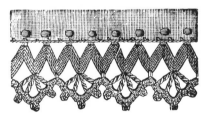

No. 33.—Wave Braid Edging.

No. 34.—Narrow Mignardese Edging.

No. 35.—Juniper Edging.

the row. **For the Heading**—Work 1 single crochet on the one chain-stitch at the top of the point, 4 chain, 1 treble in the second treble along the side, 1 treble at base of the second treble of the next point, 4 chain, and repeat. **2nd row**—Turn the work, and do * 1 double crochet in the same place the single crochet stitch is worked into, 6 chain, and repeat from *. **3rd row**—Turn the work with 4 chain, 1 treble in the second chain of last row, 1 chain, miss one, 1 treble, and continue to the end of the row.

No. 21.—NARROW WAVE BRAID EDGING.

UPON a length of wave braid, and with Coats's crochet cotton No. 18 or No. 20, work **for the Heading,** 1 double crochet on the top of each wave of the braid and 4 chain between, for the required length, and on this do a row of 1 treble, 1 chain, miss one. On the opposite side of the braid work, **1st row**—1 treble on the first wave of the braid, 5 chain, another treble in the same place, and repeat all along. **2nd row**—1 double crochet, 3 treble, 3 chain, 3 treble, 1 double crochet, all under each loop of five chain of last row.

No. 22.—FRINGE FOR FURNITURE TRIMMING.

COMMENCE with chain sufficient for the length required. **1st row**—Treble ; break off at the end of this and every row, and recommence on the right-hand side. **2nd row**—1 treble on the first treble of last row, * 5 chain, miss five treble stitches, 1 treble on the next, 5 chain, miss five, 1 treble on the next, 5 chain, another treble in the same place, 5 chain, miss five, 1 treble on the next, 5 chain, miss five, 1 treble on the next, and repeat from * to the end of the row. **3rd row**—2 double crochet 3 treble and 2 double crochet all under the first five chain of last row, miss the next loop of five chain, under the next work 5 treble, 4 chain, 5 treble, miss the next loop, and work 2 double crochet, 3 treble, 2 double crochet, under the next, and repeat. **4th row**—3 chain to begin,* 1 treble on the centre stitch of the three treble of last row, 5 chain, 7 consecutive treble stitches beginning over the five treble of last row, 4 chain, 7 more consecutive treble. 5 chain, 1 treble on the centre stitch of the three treble of

side of the tenth row. **2nd row of the Scallop**—Turn, and do 1 double crochet under the eight chain, 9 chain and 1 double crochet six times in the same place, 4 chain, 1 treble on each of the two treble stitches of the heading, which work as before. **3rd row**—Work along the heading as before, then 5 chain and one double crochet into each of the loops of nine chain round the scallop, 5 chain, and catch into the eighth row of the heading. **4th row**—Turn, 5 chain and 1 double crochet under each loop of last row, and then the heading as before. **5th row**—Work the heading, and then 5 chain and 1 double crochet into each loop of last row, and catch into the sixth row of the heading. **6th row**—2 chain, and catch into the fifth row of the heading, work 7 treble under each loop of five chain, and the heading as before. **7th row**—Work the heading, then 1 chain, 1 treble, alternately, in every other stitch of the scallop, 1 chain, and catch into the fourth row of the heading. **8th row**—2 chain, and catch into the third row of the heading, 1 chain and 1 treble under each one chain of last row, and heading as before. **9th row**—Work the heading, then 3 chain and 2 treble under each alternate one chain of last row, and catch into the second row of the heading. **10th row**—2 chain, and catch into the first row of the heading, 2 chain, * 1 double crochet between the first two treble stitches, 2 chain, 1 treble under the three chain, do 4 chain and 1 double crochet three times for a picot on the top of the treble just done, 2 chain, and repeat from * all round the scallop, and work the heading as before. Then do 1½ rows of heading only and continue.

No. 24.—HONITON LACE EDGING.

BEGIN by working a piece of hair-pin trimming about twice the length the edging is required to be. This done, commence with 18 chain, pass the cotton twice round the needle, insert the hook in the sixth chain from the needle and draw the cotton through, cotton over the needle and draw through two loops on the needle (leaving 3 on the needle), * cotton twice round the needle, miss one stitch of the foundation, insert the hook in the next stitch and draw the cotton through, cotton over the needle and draw through two loops on the needle (leaving 5 on the needle), repeat from * till you have 7 stitches worked (15 on the needle), then take the hair-pin trimming and work in the same manner 4 times in two loops of the trimming taken together, cotton once round the needle, insert the hook in the next two loops of the trimming and draw the cotton through, cotton over the needle and draw through two loops on the needle; now you work back like tricotee, cotton over the needle and draw through the first stitch, cotton over the needle and draw through the next stitch, and so on, till all are worked off. **2nd row**—2 chain to turn, miss the first treble of last row, and work the same as above on the 6 following trebles, inserting the hook so as to take up one thread only, then work same way but with cotton only once round the needle, and do 1 stitch on the space and 1 stitch on the treble for 8 stitches, do another stitch in two loops of the hair-pin trimming taken together; and work off as in previous row. **3rd row**—2 chain, miss the first treble of last row, and work 5 stitches over five treble with cotton twice round the needle, nd 8 stitches over the eight of last row with cotton once round the needle and another stitch in two loops of the hair-pin trimming taken together, and work back as in previous row. **4th row**—2 chain, miss the first treble of last row, and work 4 stitches over four treble with cotton twice round the needle, then 8 stitches over the eight of last row with cotton once round the needle, and another stitch in two loops of the hair-pin trimming taken together; and work back as in previous row. **5th row**—2 chain, miss the first treble of last row, and work 7 stitches the same as in the first row (make the last of the seven come upon the last stitch of the diamond), then 1 stitch in the same two loops of the hair-pin trimming as were worked into in last row, 3 more stitches taking up two loops of the hair-pin trimming each time, and 1 stitch in the next two loops with the cotton once round the needle; draw back as in the first row, and continue for the length required.

No 25.—RAILWAY EDGING.

THIS is worked upon a piece of fancy braid of the kind shown in the illustration. For the **Crochet Edging**, begin with 15 chain, work a single crochet in the eleventh chain from the needle, cross over the commencing chain, and along the under side of the circle work 6 single crochet, then do 10 double crochet in the circle, 1 double crochet in the fourth stitch from the end of the commencing chain, 4 chain, miss one, 1 double crochet in each of the two end stitches. **2nd row**—3 chain, 1 single into a picot of the braid, 2 chain, 1 single in the next picot, 2 chain, 1 treble on the first of the ten double crochet stitches, 1 chain and 1 treble nine times. **3rd row**—4 chain to turn, 1 double crochet under the first one chain, 1 double crochet under the next, 4 chain, 2 double crochet under two next chain, 4 chain, 2 double crochet under two next chain, 7 chain, turn the work 1 single on the second double crochet at left-hand side, turn the work, do 10 double crochet under the loop of seven chain, 1 single in the same place double crochet stitch is worked into, 4 chain, 2 double crochet under next two chain: this leaves one space of one chain *not* worked into. **4th row**—3 chain, 1 single into the second picot from the one last worked into, 2 chain, 1 single in the next picot, 2 chain, 1 treble on the first of the ten double crochet stitches, 1 chain and 1 treble nine times, 6 chain, 1 single under the loop of four chain at the point **5th row**—4 chain to turn, 1 double crochet under the loop of six chain, 4 chain and 1 double crochet five times in the same place, 4 chain, 1 double crochet under one chain, 1 double crochet under next one chain, 4 chain, 1 double crochet under one chain, 1 double crochet under next one chain, 4 chain, 1 double crochet under one chain, 1 double crochet under next one chain, 7 chain, turn the work, 1 single on the second double crochet stitch at left-hand side, turn the work, do 10 double crochet under the loop of seven chain, 1 single in the same place double crochet stitch is worked into, 4 chain, 1 double crochet under next one chain, 1 double crochet under next one chain, leave one space of one chain *not* worked into. **6th row**—3 chain, 1 single into the second picot from the one last worked

into, 2 chain, 1 single in the next picot, 2 chain, 1 treble on the first of the ten double crochet stitches, 1 chain and 1 treble nine times, 6 chain, 1 single in the third loop of four chain. **7th row**—4 chain to turn, 1 double crochet under the loop of six chain, 4 chain, 1 double crochet in the same place, 8 chain, 1 single in the fifth loop to the right, 4 chain, 1 double crochet under the loop of eight chain, 4 chain and 1 double crochet three times in the same place, 4 chain and 1 double crochet three times under the remaining part of the loop of six chain, 4 chain, 1 double crochet under 1 chain, 1 double crochet under next one chain, 4 chain, 1 double crochet under one chain, 1 double crochet under next one chain, 4 chain, 1 double crochet under 1 chain, 1 double crochet under next one chain, 7 chain, turn the work, 1 single on the second double crochet at left-hand side, turn the work, do 10 double crochet under loop of seven chain, 1 single in the same place double crochet stitch is worked into, 4 chain, 1 double crochet under next one chain, 1 double crochet under next one chain, leave one space of one chain *not* worked into. Repeat from the fourth row. For the **Heading**—On the opposite side of the braid, work **1st row**—1 single in the first picot of the braid, * 4 chain, 1 treble in the same picot, 3 chain, miss one picot, 1 single in the next, and repeat from *. **2nd row**—1 double crochet on the treble of last row, 6 chain, and repeat. **3rd row**—1 treble, 1 chain, miss one, and repeat.

No. 26.—TARGET BORDER.

BEGIN with 9 chain; join round, and work 3 long treble (cotton twice round the needle), 2 chain, eight times in the circle, join. **2nd round**—1 double crochet on the centre stitch of the three long treble, 2 chain, 1 treble in the second chain stitch, 2 chain, another treble in the same place, 2 chain, and repeat; join at the end of the round. **3rd round**—1 double crochet on the double crochet of last round, 3 chain, 1 treble, 2 long treble, and 1 treble, all under the loop of two chain between the treble stitches of last round, 3 chain, and repeat; join, and break off at the end of the round. Work a number of

No. 36.—Guipure Border.

No. 37.—Elegant Looped Border.

these circles or targets, connecting them together as you work by catching the last two long treble stitches into the first two long trebles of the preceding circle. For the **1st row of the Heading**—Work 3 long treble in between two long treble stitches of the first circle, 7 chain, 1 double crochet in between the two next long treble stitches, which is the central point of the circle, 7 chain, 3 long treble in between the next two long treble stitches, and repeat. **2nd row**—1 treble, 1 chain, miss one, and repeat. **3rd row**—1 treble under one chain of last row, 1 chain, and repeat. Work on the opposite side of the crochet circles, **1st row** and **2nd row**— Same as the first and second row above. **3rd row**—1 double crochet on the first treble stitch, * 6 chain, miss five, 1 double crochet on the next, 3 chain, 2 long treble in the same place, miss five, 2 long treble on the next, 3 chain, 1 double crochet in the same place, and repeat from *. **4th row**—1 double crochet under the loop of six chain, 4 chain, 2 long treble on top of the two long treble of last row, 3 chain, 1 double crochet in the same place, 3 chain, 2 long treble on top of the next two long treble, 4 chain, and repeat. **5th row**—1 double crochet under the loop of three chain, 3 c row 1 double crochet under next loop of three chain, 4 chain and repeat. **6th** chain —1 treble, 1 chain, miss one, and repeat. **7th row**—1 double crochet under the first one chain of last row, 2 chain, 1 treble under the next one chain, 3 chain, another treble in the same place, 2 chain, and repeat.

No. 27.—FRINGE FOR QUILTS, TOILET COVERS, &c.

MAKE a chain the length required. **1st row**—1 treble, 1 chain, miss one, and repeat; break off at the end of this and every row. **2nd row**—1 double crochet, 7 chain, miss four stitches of last row, 1 double crochet, 9 chain, miss five, and repeat. **3rd row**—1 double crochet in the centre stitch of the seven chain, 2 chain, 5 treble in the third stitch of the nine chain, 3 chain, miss three, 5 treble in the next which is the seventh stitch of the nine chain, 2 chain, and repeat. **4th row**—1 treble on the double crochet of last row, 3 chain, 5 consecutive treble over five treble of last row, 3 chain 5 more consecutive treble, 3 chain, and repeat. **5th row**—1 treble on the treble stitch of last row, 3 chain, another treble in the same place, 3 chain, miss three chain and one treble, and work 4 consecutive treble on four treble of last row, 1 chain, 4 more consecutive treble on the four following, 3 chain, and repeat. **6th row**—1 treble on the first treble stitch of last row, 3 chain, another treble in the same place, 1 chain, 1 treble on the next treble of last row, 3 chain, another treble in the same place, 3 chain. 7 treble, the centre one of these to come over the one chain-stitch of last row, 3 chain, and repeat. **7th row**—1 treble on the first treble stitch of last row, 3 chain, another treble in the same place, 1 chain, 5 treble in the single chain stitch of last row, 1 chain, 1 treble on the fourth treble stitch of last row, 3 chain, another treble in the same place, 3 chain, 5 consecutive treble over the centre five treble of last row, 3 chain, and repeat. **8th row**—1 treble on the first treble stitch of last row, 3 chain, another treble in the same place 1 chain, 1 treble in single chain stitch, 1 chain, 5 treble in the other single chain stitch, 1 chain, 1 treble on treble stitch of last row, 3 chain, another treble in the same place, 3 chain, 3 consecutive treble over the centre three treble of last row, 3 chain, and repeat. **9th row**—1 double crochet on the first treble stitch of last row, 5 chain, * 1 treble in the single chain stitch of last row, 3 chain, another treble in the same place, 1 chain, 5 treble in the one chain between the groups of treble stitches, 1 chain, 1 treble in the single chain, 3 chain, another treble in the same place, 5 chain, 1 double crochet in the loop before the three treble of last row, 5 chain, 1 double crochet in the loop after the three treble, 5 chain, and repeat from *. **10th row**—1 double crochet on double crochet of last row, 5 chain, 1 double crochet in the last stitch of the 5 chain of last row, 5 chain, 1 treble in the single chain stitch of last row, 3 chain, another treble in the same place, 1 chain, 1 treble in the next single chain of last row, 3 chain, another treble in the same place, 5 chain, 1 double crochet in the first of the five chain of last row, 5 chain, 1 double crochet on double crochet of last row, 7 chain and repeat. **11th row**—1 double crochet under the first loop of five chain, 5 chain, 1 double crochet under the next loop of five chain, 5 chain, 1 treble in the single chain stitch, 3 chain, another treble in the same place, 5 chain, 1 double crochet under the loop of five chain, 5 chain, 1 double crochet under the next loop of five chain, 7 chain, and repeat. **12th row**—1 double crochet under the first loop of five chain, 5 chain, 1 double crochet under the next loop, 5 chain, 1 double crochet under the loop of three chain, 5 chain, 1 double crochet under the loop of five chain, 5 chain, 1 double crochet under the next loop, 7 chain, and repeat. Now to form the fringe, cut the remainder of your thread or wool into 6-inch lengths, and knot six strands into every loop of the crochet beading.

No. 30.—NEAT EDGING FOR UNDERLINEN.

COMMENCE with 17 chain. **1st row**—1 treble in the seventh chain from the needle, 1 chain, miss one, 1 treble in the next, 2 chain, miss three, 1 treble in the next, 3 chain, another treble in the same place, 2 chain, miss three, 1 treble in the next, 3 chain, another treble in the same place. **2nd row**—2 chain to turn, 9 treble under the loop of three chain, 7 treble under the next loop of three chain, 1 treble on the first of the two treble stitches, 1 chain, 1 treble on the next treble, 1 chain, 1 treble on the second stitch of the chain that turned. **3rd row**—4 chain to turn, 1 treble on the first treble stitch, 1 chain, 1 treble on the next treble stitch, 2 chain. 1 treble on the centre stitch of the seven treble, 3 chain, another treble in the same place, 2 chain, 1 treble on the fourth stitch of the nine treble, 3 chain, another treble in the same place. Repeat the second and third rows for the length required.

No. 31.—POLO EDGING.

BEGIN with 16 chain. **1st row**—1 treble in the fourth chain from the needle, 8 treble worked consecutive, 1 chain, miss one, 1 treble in the next, 1 chain, miss one, 1 treble in the next. **2nd row**—4 chain to turn, 1 treble on the first treble stitch of last row, 1 chain, miss one, six consecutive treble, 3 chain. miss three, 1 treble at the end. **3rd row**—9 chain to turn, 3 treble on the three chain, 4 chain, miss four, 2 treble, 1 chain, 1 treble, 1 chain, 1 treble on the second stitch of the chain that turned. **4th row**—4 chain to turn, 1 treble on the first treble stitch of last row, 1 chain, miss one, 6 consecutive treble, 3 chain, miss three, one treble at the end. **5th row**—3 chain to turn, 9 treble in consecutive stitches 1 chain, 1 treble, one chain, 1 treble on the second stitch of the chain that turned. Repeat from the second row. Break off when you have a sufficient length, and work **for the Scallops—1st row**—1 double crochet at the corner of the commencing chain, 2 chain, 1 double crochet at the corner of the first row, * 13 treble under the loop of nine chain, 1 double crochet at the corner of the fourth row, 2 chain, 1 double crochet at the corner of the fifth row, and repeat from *. **2nd row**—1 double crochet under the loop of two chain, 1 double crochet on the second stitch of the thirteen trebles, 3 chain, miss one, one double crochet on the next five times, 3 chain, and continue.

No. 32.—SIMPLE EDGING, WORKED ON PLAIN BRAID.

HAVING a piece of plain braid, work on it with red ingrain cotton in Holbein stitch the little pattern shown in the illustration. With crochet cotton No. 18 or

No. 38.—Mignardese Edging for Baby Things.

No. 39.—Birkbeck Edging.

No. 40.—Pretty Narrow Edging.

No. 28.—PICOTEED EDGING OF WAVE BRAID.

PROCURE a length of wave braid and a skein of Coats's crochet cotton No. 18 or No. 20. Work **for the Heading**, 1 treble on the top of the first wave of the braid, * 2 chain, cotton twice round the needle, insert the hook half-way down the side of the same wave and draw the cotton through, cotton over the needle, and draw through two loops on the needle, cotton over the needle, insert the hook in the side of the next wave and draw the cotton through, cotton over the needle and draw through two loops on the needle, cotton over the needle and draw through two more loops on the needle, cotton over the needle and again draw through two loops on the needle, cotton over the needle and draw through the two last loops on the needle, 2 chain, one treble on the top of the wave, and repeat from *. On this work a row of 1 treble, 1 chain, miss one. On the opposite side of the braid work, **1st row**—1 double crochet on the top of the first wave, * 1 long treble in the side of the next wave, 3 chain, 1 treble on top of the same wave, 5 chain, another treble in the same place, 3 chain, 1 long treble in the side of the wave, 1 double crochet on the top of the next wave, and repeat from *. **2nd row**—1 double crochet in the little space between the double crochet and the long treble stitch of last row, 1 double crochet under the loop of three chain, 4 chain, 1 single in the fourth chain from the needle, 1 double crochet under the same loop of three chain, 4 chain, 1 single in the fourth chain from the needle, 1 double crochet in the same loop of three chain, and continue the piqués thus, doing 5 under the loop of five chain, and 2 under the other loop of three chain, 9 piqués in all round the scallop, 1 double crochet in the little space between the long treble and the double crochet of last row, and repeat to the end of the row.

No. 29.—SCALLOPED EDGING OF WAVE BRAID.

PROCURE a piece of wave braid and crochet cotton No. 18 or No. 20. Work **for the Heading—1st row**—1 long treble in the top of the first wave of the braid, 3 chain, another long treble in the same place, and repeat. **2nd row**—1 double crochet in every stitch of the preceding row. On the opposite side of the braid work **for the Scallops—1st row**—1 single crochet in each wave of the braid, 7 chain between. **2nd row**—1 double crochet, 9 treble, 1 double crochet, under each loop of seven chain of last row.

No. 20, work along one side of the braid **for the Heading**. 1 treble in two picots of the braid taken up together, * 3 chain, 1 treble in next two picots of the braid, and repeat from * to the end. On the other side of the braid work—**1st row**—1 double crochet in two picots of the braid taken up together, * 5 chain, 1 double crochet in next two picots of the braid, and repeat from * **2nd row**—1 double crochet under loop of five chain of last row, 5 chain, and repeat. **3rd row**—1 double crochet under five chain of last row, * 7 chain, 1 double crochet in the fifth chain from the needle, 2 chain, 1 double crochet under five chain of last row, and repeat from *.

No. 33.—WAVE BRAID EDGING.

USE Coats's crochet cotton No 18 or 20, and **for the Heading** work 2 single crochet on the first wave of the braid, 4 chain, 2 single crochet on the next wave, and continue for the length required. On the opposite side work, **1st row**—1 double crochet on the first wave of the braid, * 2 chain, 1 long treble on the next wave, 3 chain, another long treble, 3 chain, another long treble, 3 chain, another long treble, all in the same place, 2 chain, 1 double crochet in the next wave of the braid, and repeat from *. **2nd row**—2 double crochet under loop of two chain, * 2 double crochet under the loop of three chain, 4 chain, 1 single in the fourth chain from the needle, 2 more double crochet under the same three chain, repeat from * under each of the other loops of three chain, 2 double crochet under the two chain, and continue the same to the end of the row.

No. 34.—NARROW MIGNARDESE EDGING.

PROCURE a length of mignardese braid, and work with crochet cotton No. 18 or No. 20. **1st row**—1 double crochet in the first picot of the braid, 1 chain, 1 double crochet in the next picot, * 7 chain, miss one picot, 8 treble in next successive picots, 2 chain, catch with a single crochet in to the third chain stitch before the trebles, 4 chain, miss one picot, 1 double crochet in the next, chain, 1 double crochet in the next, and repeat from *. Turn with 1 chain, work 1 double crochet under one chain of last row, 8 chain, and repeat to the and Turn with 1 chain, and work double crochet in every stitch of last row.

No. 35.—JUNIPER EDGING.

THIS is worked lengthways; it looks best done with fine cotton, and is pretty for edging pincushion covers and other purposes. Begin with a chain the length required, and for the 1st row—Work 1 treble, 1 chain, miss one, and repeat. 2nd row—1 double crochet under the first space of one chain, * 9 chain, 1 single crochet in the fifth from the needle, 7 chain, 1 single in the fifth from the needle, 9 chain, 1 single in the fifth from the needle, 7 chain, 1 single in the fifth from the needle, 1 single in the fourth chain from the double crochet stitch, 3 chain, miss two spaces of one chain, 1 double crochet in the next, and repeat from * to the end of the row. 3rd row—1 double crochet under the top loop of chain between the picots of last row, 6 chain, and repeat. 4th row—2 long treble in the third chain-stitch of the preceding row, 2 long treble in the next chain-stitch, and repeat. 5th row—1 treble on the first stitch of the long treble of last row, 6 chain, 1 single in the fifth from the needle, 1 long treble on the next long treble, 6 chain, 1 single in the fifth from the needle, 1 long treble on the next long treble, 6 chain, 1 single in the fifth from the needle, 1 treble on the last long treble, and repeat to the end of the row.

No. 36.—GUIPURE BORDER.

THIS is a useful border for many purposes. If worked with ecru or grey linen thread it makes a handsome trimming for summer dresses. Commence by making a length of hair-pin trimming, rather more than twice as long as the length required for the border. 1st row—1 double crochet in the first picot of the hair-pin trimming, which hold in such a way as to keep to the *right* as you work, 3 chain, miss one picot of the trimming, 1 double crochet in the next, * 19 chain (here begins the spray), 1 single in the third picot from that last worked into, and now you are on the first leaf, for which miss the first chain stitch, work 1 double crochet in the next, 2 treble, 1 long treble, 2 treble, 1 double crochet in successive stitches ; then for the second leaf, 11 chain, 1 single in the fourth picot, and work the same ; for the third leaf (the one at the top), 8 chain, 1 single in the fifth picot, and work the same ; for the fourth leaf, 8 chain, 1 single in the fifth picot, and work the same, and do also 1 single into the second leaf and 1 single on each of the three stem stitches ; for the fifth leaf, 8 chain, 1 single in the fourth picot, and work the same, and do also 1 single into the first leaf and 1 single on each of three stem stitches ; for the sixth leaf, 8 chain, 1 single, 1 single in the third picot, and work the same, then 5 chain, and do the seventh leaf on the remaining chain stitches ; work 1 double crochet

No. 41.—Acorn Edging.

under the loop of three chain, * 8 chain, 1 single in the sixth from the needle, 1 chain, 1 single in the sixth from the needle, 2 chain, turn the work, and do 1 double crochet under the loop of five chain ; 8 chain, 1 single in the sixth from the needle, 9 chain, 1 single in the sixth from the needle, 2 chain, 1 double crochet at the tip of the last leaf ; 8 chain, 1 single in the sixth from the needle, 9 chain, 1 single in the sixth from the needle, 2 chain, 1 double crochet in the third picot from that last worked into ; 8 chain, 1 single in the sixth from the needle, 9 chain, 1 single in the sixth from that last worked into, turn the work so that you get the hair-pin trimming again to the right as you work, and repeat from * for the length required. For the Heading—1st row—Work 2 treble in the centre of every picoteed bar above the sprays of last row, 6 chain, and repeat. 2nd row—2 treble on the first two chain stitches of last row, 2 chain, miss two, 2 treble on the last two chain stitches, 2 chain, miss two treble stitches, and repeat. For the Edging—1st row—Begin at the same end of the hair-pin trimming as the first spray began upon, and work 1 double crochet in the third picot of the trimming, 6 chain, 1 single in the fourth from the needle, 2 chain, miss two picots, 2 treble in the next, * 9 chain, 1 treble in the seventh from the needle, 1 long treble in the next, 1 chain, miss one picot, 2 treble in the next, repeat from * seven times more, then 6 chain, 1 single in the fourth from the needle, 2 chain, miss two picots, 1 double crochet in the next, 2 chain, miss two picots, 1 treble in the next, miss one picot, 1 treble in the next, 2 chain, miss two picots, 1 double crochet in the next, catch with 1 single into the double crochet stitch eight picots back, 6 chain, 1 single in the fourth from the needle, 2 chain, miss two picots, 2 treble in the next, and repeat from * to the end of the scallops. 2nd row—2 double crochet under the first picot loop of last row, * 8 chain, 1 single in the sixth from the needle, 9 chain, 1 single in the sixth from the needle, 2 chain, 2 double crochet under the next picot loop of last row, repeat from * six times more, 2 chain, 1 double long treble (cotton three times round the needle, in the little space between the two treble stitches of last row, 2 chain, 2 double crochet under the first picot loop of the next scallop, and continue.

No. 37.—ELEGANT LOOPED BORDER.

THIS is suitable for a variety of purposes, and if worked with ecru thread or with coloured silk is pretty for dress trimming. Commence with 6 chain, turn, miss the first chain stitch, work 5 double crochet, turn with 1 chain, and again work 5 double crochet, inserting the hook to take up the thread at the

---

back, that the work may sit in ridges ; do 4 rows altogether of 5 double crochet, then 6 chain, and again 4 rows of 5 double crochet ; and continue till you have the length desired, when fasten off. 2nd row—Begin with 1 double crochet on the first corner of the little square, * 9 chain, 1 double crochet in the fifth chain from the needle, 5 chain, 1 double crochet in the fifth from the needle, 8 chain, 1 double crochet in the fifth from the needle, 5 chain, 1 double crochet in the fifth from the needle, 1 double crochet in the chain stitch before the first of these piqués, 3 chain, 1 double crochet on the point of the little square ; repeat from *, and after doing three chain work the double crochet stitch on the point of the next little square, and continue to the end of the row. 3rd row—Begin with 1 double crochet in the space between the second and third piques of last row, 9 chain, 1 double crochet in the fifth from the needle, * 5 chain, 1 double crochet in the fifth from the needle, and repeat from * till you have done 11 piqués, then do 1 double crochet in the chain stitch before the first of the piques, 3 chain, 1 double crochet in the space in the next circle of piqué stitches and continue. This completes the loops. Now work for the Heading—1st row—1 double crochet on the point of the first little square, * 6 chain, 1 double crochet on the point of the next little square, and repeat from * 2nd row—1 treble, 1 chain, miss one, and repeat. 3rd row—1 treble on the treble stitch of last row, 1 chain, and repeat.

No. 38.—MIGNARDESE EDGING FOR BABY THINGS.

WORK with crochet cotton No. 20 upon a piece of mignardese braid. 1st row—1 single crochet in the first picot of the braid, * 3 chain, miss one picot, 1 treble in the next, 6 chain, 1 double crochet in the lower part of the treble stitch, 3 chain, miss one picot, 1 single crochet in the next, and repeat from *. 2nd row—3 double crochet under each loop of three chain of last row, 7 double crochet under the six chain. For the Heading—Work on the other side of the braid, 2 double crochet in one picot, 1 double crochet in the next, and repeat.

No. 39.—BIRKBECK EDGING.

COMMENCE with 20 chain. 1st row—1 treble in the seventh chain from the needle, 2 more treble in the same place, 2 chain, 3 treble in the next stitch of the foundation, 3 chain, miss three, 1 double crochet in the next, 3 chain, miss three, 3 treble in the next, 2 chain, 3 treble in the next, leave three stitches unworked. 2nd row—6 chain to turn, 3 treble under two chain of last row, 2

No. 42.—Serpolette Edging.

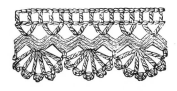

No. 43.—Scallop of Wave Braid.

chain, 3 more treble in the same place, 3 chain, 1 double crochet on the double crochet of last row, 3 chain, 3 treble under two chain, 2 chain, 3 more treble in the same place, 1 chain, 1 treble on the second stitch of the chain that turned. 3rd row—4 chain to turn, 3 treble under two chain, 2 chain, 3 more treble in the same place, 7 chain, 3 treble under two chain, 2 chain, 3 more treble in the same place, 1 chain and 1 treble seven times under the loop of six chain at the side of the edging, 1 single crochet in the stitch at the end of the foundation chain. 4th row—Work 5 chain and 1 double crochet seven times under the one chains of last row, 3 chain, 3 treble under two chain, 2 chain, 3 more treble in the same place, 3 chain, 1 double crochet in the centre stitch of the seven chain, 3 chain, 3 treble under two chain, 2 chain, 3 more treble in the same place, 1 chain, 1 treble on the second stitch of the chain that turned. 5th row—4 chain to turn, 3 treble under two chain, 2 chain, 3 more treble in the same place, 3 chain, 1 double crochet on the double crochet of last row, 3 chain, 3 treble under two chain, 2 chain, 3 more treble in the same place. 6th row—6 chain to turn, 3 treble under two chain, 2 chain, 3 more treble in the same place, 7 chain, 3 treble under two chain, 2 chain, 3 more treble in the same place, 1 chain, 1 treble on the second stitch of the chain that turned. 7th row—4 chain, 3 treble under two chain, 2 chain, 3 more treble in the same place, 3 chain, 1 double crochet in the centre stitch of the seven chain, 3 chain, 3 treble under two chain, 2 chain, 3 more treble in the same place, 1 chain and 1 treble seven times under the loop of six chain at the side of the edging, 1 single crochet under the three chain of the fourth row. 8th row—Work 5 chain and 1 double crochet seven times under the one chains of last row, 3 chain, 3 treble under two chain, 2 chain, 3 more treble in the same place, 3 chain, 1 double crochet on the double crochet of last row, 3 chain, 3 treble under 2 chain, 2 chain, 3 more treble in the same place, 1 chain, 1 treble on the second stitch of the chain that turned. Continue thus : each scallop takes four rows, and you do seven chain every third row in the centre.

No. 40.—PRETTY NARROW EDGING.

WORK upon a piece of mignardese braid with crochet cotton No. 18 or No. 20. 1st row—3 treble in every alternate picot of the braid. 2nd row—1 treble in the little space between the groups of treble stitches, 3 chain, and repeat. 3rd row—1 double crochet, 3 treble, 1 double crochet, under every space of three chain of last row. Then on the opposite side of the braid, for a heading work 1 treble in every picot and 1 chain between.

No. 41.—ACORN EDGING.

COMMENCE with 9 chain. 1st row—1 treble in the eighth chain from the needle, 2 chain, another treble in the same place, 2 chain, 1 treble in the last stitch of the foundation, 2 chain, another treble in the same place. 2nd row—5 chain to turn, 1 treble under the centre loop of two chain of last row, 2 chain and 1 treble three more times in the same place. Repeat the second row for the length desired. When a sufficient length is done, form the scallops by working along one side of the foundation, 9 treble under every loop of five chain. And on the opposite side make a heading, 2 double crochet under loop of five chain, 4 chain, and repeat.

No. 42.—SERPOLETTE EDGING.

THIS pretty edging is worked the short way. Begin with 14 chain. 1st row—1 treble in the eighth chain from the needle, 6 treble in consecutive stitches. 2nd row - 2 chain to turn, 1 treble in the third treble stitch, 1 treble on the fifth, and 1 treble on the last of the seven treble stitches, 4 chain, 7 treble under the loop at the end. 3rd row—4 chain to turn, 1 treble on the third treble stitch, 1 chain, 1 treble on the fifth, 1 chain, 1 treble on the last of the seven treble stitches, 5 chain, 7 treble under the four chain of last row, 1 treble in the first chain-stitch at the end of the row. 4th row—Same as the second row. 5th row—Same as the third row. 6th row—2 chain to turn, 1 treble on the third treble stitch, 1 treble on the fifth, and 1 treble on the last of the seven treble stitches, 4 chain, 7 treble under the five chain of last row, 9 chain, 1 single crochet in the four chain of previous point. 7th row—Turn, do 11 double crochet under the loop of nine chain, 1 chain, 1 treble on the third treble stitch, 1 chain, 1 treble on the fifth, 1 chain, 1 treble on the last of the seven treble stitches, 5 chain, 7 treble under the loop of four chain, 1 treble in the first chain stitch at the end of the row. 8th row—2 chain to turn, 1 treble on the third treble stitch, 1 treble on the fifth, and 1 treble on the last of the seven treble stitches, 4 chain, 7 treble under the loop of five chain, 1 long treble on the first stitch of the eleven double crochet, * 2 chain, 1 long treble on the next, repeat from * till 12 long treble are done, the last of these will come upon the single

1 treble in the next, 2 chain and 1 treble three times in the same place. 4th row—Same as the second row. Continue working the third and fourth rows for the length required. Then along the top of the edging work a heading of 5 chain, 1 double crochet, alternately.

No. 45.—SWISS PATTERN BORDER.

EVANS'S crochet cotton No. 24, and a very fine steel crochet needle. Begin with 26 chain. 1st row—1 treble in the tenth stitch from the needle, cotton twice round the needle, insert the hook in the same stitch of the foundation and draw the cotton through, cotton over the needle and draw through two loops on the needle, cotton over the needle, insert the hook in the third foundation stitch from that last worked into and draw the cotton through. Now there are five loops on the needle. Cotton over the needle and draw through two loops on the needle, cotton over and draw through two loops, cotton over and draw through two loops, cotton over and draw through the two last loops, 3 chain, cotton over the needle, insert the hook to take up three threads in the centre of the twisted stitch just done and draw the cotton through, cotton over the needle and draw through two loops on the needle, cotton over the needle and draw through the two last loops, 1 treble in the same stitch of the foundation already worked into 3 chain, miss three, 1 treble in the next, cotton twice round the needle and work another cross-stitch as described above and a treble stitch adjoining, 8 chain, 1 double crochet in the last stitch of the foundation. 2nd row—1 chain to turn 13 treble under the loop of eight chain, 1 treble on the first treble stitch, 5 chain, 1 treble on the next treble stitch, cotton twice round the needle and work a cross-stitch and a treble adjoining, 3 chain, 1 treble on the last treble stitch, cotton twice round the needle, work a cross-stitch and a treble adjoining upon the chain that turned. 3rd row—7 chain to turn, 1 treble on the first treble stitch of last row and work a cross and a treble stitch adjoining, 3 chain, 1 treble on the fourth treble stitch of last row, and work another cross and a treble stitch adjoining, 1 chain, 1 long treble, alternately, on each treble to the end of the scallop. 4th row—5 chain, 1 double crochet under the first loop of one chain, 5 chain and 1 double crochet under each loop of one chain, 3 chain, one treble on the first treble stitch, 3 chain, 1 treble on the second treble stitch and work a

No. 44.—Spike Edging.

No. 45.—Swiss Pattern Border.

No. 46.—Cornflower Edging.

crochet stitch at the end, catch with a single crochet into the four chain of previous point. 9th row—3 chain to turn, 1 double crochet on the second long treble stitch, 5 chain (here in succeeding scallops you catch into the scallop preceding) 1 single crochet in the top thread of the double crochet just done, 1 double crochet under the loop of two chain, 4 chain and 1 double crochet eight times under consecutive loops of two chain, 2 chain, 1 double crochet under the last loop of two chain, 1 double crochet on the long treble stitch, 2 chain, 1 treble on the third treble stitch, 1 chain, 1 treble on the fifth, 1 chain, 1 treble on the last of the seven treble stitches, 5 chain, 7 treble under the loop of four chain, 1 treble in the first chain-stitch at the end of the row. Repeat from the fourth row for the length desired.

No. 43.—SCALLOP OF WAVE BRAID.

HAVE a sufficient length of braid, and work with Coats's crochet cotton No. 18 or No. 20. 1st row—1 treble on the first wave of the braid, 3 chain, another treble in the same place, 1 chain, and repeat. 2nd row—1 treble, 1 chain, miss one, and repeat. On the opposite side of the braid work 1 double crochet on the first wave, 1 long treble on the next wave, * 4 chain, 1 single crochet in the fourth chain from the needle, 1 long treble in the same place as last long treble is worked into, repeat from * till 6 long treble are worked, then 1 double crochet in the next wave of the braid, and continue.

No. 44.—SPIKE EDGING.

THIS edging is worked the short way with Evans's crochet cotton No. 22 and a fine steel crochet needle; it is useful for trimming underlinen. Commence with 8 chain; turn, work 1 treble in the seventh chain from the needle, 2 chain, another treble in the same place, 2 chain, 1 treble in the last stitch of the foundation, 2 chain, another treble in the same place. 2nd row—6 chain to turn, miss the first loop of two chain, 1 treble in the next, 2 chain and 1 treble three times in the same place, 7 chain, 1 double crochet in the loop at the end. 3rd row—2 double crochet under the loop of seven chain, 4 chain and 2 double crochet twice in the same place, 2 chain, miss the first loop of two chain,

cross and a treble stitch adjoining, 3 chain, 1 treble on the last treble stitch and work a cross and a treble stitch adjoining on the chain that turned. 5th row—7 chain to turn, and proceed the same as the first row, and work the double crochet at the end under the first loop of five chain stitches. Repeat from the second row for the length required.

No. 46.—CORNFLOWER EDGING.

PROCURE a piece of mignardese braid, a reel of Evans's crochet cotton No. 22, and a fine steel crochet needle. 1st row—Work 1 double crochet in the first picot of the braid, 5 chain, another double crochet in the same place, * 4 chain, miss two picots of the braid, 1 double crochet in the next, 16 chain, 1 single crochet in the fourteenth from the needle, 2 chain, 1 double crochet in the same picot as last double crochet is worked into, 4 chain, miss two picots of the braid, 5 chain, another double crochet in the same place, and repeat from * for the length required. 2nd row—Beginning on the right-hand side, * 1 double crochet under the first loop of five chain, 9 chain, 1 double crochet in the same place, 11 chain, 1 double crochet in the same place, 9 chain, another double crochet in the same place, then under the loop of fourteen chain work 3 long treble stitches, 4 treble, 5 double crochet, 4 treble, 3 long treble, and repeat from *. 3rd row—1 double crochet under the loop of nine chain, 1 double crochet under the loop of eleven chain, 5 chain, another double crochet in the same place, 1 double crochet under the loop of nine chain, 4 chain, 1 double crochet on the centre stitch of the five double crochet, 5 chain, 1 single in the fifth from the needle, 5 chain, 1 single in the same place, 5 chain, 1 single in the same place, 1 double crochet in the same stitch last double crochet is worked into, 4 chain, and repeat. On the other side of the mignardese braid work a row of single crochet stitches in the picots of the braid, 1 chain between each single crochet.

WELDON'S
PRACTICAL KNITTER. EDGINGS
(SIXTH SERIES).

How to Knit Useful Edgings and Insertions for all Purposes.

THIRTY-EIGHT ILLUSTRATIONS.

The Yearly Subscription to this Magazine, post free to any Part of the World, is 2s. 6d.
Subscriptions are payable in advance, and may commence from any date and for any period.

The Back Numbers are always in print. Nos. 1 to 241 now ready, Price 2d. each, or bound in 20 Vols., price 2s. 6d. each.

No. 1.—TRELLIS BORDER.

THIS is a very pretty scalloped border, suitable for a variety of purposes, according to the quality of the material with which it is knitted. Cast on 26 stitches. Purl a row. **1st row**—Slip 1, knit 2, make 1, knit 2 together make 1, knit 2, slip 1, knit 2 together, pass the slipped stitch over, slip 1, knit 2 together, pass the slipped stitch over, make 1, knit 1, make 1, knit 2 together, make 1, knit 2 together, make 1, knit 2. **2nd row**—Knit 6, purl 9, knit 1, make 1, knit 2 together, knit 1. **3rd row**—Slip 1, knit 2, make 1, knit 2 together, make 1, knit 1, slip 1, knit 2 together, pass the slipped stitch over, knit 1, make 1, knit 3, make 1, knit 2 together, make 1, knit 2 together, make 1, knit 2. **4th row**—Knit 6, purl 10, knit 1, make 1, knit 2 together, knit 1. **5th row**—Slip 1, knit 2, make 1, knit 2 together, make 1, knit 1, slip 1, knit 2 together, pass the slipped stitch over, make 1, knit 5, make 1, knit 2 together, make 1, knit 2 together, make 1, knit 2. **6th row**—Knit 6, purl 11, knit 1, make 1, knit 2 together, knit 1. **7th row**—Slip 1, knit 2, make 1, knit 2 together, make 1, knit 2 together, knit 1, make 1, knit 7, make 1, knit 2 together, make 1, knit 2 together, make 1, knit 2. **8th row**—Knit 6, purl 13, knit 1, make 1, knit 2 together, knit 1. **9th row**—Slip 1, knit 2, make 1, knit 2 together, make 1, knit 1, make 1, knit 4, slip 1, knit 2 together, pass the slipped stitch over, knit 4, make 1, knit 2 together, make 1, knit 2 together, make 1, knit 2. **10th row**—Knit 7, purl 13, knit 1, make 1, knit 2 together, knit 1. **11th row**—Slip 1, knit 2, make 1, knit 2 together, make 1, knit 3, make 1, knit 3, slip 1, knit 2 together, pass the slipped stitch over, knit 3, make 1, knit 2 together, make 1, knit 2 together, make 1, knit 2. **12th row**—Knit 7, purl 13, knit 1, make 1, knit 2 together, knit 1. **13th row**—Slip 1, knit 2, make 1, knit 2 together, make 1, knit 5, make 1, knit 2, slip 1, knit 2 together, pass the slipped stitch over, knit 2, make 1, knit 2 together, make 1, knit 2 together, make 1, knit 2 together, knit 1. **14th row**—Knit 7, purl 13, knit 1, make 1, knit 2 together, knit 1. **15th row**—Slip 1, knit 2, make 1, knit 2 together, make 1, knit 2, slip 1, knit 2 together, pass the slipped stitch over, knit 2, make 1, knit 1, slip 1, knit 2 together, pass the slipped stitch over, knit 1, make 1, knit 2 together, make 1, knit 2 together, make 1, knit 2 together, make 1, knit 2 together, knit 1. **17th row**—Slip 1, knit 2, make 1, knit 2 together, make 1, knit 2, slip 1, knit 2 together, pass the slipped stitch over, knit 2, make 1, slip 1, knit 2 together, pass the slipped stitch over, make 1, knit 2 together, make 1, knit 2 together, knit 1. **18th row**—Knit 7, purl 9, knit 1, make 1, knit 2 together, knit 1. Repeat from the first row.

No. 1.—Trellis Border.

No. 2.—VALENCIENNES BORDER.

CAST on 26 stitches. Knit one row. **1st row**—Knit 2 together knit 1, make 1, knit 2 together, knit 5, knit 2 together, make 1, knit 2 together, knit 9, make 1, knit 2 together, knit 1. **2nd row**—Slip 1, knit 2, make 1, knit 2 together.

knit 1, knit 2 together, make 1, knit 2 together, make 1, knit 2 together. knit 2 make 1, knit 2 together, knit 3, knit 2 together, make 1, knit 3. **3rd row**—Make 1, knit 4, make 1, knit 2 together, knit 1, knit 2 together, make 1, knit 11 make 1, knit 2 together, knit 1. **4th row**—Slip 1, knit 2 make 1, knit 2 together, knit 3, make 1, knit 2 together, make 1, knit 2 together, knit 3, make 1, knit 3 together, make 1, knit 6. **5th row**—Make 1, knit 1, knit 2 together, make 2, knit 18, make 1, knit 2 together, knit 1. **6th row**—Slip 1, knit 2, make 1, knit 2 together, knit 4, make 1, knit 2 together, make 1, knit 2 together, knit 9, purl 1, knit 3. **7th row**—Knit 1, knit 2 together, make 2, knit 2 together, make 2, knit 2 together, knit 16, make 1 knit 2 together, knit 1. **8th row**—Slip 1, knit 2, make 1, knit 2 together, knit 5, make 1, knit 2 together, make 1, knit 2 together, knit 7, purl 1, knit 2, purl 1 knit 2. **9th row**—Knit 2 together, knit 1, knit 2 together, make 2, knit 2 together, knit 3, make 1, knit 1, make 1, knit 2 together, knit 11, make 1, knit 2 together, knit 1. **10th row**—Slip 1, knit 2, make 1, knit 2 together, knit 3, knit 2 together, make 1, knit 2 together, make 1, knit 3, make 1, knit 3, make 1, knit 2 together, knit 3, purl 1, knit 2 together knit 1. **11th row**—Knit 2 together, knit 3, knit 2 together, make 1, knit 5, make 1, knit 2 together, knit 10, make 1, knit 2 together, knit 1. **12th row**—Slip 1, knit 2, make 1, knit 2 together, knit 2, knit 2 together, make 1, knit 3, make 1, knit 7, make 1, knit 2 together, knit 1, knit 2 together. Begin again at the first row

No. 3.—MELON PATTERN BORDER.

CAST on 16 stitches. Purl one row. **1st row**—Slip 1, knit 1, make 2, purl 2 together, knit 4, make 1, knit 1 in the front and 1 in the back of the next stitch, make 1, knit 1 and purl 1 and knit 1 in the next, make 1, knit 1 in the front and 1 in the back of the next stitch, make 1, knit 2 together, make 2, knit 2 together, knit 1. **2nd row**—Knit 3, purl 1, knit 1, purl 10, knit 5, make 2, purl 2 together, knit 2. **3rd row**—Slip 1, knit 1, make 2, purl 2 together, knit 5, make 1, knit 3, make 1, knit 3, make 1, knit 2 together, make 1, knit 3, make 1, knit 1, make 2, purl 2 together, knit 1. **4th row**—Knit 3, purl 1, knit 2, purl 1, knit 1, purl 13, knit 2, knit 2 together, knit 1, make 2, purl 2 together, knit 2. **5th row**—Slip 1, knit 1, make 2, purl 2 together, knit 2, knit 2 together, make 1, knit 3, slip 1, knit 1, pass the slipped stitch over, knit 3, make 1, knit 1, make 2, knit 2 together, make 2, knit 2 together, make 2, knit 2 together, knit 1. **6th row**—Knit 3, purl 1, knit 2, purl 1, knit 2, purl 1, knit 1, purl 15, knit 2 together, knit 1, make 2, purl 2 together, knit 2. **7th row**—Slip 1, knit 1, make 2, purl 2 together, knit 2, knit 2 together, make 1, knit 3, slip 1, knit 1, pass the slipped stitch over, make 1, knit 3, make 1, knit 2 together, knit 2, knit 2 together, make 1, knit 11. **8th row**—Cast off 7, knit 4, purl 13, knit 2 together, knit 1, make 2, purl 2 together, knit 2. **9th row**—Slip 1, knit 1, make 2, purl 2 together, knit 2, make 1, knit 3, slip 1, knit 1, pass the slipped stitch over, make 1, knit 3, make 1, knit 2 together, knit 3, make 1, knit 2 together, make 2 knit

2 together, knit 1. **10th row**—Knit 3, purl 1, knit 1, purl 15, knit 2, make 2, purl 2 together, knit 2. **11th row**—Slip 1, knit 1, make 2, purl 2 together, knit 2 make 1, slip 1, knit 1, pass the slipped stitch over, knit 2, slip 1, knit 1, pass the slipped stitch over, make 1, knit 3, make 1, knit 2 together, knit 2, knit 2 together, make 1, knit 1, make 2, knit 1 make 2, knit 2 together, knit 1. **12th row**—Knit 3, purl 1, knit 2, purl 1, knit 1, purl 2 together, purl 3, purl 2 together, purl 1, purl 2 together, purl 3, purl 2 together, knit 2, make 2, purl 2 together, knit 2. **13th row**—Slip 1, knit 1, make 2, purl 2 together, knit 2, make 1, slip 1, knit 1, pass the slipped stitch over, knit 2, make 1, knit 3 together, make 1, knit 2, knit 2 together, make 1, knit 1, make 2, knit 2 together, make 2, knit 2 together, make 2, knit 2 together, knit 1. **14th row**—Knit 3, purl 1, knit 2, purl 1, knit 2, purl 1, knit 1, purl 2 together, purl 6, purl 2 together, knit 3, make 2, purl 2 together, knit 2. **15th row**—Slip 1, knit 1

No. 2.—Valenciennes Border.

make 2, purl 2 together, knit 3, make 1, slip 1, knit 1, pass the slipped stitch over knit 3, knit 3 together, make 1, knit 11. **16th row**—Cast off 7, knit 4, purl 2 together, purl 1, purl 2 together, knit 4, make 2, purl 2 together, knit 2. Repeat from the first row.

No. 4.—DOUBLE ROSE LEAF BORDER.

CAST on 28 stitches. Purl one row. **1st row**—Slip 1, knit 2, make 1, knit 2 together, knit 1, make 1, knit 5, make 1, slip 1, knit 2 together, pass the slipped stitch over, make 1, knit 5, make 1, knit 3, make 1, knit 2 together, knit 4. **2nd row**—Knit 6, make 1, knit 2 together, purl 18, knit 1, make 1, knit 2 together, knit 1. **3rd row**—Slip 1, knit 2, make 1, knit 2 together, knit 1, make 1, knit 1 knit 2 together, purl 1, slip 1, knit 1, pass the slipped stitch over, knit 1, make 1, knit 1, make 1, knit 1, knit 2 together, purl 1, slip 1, knit 1, pass the slipped stitch over, knit 1, make 1, knit 3, make 1, knit 2 together, make 2, knit 2 together, make 2, knit 2. **4th row**—Knit 3, purl 1, knit 2, purl 1, knit 2, make 1, knit 2 together, purl 4, knit 1, purl 3, knit 1, purl 3, knit 1, purl 5, make 1, knit 2 together, knit 1. **5th row**—Slip 1, knit 2, make 1, knit 2 together, knit 1, make 1, knit 1, knit 2 together, purl 1, slip 1, knit 1, pass the slipped stitch over, knit 1, purl 1, knit 1, knit 2 together, purl 1, slip 1, knit 1, pass the slipped stitch over, knit 1, make 1, knit 3, make 1, knit 2 together, knit 7. **6th row**—Knit 9, make 1, knit 2 together, purl 4, knit 1, purl 2, knit 1, purl 2, knit 1, purl 5, knit 1, make 1, knit 2 together, knit 1. **7th row**—Slip 1, knit 2, make 1, knit 2 together, knit 1, make 1, knit 1, make 1, knit 2 together, purl 1, slip 1, knit 1, pass the slipped stitch over, purl 1, knit 2 together, purl 1, slip 1, knit 1, pass the slipped stitch over, make 1, knit 1, make 1, knit 3, make 1, knit 2 together, make 2, knit 2 together, make 2, knit 2 together, make 2, knit 2 together, knit 1. **8th row**—Knit 3, purl 1, knit 2, purl 1, knit 2, purl 1, knit 2, make 1, knit 2 together, purl 5, knit 1, purl 1, knit 1, purl 1, knit 1, purl 6, knit 1, make 1, knit 2 together, knit 1. **9th row**—Slip 1, knit 2, make 1, knit 2 together, knit 1, make 1, knit 3, make 1, slip 1, knit 2 together, pass the slipped stitch over, purl 1, knit 3 together, make 1, knit 3, make 1, knit 3, make 1, knit 2 together, knit 10. **10th row**—Cast off 6, knit 5, make 1, knit 2 together, purl 7, knit 1, purl 8, knit 1, make 1, knit 2 together, knit 1 Recommence at the first row, and continue for the length required.

No. 5.—ANTIQUE EDGING.

CAST on 13 stitches Knit one row plain. **1st row**—Slip 1, knit 1, make 1, slip 1, knit 1, pass the slipped stitch over, make 1, knit 1, make 1, slip 1, knit 2 together, pass the slipped stitch over make 1, knit 3, make 1, knit 2. **2nd row**—Knit 4, knit 1 and purl 1 three times in the next stitch (so making six stitches out of one), purl 2, knit 1, purl 3, knit 4. **3rd row**—Slip 1, knit 1, make 1, slip 1, knit 1, pass the slipped stitch over, knit 1 and purl 1 three times in the next stitch, slip 1, knit 1, pass the slipped stitch over, purl 1, knit 2 together, cast off 5 of the six stitches you knitted in one knit 2. make 1. knit 2.

4th row—Knit 5, make 1, knit 1, purl 1, knit 1, purl 1, cast off 5 of the six stitches knitted in one, knit 4. **5th row**—Slip 1, knit 1, make 1, slip 1, knit 1, pass the slipped stitch over, make 1, knit 1, make 1, slip 1, knit 2 together, pass the slipped stitch over, make 1, knit 3, make 1, knit 2 together, make 1, knit 2. **6th row**—Knit 6, knit 1 and purl 1 three times in the next stitch, purl 2, knit 1, purl 3, knit 4. **7th row**—Slip 1, knit 1, make 1, slip 1, knit 1, pass the slipped stitch over, knit 1 and purl 1 three times in the next stitch, knit 1, purl 2, slip 1, knit 1, pass the slipped stitch over, purl 1, knit 2 together, cast off 5 of the six stitches knitted in one, knit 2, make 1, knit 2 together, make 1. knit 2. **8th row**—Cast off 4, knit 2, make 1, knit 1, purl 1, knit 1, purl 1, cast off 5 of the six stitches knitted in one, knit 4. Repeat from the first row

---

No. 6.—PIERREPOINT EDGING.

CAST on 17 stitches. Knit 1 row plain. **1st row**—Slip 1, knit 2, knit 2 together, make 1, knit 1, knit 2 together, make 1, knit 5, make 2, knit 2. **2nd row**—Knit 3, purl 1, knit 3, knit 2 together, make 1, knit 3, knit 2 together, make 1, knit 2, make 1, knit 2 together, knit 1. **3rd row**—Slip 1, knit 5, make 1, knit 2 together, knit 3, make 1, knit 2 together, knit 2, make 2, knit 2 together, make 2, knit 2. **4th row**—Knit 3, purl 1, knit 2, purl 1, knit 1, knit 2 together, make 1, knit 3, knit 2 together, make 1, knit 4, make 1, knit 2 together, knit 1. **5th row**—Slip 1, knit 7, make 1, knit 2 together, knit 3, make 1, knit 2 together, knit 3, make 2, knit 2 together, knit 2 together. **6th row**—Knit 3, purl 1, knit 5, make 1, knit 2 together, knit 3, make 1, knit 2 together, knit 3, make 1, knit 2 together, knit 1. **7th row**—Slip 1, knit 4, knit 2 together, make 1, knit 3, knit 2 together, make 1, knit 10. **8th row**—cast off 5, knit 5, make 1, knit 2 together, knit 3, make 1, knit 2 together, knit 1, make 1, knit 2 together, knit 1. Repeat the pattern from the first row

---

No. 7.—PRIMROSE EDGING.

CAST on 11 stitches. Purl one row. **1st row**—Slip 1, knit 2, make 1, knit 2 together, make 1, knit 1, make 1, knit 1, knit 2 together, make 2, knit 2 together **2nd row**—Purl 2, knit 1, purl 6, knit 1, make 1, knit 2 together knit 1. **3rd row**—Slip 1, knit 2, make 1, knit 2 together, make 1, knit 2, make 1, knit 1, knit 2 together, make 2, knit 2 together, knit 1. **4th row**—Purl 3, knit 1, purl 7, knit 1, make 1, knit 2 together, knit 1. **5th row**—Slip 1, knit 2, make 1, knit 2 together, make 1, knit 3, make 1, knit 1, knit 2 together, make 2, knit 2 together, make 2, knit 2 together. **6th row**—Purl 2, knit 1, purl 2, knit 1, purl 8, knit 1, make 1, knit 2 together, knit 1. **7th row**—Slip 1, knit 2, make 1, knit 2 together, make 1, knit 3 together, make 1, knit 1, knit 2 together, knit 7. **8th row**—Cast off 6, purl 6, knit 1, make 1, knit 2 together, knit 1. Repeat from the first row.

No. 8.—APPLE-LEAF EDGING.

THIS is a handsome open edging of medium width. Cast on 12 stitches. Purl one row. **1st row**—Slip 1, knit 1, make 1, knit 2 together, make 1, knit 1, make 1, knit 2 together, make 1, knit 2 together, make 1, knit 2 together, make 2, knit 2 together, knit

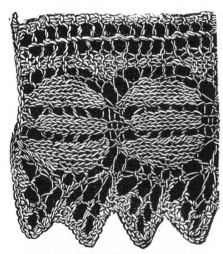

No. 3.—Melon Pattern Border.

1. **2nd row**—Knit 3, purl 1, knit 1, purl 9. **3rd row**—Slip 1, knit 1, make 1, knit 2 together, make 1, knit 3, make 1, knit 2 together, make 1, knit 2 together, make 2, knit 1, make 1, knit 2. **4th row**—Knit 2, purl 1, knit 2, purl 1, knit 1, purl 11. **5th row**—Slip 1, knit 1, make 1, knit 2 together, make 1, knit 5, make 1, knit 2 together, make 1, knit 2 together, make 2, knit 2 together, make 2, knit 2 together, knit 1. **6th row**—Knit 3, purl 1, knit 2, purl 1, knit 1, purl 13. **7th row**—Slip 1, knit 1, make 1, knit 2 together make 1, slip 1, knit 1, pass the slipped stitch over, knit 2, knit 2 together, make 1, knit 2 together, make 1, knit 2 together, make 2 and knit 2 together three

times, knit 1. **8th row**—Knit 3, purl 1, knit 2, purl 1, knit 2, purl 1, knit 1, purl 12. **9th row**—Slip 1, knit 2 together, make 1, knit 2 together, make 1, slip 1, knit 1, pass the slipped stitch over, knit 1, knit 2 together, make 1, knit 2 together, make 1, knit 2 together, make 2 and knit 2 together four times, knit 1. **10th row**—Knit 3, purl 1, knit 2, purl 1, knit 2, purl 1, knit 2, purl 1, knit 1, purl 11. **11th row**—Slip 1, knit 2 together, make 1, knit 2 together, make 1, slip 1, knit 2 together, pass the slipped stitch over, make 1, knit 2 together, make 1, knit 2 together, knit 13. **12th row**—Cast off 11, purl 11. Repeat the pattern from the first row.

No. 9.—BEECH LEAF BORDER.

CAST on 18 stitches. Purl 1 row. **1st row**—Slip 1, knit 1, make 1, knit 2 together, make 1, slip 1, knit 1, pass the slipped stitch over, make 1, knit 1, make 1, slip 1, knit 1, pass the slipped stitch over, make 1, knit 2 together,

No. 4.—Double Rose Leaf Border.

make 1, knit 2 together, make 2, knit 2 together, make 2, knit 2 together, knit 1. **2nd row**—Knit 3, purl 1, knit 2, purl 1, knit 1, purl 1, knit 1, purl 8, cotton over the needle to make a stitch, knit 2 together, knit 1. **3rd row**—Slip 1, knit 1, make 1, knit 2 together, make 1, slip 1, knit 1, pass the slipped stitch over, make 1, knit 3, make 1, slip 1, knit 1, pass the slipped stitch over, make 1, knit 2 together, make 1, knit 2 together, make 2, knit 2 together, make 1, knit 2. **4th row**—Knit 2, purl 1, knit 2, purl 1, knit 2, purl 1, knit 1, purl 1, knit 1, purl 10, cotton over the needle to make a stitch, knit 2 together, knit 1. **5th row**—Slip 1, knit 1, make 1, knit 2 together, make 1, slip 1, knit 1, pass the slipped stitch over, make 1, knit 5, make 1, slip 1, knit 1, pass the slipped stitch over, make 1 and knit 2 together five times, make 1, knit 2. **6th row**—Knit 2, purl 1 and knit 1 five times, purl 12, cotton over the needle to make a stitch, knit 2 together, knit 1. **7th row**—Slip 1, knit 1, make 1, knit 2 together, make 1, slip 1, knit 1, pass the slipped stitch over, make 1, knit 7, make 1, slip 1, knit 1, pass the slipped stitch over, make 1, knit 2 together, make 1, knit 2 together, knit 8. **8th row**—Cast off 4, purl 20, cotton over the needle to make a stitch, knit 2 together, knit 1. **9th row**—Slip 1, knit 1, make 1, knit 2 together, make 1, slip 1, knit 2 together, pass the slipped stitch over, make 1, slip 1, knit 1, pass the slipped stitch over, knit 3, knit 2 together, make 1, slip 1, knit 2 together, pass the slipped stitch over, make 1, knit 2 together, make 2, knit 1, make 2, knit 2. **10th row**—Knit 3, purl 1, knit 2, purl 1, knit 1, purl 1, knit 1, purl 12, cotton over the needle to make a stitch, knit 2 together, knit 1. **11th row**—Slip 1, knit 1, make 1, knit 2 together, make 1, slip 1, knit 1, pass slipped stitch over, make 1, slip 1, knit 2 together, pass slipped stitch over, knit 1, knit 2 together, make 1, slip 1, knit 2 together, pass the slipped stitch over, make 1, knit 2 together, make 1, knit 2 together, make 2, knit 2 together, make 2, knit 2 together, make 1, knit 2. **12th row**—Knit 2, purl 1, knit 2, purl 1, knit 2, purl 1, knit 1, purl 1, knit 1, purl 10, cotton over the needle to make a stitch, knit 2 together, knit 1. **13th row**—Slip 1, knit 1, make 1, knit 2 together, make 1, slip 1, knit 2 together, pass the slipped stitch over, make 1, slip 1, knit 2 together, pass the slipped stitch over, make 1, slip 1, knit 2 together, pass the slipped stitch over, make 1, knit 2 together, make 1, knit 2 together, knit 8. **14th row**—Cast off 4, purl 14, cotton over the needle to make a stitch, knit 2 together, knit 1. Recommence at the first row.

No. 10.—PARISIAN EDGING.

CAST on 15 stitches. Purl one row. **1st row**—Slip 1, knit 2, make 1, knit 2 together, make 1, knit 2 together, make 1, knit 3, make 1, knit 2 together, make 2, knit 3. **2nd row**—Knit 4, purl 11, cotton over the needle to make a stitch, knit 2 together, knit 1. **3rd row**—Slip 1, knit 2, make 1, knit 2 together, make 1, knit 2 together, make 1, knit 5, make 1, knit 2 together, make 2, knit 2, make 3, knit 2. **4th row**—Knit 2, purl 1 and knit 1 and purl 1 in

the three made stitches, knit 3, purl 13, cotton over the needle to make a stitch, knit 2 together, knit 1. **5th row**—Slip 1, knit 2, make 1, knit 2 together, make 1, knit 2 together, make 1, knit 7, make 1, knit 2 together, make 2, knit 2 together, knit 6. **6th row**—Cast off 5, knit 2, purl 15, cotton over the needle to make a stitch, knit 2 together, knit 1. **7th row**—Slip 1, knit 2, make 1, knit 3 together, make 1, knit 2 together, make 1, knit 3, slip 1, knit 2 together, pass the slipped stitch over, knit 2, make 1, knit 3 together, make 2, knit 3. **8th row**—Knit 4, purl 13, cotton over the needle to make a stitch, knit 2 together, knit 1. **9th row**—Slip 1, knit 2, make 1, knit 3 together, make 1, knit 2 together, make 1, knit 1, slip 1, knit 2 together, pass the slipped stitch over, knit 1, make 1, knit 3 together, make 2, knit 2, make 3, knit 2. **10th row**—Knit 2, purl 1 and knit 1 and purl 1 in the three made stitches, knit 3, purl 11, cotton over the needle to make a stitch, knit 2 together, knit 1. **11th row**—Slip 1, knit 2, make 1, knit 3 together, make 1, knit 2 together, make 1, slip 1, knit 2 together, pass the slipped stitch over, make 1, knit 3 together, make 2, knit 2, knit 6. **12th row**—Cast off 5, knit 2, purl 9, cotton over the needle to make a stitch, knit 2 together, knit 1. Repeat from the first row.

No. 11.—MARGUERITE BORDER.

CAST on 16 stitches. Purl one row. **1st row**—Slip 1, knit 1, make 1, knit 2 together, make 1, knit 2 together, make 1, knit 3, make 1, knit 2 together, make 2, knit 2 together, make 2, knit 2 together, knit 1. **2nd row**—Knit 3, purl 1, knit 2, purl 8, cotton over the needle to make a stitch, knit 2 together, make 1, knit 2 together, knit 1. **3rd row**—Slip 1, knit 1, make 1, knit 2 together, make 1, slip 1, knit 2 together, pass the slipped stitch over, knit 2 together, make 1, knit 3, make 2, knit 2 together, make 2, knit 2 together, knit 1. **4th row**—Knit 3, purl 1, knit 2, purl 9, cotton over the needle to make a stitch, knit 2 together, make 1, knit 2 together, knit 1. **5th row**—Slip 1, knit 1, make 1, knit 2 together, make 1, knit 2 together, make 1, slip 1, knit 2 together, pass the slipped stitch over, make 1, knit 2, make 1, knit 2 together, knit 2, make 2, knit 2 together, make 2, knit 2 together, knit 1. **6th row**—Knit 3, purl 1, knit 2, purl 11, cotton over the needle to make a stitch, knit 2 together, make 1, knit 2 together, knit 1. **7th row**—Slip 1, knit 1, make 1, knit 2 together, make 1, knit 2 together, knit 2 together, make 1, knit 1, make 1, knit 2 together, knit 6, make 2, knit 2, together, make 2, knit 2 together, knit 1. **8th row**—Cast off 8 (take up at the back the second loop of the two made stitches, or they will slip), purl 10, cotton over the needle to make a stitch, knit 2 together, make 1, knit 2 together, knit 1. Repeat from the first row of the pattern.

No. 12.—WIDE HANDSOME BORDER FOR MANTEL DRAPE.

THIS may be worked with silk, with coloured cotton or linen thread, or with one of the new fancy wools. The pattern is also suitable for bordering a quilt or for any purpose for which a wide scalloped trimming is desired. Cast on 30 stitches. Knit 1 plain row. **1st row**—Slip 1, knit 3, make 1, knit 2 together, knit 10, make 1, knit 2 together, knit 11, knit 2 together, make 1, knit 2.

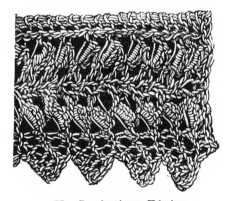

No 5.—Antique Edging.

2, knit 2 together, knit 1. The second half of the make 2 at *this end* of the row is always to be dropped in the next row, as it is turned twice simply to make the edge sit easy. **2nd row**—Make 1, knit 2 together, knit 18, make 1, knit 2 together, knit 10, make 1, knit 2 together. knit 2. **3rd row**—Slip 1, knit 3, make 1, knit 2 together, knit 2, knit 2 together, make 2, knit 2 together, knit 4, make 1, knit 2 together, knit 10, knit 2 together, make 1, knit 4, make 2, knit 2. **4th row**—Make 1, knit 2 together, knit 19, make 1, knit 2 together, knit 4, purl 1, knit 5, make 1, knit 2 together, knit 2. **5th row**—Slip 1, knit 3, make 1, knit 2 together, knit 2 together, make 2, knit 2 together, knit 2 together, make 2, knit 2 together, knit 2, make 1, knit 2 together, knit 9, knit 2 together, make 1, knit 6, make 2, knit 2. **6th row**—Make 1, knit 2 together, knit 20, make 1, knit 2 together, knit 2, purl 1, knit 3, purl 1, knit 3, make 1, knit 2 together, knit 2. **7th row**—Slip 1, knit 3, make 1, knit 2 together, knit 2, knit 2 together, make 2, knit 2 together, knit 4, make 1, knit 2 together, knit 8, knit 2 together, make 2, knit 2 together, make 2, knit 2 together, knit 2, make 2, knit 2. **8th row**—Make 1, knit 2 together, knit 5, purl 1, knit 15, make 1, knit 2 together, knit 4, purl 1, knit 5, make 1, knit 2 together, knit 2. **9th row**

—Slip 1, knit **3**, make 1, knit 2 together, knit 2 together, make 2, knit 2 together, knit 2 together, make 2, knit 2 together, knit 2, make 1, knit 2 together, knit 7, knit 2 together, make 1, knit 1, knit 2 together, make 2, knit 2 together, knit 2 together, make 2, knit 2 together, knit 1, make 2, knit 2. **10th row**—Make 1, knit 2 together, knit 4, purl 1, knit 3, purl 1, knit 13. make 1, knit 2 together, knit 2, purl 1, knit 3, purl 1, knit 3, make 1, knit 2 together, knit 2. **11th row**—Slip 1, knit 3, make 1, knit 2 together, knit 2, knit 2 together, make 2, knit 2 together, knit 4, make 1, knit 2 together, knit 6, knit 2 together, make 1, knit 4, knit 2 together, make 2, knit 2 together, knit 4, make 2, knit 2. **12th row**—Make 1 knit 2 together, knit 7, purl 1, knit 15, make 1, knit 2 together, knit 4, purl 1, knit 5, make 1, knit 2 together, knit 2. **13th row**—Slip 1, knit 3, make 1, knit 2 together, knit 10, knit 2 together, knit 5, knit 2 together, make 1, knit 3, knit 2 together, make 2, knit 2 together, knit 2 together, make 2, knit 2 together, knit 3, make 2, knit 2. **14th row**—Make 1, knit 2 together, knit 6, purl 1, knit 3, purl 1, knit 13, make 1, knit 2 together, knit 10, make 1, knit 2 together, knit 2. **15th row**—Slip 1, knit 3, make 1, knit 2 together, knit 10, make 1, knit 2 together, knit 4, knit 2 together, make 1, knit 6, knit 2 together, make 2, knit 2 together, knit 6, make 2, knit 2. **16th row**—Make 1, knit 2 together, knit 9, purl 1, knit 15, make 1, knit 2 together, knit 10, make 1, knit 2 together, knit 2. **17th row**—Slip 1, knit 3, make 1, knit 2 together, knit 2, knit 2 together, make 2, knit 2 together, knit 4, make 1, knit 2 together, knit 3, knit 2 together, make 1, knit 2, knit 2 together, make 2, knit 2 together, knit 6, knit 2 together, make 2, knit 2 together, knit 2, make 2, knit 2. **18th row**—Make 1, knit 2 together, knit 5, purl 1, knit 9, purl 1, knit 10, make 1, knit 2 together, knit 4, purl 1, knit 5, make 1, knit 2 together, knit 2. **19th row**—Slip 1, knit 3, make 1, knit 2 together, knit 2 together, make 2, knit 2 together, knit 2 together, make 2, knit 2 together, knit 2, make 1, knit 2 together, knit 2, knit 2 together, make 1, knit 1, knit 2 together, make 2, knit 2 together, knit 2 together, make 2, knit 2 together, knit 2, knit 2 together, make 2, knit 2 together, knit 2 together, make 2, knit 2 together, make 2, knit 2 together, knit 1, make 2, knit 2. **20th row**—Make 1, knit 2 together, knit 4, purl 1, knit 3, purl 1, knit 5, purl 1, knit 3, purl 1, knit 8, make 1, knit 2 together, knit 2, purl 1, knit 3, purl 1, knit 3, make 1, knit 2 together, knit 2. **21st row**—Slip 1, knit 3, make 1,

knit 4, purl 1, knit 5, make 1, knit 2 together, knit 2. **33rd row**—Slip 1, knit 3, make 1, knit 2 together, knit 2 together, make 2, knit 2 together, make 2, knit 2 together, knit 2, make 1, knit 2 together, knit 8 make 1, knit 2 together, knit 2 together, make 2, knit 2 together, knit 2 together, knit 2 together, knit 2 together, make 2, knit 2 together, knit 1. **34th row**—Make 1, knit 2 together, knit 4, purl 1, knit 3, purl 1, knit 13, make 1, knit 2 together, knit 2, purl 1, knit 3, purl 1, knit 3, make 1, knit 2 together, knit 2. **35th row**—Slip 1, knit 3, make 1, knit 2 together, knit 2 together, make 2, knit 2 together, knit 4, make 1, knit 2 together, knit 9, make 1, knit 2 together, knit 1, knit 2 together make 2, knit 2 together, knit 1, make 2, knit 2 together, knit 1 **36th row**—Make 1, knit 2 together, knit 5, purl 1, knit 15, make 1, knit 2 together, knit 4, purl 1, knit 5, make 1, knit 2 together, knit 2. **37th row**—Slip 1, knit 3, make 1, knit 2 together, knit 2 together, make 2, knit 2 together, knit 2 together, make 2, knit 2 together, knit 2, make 1, knit 2 together, knit 10, make 1, knit 2 together, knit 4, knit 2 together, make 2, knit 2 together, knit 1. **38th row**—Make 1, knit 2 together, knit 20, make 1, knit 2 together, knit 2, purl 1, knit 3, purl 1, knit 3, make 1, knit 2 together, knit 2. **39th row**—Slip 1, knit 3, make 1, knit 2 together, knit 2, knit 2 together, make 2, knit 2 together, knit 4, make 1, knit 2 together, knit 11, make 1, knit 2 together, knit 2 together, make 2, knit 2 together, knit 1. **40th row**—Make 1, knit 2 together, knit 19, make 1, knit 2 together, knit 4, purl 1, knit 5, make 1, knit 2 together, knit 2. **41st row**—Slip 1, knit 3, make 1, knit 2 together, knit 10, make 1, knit 2 together, knit 12, make 1, knit 2 together, knit 2 together, make 2, knit 2 together, knit 1. **42nd row**—Make 1, knit 2 together, knit 18, make 1, knit 2 together, knit 10, make 1, knit 2 together, knit 2. Repeat from the first row for the length required.

No. 13.—ASPEN LEAF BORDER.

CAST on 24 stitches. Knit one row plain. **1st row**—Slip 1, knit 2, make 1 knit 2 together, knit 1, make 1, knit 2 together, knit 2, make 1, knit 2 together, make 1, knit 2 together, knit 5, make 2, knit 2 together, make 2, knit 2

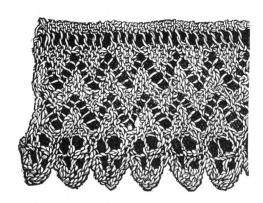

No. 6.—Pierrepoint Edging.

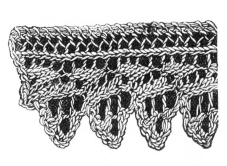

No. 7.—Primrose Edging.

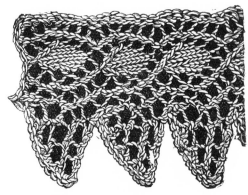

No. 8.—Apple Leaf Edging.

knit 2 together, knit 2, knit 2 together, make 2, knit 2 together, knit 4, make 1, knit 2 together, knit 1, knit 2 together, make 1, knit 4, knit 2 together, make 2, knit 2 together, knit 6, knit 2 together, make 2, knit 2 together, knit 4, make 2, knit 2. **22nd row**—Make 1, knit 2 together, knit 7, purl 1, knit 9, purl 1, knit 10, make 1, knit 2 together, knit 4, purl 1, knit 5, make 1, knit 2 together, knit 2. **23rd row**—Slip 1, knit 3, make 1, knit 2 together, knit 2 together, make 2, knit 2 together, make 2, knit 2 together, knit 2, make 1, knit 2 together, knit 3, make 1, knit 2 together, knit 2 together, make 2, knit 2 together, knit 2, knit 2 together, make 2, knit 2 together, make 2, knit 2 together, make 2, knit 2 together, knit 2 together, make 2, knit 2 together, knit 1. **24th row**—Make 1, knit 2 together, knit 4, purl 1, knit 3, purl 1, knit 5, purl 1, knit 3, purl 1, knit 8, make 1, knit 2 together, knit 2, purl 1, knit 3, purl 1, knit 3, make 1, knit 2 together, knit 2. **25th row**—Slip 1, knit 3, make 1, knit 2 together, knit 2, knit 2 together, make 2, knit 2 together, knit 4, make 1, knit 2 together, knit 4, make 1, knit 2 together, knit 1, knit 2 together, make 2, knit 2 together, knit 6, knit 2 together, make 2, knit 2 together, knit 1, knit 2 together, make 2, knit 2 together, knit 1. **26th row**—Make 1, knit 2 together, knit 5, purl 1, knit 9, purl 1, knit 10, make 1, knit 2 together, knit 4, purl 1, knit 5, make 1, knit 2 together, knit 2. **27th row**—Slip 1, knit 3, make 1, knit 2 together, knit 10, make 1, knit 2 together, knit 5, make 1, knit 2 together, knit 5, knit 2 together, make 2, knit 2 together, knit 5, knit 2 together, make 2, knit 2 together, knit 1. **28th row**—Make 1, knit 2 together, knit 9, purl 1, knit 15, make 1, knit 2 together, knit 10, make 1, knit 2 together, knit 2. **29th row**—Slip 1, knit 3, make 1, knit 2 together, knit 10, make 1, knit 2 together, knit 6, make 1, knit 2 together, knit 2, knit 2 together, make 2, knit 2 together, knit 2 together, make 2, knit 2 together, knit 1. **30th row**—Make 1, knit 2 together knit 6, purl 1, knit 3, purl 1, knit 13, make 1, knit 2 together, knit 10, make 1, knit 2 together, knit 2. **31st row** — Slip 1, knit 3, make 1, knit 2 together, knit 2, knit 2 together, make 2, knit 2 together, knit 4, make 1, knit 2 together, knit 7, make 1, knit 2 together, knit 3, knit 2 together, make 2, knit 2 together, knit 3, knit 2 together, make 2, knit 2 together, knit 1. **32nd row**—Make 1, knit 2 together, knit 7, purl 1, knit 15, make 1, knit 2 together,

together, knit 1. **2nd row**—Knit 3, purl 1, knit 2, purl 1, knit 13, make 1, knit 2 together, knit 1, make 1, knit 2 together, knit 1. **3rd row**—Slip 1, knit 2, make 1, knit 2 together, knit 1, make 1, knit 2 together, knit 3, make 1, knit 2 together, make 1 knit 2 together, knit 6, make 2, knit 2 together, make 2, knit 2 together, knit 1. **4th row**—Knit 3, purl 1, knit 2, purl 1, knit 15, make 1, knit 2 together, knit 1, make 1, knit 2 together, knit 1. **5th row**—Slip 1, knit 2, make 1, make 1, knit 2 together, knit 1, make 1, knit 2 together, knit 4, make 1, knit 2 together, make 1, knit 2 together, knit 7, make 2, knit 2 together, make 2, knit 2 together, knit 1. **6th row**—Knit 3, purl 1, knit 2, purl 1, knit 17, make 1, knit 2 together, knit 1, make 1, knit 2 together, knit 1. **7th row**—Slip 1, knit 2, make 1, knit 2 together, knit 1, make 1, knit 2 together, knit 5, make 1, knit 2 together, make 1, knit 2 together, knit 8, make 2, knit 2 together, make 2, knit 2 together, knit 1. **8th row**—Knit 3, purl 1, knit 2, purl 1, knit 19, make 1, knit 2 together, knit 1, make 1, knit 2 together, knit 1. **9th row**—Slip 1, knit 2, make 1, knit 2 together, knit 1, make 1, knit 2 together, knit 24. **10th row**—Cast off 8, knit 17, make 1, knit 2 together, knit 1, make 1, knit 2 together, knit 1. Repeat from the first row of the pattern.

No. 14.—HANDSOME WIDE BORDER FOR BRACKETS.

THIS looks well worked with rather coarse ingrain cotton and knitting needles of suitable size. Cast on 28 stitches. Knit 1 plain row. **1st row**—Slip 1, knit 4, make 1, knit 2 together, knit 1, make 2, knit 2 together, knit 11, make 2 and knit 2 together three times, knit 1. **2nd row**—Slip 1, knit 2, purl 1, knit 2, purl 1, knit 2, purl 1, knit 13, purl 1, knit 3, make 1, knit 2 together, knit 3. **3rd row**—Slip 1, knit 4, make 1, knit 2 together, knit 25 **4th row** knit 26, make 1, knit 2 together, knit 3. **5th row**—Slip 1, knit 4, make 1, knit 2 together, knit 1, make 2, knit 2 together, make 2, knit 2 together, knit 13, make 2 and knit 2 together three times, knit 1. **6th row**—Slip 1, knit 2, purl 1, knit 2, purl 1, knit 2, purl 1, knit 15, purl 1, knit 2, purl 1, knit 3, make 1, knit 2 together, knit 3. **7th row**—Slip 1, knit 4, make 1, knit 2 together knit 50. **8th row**—Slip 1, knit 31, make 1, knit 2 together, knit 3 **9th row**—Slip 1, knit 4, make 1, knit 2 together, knit 1, make 2, knit 2 together, make 2, knit 2 together, make 2, knit 2 together, knit 16, make 2 and knit 2 together three times, knit 1. **10th row**—Slip 1, knit 2, purl 1, knit 2, purl 1, knit 2, purl 1, knit 18, purl 1, knit 2, purl 1, knit 2, purl 1, knit 3, make 1, knit 2 together, knit 3. **11th row**—Slip 1, knit 4, make 1, knit 2 together, knit 36. **12th row**—Slip 1, knit 37, make 1, knit 2 together, knit 3. **13th row**—Slip 1, knit 4, make 1, knit 2 together, knit 1, make 2, knit 2 together, make 2 and knit 3 together ten times, make 2, knit 2 together, knit 1. **14th row**—Slip 1, knit 2, purl 1, knit 2 and purl 1 eleven times, knit 3, make 1, knit 2 together, knit 3. **15th row**—Slip 1, knit 4, make 1, knit 2 together, knit 38. **16th row**—Slip 1, knit 39, make 1, knit 2 together, knit 3. **17th row**—Slip 1, knit 4, make 1, knit 2 together, knit 1, make 2 and knit 3 together twelve times, knit 1. **18th row**—Slip 1, knit 2, purl 1, knit 2 and purl 1 eleven times, knit 3, make 1, knit 2 together, knit 3. **19th row**—Slip 1, knit 4, make 1, knit 2 together, knit 38. **20th row**—Slip 1, knit 39, make 1, knit 2 together, knit 3. **21st row**—Slip 1, knit 4, make 1, knit 2 together, knit 1, make 2 and knit 3 together twelve times, knit 1. **22nd row**—Slip 1, knit 2, purl 1, knit 2 and purl 1 eleven times, knit 3, make 1, knit 2 together, purl 1, knit 2 and purl 1 eleven times, knit 3, make 1, knit 2 together, knit 3. **23rd row**—Slip 1, knit 4, make 1, knit 2 together, knit 38. **24th row**—Cast off 17, knit 22, make 1, knit 2 together, knit 3. Repeat from the first row of the pattern.

No. 15.—TRIPLE VANDYKE BORDER.

This is a suitable trimming for quilts, for edging window blinds, or for any purpose for which a handsome wide border is desired. Cast on 18 stitches, Knit 1 plain row. **1st pattern row**—Slip 1, knit 3, make 1, knit 2 together, knit 1, make 1 and knit 2 together three times, make 1, knit 2, make 2, knit 2 together, knit 1. **2nd row**—Knit 3, purl 1, knit 12, make 1, knit 2 together,

and knit 2 together four times, knit 2, make 1, knit 2 together, knit 4, make 1, knit 2 together, knit 2. **23rd row**—Slip 1, knit 3, make 1, knit 2 together, knit 26. **24th row**—Cast off 7, knit 3, knit 2 together, make 1 and knit 2 together four times, knit 2, make 1, knit 2 together, knit 3, make 1, knit 2 together, knit 2. **25th row**—Slip 1, knit 3, make 1, knit 2 together, knit 15, make 2, knit 2 together, knit 1. **26th row**—Knit 3, purl 1, knit 1, knit 2 together, make 1 and knit 2 together four times, knit 6, make 1, knit 2 together, knit 2. **27th row**—Slip 1, knit 3, make 1, knit 2 together, knit 18. **28th row**—Knit 5, knit 2 together, make 1 and knit 2 together four times, knit 5, make 1, knit 2 together, knit 2. **29th row**—Slip 1, knit 3, make 1, knit 2 together, knit 13, make 2, knit 2 together, make 2, knit 2. **30th row**—Knit 3, purl 1, knit 2, purl 1, knit 1, knit 2 together, make 1 and knit 2 together four times, knit 4, make 1, knit 2 together, knit 2. **31st row**—Slip 1, knit 3, make 1, knit 2 together, knit 19. **32nd row**—Knit 8, knit 2 together, make 1 and knit 2 together four times, knit 13, make 1, knit 2 together, knit 2. **33rd row**—Slip 1, knit 3, make 1, knit 2 together, knit 11, make 2, knit 2 together, make 2, knit 2 together, make 2, knit 2 together, knit 1. **34th row**—Knit 3, purl 1, knit 2, purl 1, knit 1, knit 2 together, make 1 and knit 2 together four times, knit 2, make 1, knit 2 together, knit 2. **35th row**—Slip 1, knit 3, make 1, knit 2 together, knit 20. **36th row**—Cast off 7, knit 3, knit 2 together, knit 9, make 1, knit 2 together, knit 2. This completes the pattern; repeat from the first row.

No. 16.—DIAMOND INSERTION.

Cast on 15 stitches. Purl one row. **1st row**—Slip 1, k 2, make 1, k 2 together, make 1, k 2 together, make 1, k 1, make 1, slip 1, k 1, pass the slipped stitch over, make 1, k 2, make 1, k 2 together, k 1. **2nd row**—Slip 1, knit 2, make 1, knit 2 together, purl 8, knit 1, make 1, knit 2 together, knit 1. **3rd row**—Slip 1, knit 2, make 1, knit 2 together, make 1, knit 2 together, make 1, knit 3

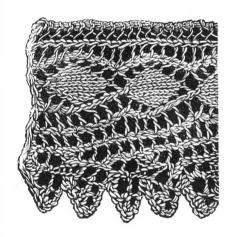

No. 9.—Beech Leaf Border.

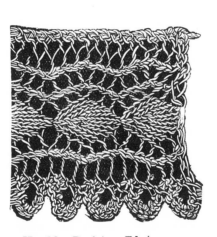

No. 10.—Parisian Edging.

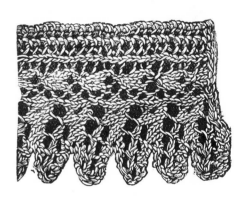

No. 11.—Marguerite Border.

knit 2. **3rd row**—Slip 1, knit 3, make 1, knit 2 together, knit 2 make 1 and knit 2 together three times, make 1, knit 6. **4th row**—Knit 17, make 1, knit 2 together, knit 2. **5th row**—Slip 1, knit 3, make 1, knit 2 together, knit 3, make 1 and knit 2 together three times, make 1, knit 2, make 2, knit 2 together, make 2, knit 2 **6th row**—Knit 3, purl 1, knit 2, purl 1, knit 14, make 1, knit 2 together, knit 2. **7th row**—Slip 1, knit 3, make 1, knit 2 together, knit 4, make 1 and knit 2 together three times, make 1, knit 9. **8th row**—Knit 22, make 1, knit 2 together, knit 2. **9th row**—Slip 1, knit 3, make 1, knit 2 together, knit 5, make 1 and knit 2 together three times, make 1, knit 2, make 2, knit 2 together, make 2, knit 2 together, make 2, knit 2 together, knit 1. **10th row**—Knit 3, purl 1, knit 2, purl 1, knit 2, purl 1, knit 16, make 1, knit 2 together, knit 2. **11th row**—Slip 1, knit 3, make 1, knit 2 together, knit 2, make 1, knit 2 together, knit 2, make 1 and knit 2 together three times, make 1, knit 12. **12th row**—Cast off 7, knit 19, make 1, knit 2 together, knit 2. **13th row**—Slip 1, knit 3, make 1, knit 2 together, knit 3, make 1, knit 2 together, knit 2, make 1 and knit 2 together three times, make 1, knit 2, make 2, knit 2 together, knit 1. **14th row**—Knit 3, purl 1, knit 18, make 1, knit 2 together, knit 2. **15th row**—Slip 1, knit 3, make 1, knit 2 together, knit 4, make 1 and knit 2 together three times, make 1, knit 6. **16th row**—Knit 23, make 1, knit 2 together, knit 2. **17th row**—Slip 1, knit 3, make 1, knit 2 together, knit 2, make 1, knit 2 together, knit 1, make 1, knit 2 together, knit 2, make 1 and knit 2 together three times, make 1, knit 2, make 2, knit 2 together, make 2, knit 2. **18th row**—Knit 3, purl 1, knit 2, purl 1, knit 20, make 1, knit 2 together knit 2 **19th row**—Slip 1, knit 3, make 1, knit 2 together, knit 25. **20th row**—Knit 8, knit 2 together, make 1 and knit 2 together four times, knit 2, make 1, knit 2 together, knit 5, make 1, knit 2 together, knit 2. **21st row**—Slip 1, knit 3, make 1, knit 2 together, knit 17, make 2, knit 2 together, make 2, knit 2 together, make 2, knit 2 together, knit 1. **22nd row**—Knit 3, purl 1, knit 2, purl 1, knit 2, purl 1, knit 1, knit 2 together, make 1

make 1, slip 1, knit 1, pass the slipped stitch over, make 1, knit 2, make 1, knit 2 together, knit 1. **4th row**—Slip 1, knit 2, make 1, knit 2 together, purl 10, knit 1, make 1, knit 2 together, knit 1. **5th row**—Slip 1, knit 2, make 1, knit 2 together, make 1, knit 5, make 1, slip 1, knit 1, pass the slipped stitch over, make 1, knit 2, make 1, knit 2 together, knit 1. **6th row**—Slip 1, knit 2, make 1, knit 2 together, purl 12, knit 1, make 1, knit 2 together, knit 1. **7th row**—Slip 1, knit 2, make 1, knit 2 together, make 1, knit 7, make 1, slip 1, knit 1, pass the slipped stitch over, make 1, knit 2, make 1, knit 2 together, knit 1. **8th row**—Slip 1, knit 2, make 1, knit 2 together, purl 14, knit 1, make 1, knit 2 together, knit 1. **9th row**—Slip 1, knit 2, make 1, knit 2 together, make 1, knit 3 together, make 1, slip 1, knit 1, pass the slipped stitch over, knit 3, knit 2 together, make 1, knit 2 together, make 1, knit 2 together, knit 1, make 1, knit 2 together, knit 1. **10th row**—Slip 1, knit 2, make 1, knit 2 together, purl 12, knit 1, make 1, knit 2 together, knit 1. **11th row**—Slip 1, knit 2, make 1, knit 2 together, make 1, knit 3 together, make 1, slip 1, knit 1, pass the slipped stitch over, knit 1, knit 2 together, make 1, knit 2 together, make 1, knit 2 together, knit 1, make 1, knit 2 together, knit 1. **12th row**—Slip 1, knit 2, make 1, knit 2 together, purl 10, knit 1, make 1, knit 2 together, knit 1. **13th row**—Slip 1, knit 2, make 1, knit 2 together, make 1, knit 3 together, make 1, slip 1, knit 2 together, pass the slipped stitch over, make 1, knit 2 together, make 1, knit 2 together, knit 1, make 1, knit 2 together, knit 1. **14th row**—Slip 1, knit 2, make 1, knit 2 together, purl 8, knit 1, make 1, knit 2 together, knit 1. **15th row**—Slip 1, knit 2, make 1, knit 2 together, make 1, knit 3 together, make 1, slip 1, knit 2 together, pass the slipped stitch over, make 1, knit 2 together, knit 1, make 1, knit 2 together, knit 1. **16th row**—Slip 1, knit 2, make 1, knit 2 together, purl 6, knit 1, make 1, knit 2 together, knit 1. Repeat from the first row.

No. 17.—STAR PATTERN BORDER.

CAST on 12 stitches. Knit 1 plain row. **1st row**—Slip 1, knit 2, make 1, knit 2 together, knit 7. **2nd row**—Make 1, knit 3, make 1, knit 2 together, make 1, knit 1, knit 2 together, knit 1. **3rd row**—Slip 1, knit 2, make 1, knit 2 together, knit 8. **4th row**—Make 1, knit 5, make 1, knit 2 together, knit 3, make 1, knit 2 together, knit 1. **5th row**—Slip 1, knit 2, make 1, knit 2 together, knit 9. **6th row**—Make 1, knit 1, knit 2 together, make 1, knit 1, make 1 knit 1, knit 2 together, make 1, knit 2 together, knit 2, make 1, knit 2

No. 12.—Wide Handsome Border for Mantel Drape.

together, knit 1. **7th row**—Slip 1, knit 2, make 1, knit 2 together, knit 10. **8th row**—Make 1, knit 1, knit 2 together, make 1, knit 3, make 1, knit 2 together, knit 1 make 1 knit 2 together, knit 1, make 1, knit 2 together, knit 1. **9th row**—Slip 1, knit 2, make 1, knit 2 together, knit 11. **10th row**—Make 1, knit 3 toge ther, knit 1, make 1, knit 3 together, make 1, knit 1, knit 2 together, make 1, knit 3, make 1, knit 2 together, knit 1. **11th row**—Slip 1, knit 2, make 1, knit 2 together, knit 10. **12th row**—Make 1, knit 3 together, knit 3, knit 2 together, make 1, knit 4, make 1, knit 2 together, knit 1. **13th row** — Slip 1, knit 2, make 1, knit 2 together, knit 9. **14th row**—Make 1, knit 3 together, knit 1, knit 2 together, make 1, knit 5, make 1, knit 2 together, knit 1. **15th row**—Slip 1, knit 2, make 1, knit 2 together, knit 5, knit 2 together, knit 1. **16th row**—Make 1, knit 3 together, make 1, knit 6, make 1, knit 2 together knit 1 Repeat from the first row.

No. 18.—GRECIAN LACE.

CAST on 15 stitches. Purl one row. **1st row**—Slip 1, knit 1, make 1, knit 2 together, make 1, knit 2 together, make 1, knit 2 together, knit 1, make 1, make 1, knit 1, knit 2 together, make 2, knit 2 together. **2nd row**—Knit 2, purl 13, knit 2. **3rd row**—Slip 1, knit 1, knit 2 together, make 1, knit 2 together, make 1, knit 2 together, knit 1, make 1, knit 2, make 1, knit 1, knit 2 together, make 2, knit 2 together, knit 1. **4th row**—Knit 3, purl 14, knit 2. **5th row**—Slip 1, knit 1, make 1, knit 2 together, make 1, knit 2 together, make 1, knit 1, knit 2 together, knit 1, make 1, knit 3, make 1, knit 1, knit 2 together, make 2, knit 2 together, make 2, knit 2 together. **6th row**—Knit 2, purl 1, knit 2, purl 14, knit 2. **7th row**—Slip 1, knit 1, make 1, knit 1, make 1, knit 2 together, make 1, knit 2 together, make 1, knit 2 together, knit 1, slip 1, knit 2 together, pass the slipped stitch over, make 1, knit 1, knit 2 together, knit 6. **8th row**—Cast off 6, purl 12, knit 2. Repeat from the first row of the pattern

---

No. 19.—COCKLE SHELL EDGING.

THIS pretty edging may be worked with any cotton suitable to the purpose for which it is required. Cast on 16 stitches. Knit 1 plain row. **1st row**—Slip 1, knit 2, cotton twice round the needle, purl 2 together, knit 10, purl 1. **2nd row**—Make 1, knit 2 together, knit 1, make 1, knit 8, cotton twice round the needle, purl 2 together, knit 3. **3rd row**—Slip 1, knit 2, cotton twice round the needle, purl 2 together, knit 11, purl 1. **4th row**—Make 1, knit 2

together, knit 1, make 1, knit 2 together, make 1, knit 7, cotton twice round the needle, purl 2 together, knit 3. **5th row**—Slip 1, knit 2, cotton twice round the needle, purl 2 together, knit 12, purl 1. **6th row**—Make 1, knit 2 together, knit 1, make 1, knit 2 together, make 1, knit 2 together, make 1, knit 6, cotton twice round the needle, purl 2 together, knit 3. **7th row**—Slip 1, knit 2, cotton twice round the needle, purl 2 together, knit 13, purl 1. **8th row**—Make 1, knit 2 together, knit 1, make 1 and knit 2 together three times, make 1, knit 5, cotton twice round the needle, purl 2 together, knit 3. **9th row**—Slip 1, knit 2, cotton twice round the needle, purl 2 together, knit 14, purl 1. **10th row**—Make 1, knit 2 together, knit 1, make 1 and knit 2 together four times, make 1, knit 4, cotton twice round the needle, purl 2 together, knit 3. **11th row**—Slip 1, knit 2, cotton twice round the needle, purl 2 together, knit 15, purl 1. **12th row**—Make 1 knit 2 together, knit 1, make 1 and knit 2 together five times, make 1, knit 3, cotton twice round the needle, purl 2 together, knit 3. **13th row**—Slip 1, knit 2, cotton twice round the needle, purl 2 together, knit 16, purl 1. **14th row**—Make 1, knit 2 together, knit 2 together, make 1 and knit 2 together five times, knit 3, cotton twice round the needle, purl 2 together, knit 3. **15th row**—Slip 1, knit 2, cotton twice round the needle, purl 2 together, knit 15, purl 1. **16th row**—Make 1, knit 2 together, knit 2 together, make 1 and knit 2 together four times, knit 4, cotton twice round the needle, purl 2 together, knit 3. **17th row**—Slip 1, knit 2, cotton twice round the needle, purl 2 together, knit 14, purl 1. **18th row**—Make 1, knit 2 together, knit 2 together, make 1 and knit 2 together three times, knit 5, cotton twice round the needle, purl 2 together, knit 3 **19th row**—Slip 1, knit 2, cotton twice round the needle, purl 2 together knit 13, purl 1. **20th row**—Make 1, knit 2 together, knit 2 together, make 1, knit 2 together, make 1, knit 2 together, knit 6, cotton twice round the needle, purl 2 together, knit 3. **21st row**—Slip 1, knit 2, cotton twice round the needle, purl 2 together, knit 12, purl 1. **22nd row**—Make 1, knit 2 together, knit 2 together, make 1, knit 2 together, knit 7, cotton twice round the needle, purl 2 together, knit 3. **23rd row**—Slip 1, knit 2, cotton twice round the needle, purl 2 together, knit 11, purl 1. **24th row**—Make 1, knit 2 together, knit 2 together, knit 8, cotton twice round the needle, purl 2 together, knit 3. Repeat from the first row

---

No. 20.—VICTORIA BORDER.

CAST on 16 stitches. Knit 1 plain row. **1st row**—Slip 1, knit 3, make 1, knit 2 together, knit 1, make 2, knit 2 together, knit 7. **2nd row**—Knit 9, purl 1, knit 3, make 1, knit 2 together, knit 2. **3rd row**—Slip 1, knit 3, make 1, knit 2 together, knit 11. **4th row**—Knit 13, make 1, knit 2 together knit 2. **5th row**—Slip 1, knit 3, make 1, knit 2 together, knit 1, make 2, knit 2 together, make 2, knit 2 together, knit 6. **6th row**—Knit 8, purl 1, knit 2, purl 1, knit 3, make 1, knit 2 together, knit 2. **7th row**—Slip 1, knit 3, make 1, knit 2 together, knit 13. **8th row**—Knit 15, make 1, knit 2 together, knit 2. **9th row**—Slip 1, knit 3, make 1, knit 2 together, knit 1, make 2, knit 2 together, make 2, knit 2 together, make 2, knit 2 together, knit 6. **10th row**—Knit 8, purl 1, knit 2, purl 1, knit 2, purl 1, knit 3, make 1, knit 2 together, knit 2. **11th row**—Slip 1, knit 3, make 1, knit 2 together, knit 16. **12th row**—Cast off 6, knit 11, make 1, knit 2 together, knit 2. Repeat from the first row for the length desired.

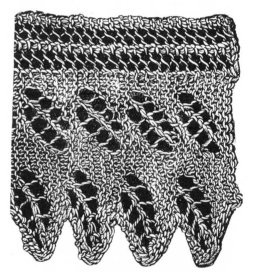

No. 13.—Aspen Leaf Border.

No. 21.—LEAF AND BERRY PATTERN.

CAST on 12 stitches. Purl one row. **1st row**—Slip 1, knit 2 together, make 2, knit 2 together, make 1, knit 1, make 1, knit 1 and purl 1 and knit 1 all in the next stitch, make 1, knit 1, make 1, knit 1, make 2, knit 2 together, knit 1 **2nd row**—Knit 3, purl 1, knit 1, purl 9, knit 2, purl 1, knit 2 **3rd row**—Slip 1, knit 2 together, make 2, knit 2 together, make 1, knit 3, make 1, knit 3, make 1, knit 3, make 1, knit 1, make 1, knit 1, make 2, knit 2 together, knit 1, **4th row**—Knit 3, purl 1, knit 2, purl 1, knit 1, purl 5, purl 3 together, purl 5, knit 2, purl 1, knit 2. **5th row**—Slip 1, knit 2 together, make 2, knit 2 together, make 1, slip 1, knit 1, pass the slipped stitch over, knit 1, knit 2 together, make 1, knit 1, make 1, slip 1, knit 1, pass the slipped stitch over, knit 1, knit 2 together, make 1, knit 1, make 1, knit 2 together, make 2, knit 2 together, make 2, knit 2 together, knit 1. **6th row**—Knit 3, purl 1, knit 2, purl 1, knit 2, purl 1, knit 1, purl 2 together, purl 1, purl 2 together, purl 1, purl 2 together, purl 1, purl 2 together, knit 2, purl 1, knit 2. **7th row**—Slip 1, knit 2 together, make 2, knit 2 together, make 2, knit 2 together, pass the slipped stitch over, knit 1, slip 1, knit 2 together, pass the slipped stitch over, knit 11. **8th row**—Cast off 7, knit 4, purl 3 together, knit 3, purl 1, knit 2. Repeat from the first row for the length required

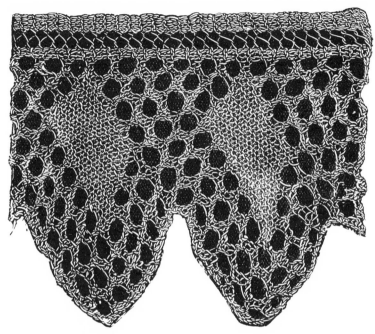

No. 14.—Handsome Wide Border for Brackets.

No. 22.—FLUTED BORDER.

Cast on 16 stitches. Knit 1 plain row. **1st row**—Slip 1, knit 2, make 1, knit 2 together, purl 10, knit 1 and purl 1 in the last stitch. **2nd row**—Knit 17. **3rd row**—Slip 1, knit 2, make 1, knit 2 together, purl 11, knit 1 and purl 1 in the last stitch. **4th row**—Knit 13, turn the work. **5th row**—Slip the first stitch, purl 11, knit 1 and purl 1 in the last stitch. **6th row**—Knit 19. **7th row**—Slip 1, knit 2, make 1, knit 2 together, purl 1, make 1 and purl 2 together six times, purl 1. **8th row**—Knit 14, turn the work. **9th row**—Slip the first stitch, purl 11, purl 2 together. **10th row**—Knit 18. **11th row**—Slip 1, knit 2, make 1, knit 2 together, purl 11, purl 2 together. **12th row**—Knit 17. **13th row**—Slip 1, knit 2, make 1, knit 2 together, purl 10, purl 2 together. **14th row**—Knit 16. **15th row**—Slip 1, knit 2, make 1, knit 2 together, purl 1, knit 10. **16th row**—Purl 10, turn the work. **17th row**—Slip the first stitch, knit 9. **18th row**—Purl 10, turn the work. **19th row**—Slip the first stitch, knit 9. **20th row**—Purl 10, knit 6. Repeat from the first row.

No. 23.—DOLPHIN LACE.

Cast on 20 stitches. Knit 1 plain row. **1st row**—Slip 1, knit 1, knit 2 together, make 2, knit 2 together, knit 2 together, make 2, knit 2 together, knit 4, draw the second stitch over the last, knit 1, draw another stitch over, knit 2, make 2, knit 2 together, knit 1. **2nd row**—Knit 3, purl 1, knit 3, cast on 5, knit 1, purl 1, knit 3, purl 1, knit 3. **3rd row**—Slip 1, knit 1, knit 2 together, make 2, knit 2 together, knit 2 together, make 2, knit 2 together, knit 11, make 2, knit 2 together, knit 1. **4th row**—Knit 3, purl 1, knit 2 together, knit 11, purl 1, knit 3, purl 1, knit 3. **5th row**—Slip 1, knit 1, knit 1, knit 2 together, make 2, knit 2 together, knit 2 together, make 2, knit 2 together, make 2, knit 2 together, knit 7, knit 2 together, make 2, knit 2 together, knit 1. **6th row**—Knit 3, purl 1, knit 2 together, knit 8, purl 1, knit 2, purl 1, knit 3, purl 1, knit 3. **7th row**—Slip 1, knit 1, knit 2 together, make 2, knit 2 together, make 2, knit 2 together, make 2, knit 2 together, make 2, knit 2 together, knit 5, knit 2 together, make 2, knit 2 together, knit 1. **8th row**—Knit 3, purl 1, knit 2 together, knit 3, knit 2 together, knit 1, purl 1, knit 4, purl 1, knit 3, purl 1, knit 3. **9th row**—Slip 1, knit 1, knit 2 together, make 2, knit 2 together, knit 4, make 2, knit 2 together, knit 2, knit 2 together, make 2, knit 2 together, knit 1. **10th row**—Knit 3, purl 1, knit 2 together, knit 2 together, knit 1, purl 1, knit 6, purl 1, knit 3, purl 1, knit 3. **11th row**—Slip 1, knit 1, knit 2 together, make 2, knit 2 together,

knit 2 together, make 2, knit 2 together, knit 6, make 2, knit 2 together, knit 4 **12th row**—Cast off 3, knit 2, purl 1, knit 8, purl 1, knit 3, purl 1, knit 3. Repeat from the first row for the length required.

No. 24.—BUTTON-HOLE PATTERN.

Cast on 16 stitches. Purl one row. **1st row**—Slip 1, knit 4, make 1, knit 2 together, knit 3, knit 2 together, make 1, knit 1, make 1, knit 2 together, knit 1. **2nd row**—Make 1, knit 2, purl 9, make 1, purl 2 together, knit 3. **3rd row**—Slip 1, knit 4, make 1, knit 2 together, knit 2, knit 2 together, make 1, knit 3, make 1, knit 2 together, knit 1. **4th row**—Make 1, knit 2, purl 10, make 1, purl 2 together, knit 3. **5th row**—Slip 1, knit 4, make 1, knit 2 together, knit 1, knit 2 together, make 1, knit 5, make 1, knit 2 together, knit 1. **6th row**—Make 1, knit 2, purl 11, make 1, purl 2 together, knit 3. **7th row**—Slip 1, knit 4, make 1, knit 2 together, knit 2 together, make 1, knit 3, draw the second stitch over the last, cast off 4 more in the ordinary manner, make 1, knit 2 together, knit 1. **8th row**—Make 1, knit 2, purl 2, cast on 5, purl 5, make 1, purl 2 together, knit 3. **9th row**—Slip 1, knit 4, make 1, knit 2 together, knit 1, make 1, slip 1, knit 1, pass the slipped stitch over, knit 6, make 1, knit 1, make 1, knit 2 together, knit 1. **10th row**—Make 1, knit 2, purl 14, make 1, purl 2 together, knit 3. **11th row**—Slip 1, knit 4, make 1, knit 2 together, knit 2, make 1, slip 1, knit 1, pass slipped stitch over, k 3, k 2 together, m 1, k 3, m 1, knit 2 together, knit 1. **12th row**—Make 1, knit 2, purl 15, make 1, purl 2 together, knit 3. **13th row**—Slip 1, knit 4, make 1, knit 2 together, knit 3, make 1, slip 1, knit 1, pass the slipped stitch over, knit 1, knit 2 together, make 1, knit 5, make 1, knit 2 together, knit 1. **14th row**—Make 1, knit 2, purl 16, make 1, purl 2 together, knit 3. **15th row**—Slip 1, knit 4, make 1, knit 2 together, knit 4, make 1, slip 1, knit 2 together, pass the slipped stitch over, make 1, knit 3, draw the second stitch over the last, cast off 4 more in the ordinary manner, make 1, knit 2 together, knit 1. **16th row**—Make 1, knit 2, purl 2, cast on 5, purl 10, make 1, purl 2 together, knit 3. **17th row**—Slip 1, knit 4, make 1, knit 2 together, knit 3, knit 2 together, make 1, knit 1, make 1, slip 1, knit 1, pass the slipped stitch over, knit 5, make 1, knit 2 together, make 1, knit 2 together, knit 1. **18th row**—Make 1, knit 2 together, purl 17, make 1, purl 2 together, knit 3. **19th row**—Slip 1, knit 4, make 1, knit 2 together, knit 2, knit 2 together, make 1, knit 3, make 1, slip 1, knit 1, pass the slipped stitch over, knit 3, knit 2 together, make 1, knit 2 together, knit 1. **20th row**—Make 1, knit 2 together, purl 16, make 1, purl 2 together, knit 3. **21st row**—Slip 1, knit 4, make 1, knit 2 together, knit 1, knit 2 together, make 1, knit 5, make 1, slip 1, knit 1, pass the slipped stitch over, knit 1, knit 2 together, make 1, knit 2 together, knit 1. **22nd row**—Make 1, knit 2 together, purl 15, make 1, purl 2 together, knit 3. **23rd row**—Slip 1, knit 4, make 1, knit 2 together, knit 2 together, make 1, knit 3, draw the second stitch over the last, cast off 4 more in the ordinary manner, make 1, slip 1, knit 2 together, pass the slipped stitch over, make 1, knit 2 together, knit 1. **24th row**—Make 1, knit 2 together, purl 4, cast on 5, purl 5, make 1, purl 2 together, knit 3. **25th row**—Slip 1, knit 4, make 1, knit 2 together, knit 1, make 1, slip 1, knit 1, pass the slipped stitch over, knit

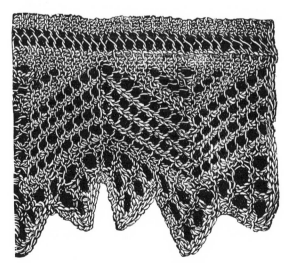

No. 15.—Triple Vandyke Border.

5, knit 3 together, make 1, knit 2 together, knit 1. **26th row**—Make 1, knit 2 together, purl 12, make 1, purl 2 together, knit 3. **27th row**—Slip 1, knit 4, make 1, knit 2 together, knit 2, make 1, slip 1, knit 1, pass the slipped stitch over, knit 3, knit 2 together, make 1, knit 2 together, knit 1. **28th row**—Make 1, knit 2 together, purl 11, make 1, purl 2 together, knit 3. **29th row**—Slip 1, knit 4, make 1, knit 2 together, knit 3, make 1, slip 1, knit 1, pass the slipped stitch over, knit 1, knit 2 together, make 1, knit 2 together, knit 1. **30th row**—Make 1, knit 2 together, purl 10, make 1, purl 2 together, knit 3. **31st row**—Slip 1, knit 4, make 1, knit 2 together, knit 4, make 1, slip 1, knit 2 together, pass the slipped stitch over, make 1, knit 2 together, knit 1. **32nd row**—Make 1, knit 2 together, purl 9, make 1, purl 2 together, knit 3. Recommence at the first row, and continue for the length required.

No. 25.—DEWDROP EDGING.

CAST on 13 stitches. Knit 1 plain row. **1st row**—Slip 1, knit 2, make 1, knit 2 together, knit 2 together, make 1, knit 6. **2nd row**—Knit 1, make 2, knit 2 together, make 2, knit 2 together, knit 1, purl 2, knit 2, make 1, knit 2 together, knit 1. **3rd row**—Slip 1, knit 2, make 1, knit 2 together, knit 2 together, make 1, knit 3, purl 1, knit 2, purl 1, knit 1. **4th row**—Knit 8, purl 1, knit 2, make 1, knit 2 together, knit 1. **5th row**—Slip 1, knit 2, make 1, knit 2 together, knit 2 together, make 1, knit 1, make 2, knit 2 together, make 2, knit 2 together, make 2, knit 2 together, knit 1. **6th row**—Knit 3, purl 1, knit 2, purl 1, knit 2, purl 4, knit 2, make 1, knit 2 together, knit 1. **7th row**—Slip 1, knit 2, make 1, knit 2 together, knit 2 together, make 1, knit 11. **8th row**—Cast off 5, make 2, knit 2 together, make 2, knit 2 together, knit 1, purl, knit 2, make 1, knit 2 together, knit 1. Repeat from the third row.

No. 16.—Diamond Insertion.

No. 26.—WHEAT-EAR PATTERN.

CAST on 20 stitches. Purl one row. **1st row**—Slip 1, knit 1, make 1, knit 2 together, make 1, knit 2 together, knit 2 together, knit 2 together, knit 2, make 1, knit 3, make 1, knit 2 together, make 1, knit 1, make 2, knit 2. **2nd row**—Knit 3, purl 1, knit 3, purl 13, knit 2. **3rd row**—Slip 1, knit 1, make 1, knit 2 together, make 1, knit 3 together, knit 3 together, make 1, knit 1, make 1, knit 2, knit 2 together, make 1, knit 2 together, make 1, knit 5. **4th row**—Cast off 2, knit 4, purl 8, purl 2 together, purl 1, knit 2. **5th row**—Slip 1, knit 1, make 1, knit 3 together, make 1, knit 3, make 1, knit 2, knit 2 together, make 1, knit 2 together, make 1, knit 1, make 2, knit 2. **6th row**—Knit 3, purl 1, knit 3, purl 11, knit 2. **7th row**—Slip 1, knit 1, make 1, knit 2 together, make 1, knit 1, make 1, knit 2, knit 2 together, make 1, knit 2, knit 2 together, make 1, knit 2 together, make 1, knit 5. **8th row**—Cast off 2, knit 4, purl 13, knit 2. **9th row**—Slip 1, knit 1, make 1, knit 2 together, make 1, knit 3, make 1, knit 2, knit 2 together, make 1, slip 1, knit 1, pass the slipped stitch over, slip 1, knit 1, pass the slipped stitch over, make 1, knit 2 together, make 1, knit 1, make 1, knit 2. **10th row**—Knit 3, purl 1, knit 3, purl 14, knit 2. **11th row**—Slip 1, knit 1, make 1, knit 2 together, make 1, knit 2 together, knit 2, make 1, knit 1, make 1, slip 1, knit 1, pass the slipped stitch over, slip 1, knit 1, pass the slipped stitch over, make 1, knit 2 together, make 1, knit 5. **12th row**—Cast off 2, knit 3, purl 3 together, purl 2 together, purl 9, knit 2. **13th row**—Slip 1, knit 1, make 1, knit 2 together, make 1, knit 2 together, knit 2, make 1, knit 3, make 1, slip 1, knit 1, pass the slipped stitch over, make 1, knit 1, make 2, knit 2. **14th row**—Knit 3, purl 1, knit 3, purl 11, knit 2. **15th row**—Slip 1, knit 1, make 1, knit 2 together, make 1, knit 2 together, knit 2, make 1, knit 2 together, knit 2, make 1, knit 1, make 1, knit 2 together, make 1, knit 5. **16th row**—Cast off 2, knit 4, purl 13, knit 2. Repeat from the first row.

No. 27.—POINT LACE BORDER.

CAST on 15 stitches. Knit 1 plain row. **1st row**—Slip 1, knit 2, make 1, slip 1, knit 2 together, pass the slipped stitch over, make 1, knit 3, make 1, knit 2 together, make 2, knit 2 together, make 2, knit 2 together. **2nd row**—Make 1, knit 2, purl 1, knit 2, purl 1, knit 1, purl 6, knit 1, make 1, knit 2 together, knit 1. **3rd row**—Slip 1, knit 2, make 1, knit 2 together, make 1, slip 1, knit 1, pass the slipped stitch over, knit 1, knit 2 together, make 1, knit 8. **4th row**—Cast off 3, knit 4, purl 6, knit 1, make 1, knit 2 together, knit 1. **5th row**—Slip 1, knit 2, make 1, knit 2 together, knit 1, make 1, slip 1, knit 2 together, pass the slipped stitch over, make 1, knit 2, make 2, knit 2 together, make 2, knit 2 together. **6th row**—Make 1, knit 2, purl 1, knit 2, purl 1, knit 1, purl 6, knit 1, make 1, knit 2 together, knit 1. **7th row**—Slip 1, knit 2, make 1, knit 2 together, knit 2 together, make 1, knit 1, make 1, knit 2 together, knit 8. **8th row**—Cast off 3, knit 4, purl 6, knit 1, make 1, knit 2 together, knit 1. Repeat from the first row for the length required.

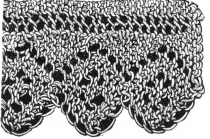

No. 17.—Star Pattern Border.

No. 28.—BOX-LEAF EDGING.

THIS is a pretty edging for underlinen and children's things, working with No. 24 crochet cotton and No. 18 steel knitting needles. Cast on 10 stitches. Knit 1 plain row. **1st row**—Slip 1, knit 2, cotton twice round the needle, purl 2 together, knit 2, make 2, knit 2 together, knit 1. **2nd row**—Knit 3, purl 1, knit 1, purl 1, make 1, purl 2 together, purl 1, knit 2. **3rd row**—Slip 1, knit 2, cotton twice round the needle, purl 2 together, knit 3, make 2, knit 2 together, knit 1. **4th row**—Knit 3, purl 1, knit 2, purl 1, make 1, purl 2 together, purl 1, knit 2. **5th row**—Slip 1, knit 2, cotton twice round the needle, purl 2 together, knit 4, make 2, knit 2 together, knit 1. **6th row**—Knit 3, purl 1, knit 3, purl 1, make 1, purl 2 together, purl 1, knit 2. **7th row**—Slip 1, knit 2, cotton twice round the needle, purl 2 together, knit 5, make 1, knit 2 together, knit 1. **8th row**—Knit 3, purl 1, knit 4, purl 1, make 1, purl 2 together, purl 1, knit 2. **9th row**—Slip 1, knit 2, cotton twice round the needle, purl 2 together, knit 6, make 2, knit 2 together, knit 1. **10th row**—Knit 3, purl 1, knit 5, purl 1, make 1, purl 2 together, purl 1, knit 2. **11th row**—Slip 1, knit 2, cotton twice round the needle, purl 2 together, knit, 10. **12th row**—Cast off 5, knit 3, purl 1, make 1, purl 2 together, purl 1, knit 2. Repeat from the first row.

No. 29.—LEAF INSERTION.

CAST on 18 stitches. **1st row**—Slip 1, knit 2, make 1, slip 1, knit 1, pass the slipped stitch over, knit 1, make 1, knit 2 together, make 1, knit 2 together, knit 5, make 1, knit 2 together, knit 1. **2nd row**—Slip 1, knit 2, cotton twice round the needle, purl 2 together, purl 9, knit 1, make 1, knit 2 together, knit 1. **3rd row**—Slip 1, knit 2, make 1, slip 1, knit 1, pass the slipped stitch over, knit 2, make 1, knit 2 together, make 1, knit 2 together, knit 4, make 1, knit 2 together, knit 1. **4th row**—Same as the second row. **5th row**—Slip 1, knit 2, make 1, slip 1, knit 1, pass the slipped stitch over, knit 3, make 1, knit 2 together, make 1, knit 2 together, knit 3, make 1, knit 2 together, knit 1. **6th row**—Same as the second row. **7th row**—Slip 1, knit 2, make 1, slip 1, knit 1, pass the slipped stitch over, knit 4, make 1, knit 2 together, make 1, knit 2 together, knit 2, make 1, knit 2 together, knit 1. **8th row**—Same as the second row. **9th row**—Slip 1, knit 2, make 1, slip 1, knit 1, pass the slipped stitch over, knit 10, make 1, knit 2 together, knit 1. **10th row**—Same as the second row. Repeat from the first row for the length required.

No. 30.—UNIT EDGING.

CAST on 12 stitches, and knit plain along them. **1st row**—Slip 1, knit 2, make 1, knit 2 together, knit 2 together, make 2, knit 2 together, purl 3. **2nd row**—Make 1, knit 5, purl 1, knit 6. **3rd row**—Slip 1, knit 2, make 1, knit 2 together, knit 2 together, make 2, knit 2 together, purl 4. **4th row**—Make 1, knit 6, purl 1, knit 6. **5th row**—Slip 1, knit 2, make 1, knit 2 together, knit 2 together, make 2, knit 2 together, purl 5. **6th row**—Make 1, knit 7, purl 1, knit 6. **7th row**—Slip 1, knit 2, make 1, knit 2 together, knit 2

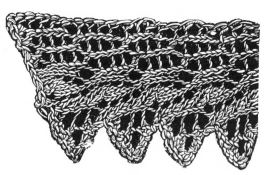

No. 18.—Grecian Lace.

together, make 2, knit 2 together, purl 6. **8th row**—Make 1, knit 2, knit 2 together, make 2, knit 2 together, knit 2, purl 1, knit 6. **9th row**—Slip 1, knit 2, make 1, knit 2 together, knit 2 together, make 2, knit 2 together, purl 2, knit 1, purl 4. **10th row**—Knit 2 together, knit 7, purl 1, knit 6. **11th row**—Slip 1, knit 2, make 1, knit 2 together, knit 2 together, make 2, knit 2 together, purl 6. **12th row**—Knit 2 together, knit 6, purl 1, knit 6. **13th row**—Slip 1, knit 2, make 1, knit 2 together, knit 2 together, make 2, knit 2 together, purl 5. **14th row**—Knit 2 together, knit 5, purl 1, knit 6. **15th row**—Slip 1, knit 2, make 1, knit 2 together, knit 2 together, make 2, knit 2 together, purl 4. **16th row**—Knit 2 together, knit 4, purl 1, knit 6. Repeat the pattern from the first row.

No. 31.—GILBERT EDGING.

CAST on 9 stitches. Knit 1 plain row. **1st row**—Slip 1, knit 2, make 1, knit 2 together, knit 1, pass the cotton 6 times round the needle, knit 2 together, knit 1. **2nd row**—Knit 3, purl 1, knit 1, purl 1, knit 1, purl 1, knit 3, make 1, knit 2 together, knit 1. **3rd row**—Slip 1, knit 2, make 1, knit 2 together, knit 9. **4th row**—Knit 11, make 1, knit 2 together, knit 1. **5th row**—Slip 1, knit 2, make 1, knit 2 together, make 2 and knit 2 together four times, knit 1. **6th row**—Knit 3, purl 1, knit 2, purl 1, knit 2, purl 1, knit 2, purl 1, knit 2, make 1, knit 2 together, knit 1. **7th row**—Slip 1, knit 2, make 1, knit 2 together, knit 13. **8th row**—Knit 15, make 1, knit 2 together, knit 1. **9th**

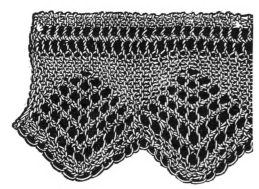

No. 19.—Cockle Shell Edging.

row—Slip 1, knit 2, make 1, knit 2 together, knit 13. **10th row**—Knit 15, make 1, knit 2 together, knit 1. **11th row**—Slip 1, knit 2, make 1, knit 2 together, knit 13. **12th row**—Cast off 9, knit 5, make 1, knit 2 together, knit 1. Repeat from the first row.

BIRD'S-EYE EDGING.

CAST on 16 stitches. Knit 1 plain row. **1st row**—Slip 1, knit 2, make 1, knit 2 together, knit 2, make 1, slip 1, knit 2 together, pass the slipped stitch over, make 1, knit 6. **2nd row**—Knit 13, make 1, knit 2 together, knit 1. **3rd row**—Slip 1, knit 2, make 1, knit 2 together, knit 2 together, make 1, knit 3, make 1, knit 2 together, knit 1, make 2, knit 2 together, knit 1. **4th row**—Knit 3, purl 1, knit 11, make 1 knit 2 together, knit 1. **5th row**—Slip 1, knit 2, make 1, knit 2 together, knit 2, make 1, slip 1, knit 2 together, pass the slipped stitch over, make 1, knit 3, make 2, knit 2 together, make 2, knit 2 together, knit 1. **6th row**—Knit 3, purl 1, knit 2, purl 1, knit 9, make 1, knit 2 together, knit 1. **7th row**—Slip 1, knit 2, make 1, knit 2 together, knit 2 together, make 1, knit 3, make 1, knit 2 together, knit 7. **8th row**—Cast off 3, knit 12, make 1, knit 2 together, knit 1. Repeat from the first row.

WIDE OPEN BORDER.

CAST on 16 stitches. Knit 1 plain row. **1st row**—Slip 1, knit 3, make 2 and knit 2 together six times. **2nd row**—Knit 2 and purl 1 six times, knit 4. **3rd row**—Slip 1, knit 3, make 2 and knit 2 together nine times. **4th row**—Knit 2 and purl 1 nine times, knit 4. **5th row**—Slip 1, knit 3, make 2, knit 2 together, make 1 and knit 2 together twelve times, knit 1. **6th row**—Knit 27, purl 1, knit 4. **7th row**—Slip 1, knit 3, make 2, knit 2 together, make 1 and knit 2 together thirteen times. **8th row**—Knit 28, purl 1, knit 4. **9th row**—Slip 1, knit 3, make 2, knit 2 together, make 1 and knit 2 together thirteen times, make 1, knit 1. **10th row**—Knit 30, purl 1, knit 4. **11th row**—Knit 35. **12th row**—Cast off 10, knit 2 together nine times, knit 6. Repeat from the first row.

WIDE LEAF EDGING.

CAST on 19 stitches, and knit 1 plain row. **1st row**—Slip 1, knit 2 together, make 1, knit 3, make 1, knit 2 together, knit 1, make 1, knit 2 together, knit 1, make 1, knit 2 together, make 1, knit 2 together, knit 1, make 1, knit 2 together, knit 1. **2nd row**—Slip 1, knit 2, purl 1, knit 10, make 1, knit 2 together, knit 4. **3rd row**—Slip 1, knit 2 together, make 1, knit 3, make 1, knit 2 together, knit 1, make 1, knit 2 together, knit 2, make 1, knit 2 together, make 1, knit 2 together, make 1, knit 2 together, knit 1. **4th row**—Slip 1, knit 2, purl 1, knit 2 together, knit 1, purl 1, knit 11, make 1, knit 2 together, knit 4. **5th row**—Slip 1, knit 2 together, make 1, knit 3, make 1, knit 2 together, knit 1, make 1, knit 2 together, knit 3, make 1, knit 2 together, make 1, knit 2 together, make 1, knit 2 together, knit 1. **6th row**—Slip 1, knit 2, purl 1, knit 12, make 1, knit 2 together, knit 4. **7th row**—Slip 1,

knit 2 together, make 1, knit 3, make 1, knit 2 together, knit 1, make 1, knit 2 together, knit 4, make 1, knit 2 together, make 1, knit 2 together, make 1, knit 2 together, knit 1. **8th row**—Slip 1, knit 2, purl 1, knit 13, make 1, knit 2 together, knit 4. **9th row**—Slip 1, knit 2 together, make 1, knit 3, make 1, knit 2 together, knit 1, make 1, knit 2 together, knit 5, make 1, knit 2 together, make 1, knit 2 together, knit 1. **10th row**—Slip 1, knit 2, purl 1, knit 14, make 1 knit 2 together, knit 4. **11th row**—Slip 1, knit 2 together, make 1, knit 3, make 1, knit 2 together, knit 1, make 1, knit 2 together, knit 6, make 1, knit 2 together, make 1, knit 2 together, knit 1. **12th row**—Slip 1, knit 2, purl 1, knit 15, make 1, knit 2 together, knit 4. **13th row**—Slip 1, knit 2 together, make 1, knit 3, make 1, knit 2 together, knit 1, make 1, knit 2 together, knit 7, make 1, knit 2 together, make 1, knit 2 together, knit 1. **14th row**—Slip 1, knit 2, purl 1, knit 16, make 1, knit 2 together, knit 4. **15th row**—Slip 1, knit 2 together, make 1, knit 3, make 1, knit 2 together, knit 1, make 1, knit 2 together, knit 15. **16th row**—Cast off 7, knit 12, make 1, knit 2 together, knit 4. Repeat from the first row for the length required.

LEAF PATTERN EDGING.

CAST on 11 stitches, and knit 1 plain row. **1st row**—Slip 1, knit 2, make 1, knit 2 together, knit 1, make 2, knit 2 together make 2, knit 2 together, knit 1. **2nd row**—Slip 1, knit 2, purl 1, knit 2, purl 1, knit 3, make 1, knit 2 together, knit 1. **3rd row**—Slip 1, knit 2, make 1, knit 2 together, knit 3, make 2, knit 2 together, make 2, knit 2 together, knit 1. **4th row**—Slip 1, knit 2, purl 1, knit 2, purl 1, knit 5, make 1, knit 2 together, knit 1. **5th row**—Slip 1, knit 2, make 1, knit 2 together, knit 5, make 2, knit 2 together, make 2, knit 2 together, knit 1. **6th row**—Slip 1, knit 2, purl 1, knit 2, purl 1, knit 7, make 1, knit 2 together, knit 1. **7th row**—Slip 1, knit 2, make 1, knit 2 together, knit 7, make 2, knit 2 together, make 2, knit 2 together, knit 1. **8th row**—Slip 1, knit 2, purl 1, knit 2, purl 1, knit 9, make 1, knit 2 together, knit 1. **9th row**—Slip 1, knit 2, make 1, knit 2 together, knit 9, make 2, knit 2 together, knit 1. **10th row**—Slip 1, knit 2, purl 1, knit 2, purl 1, knit 11, make 1, knit 2 together, knit 1. **11th row**—Slip 1, knit 2, make 1, knit 2 together, knit 11, make 2, knit 2 together, knit 1. **12th row**—Slip 1, knit 2, purl 1, knit 2, purl 1, knit 13, make 1, knit 2 together, knit 1. **13th row**—Slip 1, knit 2, make 1, knit 2 together, knit 18. **14th row**—Cast off 12, knit 7, make 1, knit 2 together, knit 1. Repeat from the first row.

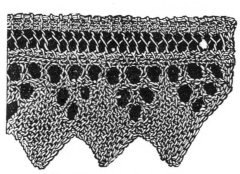

No. 20.—Victoria Border.

EPSOM BORDER.

CAST on 12 stitches, and knit 1 plain row. **1st row**—Slip 1, knit 2, make 1, knit 2 together, knit 1, make 2, knit 2 together, make 2, knit 4. **2nd row**—Slip 1, knit 4, purl 1, knit 2, purl 1, knit 3, make 1, knit 2 together, knit 1. **3rd row**—Slip 1, knit 2, make 1, knit 2 together, knit 10. **4th row**—Cast off 3, knit 8, make 1, knit 2 together, knit 1. Repeat from the first row.

VANDYKE BORDER.

CAST on 17 stitches and knit 1 plain row. **1st row**—Slip 1, knit 3, make 1, knit 2 together, knit 1, make 1, knit 2 together, make 1, knit 2 together, make 1, knit 2 together, make 2, knit 2 together, knit 2 together. **2nd row**—Make 1, knit 2 together, knit 1, purl 1, knit 9 make 1, knit 2 together knit 2. **3rd**

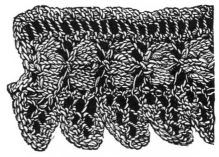

No. 21.—Leaf and Berry Pattern.

row—Slip 1, knit 3, make 1, knit 2 together, knit 2, make 1, knit 2 together, make 1, knit 2 together, make 1, knit 2 together, make 2, knit 2 together, knit 1. **4th row**—Make 1, knit 2 together, knit 1, purl 1, knit 10, make 1, knit 2 together, knit 2. **5th row**—Slip 1, knit 3, make 1, knit 2 together, knit 3, make 1, knit 2 together, make 1, knit 2 together, make 1, knit 2 together, make 2, knit 2 together, knit 1. **6th row**—Make 1, knit 2 together, knit 1 purl 1, knit 11, make 1, knit 2 together, knit 2. **7th row**—Slip 1, knit 3, make 1, knit 2 together, knit 4, make 1, knit 2 together, make 1, knit 2 together, make 1, knit 2 together, make 2, knit 2 together, knit 1. **8th row**—Make 1, knit 2 together, knit 1, purl 1, knit 12, make 1, knit 2 together knit 2. **9th row**—Slip 1, knit 3, make 1, knit 2 together, knit 5, make 1, knit 2 together, make 1, knit 2 together, make 1, knit 2 together, make 2, knit 2 together, knit 1. **10th row**—Make 1, knit 2 together, knit 1, purl 1, knit 13, make 1, knit 2 together, knit 2. **11th row**—Slip 1, knit 3, make 1, knit 2 together, knit 6, make 1, knit 2 together, make 1, knit 2 together, make 1, knit 2 together, make 2, knit 2 together, knit 1. **12th row**—Make 1, knit 2 together, knit 1, purl 1, knit 14, make 1, knit 2 together, knit 2. **13th row**—Slip 1, knit 3, make 1, knit 2 together, knit 7, make 1, knit 2 together, make 1, knit 2 together, make 2, knit 2 together, knit 1. **14th row**—Make 1, knit 2 together, knit 1, purl 1, knit 15, make 1, knit 2 together, knit 2. **15th row**—Slip 1, knit 3, make 1, knit 2 together, knit 8, make 1, knit 2 together, make 1, knit 2 together, make 1, knit 2 together, make 2, knit 2 together, knit 1. **16th row**—Make 1, knit 2 together, knit 1, purl 1, knit 16, make 1, knit 2 together, knit 2. **1 th row**—Slip 1, knit 3, make 1, knit 2 together, knit 6, knit 2 together, make 1, knit 2 together, make 1, knit 2 together, make 1, knit 2 together, make 2, knit 2 together, knit 2 together. **18th row**—Make 1, knit 2 together, knit 1, purl 1, knit 15, make 1, knit 2 together, knit 2. **19th row**—Slip 1, knit 3, make 1, knit 2 together, knit 5, knit 2 together, make 1, knit 2 together, make 1, knit 2 together, make 1, knit 2 together, make 2, knit 2 together, knit 2 together. **20th row**—Make 1, knit 2 together, knit 1, purl 1, knit 14, make 1, knit 2 together, knit 2. **21st row**—Slip 1, knit 3, make 1, knit 2 together, knit 4, knit 2 together, make 1, knit 2 together, make 1, knit 2 together, make 1, knit 2 together, make 2 knit 2 together, knit 2 together. **22nd row**—Make 1, knit 2 together, knit 1, purl 1, knit 13, make 1, knit 2 together, knit 2. **23rd row**—Slip 1, knit 3, make 1, knit 2 together, knit 3, knit 2 together, make 1, knit 2 together, make 1, knit 2 together, make 1, knit 2 together, make 2, knit 2 together, knit 2 together. **24th row**—Make 1, knit 2 together, knit 1, purl 1, knit 12, make 1, knit 2 together, knit 2. **25th row**—Slip 1, knit 3, make 1, knit 2 together, knit 2, knit 2 together, make 1, knit 2 together, make 1, knit 2 together, make 1, knit 2 together make 2 knit 2 together knit 2 together. **26th row**—Make 1, knit 2

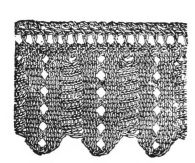

No. 22.—Fluted Border.

together, knit 1, purl 1, knit 11, make 1, knit 2 together, knit 2. **27th row**—Slip 1, knit 3, make 1, knit 2 together, knit 1, knit 2 together, make 1, knit 2 together, make 1, knit 2 together, make 1, knit 2 together, make 2, knit 2 together, knit 2 together. **28th row**—Make 1, knit 2 together, knit 1, purl 1, knit 10, make 1, knit 2 together, knit 2. **29th row**—Slip 1, knit 3, make 1, knit 2 together, knit 2 together, make 1, knit 2 together, make 1, knit 2 together, make 1, knit 2 together, make 2, knit 2 together, knit 2 together. **30th row**—Make 1, knit 2 together, knit 1, purl 1, knit 9, make 1, knit 2 together, knit 2. Repeat from the first row.

FLORENTINE EDGING.

Cast on 13 stitches, and knit 1 plain row. **1st row**—Slip 1, knit 2, make 2, knit 2 together, make 1 and knit 2 together four times. **2nd row**—Make 1, knit 10, purl 1, knit 3. **3rd row**—Slip 1, knit 2, make 2, knit 2 together, make 1 and knit 2 together five times. **4th row**—Cast off 3, knit 8, purl 1, knit 3. Repeat from the first row.

SMALL DIAMOND SPOT EDGING.

Cast on 10 stitches. Knit 1 plain row. **1st row**—Slip 1, knit 2, knit 2 together, make 1, knit 2 together, make 1, knit 1, make 2, knit 2. **2nd row, and every alternate row**—Plain knitting, and in places where make 2 occurred in previous row drop the second half of the made stitch, as it is turned twice simply to make the edge sit easy. **3rd row**—Slip 1, knit 1, knit 2 together, make 1, knit 2 together, make 1, knit 3, make 2, knit 2. **5th row**—Slip 1, knit 2 together, make 1, knit 2 together, make 1, knit 5, make 2, knit 2. **7th row**—Slip 1, knit 2, make 1, knit 2 together, make 1, knit 2 together, knit 1, knit 2 together, make 2, knit 3 together. **9th row**—Slip 1, knit 3, make 1, knit 2 together, make 1, slip 1, knit 2 together, pass the slipped stitch over, make 2

knit 2 together. **11th row**—Slip 1, knit 2, knit 2 together, make 1, knit 2 together, make 1, knit 1, make 2, knit 2 together. **12th row**—Plain, and repeat the pattern from the third row.

WHEEL EDGING.

Cast on 12 stitches and knit 1 plain row. **1st row**—Slip 1, knit 2 together, make 1, knit 2, make 1, knit 2 together, knit 1, make 2, knit 2 together, make 2, knit 2. **2nd row**—Slip 1, knit 2, purl 1, knit 2, purl 1, knit 8. **3rd row**—Slip 1, knit 2 together, make 1, knit 2, make 1, knit 2 together, knit 8, **4th row**—Slip 1, knit 14. **5th row**—Slip 1, knit 2 together, make 1, knit 2, make 1, knit 2 together, knit 1, make 2, knit 2 together, make 2, knit 2 together, make 2 knit 2 together, knit 1. **6th row**—Slip 1, knit 2, purl 1, knit 2, purl 1 knit 2, purl 1, knit 8. **7th row**—Slip 1, knit 2 together, make 1, knit 2 make 1, knit 2 together, knit 11. **8th row**—Slip 1, knit 2 together, knit 1 **9th row**—Slip 1, knit 2 together, make 1, knit 2, make 1, knit 2 together knit 4, make 2, knit 2 together, make 2, knit 2 together. **10th row**—Slip 1, knit 2, purl 1, knit 2, purl 1, knit 11. **11th row**—Slip 1, knit 2 together, make 1, knit 2, make 1, knit 2 together, knit 11 **12th row**—Cast off 6, knit 11. Repeat from the first row.

PRETTY EDGING FOR TRIMMING BABY THINGS.

Cast on 6 stitches, and knit 1 plain row. **1st row**—Slip 1, knit 1 make 1, knit 2 together, make 2, knit 2. **2nd row**—Slip 1, knit 2, purl 1, knit 4. **3rd row**—Slip 1, knit 1, make 1, knit 2 together, knit 4. **4th row**—Cast off 2 knit 5. Repeat from the first row.

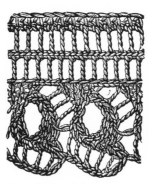

No 23.—Dolphin Lace.

No. 24.—Button-Hole Pattern.

LOCKINGTON BORDER.

Cast on 13 stitches. Knit 1 plain row. **1st row**—Slip 1, knit 9, make 2, knit 2 together, knit 1. **2nd row**—Knit 3, purl 1, knit 10. **3rd row**—Slip 1, knit 10, make 2, knit 2 together, knit 1. **4th row**—Knit 3, purl 1, knit 11. **5th row**—Slip 1, knit 4, knit 2 together, make 2, knit 2 together, knit 3, make 2, knit 2 together, knit 1. **6th row**—Knit 3, purl 1, knit 5, purl 1, knit 6. **7th row**—Slip 1, knit 12, make 2, knit 2 together, knit 1. **8th row**—Knit 3, purl 1, knit 13. **9th row**—Slip 1, knit 2, knit 2 together, make 2, knit 2 together, knit 2 together, make 2, knit 3, make 2, knit 2 together, knit 1. **10th row**—Knit 3, purl 1, knit 5, purl 1, knit 3, purl 1, knit 4. **11th row**—Slip 1, knit 11, make 2, knit 2 together, knit 11. **12th row**—Knit 3, purl 1, knit 13. **13th row**—Slip 1, knit 4, knit 2 together, make 2, knit 2 together, knit 2, knit 2 together, make 2, knit 2 together, knit 2 together. **14th row**—Knit 3, purl 1, knit 5, purl 1, knit 6. **15th row**—Slip 1, knit 9, knit 2 together, make 2, knit 2 together, knit 2 together. **16th row**—Knit 3, purl 1, knit 11. **17th row**—Slip 1, knit 8, knit 2 together, make 2, knit 2 together, knit 2 together. **18th row**—Knit 3, purl 1, knit 10. **19th row**—Slip 1, knit 7, knit 2 together, make 2, knit 2 together, knit 2 together. **20th row**—Knit 3, purl 1, knit 9. Repeat from the first row for the length required.

FLEUR-DE-LIS EDGING.

Cast on 14 stitches. Knit 1 plain row. **1st row**—Slip 1, knit 1, make 1 knit 2 together, knit 5, knit 2 together, make 1, knit 2 together, knit 1. **2nd row**—Make 1, knit 2 together, cotton twice round the needle to make a stitch purl 1, make 1, purl 2 together, purl 4, knit 4. **3rd row**—Slip 1, knit 1, make 1, knit 2 together, knit 3, knit 2 together, make 1, knit 3, make 2 knit 2 together knit 2. **4th row**—Make 1, knit 2 together, cotton twice round the needle to make a stitch, purl 1, make 1, purl 3 together, make 1, purl 1, make 1, purl 2 together, purl 2, knit 4. **5th row**—Slip 1, knit 1, make 1, knit 2 together, knit 1, knit 2 together make 1, knit 3, make 1 knit 1, make 1, knit 3 make 1, knit 2. **6th** row—Make 1, knit 2 together, purl 1, purl 3 together, make 1, purl 3 together, purl 1, make 1, purl 2 together, knit 4. **7th row**—Slip 1, knit 1, make 1, knit 2 together, make 1, knit 2 together, pass the slipped stitch over, make 1, knit 3, make 1, slip 1, knit 2 together, pass the slipped stitch over, make 1, knit 2. **8th row**—Make 1, knit 2 together, purl 2 together, purl 1, purl 3 together, purl 2 together, make 1, purl 3, knit 4. **9th row**—Slip 1, knit 1, make 1, knit 2 together, knit 4, make 1, slip 1, knit 3 together, pass the slipped stitch over, make 1, knit 2. **10th row**—Make 1, knit 2 together, purl 2 together, make 1, purl 5, knit 4. **11th row**—Slip 1, knit 1, make 1, knit 2 together, knit 6, make 1, knit 1, make 1, knit 2. **12th row**—Make 1, knit 2 together, purl 2 together, purl 7, knit 4. Repeat from the first row.

FLORENCE INSERTION AND EDGING.

CAST on 22 stitches. **1st row**—Slip 1, knit 2, make 1, knit 2 together, knit 2, slip 1, knit 1, pass the slipped stitch over, make 1, knit 1, make 1, knit 2 together, knit 3, make 2 and knit 2 together three times, knit 1. **2nd row**—Knit 3, purl 1, knit 2, purl 1, knit 2, purl 13, make 1, knit 2 together, knit 1. **3rd row**—Slip 1, knit 2, make 1, knit 2 together, make 1, slip 1, knit 1, pass the slipped stitch over, make 1, knit 3, make 1, knit 2 together, knit 12. **4th row**—Cast off 3, knit 6, purl 12, make 1, knit 2 together, knit 1. **5th row**—Slip 1 knit 2, make 1, knit 2 together, slip 1, knit 1, pass the slipped stitch over, make 1, knit 5, make 1, knit 2 together, knit 1, make 2 and knit 2 together three times, knit 1. **6th row**—Knit 3, purl 1, knit 2, purl 1, knit 2, purl 13, make 1, knit 2 together, knit 1. **7th row**—Slip 1, knit 2, make 1, knit 2 together, knit 1, make 1, slip 1, knit 1, pass the slipped stitch over, knit 3, knit 2 together, make 1, knit 12. **8th row**—Cast off 3, knit 6, purl 12, make 1, knit 2 together, knit 1. **9th row**—Slip 1, knit 2, make 1, knit 2 together, knit 1, make 1, slip 1, knit 1, pass the slipped stitch over, knit 3, knit 2 together, make 1, knit 2, make 2 and knit 2 together 3 times, knit 1. **10th row**—Knit 3, purl 1, knit 2, purl 1, knit 2, purl 13, make 1, knit 2 together, knit 1. **11th row**—Slip 1, knit 2, make 1, knit 2 together, knit 1, make 1, slip 1, knit 1, pass the slipped stitch over, knit 3, knit 2 together, make 1, knit 12. **12th row**—Cast off 3, knit 6, purl 12, make 1, knit 2 together, knit 1. **13th row**—Slip 1

together, knit 15. **27th row**—Slip 1, knit 1, make 1, knit 2 together, knit 8, make 1, knit 2 together, knit 4. **28th row**—Make 1, knit 2 together, knit 2 together, knit 14. **29th row**—Slip 1, knit 1, make 1, knit 2 together, knit 9, make 1, knit 2 together, knit 2. **30th row**—Make 1, knit 2 together, knit 2 together, knit 13. Repeat from the first row.

FRISBY EDGING.

CAST on 15 stitches. Knit 1 plain row **1st row**—Slip 1, knit 2, make 1, knit 2 together, knit 1, make 2 and knit 2 together four times, knit 1. **2nd row**—Knit 3, purl 1, knit 2, purl 1, knit 2, purl 1, knit 2, purl 1, knit 3, make 1, knit 2 together, knit 1. **3rd row**—Slip 1, knit 2, make 1, knit 2 together, knit 14. **4th row**—Cast off 4, knit 11, make 1, knit 2 together, knit 1. Repeat from the first row.

SPIRAL EDGING.

CAST on 11 stitches. Knit 1 plain row. **1st row**—Slip 1, knit 1, make 2, knit 2 together, knit 5, make 1, knit 2. **2nd row**—Knit 2, make 2, knit 1, make 1, knit 2 together, knit 5, purl 1, knit 2. **3rd row**—Slip 1, knit 6, knit 2 together make 1, knit 3, purl 1, knit 2. **4th row**—Knit 2, make 2, knit 5, make 1, knit 2 together, knit 3, knit 2 together, knit 1. **5th row**—Slip 1, knit 1, make 1, knit 2 together, knit 2 together, make 1, knit 7, purl 1, knit 2. **6th row**—Knit 2, make 2, knit 9, make 1, knit 2 together, knit 1, purl 1, knit 2. **7th row**—Slip 1, knit 15, purl 1, knit 2. **8th row**—Cast off 7, knit 8, knit 2 together, knit 1. Repeat from the first row.

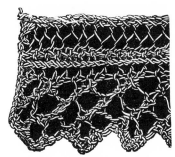
No. 25.—Dewdrop Edging.

No. 26.—Wheat-Ear Border.

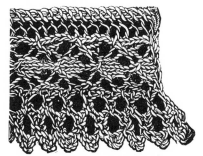
No. 27.—Point Lace Border

knit 2, make 1, knit 2 together, knit 2, make 1, slip 1, knit 1, pass the slipped stitch over, knit 1, knit 2 together, make 1, knit 3, make 2 and knit 2 together three times, knit 1. **14th row**—Knit 3, purl 1, knit 2, purl 1, knit 2, purl 13, make 1, knit 2 together, knit 1. **15th row**—Slip 1, knit 2, make 1, knit 2 together, knit 3, make 1, slip 1, knit 2 together, pass the slipped stitch over, make 1, knit 14. **16th row**—Cast off 3, knit 6, purl 12, make 1, knit 2 together, knit 1. Repeat from the first row.

WAVE PATTERN BORDER.

CAST on 16 stitches. Knit 1 plain row. **1st row**—Slip 1, knit 1, make 1, knit 2 together, knit 8, knit 2 together, make 1, knit 2. **2nd row**—Make 1, knit 16. **3rd row**—Slip 1, knit 1, make 1, knit 2 together, knit 7, knit 2 together, make 1, knit 4 **4th row**—Make 1, knit 17. **5th row**—Slip 1, knit 1, make 1, knit 2 together, knit 6, knit 2 together, make 1, knit 6. **6th row**—Make 1, knit 18. **7th row**—Slip 1, knit 1, make 1, knit 2 together, knit 5, knit 2 together, make 1, knit 8. **8th row**—Make 1, knit 19. **9th row**—Slip 1, knit 1, make 1, knit 2 together, knit 4, knit 2 together, make 1, knit 10. **10th row**—Make 1, knit 20. **11th row**—Slip 1, knit 1, make 1, knit 2 together, knit 3, knit 2 together, make 1, knit 12. **12th row**—Make 1, knit 21. **13th row**—Slip 1, knit 1, make 1, knit 2 together, knit 2, knit 2 together, make 1, knit 14. **14th row**—Make 1, knit 22. **15th row**—Slip 1, knit 1, make 1, knit 2 together, knit 1, knit 2 together, make 1, knit 16. **16th row**—Make 1, knit 2 together, knit 21. **17th row**—Slip 1, knit 1, make 1, knit 2 together, knit 3, make 1, knit 2 together, knit 14. **18th row**—Make 1, knit 2 together, knit 2 together, knit 19. **19th row**—Slip 1, knit 1, make 1, knit 2 together, knit 4, make 1, knit 2 together, knit 12. **20th row**—Make 1, knit 2 together, knit 2 together, knit 18 **21st row**—Slip 1, knit 1, make 1, knit 2 together, knit 5, make 1, knit 2 together, knit 10. **22nd row**—Make 1, knit 2 together knit 2 together, knit 17. **23rd row**—Slip 1, knit 1, make 1, knit 2 together, knit 6, make 1, knit 2 together knit 8. **24th row**—Make 1, knit 2 together, knit 2 together, knit 16. **25th row**—Slip 1, knit 1, make 1, knit 2 together, knit 7, make 1, knit 2 together, knit 6. **26th row**—Make 1, knit 2 together, knit 2

LOZENGE BORDER.

CAST on 15 stitches. Knit 1 plain row. **1st row**—Slip 1, knit 2, make 1, knit 2 together, knit 1, make 2, knit 7, make 2, knit 2. **2nd row**—Knit 2 purl 1, knit 8, purl 1, knit 6. **3rd row**—Slip 1, knit 2, make 1, knit 2 together knit 1, make 2, knit 2 together, make 2, knit 2 together, knit 3, knit 2 together, make 2, knit 4. **4th row**—Knit 5, purl 1, knit 6, purl 1, knit 2, purl 1, knit 6. **5th row**—Slip 1, knit 2, make 1, knit 2 together, knit 1, make 2, knit 2 together, knit 1, knit 2 together, make 2, knit 2 together, knit 1, knit 2 together, make 2, knit 6. **6th row**—Knit 7, purl 1, knit 4, purl 1, knit 4, purl 1, knit 6, purl 1, knit 6. **7th row**—Slip 1, knit 2, make 1, knit 2 together, knit 1, make 2, knit 2 together, knit 3, knit 2 together, make 2, slip 1, knit 2 together, pass the slipped stitch over, make 2, knit 8. **8th row**—Knit 9, purl 1, knit 2, purl 1, knit 6, purl 1, knit 6. **9th row**—Slip 1, knit 2, make 1, knit 2 together, knit 21. **10th row**—Cast off 10 knit 8, knit 2 together, knit 5. Recommence at the first row

BUTTERCUP EDGING.

CAST on 7 stitches. Knit 1 plain row. **1st row**—Slip 1, knit 2, make 1, knit 2 together, make 2, knit 2 **2nd row**—Knit 3, purl 1, knit 2, make 1, knit 2 together, knit 1. **3rd row**—Slip 1, knit 2, make 1, knit 2 together, make 2, knit 2 together, make 2, knit 2 together. **4th row**—Knit 2, purl 1, knit 2, make 1, knit 2 together, knit 1. **5th row**—Slip 1, knit 2, make 1, knit 2 together, knit 6. **6th row**—Cast off 4, knit 3, make 1, knit 2 together, knit 1. Repeat from the first row.

NARROW DICE EDGING.

Cast on 6 stitches. Knit 1 plain row. **1st row**—Slip 1, knit 3, make 1, knit 2. **2nd row**—Knit 2, make 1, knit 1, make 1, knit 1, make 1, knit 2 together, knit 1. **3rd row**—Slip 1, knit 3, make 1, knit 3, make 1, knit 2. **4th** row—Knit 2, make 1, knit 5, make 1, knit 1, make 1, knit 2 together, knit 1. **5th row**—Slip 1, knit 3, make 1, knit 2 together, knit 3, knit 2 together, make 1, knit 2. **6th row**—Knit 3, make 1, knit 2 together, knit 1, knit 2 together, make 1, knit 2, make 1, knit 2 together, knit 1. **7th row**—Slip 1, knit 5, make 1, slip 1, knit 2 together, pass the slipped stitch over, make 1, knit 4. **8th row**—Cast off 7, knit 2, make 1, knit 2 together, knit 1. Recommence at the first row.

ESCUTCHEON BORDER.

Cast on 20 stitches. Knit 1 plain row. **1st row**—Slip 1, knit 1, make 1, knit 2 together, make 1, knit 2 together, make 1, knit 2 together knit 6, make 1, slip 1, knit 1, pass the slipped stitch over, make 1, slip 1, knit 1, pass the slipped stitch over, make 1, knit 2. **2nd row**—Knit 14, make 1, knit 2 together, make 1, knit 2 together, make 1, knit 2 together, knit 1. **3rd row**—Slip 1, knit 1, make 1, knit 2 together, make 1, knit 2 together, make 1, knit 2 together, knit 7, make 1, slip 1, knit 1, pass the slipped stitch over, make 1, slip 1, knit 1, pass the slipped stitch over, make 1, knit 2. **4th row**—Knit 15, make 1, knit 2 together, make 1, knit 2 together, make 1, knit 2 together, knit 1. **5th row**—Slip 1, knit 1, make 1, knit 2 together make 1, knit 2 together, make 1, knit 2 together, knit 2, knit 2 together, make 2, knit 2 together, knit 2, make 1, slip 1, knit 1, pass the slipped stitch over, make 1, slip 1, knit 1, pass the slipped stitch over, make 1, knit 2. **6th row**—Knit 11, purl 1, knit 4, make 1, knit 2 together, make 1, knit 2 together, make 1, knit 2 together, knit 1. **7th row**—Slip 1, knit 1, make 1, knit 2 together, make 1, knit 2 together, knit 9, make 1, slip 1, knit 1, pass the slipped stitch over, make 1, slip 1, knit 1, pass the slipped stitch over, make 1, knit 2. **8th row**—Knit 17, make 1, knit 2 together, make 1, knit 2 together, make 1, knit 2 together, knit 1. **9th row**—Slip 1, knit 1, make 1, knit 2 together, make 1, knit 2 together, make 1, knit 2 together, knit 2 together, make 2, knit 2 together, knit 6, make 1, slip 1, knit 1, pass the slipped stitch over, make 1, slip 1, knit 1, pass the slipped stitch over, make 1, knit 2. **10th row**—Knit 15, purl 1, knit 2, make 1, knit 2 together, make 1, knit 2 together, make 1, knit 2 together, knit 1. **11th row**—Slip 1, knit 1, make 1, knit 2 together, make 1, knit 2 together, make 1, knit 2 together, knit 11, make 1, slip 1, knit 1, pass the slipped stitch over, make 1, slip 1, knit 1, pass the slipped stitch over, make 1, knit

No. 28.—Box Leaf Edging.

2. **12th row**—Knit 19, make 1, knit 2 together, make 1, knit 2 together, make 1, knit 2 together, knit 1. **13th row**—Slip 1, knit 1, make 1, knit 2 together, make 1, knit 2 together, make 1, knit 2 together, knit 2, knit 2 together, make 2, knit 2 together, knit 2 together, make 2, knit 2 together, knit 2, make 1, slip 1, knit 1, pass the slipped stitch over, make 1, knit 2. **14th row**—Knit 11, purl 1, knit 3, purl 1, knit 4, make 1, knit 2 together, make 1, knit 2 together, make 1, knit 2 together, knit 1. **15th row**—Slip 1, knit 1, make 1, knit 2 together, make 1, knit 2 together, make 1, knit 2 together, knit 10, knit 2 together, make 1, knit 2 together, make 1, knit 2 together, make 1, knit 2 together, knit 1. **16th row**—Knit 19, make 1, knit 2 together, make 1, knit 2 together, make 1, knit 2 together, knit 1. **17th row**—Slip 1, knit 1, make 1, knit 2 together, make 1, knit 2 together, make 1, knit 2 together, make 1, knit 2 together, make 2, knit 2 together, knit 5, knit 2 together, make 1, knit 2 together, make 1, knit 2 together, make 1, knit 2 together, knit 1. **18th row**—Knit 15, purl 1, knit 2 make 1, knit 2 together, make 1, knit 2 together, make 1, knit 2 together, knit 1. **19th row**—Slip 1, knit 1, make 1, knit 2 together, make 1, knit 2 together, knit 8, knit 2 together, make 1, knit 2 together, make 1, knit 2 together, make 1, knit 2 together, knit 1. **20th row**—Knit 17, make 1, knit 2 together, make 1, knit 2 together, make 1, knit 2 together, knit 1. **21st row**—Slip 1, knit 1, make 1, knit 2 together, make 1, knit 2 together, knit 2, knit 2 together, make 2, knit 2 together, knit 1, knit 2 together, make 1, knit 2 together, make 1, knit 2 together, make 1, knit 2 together, knit 1. **22nd row**—Knit 11, purl 1, knit 4, make 1, knit 2 together, make 1, knit 2 together, make 1, knit 2 together, knit 1. **23rd row**—Slip 1, knit 1, make 1, knit 2 together, make 1, knit 2 together, make 1, knit 2 together, knit 6, knit 2 together, make 1, knit 2 together, make 1, knit 2 together, make 1, knit 2 together, knit 1. **24th row**—Knit 15 make 1, knit 2 together, make 1, knit 2 together, make 1, knit 2 together, knit 1. **25th row**—Slip 1, knit 2, make 1, knit 2 together, make 1, knit 2 together, make 1, knit 2 together, knit 5, knit 2 together, make 1, knit 2 together, make 1, knit 2 together, make 1, knit 2 together, knit 1. **26th row**—Knit 14, make 1, knit 2 together, make 1, knit 2 together, make 1, knit 2 together, knit 1. **27th row**—Slip 1, knit 1, make 1, knit 2 together, make 1, knit 2 together, make 1, knit 2 together, knit 4, knit 2 together, make 1, knit 2 together, make 1, knit 2

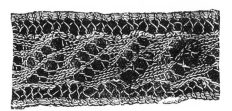

No. 29.—Leaf Insertion.

No. 30.—Unit Edging.

together, make 1, knit 2 together, knit 1. **28th row**—Knit 13, make 1, knit 2 together, make 1, knit 2 together, make 1, knit 2 together, knit 1. Repeat from the first row.

CHERRY-LEAF BORDER.

Cast on 24 stitches. Knit 1 plain row. **1st row**—Slip 1, knit 2, make 1, knit 2 together, knit 1, make 1, knit 2 together, knit 2, make 1, knit 2 together, make 1, knit 2 together, knit 5, make 2, knit 2 together, make 2, knit 2 together, knit 1. **2nd row**—Knit 3, purl 1, knit 2, purl 1, knit 13, make 1, knit 2 together, knit 1, make 1, knit 2 together, knit 1. **3rd row**—Slip 1, knit 2, make 1, knit 2 together, knit 1, make 1, knit 2 together, knit 3, make 1, knit 2 together, make 1, knit 2 together, knit 6, make 2, knit 2 together, make 2, knit 2 together, knit 1. **4th row**—Knit 3, purl 1, knit 2, purl 1, knit 15, make 1, knit 2 together, knit 1, make 1, knit 2 together, knit 1. **5th row**—Slip 1, knit 2, make 1, knit 2 together, knit 1, make 1, knit 2 together, knit 4, make 1, knit 2 together, make 1, knit 2 together, knit 7, make 2, knit 2 together, make 2, knit 2 together, knit 1. **6th row**—Knit 3, purl 1, knit 2, purl 1, knit 17, make 1, knit 2 together, knit 1, make 1, knit 2 together, knit 1. **7th row**—Slip 1, knit 2, make 1, knit 2 together, knit 1, make 1, knit 2 together, knit 5, make 1, knit 2 together, make 1, knit 2 together, knit 8, make 2, knit 2 together, make 2, knit 2 together, knit 1. **8th row**—Knit 3, purl 1, knit 2, purl 1, knit 19, make 1, knit 2 together, knit 1, make 1, knit 2 together, knit 1. **9th row**—Slip 1, knit 2, make 1, knit 2 together, knit 1, make 1, knit 2 together, knit 6, make 1, knit 2 together, make 1, knit 2 together, knit 9, make 2, knit 2 together, make 2, knit 2 together, knit 1. **10th row**—Knit 3, purl 1, knit 2, purl 1, knit 21 make 1, knit 2 together, knit 1, make 1, knit 2 together, knit 1. **11th row**—Slip 1, knit 2, make 1, knit 2 together, knit 1, make 1, knit 2 together, knit 26. **12th row**—Cast off 10, knit 17, make 1, knit 2 together, knit 1, make 1, knit 2 together, knit 1. Recommence at the first row, and continue for the length required.

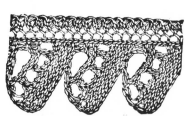

No. 31.—Gilbert Edging.

WIDE FLUTED BORDER.

Cast on 20 stitches. Knit 1 plain row. **1st row**—Slip 1, knit 5, purl 13, knit 1 and purl 1 in the last stitch. **2nd row**—Knit 16, purl 5. **3rd row**—Slip 1, knit 3, purl 16, knit 1 and purl 1 in the last stitch. **4th row**—Knit 18, purl 4. **5th row**—Slip 1, knit 1, purl 18, knit 1 and purl 1 in the last stitch. **6th row**—Knit 20, purl 3. **7th row**—Slip 1, knit 1, purl 20, knit 1 and purl 1 in the last stitch. **8th row**—Knit 22, purl 2. **9th row**—Slip 1, knit 1, purl 20, purl 2 together. **10th row**—Knit 21, purl 2. **11th row**—Slip 1, knit 2, purl 18, purl 2 together. **12th row**—Knit 19, purl 3. **13th row**—Slip 1, knit 3, purl 16, purl 2 together. **14th row**—Knit 16, purl 5. **15th row**—Slip 1, knit 5, purl 13, purl 2 together. **16th row**—Knit 15, purl 5. **17th row**—Slip 1, knit 2, make 1 and knit 2 together eight times, knit 1. **18th row**—Knit 17, purl 3. Repeat from the first row for the length required. Then pick up the stitches along the top edge of the knitting, and for the **Heading** work: **1st row**—Plain. **2nd row**—Purl. **3rd row**—Plain. **4th row**—Knit 2, * make 1, knit 2 together, knit 3, and repeat from * to the end of the row. **5th row**—Purl. **6th row**—Knit 3, make 1, knit 2 together, and repeat. **7th row**—Purl. **8th row**—Knit 4, * make 1, knit 2 together, knit 3, and repeat from *. **9th row**—Purl. **10th row**—Knit 5, * make 1, knit 2 together, knit 3, and repeat from * **11th row**—Plain. **12th row**—Purl. **13th row**—Plain. Cast off all.

KNITTED FRINGE.

Cast on 12 stitches. **1st row**—Slip 1, knit 2 together, make 2, knit 2 together, make 1 knit 2 together, knit 2 together, make 2, knit 2 together, make 2, knit 2 together, knit 1. **2nd row**—Slip 1, knit 2, purl 1, knit 5, purl 1, knit 2. **3rd row**—Slip 1, knit 4, knit 2 together, make 1, knit 5. **4th row**—Slip 1, knit 11. Repeat these four rows for the length required, when cast off. Cut strands of cotton about 6 inches in length, and knot 8 strands into each hole along one side of the heading.